METAPHORS OF SPAIN

Studies in Latin American and Spanish History

Series Editors:
Scott Eastman, Creighton University, USA
Vicente Sanz Rozalén, Universitat Jaume I, Spain

Editorial Board:
Carlos Illades, Universidad Autónoma Metropolitana, Mexico
Mercedes Yusta, Université Paris 8, France
Xosé Manoel Núñez-Seixas, Ludwig-Maximilians Universität, Munich, Germany
Dominique Soucy, Université de Franche-Comté, France
Gabe Paquette, Johns Hopkins University, USA
Karen Racine, University of Guelph, Canada
David Sartorius, University of Maryland, USA
Claudia Guarisco, El Colegio Mexiquense, Mexico
Natalia Sobrevilla Perea, University of Kent, United Kingdom

This series bridges the divide between studies of Latin America and peninsular Spain by employing transnational and comparative approaches that shed light on the complex societies, cultures, and economies of the modern age. Focusing on the cross-pollination that was the legacy of colonialism on both sides of the Atlantic, these monographs and collections explore a variety of issues such as race, class, gender, and politics in the Spanish-speaking world.

Volume 1
Metaphors of Spain: Representations of Spanish National Identity in the Twentieth Century
Edited by Javier Moreno-Luzón and Xosé M. Núñez Seixas

Volume 2
Conflict, Domination and Violence: Episodes in Mexican Social History
Carlos Illades

Metaphors of Spain

Representations of Spanish National Identity in the Twentieth Century

Edited by

Javier Moreno-Luzón and Xosé M. Núñez Seixas

berghahn
NEW YORK · OXFORD
www.berghahnbooks.com

Published in 2017 by
Berghahn Books
www.berghahnbooks.com

© 2017 Javier Moreno-Luzón and Xosé M. Núñez Seixas

Translation from Spanish of chapters 1, 2, 3, 4 and 12:
Nick Rider

Translation from Spanish of introduction, as well as chapters 5, 8, 9 and 10:
Andrea & Daniel Blanch

Library of Congress Cataloging-in-Publication Data

Names: Moreno Luzon, Javier, 1967-editor of compilation. | Nunez Seixas,
Xose M. (Xose Manoel), 1966-editor of compilation. | Universitat Jaume I.
Title: Metaphors of Spain : representations of Spanish national identity in the
twentieth century / edited by Javier Moreno Luzon and Xose M. Nunez Seixas.
Description: New York : Berghahn Books, 2017. | Series: Studies in Latin
American and Spanish history ; volume 1 | Includes bibliographical refer-
ences and index.
Identifiers: LCCN 2016053585 (print) | LCCN 2016058753 (ebook) | ISBN
9781785334665 (hardback : alkaline paper) | ISBN 9781785334672 (ebook)
Subjects: LCSH: Spain—Politics and government—20th century. |
Nationalism—Spain—History—20th century. | Regionalism—Spain—
History—20th century. | Politics and culture--Spain—History—20th century.
| Spain—Social life and customs—20th century. | Spain—Social conditions—
20th century.
Classification: LCC DP233 .M48 2017 (print) | LCC DP233 (ebook) |
DDC 946.08—dc23
LC record available at https://lccn.loc.gov/2016053585

British Library Cataloguing in Publication Data

A catalogue record for this book is available from the British Library

ISBN 978-1-78533-466-5 hardback
ISBN 978-1-78533-467-2 ebook

Contents

Introduction
The Nation and Its Metaphors

Javier Moreno-Luzón and Xosé M. Núñez Seixas

For some years now, culture has retained a central place in the immense territory occupied by nationalism studies. Though earlier examples can be found, the works that have exerted the greatest influence on specialists in these fields appeared during the 1980s, an authentic incubator of groundbreaking research. Among the authors who paved the way for studies such as those distilled here, two at least should be mentioned. In 1983, Benedict Anderson published *Imagined Communities: Reflections on the Origin and Spread of Nationalism*. This author examined nations as modern cultural artefacts that emerged at a specific point, were transformed and under certain circumstances acquired extraordinary strength. His most prominent thesis defined the nation as an 'imagined community' capable of integrating very diverse individuals, even those unknown to each other. This type of political community is conceived as fraternal, limited within specific territorial borders and inherently sovereign: free to govern itself. In 1984, the first of the seven-volume *Les lieux de mémoire* (Realms of Memory) began to appear under the guidance of French historian Pierre Nora.[1] These books examined the trajectory of some key elements in French identity: physical and figurative places where 'national memory' crystallized. The inventory – coloured in a certain essentialism – included commemorations, festivities and rituals, emblems and historical personalities, books, monuments and museums, buildings and laws, landscapes, cuisine, concepts, mottos and leitmotivs. Where history intersects the living reality of a nation, these may undergo alteration and reinterpretation but remain resilient over time.

These foundational perspectives have been criticized but still inspire historians and social scientists interested in the inherently interdisciplinary field of nationalism, where many others have also made significant contributions, emphasizing the importance of not losing sight of the political character of nations, which are unintelligible apart from state action and the interests and strategies of nationalist elites inside and outside of government.[2] Culture does not consist of a coherent, harmonious whole; it is negotiated and disputed by opposing sectors of the public sphere. Multiple and at times paradoxical combinations can occur in the extremely complex processes that shape identities and identification, whether collective or individual, territorial or otherwise. Later on, Nira Yuval-Davis (1997) drew attention to the ubiquitous gender dimension in nationalist discourses and constructions, outlining how these were affected by the roles of men and women. Significant horizons also open for the researcher when exploring popular culture and daily life. There, nationalism is reproduced through various means and penetrates worldviews through conscious or semi-conscious mechanisms. Along these lines, sociologist Michael Billig (1995) coined the term *banal nationalism*; it has since been applied to analyse almost everything, from sporting events to commercial brands. Recently, the spotlight has shifted away from elitist initiatives and focussed predominately on ordinary people, local contexts, civil society and grass-roots movements to explain the rise, development and spread of national identities, even when confused with nationalism.[3] Similarly, abundant perspectives have emerged that emphasize the variable territorial geometry of all collective identities.[4]

Recognizing the cultural nature of nations necessarily leads to the analysis of symbols and symbolic practices. Here, we can even discover a feature common to both representatives and successors of the interpretative schools that have traditionally divided academic circles. The ethno-symbolist school, represented mainly by Anthony D. Smith, includes symbols among the long-term resources that guarantee the transition of ethnic groups into nationalities.[5] However, even modernist approaches that ascribe contemporary origins to nations – such as that of Anderson – recognize the importance of symbols as representations and projections of essential values in the construction or reconstruction of the imagined communities known as nations.[6] In reality, Nora's *lieux de mémoire* were simply nexuses or multiform symbolic spaces, condensers of meanings and emotions. Symbols appeal to sentiments but also represent a rational appeal that nationalists develop and use to serve their diverse aims. National symbols thus acquire at least five primordial functions: they condense elements of shared ideology by simplifying it, thereby creating a degree of unanimity but also dissent in their spheres; they establish group identity markers, for internal and external use; they create emotions and connect people with collective identities; they sometimes serve as an effective community cement that overcomes social divisions; and, finally, mere sight or evocation of them can move people to action.[7]

This volume does not incite the search for, or defence of, national essences. Rather, it examines the vicissitudes of the Spanish national identity and its core of symbols and symbolic practices, which have been subjected to very diverse interpretations by multiple actors throughout the twentieth century. Resisting the tendency to define the contours of a supposedly timeless and metaphysical 'Spanish being' or *Volksgeist*, we search for what it meant to *be Spanish* in the past century, as a constructed identity. Consequently, the use of the word *metaphor* in the book's title refers to very diverse twentieth-century expressions of 'Spanishness'. We do not attempt to construct a Spanish version of *Les lieux de mémoire*, nor is this collection of essays comparable to more exhaustive thematic compilations on other state – or stateless – nationalisms and national identities: including German, Italian, Swiss, Basque or Flemish cases.[8] Furthermore, this volume does not emphasize the images or visual aspects of comparative national iconology.[9] We have simply selected – while acknowledging the debatable nature of our selection – some elements that to us seem indisputably relevant to Spanish nationalist imaginaries. Here, we encounter a parade of historical myths, official emblems such as flags and hymns, the republic and the monarchy, the role of gender, religion and language, and the symbolic dimension of the former empire in the Americas. Special attention is given to mass culture in the twentieth century, which became a crucial nationalizing element through sports, music, tourism and the Spanish national metaphor par excellence, bullfighting.

This volume focuses on a cultural history of politics while exhibiting the distinctiveness of each author. The work goes beyond describing the formal features of symbols or places of memory, which are not here considered static, perennial or an expression of the intrinsic continuity of nations. Rather, the authors look at the metaphors within their contexts, spaces and interactive dynamics, analysing their political and social uses as well as their conflictive, changing meanings. Among the very diverse actors addressed we find state and political parties, intellectual elites, all sorts of associations and specific enterprises, including those of emigrants established far from Spain. Here also, we avoid any historiographic exceptionalism, a feature that has characterized a great part of twentieth-century historiography on Spain. Far from any Iberian *Sonderweg*, the Spanish case was not anomalous within the European context; it was conditioned by factors also present in neighbouring areas. As in other places, various versions of hegemonic nationalism – liberal and traditionalist, republican and conservative, centralist and regionalized – clashed in Spain. However, 'Spanishness' was forged in a way that was less frequent in Europe but not singular: in the heat of constant struggle with sub-state nationalisms, notably the Catalan, Basque and Galician movements. One cannot be understood without the other; each fed the other's flame. From this emerges a complex and fascinating narrative of the Spanish twentieth century.

The century opened with abundant angst among Spanish political and intellectual elites regarding national identity: its content, its potential and its diffusion. The colonial Disaster of 1898 – the loss of Spain's last overseas colonies (Cuba, Puerto Rico and the Philippines) after a short war with the United States – marked a decisive turning point in the history of Spanish identities. This launched a phase of identitary shipwreck that was to continue throughout the first four decades of the twentieth century. During this phase, renewed forms of Spanish nationalism assumed the task of regenerating the homeland, deploying multiple tactics to counter the rise of sub-state nationalisms. José Álvarez Junco describes how intellectuals in this setting searched incessantly for the national spirit – or Spanish *Volksgeist* – in a history with *the nation* as a living, enduring organism and the main actor. While musicians, painters and architects searched incessantly for a genuine Spanish style, many thinkers sought the keys to the present somewhere in the past, hoping to discover there the origins of *el problema de España* (the problem of Spain) and its possible solutions. This essentialist question remained fashionable at least until the 1960s. Inmaculada Blasco Herranz shows how regenerationism diagnosed the homeland with a loss of virility and fostered the eventual political participation of women, though their role was limited to that of mothers and educators of patriots. In turn, the State launched into various strategies of nation-building guided by the military and the monarchy. As in other European countries, the Crown spearheaded national renewal. In Spain, however, the king would ultimately trespass constitutional limits, as Javier Moreno-Luzón explains.

From 1923 on, the dictatorship of General Primo de Rivera set in motion much more intense and repressive policies that were linked to Catholic reactionary nationalism and sought to re-nationalize the country. Emerging symbols of the alternative nationalisms were repressed and Spanish symbols were repeatedly promoted and exhibited in all sorts of patriotic ceremonies. Under this military regime, the celebrations of 12 October as the *Día de la Raza*, or Day of the [Hispanic] Race, reached their maximum expression. Marcela García Sebastiani and David Marcilhacy describe how this holiday became official in 1918 after decades of propaganda by Americanist associations succeeded in convincing almost everyone of the need to prioritize the Americas in the Spanish imaginary. Both variants of this durable, multifaceted myth – the Catholic traditionalist and the liberal-democratic versions – survived until the end of the twentieth century. In the 1920s also, mass sporting events such as football arose as a projection of nationalist sentiments. Alejandro Quiroga identifies how these impulses converged in a series of narratives that oscillated between exaltation of Spanish fury as proof of its masculinity and courage, and lament over the cursed fate of the nobleman. After 1898, harsh critique was levelled against another great popular spectacle, bullfighting, as a symptom of Spanish backwardness. However, Rafael Núñez Florencio argues that it encapsulated what many perceived as the supreme art and symbol of a nation where life and death were tangled in a reckless game.

In 1931, the official discourse of the Spanish Second Republic replaced the monarchic emphasis on religious and imperial traditions with features of another form of *españolismo* that had also been distilled in the nineteenth and early twentieth centuries. Àngel Duarte expands on how being Republican was a way of being Spanish. The Republic was identified with Spain and the nation with the people: a nation composed of free and virtuous citizens. This language remained operative even though the new democratic system lacked both efficacy and the time needed to establish its patriotic symbology.

The 1936–39 Civil War exacerbated various Spanish nationalist expressions and the violent clashes among them. It also revealed the high degree of nationalization that had been achieved in the first third of the century. This was not the first time Spanish history featured intense political mobilization. After a civil war and extensive repression of any suspicious exhibition of sub-state national identities, in its first two decades, the Franco dictatorship reproduced many of the renationalizing initiatives of Primo de Rivera. These were radicalized and inserted in a fascist-rooted narrative about a new beginning. In the realm of linguistic policy, with the turn of the century the Castilian language became the essential Spanish identity marker. The various Spanish nationalist currents felt that the nation should have a single language for administration and education. Regional languages were considered national heritage that could be preserved in the private sphere as folklore and in certain literary genres. Xosé M. Núñez Seixas describes how Francoism carried these postulates to their full legal consequences, though inherited contradictions persisted. Nationalist use of culture by public authorities even extended to music, where Francoist folklore turned regional songs and dances into a collective expression of the Spanish people. According to Sandie Holguín, this acted as both a unifying barrier against infectious foreign rhythms and a channel for projecting the image of Spain – spiced with flamenco and *canción española* – to the outside world.

The nationalizing and propagandistic push of Francoism reached such remote locations as Equatorial Guinea. However, public authorities did not succeed in controlling the complex culture that took hold with the accelerated economic development that began in the 1950s. Not even the Catholic Church remained untouched: though a pillar of the regime, and though Francoist religious revival presented itself as the return to the authentic Spain, Mary Vincent explains that the Church remained universal and plural. Significant currents within the Catholic Church embraced left-wing movements and were cordial to sub-state nationalists. According to Eric Storm, one of the main indicators of cultural change derived from mass tourism was an overhaul of the promotional image of Spain, which until then had been sold to travellers as an ancient culture of monumental cities. The touristic explosion imposed sun and beach, bullfights and *tablaos flamencos*. Romantically rooted exoticism remained, though spiced with touches of modernity. The new cinematographic *españoladas* declared that it was possible to be modern and also Spanish, as prohibitions on alternative national symbols relaxed with the decline of dictator.

After the death of Franco in 1975, the transition to democracy brought decades of nationalist rhetoric to an end. Youthful Spain aspired to a place among the democratic States of Europe and reformulated its symbolic representations, giving new meanings to old emblems. The Crown again embodied the aspirations of national renewal: the new monarch willingly ceded political power to retain a ceremonial role, while also acting as the definitive guarantor of the democratic system. Meanwhile, 12 October became an itinerant festival of Hispano-Americanism until it was declared the National Holiday. Extensive preparations for the fifth centenary of the discovery of the Americas in 1992 marked the apotheosis of modernity. The red-and-gold standard was reinvented as the *constitutional flag*. Though its legitimacy remained doubtful for Francoist opponents and those who remembered the Republic, the emblem endured in poor but invincible health and fared much better than the national anthem, as Javier Moreno-Luzón and Xosé M. Núñez Seixas analyse in their joint chapter. For the first time, a certain consensus arose around Spanish symbols that could be used without recurring to repressive threats. Secularization also extinguished the old cultural war between clerical and anti-clerical positions. Night life re-energized the capital, which had been devastated by speculation, as the Madrid *movida* took hold and updated clichés such as bullfighting and folkloric music. Finally, as the resurgence of sub-state nationalisms that first stimulated the creation of the State of the Autonomies became consolidated, it generated a renaissance of Spanish nationalism, which had hit a low point in the 1970s and 1980s. Demand for the normalized presence of national symbolism set the stage for a clash, the effects of which have only intensified in the twenty-first century.

This volume is one of the main results of two research projects financed by the government of Spain between 2009 and 2015: *Imaginarios nacionalistas e identidad nacional española en el siglo XX* (HAR2008-06252-C02) and *La nación desde la raíz. Nacionalismo español y sociedad civil en el siglo XX* (HAR2012-37963-C02). After bringing together specialists from diverse locations and institutions, hotly debated papers from two colloquia in Madrid and Santiago de Compostela became chapters. Prior to this, the outcomes of these two projects were published in Spanish in two volumes: *Ser españoles*, eds Moreno-Luzón and Núñez Seixas (2013), and *Imaginarios y representaciones de España durante el franquismo*, eds Stéphane Michonneau and Núñez Seixas (2014), along with a dossier edited by Moreno-Luzón (*Imaginarios nacionalistas españoles en el primer tercio del siglo XX*, 2013) in the Spanish journal *Hispania*. We would like to express our appreciation to all the participants in these collective works and to Berghahn Books, with particular thanks to Scott Eastman and Vicent Sanz for their interest in launching with this volume a new series, Studies in Latin American and Spanish History. The *Hiwis* of the chair of Modern European History at the Ludwig-Maximilians University (Sabina De Luca, Lisa Leuschel, Sarafina Märtz and Emanuel Steinbacher) provided great assistance in formatting the final bibliography. We hope that these essays may somehow invite a bit of reflection and rationality on topics that so often unleash passions.

Madrid and Munich, December 2015

Javier Moreno-Luzón is Professor of Political History at the Complutense University of Madrid. He has been visiting scholar at the London School of Economics and Political Science, L'École des Hautes Études en Sciences Sociales (Paris), Harvard University, and the University of California, San Diego, and written several books and articles on political clientelism, elections and parties, elites and parliament, liberalism, nationalism and monarchy in Spanish modern history. Among his publications in English is *Modernizing the Nation: Spain During the Reign of Alfonso XIII, 1902–1931* (Brighton, 2012).

Xosé M. Núñez Seixas is Professor of Modern History at the University of Santiago de Compostela (on leave) and Ludwig-Maximilians University Munich. He has been visiting professor at Paris X, the City University of New York and Stanford University, and has written several monographs on comparative Iberian and European nationalism, migration studies and cultural history of war. Among his last monographs are *Patriotas y demócratas. El discurso nacionalista español después de Franco* (Madrid, 2010), *Icônes littéraires et stéréotypes sociaux: L'image des immigrants galiciens en Argentine (1800–1960)* (Besançon, 2013) and *Die spanische Blaue Division an der Ostfront. Zwischen Kriegserfahrung und Erinnerung* (Münster 2016).

Notes

1. See Nora (1984, 1986, 1992–94)
2. See e.g. Özkirimli (2000); Kolár and Rezník (2012). Breuilly (1985).
3. See e.g. Van Ginderachter and Beyen (2012).
4. Augusteijn and Storm (2012).
5. Smith (1999, 2009).
6. Marsland (2001).
7. See Casquete and Mees (2012).
8. See François and Schulze (2002), Isnenghi (1996, 1997a, 1997b), Kreis (2010), De Pablo et al. (2012) and Simons et al. (1998).
9. See Beller and Leerssen (2007).

Chapter 1

History and National Myth

José Álvarez Junco

The Twentieth Century, under the Impact of 1898: Regenerationism and *Institucionismo*

History written in Spain in the twentieth century was strongly marked, from its first beginnings, by the legacy of two opposing historiographical visions inherited from the previous century – one secular and liberal, the other Catholic-conservative. The attempts that were undertaken to professionalize the writing of history by Antonio Cánovas del Castillo – architect and several times prime minister of the Restoration regime after 1874, but also a substantial historical writer – Rafael Altamira or later Ramón Menéndez Pidal were due not only to the natural evolution of knowledge, or the permanent influence of French culture within Spain, but also to a desire to overcome this polarization.

At the same time, Spain's twentieth century was born under the impact of 1898, when it had lost all its major colonies in Cuba, Puerto Rico and the Philippines, and a huge amount of its pride, in a war of just ten weeks with the United States. It was not that there had never previously been any literature on the 'problem of Spain', but that episode inaugurated the tradition of what Juan Marichal called Spanish 'historical introspection'. The great question, for both historians and political analysts, lay in explaining the causes of the 'Spanish anomaly', as Santos Juliá has put it – that is, what made Spain different from Europe; whether it was economic backwardness, or its unjust social structure, or its incapacity to establish a participatory political system that would be of use to its citizens.[1] In their efforts to answer this question, writers resorted not to political or socioeconomic analyses but historical observations, which in fact contained a strong element of metaphysics. This leap into metaphysics came with the work of Miguel de Unamuno and Ángel Ganivet, precisely at the time when the war in Cuba was beginning in the 1890s. The former launched the idea of *intrahistoria*, or 'intrahistory', in 1895, a kind of *Volksgeist* that explained the history of a people; Spanish intrahistory was, for Unamuno, identified with a Quixotic spirit, the opposite of European rationalism. In a similar vein, two years later Ganivet explained the Spanish enigma in his *Idearium español* in the light of the mystery of the Immaculate Conception. Spain had a spiritual essence, he said, and the solution to its problems was not to open itself up to modern and materialist Europe, but to concentrate its energies on itself and experience its particular and singular historic trajectory in all its intensity.[2]

At the same time as these ideas were coming into circulation, efforts were continuing to professionalize the study of history. The best example at the turn of the century was the work of Rafael Altamira. However, not even he could avoid combining this modern scientific approach with a constant preoccupation with the essence of the nation. In Paris in 1890, he had met Ernest Lavisse, Charles Seignobos, Alfred Morel-Fatio and Ernest Renan, and he had also been in contact with British and German historians. He was especially impressed by the recently initiated discipline of sociology, which he felt would eventually replace the deliberations of the 'philosophy of history'. He set out to explain this as early as 1891, when he announced his attention to distance himself radically from traditional histories of Spain, full of 'fables, calumnies and false patriotisms'. It was necessary to reduce 'external history' (politics, wars, great names) to a minimum, and base oneself in the emerging social sciences: sociology, law, economics, the study of institutions, archaeology, geography, art, folklore. One had, in short, to replace individuals with collective groupings as the subjects of human events. This was what he attempted to do in his seminal *Historia de España y de la civilización española* (1900–1911).

In principle, Altamira was far from being a nationalist. He adopted comparative methods, was profoundly pro-European and felt a special interest in the Americas, a crucial element for the understanding of Spain. However, the deep nationalism that permeated the vision of reality at that time could make itself felt even in an individual as determined as he was to impose methodological rigour ahead of any kind of idealist apriorism. For he made the leading protagonist of his history the 'Spanish people', the subject and object of a narrative understood as an 'organic whole', the different parts of which were inter-related like those of a biological organism. Although, he explained, the great figures of history appeared to be the 'directors of national life', they could only be so depending on the degree to which they 'were in accordance with and accommodated themselves to the collective spirit which they sought to influence', and the contributions of 'outstanding individuals' needed to be understood as expressions of a 'collective spirit'. His own *Historia de España y de la civilización española* began with a declaration that the value of history lies in the fact that 'it leads the researcher to penetrate the most intimate [part] of the spirit of the different peoples', a knowledge that supplies us with 'the surest north for the direction of collective groups'.

To understand his *Historia,* in addition, one must consider it in relation to his *Psicología del pueblo español,* which appeared at virtually the same time and followed very faithfully the style of Alfred Fouillée's *Psychologie du peuple français.* 'The Necessity and Essential Nature of Nations' was the title of its first chapter, and the entire book was based on the presumption that there is a particularly Spanish 'psychological unity', a 'common Iberian root', a 'national genius that does not change', knowledge of which, he admitted, would be gained through the study of history.

Altamira was, as Antonio Morales has written, the 'true historian of the generation of 1898'.[3] This was so because his work not only dealt with the national fabric but also sought to be of use in the task of 'national regeneration'. In the gloom-laden climate of the beginning of the university year of 1898–99, in Oviedo, he chose as the subject of his inaugural lecture 'Patriotism in the University'. He spoke about the political impact of historical interpretations, which lay in the fact that they aided the creation of a 'national consciousness', for which purpose the 'scientific' history that he was proposing was far more suitable than one based on legends. Hence books on history had to be readable as well as rigorous, so that they could reach the people, who would thus learn to know themselves and gain faith in their own qualities. An enthusiastic admirer of the German philosopher Johann-Gottlieb Fichte, Altamira said that with his work he sought to provoke a patriotic reaction similar to the one seen in Germany after the defeat at Jena, an 'internal regeneration, the correction of our faults, the vigorous effort that has to lead us out of our deep national decadence'. Basing himself on a 'conviction that there was something great and noble in the Spanish past', through his work he hoped to give back to the Spanish people 'faith in their native qualities and in their aptitude for civilized life'.

Also part of the same generation as Altamira, and similarly moulded by the atmosphere of 1898, was Ramón Menéndez Pidal, a great historian of language and literature and the father of modern Spanish philology. Pidal differed from previous historians in that he brought together a dual affiliation, both traditionalist and liberal. A member of the Pidal family, bastions of Catholic conservatism in Asturias, and a student of the pre-eminent Catholic historian Marcelino Menéndez Pelayo, he nevertheless moved away from traditionalism and came into contact with the liberal-positivist circles influenced by the ideas of the German philosopher Karl C. F. Krause – who combined an emphasis on scientific rationalism and a liberal commitment to individual freedom with Christian spirit – and centred on the *Institución Libre de Enseñanza* (Free Educational Institution), the school founded by Francisco Giner de los Ríos and other liberal academics in Madrid in 1876. Immensely influential, the *Institución* and the liberal ethos it inspired – collectively known as *institucionismo* – became the leading exponents of a newly questioning, rationalist approach in virtually every area of Spanish intellectual life in the years from the 1880s up to the Civil War. Pidal appeared destined to join the *institucionistas* due to his austere, level-headed, hard-working character, open to Europe, rigorous in his research and respectful of the opinions and beliefs of others. He never felt any special fervour for Catholicism, but he was equally untouched by any kind of aggressive anti-clericalism.

Pidal began his career with careful research into the origins of the Castilian language and its literature, but always combined his protestations of scientific positivism with a profound romantic belief in the *Volksgeist*. In language he was interested 'not only in isolated words and phrases, but in the word as instrument of an idea, of a task, of a literature'; philology, he insisted, should lead to a scientific understanding of 'those manifestations of "the spirit of a people" that are expressed through the medium of language'. In the case of Spain there was, he believed, a profound symbiosis between its epic literature and 'national' history. The *cantares de gesta*, medieval poems of 'heroic feats' recounting stories of warrior heroes, were 'a privileged manifestation of the "popular soul"', in which there 'is no distinction between the author and the common people'. These romances were inspired by a 'deep national spirit' and were 'the most sincere and complete expression of the high ideals of the nation', so that as a result they enabled Spaniards to connect with 'that race of long-gone men, with whom, however strange it may make us feel, we are united by an ineluctable atavism'.[4]

The most important of the epic poems that he studied was the cycle associated with Rodrigo Díaz de Vivar, the eleventh-century knight known as *El Cid* who is the central subject of the most famous of all the *cantares*, the *Cantar de Mio Cid*, upon which Pidal worked for decades. In 1908 he 'reconstructed' and published a comprehensive edition of the poem and in 1929 he produced a purely historical survey of the time, *La España del Cid* (The Spain of the Cid). He fervently rejected any questioning of the historical veracity of the *Cantar de Mio Cid*, as put forward by the Dutch Arabist Reinhart Dozy. For Menéndez Pidal, not only was the historical reality of the figure of *El Cid* indisputable, he was equally the embodiment of a national hero. Pidal considered him a 'man of the people', as an *infanzón* or member of the lower nobility without a hereditary title, and saw him as endowed with the best Castilian popular virtues: loyal, chivalrous, devout and valiant, but with a sense of justice, and capable of calling the king himself to account in the name of the kingdom. *El Cid*, in short, 'in his own self gave shape to the national idea throughout the whole of his adventurous life'.

In the midst of the crisis following 1898, moreover, this 'terror of kings and Moors' could also be a regenerative myth. The exemplary nature of *El Cid* could be a salutary remedy against 'this current weakness of the collective spirit'. In reality, 'all the great historical records', but especially epic poetry, could fulfil this function of reactivating patriotism. *El Cid* also lacked, Pidal argued, what he considered to be the 'capital Iberian defect', the 'exclusivist regional spirit' that led people 'not to feel a sense of solidarity between the regions of Spain as a whole'. According to Pidal, Rodrigo Díaz had sought the unity of all the peoples of the Iberian peninsula – including the 'Spanish Moors' – against the invasion of the Almoravids, the originally Moroccan Islamic revivalist movement that seized Muslim Spain in the 1090s. Thanks to this zeal for integrating the different territories of the Iberian peninsula, this lack of exclusive selfishness, it had been Castile that had been capable of overcoming the 'imperialism' of the old kingdom of León, based on mere force, and leading the process that united Spain at the end of the Middle Ages. And if *El Cid* was the very image of Castile, so too Castile was the image of Spain.

The enterprises undertaken by Castile were not just political or military, but above all cultural: Castile created the language and literature that would go on to become national. For Pidal, culture expressed a communitarian identity, and a language was the highest expression of a culture. Hence the new slant he gave to the problem of the 'two Spains', supposedly articulated around adherence or opposition to Catholicism and monarchical authority. In order to overcome this political and religious abyss between the conservative and progressive elites, Pidal proposed, as a unifying factor for Spain, the language: the one that had been referred to as *Castellano*, Castilian, in Spain, but which on Pidal's initiative began to be called *Español*, Spanish, in the dictionary of the Spanish Royal Academy.

Like that of Altamira, Menéndez Pidal's nationalism did not signify a closed attitude to the outside world, a rejection of the foreign. Pidal was pro-European, in the sense that he saw Spain as fundamentally a part of European culture, in opposition to the orientalist vision of the romantics. Spain, the birthplace of two great Roman emperors, had defended European civilization in its long battle with Islam. When it imposed its hegemony, it created a fully European empire, a successor to that of Rome. As a historian, Pidal thus defended the nation's achievements, and sought to cultivate among his readers a pride in feeling Spanish. His nationalism, however, at times also led him to adopt positions that were inappropriate in a pro-European, post-Enlightenment intellectual, such as his disdain for the Renaissance and the Enlightenment itself as 'anti-national' eras. Only the medieval epic authentically expressed the national being.

Menéndez Pidal, in sum, was a great intellectual, one who made vital contributions to the fields of philology, the history of grammar, the origins of the Spanish language and toponymics. However, the general inferences he made, which went beyond his specialized field, were weighed down by the nationalism of his era. Pidal reasoned in the manner that was current at the end of the nineteenth century, or as someone like Spengler still did in the first third of the twentieth.[5]

Ortega y Gasset: Invertebrate Spain

The generation of 1898 gave way to that of 1914, less metaphysically inclined, with a more professional education and direct experience of a Europe in which many had studied. Its great representative was José Ortega y Gasset, a philosopher who based his theories precisely on the concept of 'historical reason' or 'narrative reason', which he distinguished from physical and mathematical reason, and so deserves a space in this survey of historical viewpoints.

Between 1920 and 1922, Ortega published his *España invertebrada: Bosquejo de algunos pensamientos históricos* (Invertebrate Spain: An Outline of Some Thoughts on History),[6] an attempt to investigate the national political problem in order to diagnose the malaise and offer remedies that could 'revitalize' the country. He conceived the object of his study, the nation as a body, in a manner part-way between a historical approach and an organic, essentialist one. In accordance with the ideas of his time, he took as his starting point the existence of 'peoples', 'nations' or 'races', which he described as organic entities, affected by vital cycles of birth, growth, decline and death. Spain was in this case, according to Ortega, a 'social organism', a 'historic animal that belongs to a particular species', with 'a specific structure identical to those of

France, England and Italy'. However, these historical subjects were also atemporal, immutable psychological entities; each nation had its own particular and unmistakeable 'genius' or 'talent', and there was a distinct 'national way of looking at things', a 'way of living', a 'style of life', as captured in its art, its cultural creations, its customs and its political institutions.

At the same time, nations were products of their history, the subject that concerns us here. With *España invertebrada*, Ortega wanted to compensate for the absence of 'real books on the history of Spain' – that is, for him, books that offered a global interpretation. The explanation he offered began with the Roman Empire, 'the only complete historical trajectory of a national organism of which we have knowledge'. This trajectory consisted of a process of aggregating cultures and peoples around a nucleus that offered an 'attractive project of life in common'. This nucleus had been Rome, similar to Castile in the case of Spain. Both possessed a 'nationalizing talent', a *'quid divinum,* a genius or talent as particular as one for poetry, music or religious invention', based on 'knowing how to love, and have strength, and knowing how to command'.

Many aspects of this argument would be questioned today by specialists in nationalism. However, Ortega at least took as his starting point the nation as a historical entity, which was not a bad beginning. There was no primordialism in his opening lines. He had read Renan, and embraced the idea of the 'daily plebiscite'. Modern nations were a 'community of purposes, desires, of great practical utilities. We do not live together in order *to be* together, but in order *to do* something together.' The Spain that Ortega was thinking of was orientated to the future, not the past.

From this point, *España invertebrada* turned towards an inquiry into the historical roots of the 'Spanish problem', which for the philosopher was found in the absence or weakness of feudalism. This was due to the Visigoths who had taken over Iberia after the fall of Rome, a 'decadent' Germanic people 'drunken on Romanism' who had lost the 'lordly vitality' of their Aryan spirit and lacked a 'select minority'. The key to the Hispanic character, the root of its problems, lay precisely in the Visigoths' inability to construct a feudal society, with powerful 'guiding minorities'. Ever since then, Spain had been a country in which *señores* or 'lords' were few in number, and weak.

For Ortega, as is well known, a healthy social organism was one in which the 'masses' submitted to the guidance of a 'select' or 'eminent' minority. Spain, in contrast, had been delivered up by the Visigoths to the 'domination of the masses'. The defect of the 'race', the 'real root of the great Hispanic failure', consisted of the fact that the masses 're-fused to be the mass' and did not resign themselves to their role, they were 'not disposed [to adopt] the humble attitude of listening', so that instead a 'hatred of those who are best' reigned. This was the source of all the other ills that contributed to the unintegrated and 'invertebrate' nature of the country: 'particularism', a lack of solidarity, congenital individualism, an inability to cooperate, to be disciplined, to submit to the norms of a modern state.

Ortega thus abandoned history in favour of an atemporal, organicist analysis, moving away from Renan to move closer to the primordial-ism of Herder or Fichte. The 'ethnic vices' of Spain, its 'infirm' com-position, are pre-political and permanent. They can be summed up as two: *plebeyismo,* 'plebeianism' or 'aristophobia', and 'particularism', the weakness of any unitary idea of coexistence. At this stage in his argument, liberal or democratic considerations also lost priority. Or-tega was concerned about chaos, the reign of 'direct action' that he saw as derived from particularism, and the only solution that occurred to him was to demand obedience. He was not so worried by the ques-tion of how the power that corresponded to 'the best', the 'vigorous' or 'eminent men' was to be controlled and limited. Some critics of Or-tega have taken advantage of this vein in his thinking to speak of his 'pre-Fascism'. However, it was a feature of the time: Gaetano Mosca and Vilfredo Pareto in Italy, and such well-accredited Spanish republi-cans as José Gaos or María Zambrano, all said similar things.

España invertebrada is without doubt a complex book, as well as being very elegantly written, and one that has been analysed a thou-sand times in philosophical, political or literary terms. From a histor-ical point of view, it was an excessively bold work. Its entire reasoning is based on one very simple dichotomy: the opposition between Ger-manic culture and that of Rome. The former represents everything aristocratic, reflective and creative, masculine or 'vertebrate'; the latter, whatever is disorganized, decadent and submissive, that is, the 'inver-tebrate' or feminine, a mere 'mass' of voluptuous flesh, sensitive and spontaneous but lacking in solidity. All the ills of Spain are due to a simple historic fact: the arrival of the Goths, a people that Ortega cate-gorized, without taking the trouble to support his argument, as insuffi-ciently Germanic, and therefore invertebrate and feminine.

Many things remain unexplained in such an audacious exercise in speculative essay-writing. For example, the question of how Spain managed to attain the political unity driven forward by Castile and went on to reach the peak of its imperial power, when the cause of its failings – the culture of the Goths – had by then been established in the country for more than a millennium. In other words, why the factor that supposedly explains its decline did not play any role at the time when the nation was rising, when it was taking shape and attaining its *plenitud vital,* or 'fullness of life'. A difficult question, which Ortega resolved with one stroke of his pen: 'the unity of Spain was achieved so early because Spain was weak', he wrote, because it lacked 'a strong sense of pluralism sustained by great figures in the feudal manner', and there were no institutions capable of resisting a violent drive for unification. Hence, Spain's moment of 'plenitude' was in reality not a 'symptom of vital powers' but artificial, premature and feeble.

Overall, the work by Ortega y Gasset that can most legitimately be classed as historical contradicts subsequent positions he developed, of much greater interest, which take as their basis the idea that 'man is not nature, but history' – that is, that a human being is not a fixed, definite substance in the Parmenidean sense, but creates himself in the course of his life.

Francoism: Imperial History

Altamira, Menéndez Pidal and Ortega created the intellectual climate that predominated in the best minds of the Spain of the Second Republic. It is no exaggeration to say that in the radical political turnaround of 1931, the *institucionistas,* the followers of Ortega and the generations that had been trained abroad in other parts of Europe thanks to the *Junta para Ampliación de Estudios* – in the historical field, the great swathe of researchers that had emerged from the Centre of Historical Studies, under Menéndez Pidal – arrived in power.[7]

However, there was also another conservative intellectual community, which had been drawing up the outlines of a nationalist and authoritarian alternative as a renewal of the National-Catholicism inherited from the nineteenth century, and which of course found itself excluded from power in 1931. It was these circles that nourished the intellectual ambience that was taking shape around those who set themselves up in opposition to the Second Republic. As one might expect, no great new contributions in the historical field formed part of this renovation of conservatism. In the 1930s, the only debates that took place on history were restricted to battles for the control of institutions and for the publicizing of existing ideas. In these controversies, the conservatives were content to resort to old, simple myths, such as that of Tubal, the grandson of Noah who was said to have been the first settler in Iberia, or of Saint James the Apostle, Spain's first Christian

evangelist. They also repeated previous attacks on the Spanish followers of the Enlightenment and the liberals of the Cádiz Parliament of
1812, as servile imitators of French ideas, and the customary conservative glorification of the Spanish Empire as the crowning moment in the
nation's history, in opposition to the long-established liberal detach-
ment from an enterprise that progressives saw as driven by dynastic
interest and unbefitting a people characterized by an obstinate defence
of their own independence in the face of repeated foreign invasions.

Of the conservative historians of that period, the names of Pío Za-
bala, Melchor Fernández Almagro and Gabriel Maura deserve to be
remembered. Also notable as an overview was the voluminous *Historia
de España y su influencia en la Historia Universal* by Antonio Ballesteros Beretta, published between 1919 and 1941. In this latter work,
there are, as with any author of the period, constant references to the
'spirit of the race' as a mechanism for explaining the conduct of the
inhabitants of Iberia. However, what makes the book stand out is its
assertive, vindicatory tone and its marked Castilianism. For Ballesteros, the culminating period in national history began with the reign
of the Catholic Monarchs Ferdinand and Isabella, 'the most glorious
of all the reigns that there have been in Spain', and extended to the
older Habsburgs, so that he thus distanced himself from the liberal
critique of the Habsburgs' suppression of traditional native liberties,
most notably in the crushing of the *Comuneros* revolt in Castile by
Charles V in 1520–21. In his first edition, he criticized the imperial
enterprises of Charles V as a 'continual draining away of energies that
won us many laurels, [but] without any positive result', but this phrase
disappeared from editions produced after the Civil War. He similarly
rectified his opinion of the *Comuneros*, described in 1924 as 'defenders
of the liberties specified in the requirement to convene a *Cortes* (parliament), and the petition for constitutional guarantees regarding the
collection of financial subsidies ... the basis of fundamental modern
freedoms', but of whom he wrote in 1942 that 'they did not understand
the spiritual greatness of the Empire ... preferring their own mean
self-interest to lofty prospects'. He went over the contemporary era
more rapidly, but said that the coup d'état of Primo de Rivera 'gave
Spain six years of effective peace and public order'. In post–Civil War
editions, he also added a chapter on 'The Republic, the Revolution and
the War of Liberation'.[8]

Under the dictatorship of Franco, one historian who was close to
the regime but maintained an unquestionable level of professionalism
was Ciriaco Pérez Bustamante, the author of a *Compendio de Historia
Universal* and a *Síntesis de la Historia de España*, both published in

1939. In his works, abundant and carefully gathered factual research cohabits with references to 'the character of the primitive Hispanic peoples', the 'Spanish' Roman emperors or the 'Spanishness' of the Córdoba-born Seneca. Writing on the Middle Ages, he pointed out the transition 'from a horde to a nation' of the Visigoths, the 'royal blood' of Don Pelayo, who inflicted the first defeat on the Moors at Covadonga some time around 722, and the extent to which the *Reconquista* of the peninsula from the Moors was a 'national undertaking'. Nor did he have any doubt that the Catholic monarchs had forged 'national unity', to which they added a 'spiritual unity' that required a 'cruel cleansing of the race of all kinds of contaminations and foreign elements encrusted into the national organism'. The Inquisition 'avoided the religious struggles that covered other countries in blood'; Philip II was a 'memorable prince' who struggled tirelessly against heresy 'with an idealism ... that went against his own interests'; and Spain's subsequent decline had been due to the inadequacies of his successors on the throne and the corruption of their ministers. The eighteenth century had been given over to 'spiritual and political *afrancesamiento* ('Frenchification')', and the Enlightenment reforms of Charles III after 1759, though laudable in intent, had opened Spain up to 'unbelieving philosopher-ism ... and Freemasonry'. The liberals of the early nineteenth century were 'a minority opposed to the religious and monarchist sentiments of Spaniards' who provoked 'the destruction of the political and religious unity of Spain', although the 'repressive policy' deployed against them by Ferdinand VII after 1814 'lacked the necessary equanimity'. There was no room for halftones, however, in Pérez Bustamante's approach to Primo de Rivera, who had 'brought an end to the crisis in employment' and managed to extend 'material well-being' throughout the country. His fall was due to the hostility of the intellectuals and the old political class and 'a devious, permanent offensive by Freemasonry'. The republic naturally signified 'chaos, anarchy', with daily 'riots, murders, strikes and disturbances'. This went on until, under the government of the Popular Front, when it was no longer possible 'to wait any more', and 'all legal recourse' had been exhausted, the army rose up in revolt, 'led by its most clear-headed commanders', 'austere men, removed from politics', who were joined by everything 'healthy' in Spanish society: 'the Falange, the Carlist militia, the masses of the right'.

On the Spanish Empire, the subject of so many panegyrics in Francoist speeches and pamphlets, scarcely any historical works worth mentioning were produced in this period. The most notable was *La fundación de un Imperio*, also by Pérez Bustamante, from 1940, which was later extended to become a *Historia del Imperio español*. Once again, this was not a speculative essay but a study heavily packed with facts, with a clear conservative message. To sum up its argument, the entire imperial enterprise in the Americas had as its aim the conversion of the indigenous peoples to Christianity, and the thousands of millions of pesos in precious metals that Spain received from America were a 'well-deserved compensation for a gigantic effort'. For the country had placed 'its blood, the best of its population, its beliefs, its culture, the produce of its soil and the products of its factories ... at the service of the newly discovered countries and races', and 'however great may have been the benefit it received in return for such sacrifice, it would never be excessive as a reward for the civilization of a whole world, and a task so well done for the cause of Humanity'.[9]

The aim of Francoist historiography was not to gain knowledge of the past but to provide political indoctrination. The manifestation of this idea with the greatest impact at the time was in the courses referred to as *Formación del Espíritu Nacional* (Formation of the National Spirit), which were fundamentally historical in content and compulsory in all levels and branches of education. Several other works created to serve this objective, such as *La Historia de España contada con sencillez*, written for schools by José María Pemán, were also distributed very widely across the country.[10]

Metaphysical Debates from across the Atlantic

While all these developments were taking place within Spain, among the exiles abroad the most resounding of the historiographical polemics of the twentieth century was underway; the one maintained between Américo Castro and Claudio Sánchez Albornoz in the 1940s and 1950s.

Castro was a philologist and historian of literature, born in Brazil and educated in Spain, France and Germany. Exiled after the Civil War, he eventually moved to the United States, where he taught for thirty years. His first works had dealt with authors and cultural artefacts that were a little marginal with respect to the dominant Catholic culture – that is, the peoples who had been defeated in 1492 and then regarded with incomprehension by the common people and persecuted by church and state. From exile, he presented these ideas in systematic form in *España en su historia. Cristianos, moros y judíos* (Spain in its History: Christians, Moors and Jews), first published in Buenos Aires in 1948 and reissued in 1954 with the title *La realidad histórica de España* (The Historical Reality of Spain).

His first point of originality was that, in the face of the habitual essentialist approach, he declared that he did not believe in an 'eternal Spaniard' or an 'atemporal Spain', and sought instead to offer a historical explanation of the question. Existence precedes essence, he observed, following Ortega. The Spanish 'being' did not go back into the far reaches of time, and one could not call the ancient Iberians, the Goths or 'whichever illustrious Roman who was born in *Hispania*' by the name Spaniards. The decisive moment in Iberian history, the one that had originated a radically different situation by comparison with the rest of Europe, had been the arrival of the Muslims, the origin of a difficult coexistence of three 'castes' and a process of psychic and physical intermixing unknown in other European countries. To this was added, at the end of the fifteenth century, the repression of the defeated minorities by the Catholic majority, which represented a shift from coexistence, *convivencia,* to 'tearing apart', or *desgarro*. In the following centuries, the cultural creators of the country – by this time fully 'Spaniards' – lived in an 'agonizing' situation of radical insecurity, in a constant 'embittered life' of 'denying one's own identity'. This was the interpretation Castro made of the principal intellectual and literary figures of the sixteenth century, including such great names as Luis Vives, Friar Luis de León and Miguel de Cervantes, all of whom were, for him, *conversos* (converts) from Judaism or Islam. Like Saint Teresa of Ávila or Saint John of the Cross, in whose mystical writings 'the distant and hidden currents of the Islamic sensibility blossomed into life', or the writers of ascetic and picaresque literature, 'twin daughters of a Judaism made into a church'. Spain, in short, owed 'the great summits of its literary and intellectual civilization' to 'the anguish of the converts'.

Castro's initial proposition was highly innovative, compared with what had been written up to that time. Although the Jewish and Muslim past of the peninsula had been studied for a long time, no one had dared locate it at the very centre of the national culture. Castro's theses were the perfect antithesis to the Catholic vision of Menéndez Pelayo. Nevertheless, he too eventually fell into the trap of national essences. His idea was, ultimately, that the 'real' Spain had not existed before the arrival of the Arabs; however, after the intimate cohabitation with Arabs and Jews between the eighth century and the end of the fifteenth, in contrast, and above all after the forced conversion and subsequent marginalization of their descendants, it did then fully exist. The important point was not so much Castro's answer, very different from that of his predecessors, as the question, which was identical to theirs: what was it that defined Spanish identity?

Although his point of departure had been existentialism, Castro's ship eventually ran aground in national essentialism. The objective of historiography, he announced from the beginning of his study, was to 'set down the identity of a people'. The historian is a 'biographer of peoples', and in his case he wished to capture the 'intimate feelings' of the Spaniards of the past, and write their 'internal history', in the sense of the underlying foundations of history as used by Unamuno. Following Ortega, who distinguished between the 'styles of life' of different peoples or 'races', Castro spoke of the special *morada vital*, or 'essential dwelling place', the 'living stance' and the 'vital motives' of Spaniards. At the root of all these distinctive elements he found that original trauma, the remains of convert culture – which at times he referred to as 'Hebrew' and at others 'Semitic', since it was mixed with Arabic elements – and he gave less importance to or excluded as non-Spanish anyone or anything that did not fit into his model of a convert or 'New Christian', with his anguish, his divided soul, his bitterness inside, his resentment towards society, his tendency to take refuge in a kind of internal emigration. This intellectual nucleus of the country had found itself persecuted and treated with incomprehension by the 'mass' of the old Christians, welded to Counter-Reformation Catholicism, uncultured ('a lack of culture guaranteed that one had no Jewish blood'), dedicated to maintaining and glorying in their caste privileges, ignorant of the 'art of producing and moving wealth' and even incapable of politically uniting the country. This, in turn, explained the intellectual output that had made Spain so singular. Outside Spain, on the other hand, it appeared from his account that there was no other country where one could find repressed cultural minorities, or aristocrats who considered manual labour degrading, or 'magical' cultures – at least, not in Europe. The East was another thing. These key cultural elements, omnipresent and exclusive, had converted the distance that separated Spain from the rest of Western culture into an abyss.

A still graver flaw in his argument was the permanence with which he endowed this identity, converted into an immutable *Volksgeist*, impermeable to all subsequent historical changes and impossible to dismantle once it had been established – rather than a 'vital dwelling place', wrote Eugenio Asensio, Castro had constructed a 'prison' – in a manner that precisely contradicted his initial, promising historicist approach. That first fundamental trauma had been the source not just of Spanish mystical writing, the picaresque or the lyric works of the Golden Age, but of all the great phenomena of contemporary Spanish history: the impossibility of constructing an effective state or an industrial economy, regionalism, anarchism and the fratricidal war of 1936, which for Castro was due to the fact that 'the need had become endemic among us to expel from the country or exterminate whoever it is that dissents from what is believed and desired by the most powerful'.[11]

The work of Américo Castro had a great impact in exile circles and among Hispanists internationally, in part because he was combating the socioeconomic focus in vogue in the academic world in the 1950s and 1960s in the name of a strictly cultural approach that would become more prominent in the following decades. Castro proclaimed 'caste', rather than 'class', as a challenge. This also explains the success of his work in the United States, where there was so much interest in the Jewish past and where the field of 'cultural studies' was beginning to develop.

Américo Castro's work was, then, an audacious effort, attractive, erudite and written with strength and style. It aided the retrieval of individuals and features that had been forgotten or repressed in Spanish history. However, his daring would have been more fruitful if he had seen his way to distinguishing distant historical problems from those of his own time and avoided entering the murky territory of national essences. Because for him, the Jews represented the modern intelligentsia; the 'Moors', the working class; and the 'old Christians', the obstacle to the modernization of Spain. That obstacle that everyone sought to identify, and that Joaquín Costa, foremost proponent of 'regenerationism' at the turn of the century, had seen in the binomial of 'oligarchy and *caciquismo* (political clientelism)', Ortega in the absence of feudalism, Catalan nationalists in 'Castile' and subsequently Manuel Tuñón de Lara (see below) in the 'power bloc'. Their preoccupation with the present was, for all of them, a serious obstacle to their understanding the past.

The academic world of Francoist Spain, despite feeling offended by a work that highlighted areas so radically distant from Catholic and imperial stereotypes, lacked the necessary intellectual strength to elaborate a reply. This came instead from within the exile circles themselves, from Argentina and under the name of a medieval historian of high reputation, Claudio Sánchez Albornoz, a student of Menéndez Pidal and Eduardo Hinojosa and a former colleague of Castro at the Centre for Historic Studies. Sánchez Albornoz had built up a solid reputation as a researcher into Roman Spain, initially, and later into the medieval period. Although he did not share in Ortega's negative vision of the Visigoths, he did believe that the absence or weakness of feudalism in Spain was the key factor in its 'abnormality'. He had documented this thesis by analysing the repopulation of the two great *mesetas* or plains of Castile following their conquest from the Muslims, which had given rise to a rare and unusual political structure with a powerful monarchy ruling over an inorganic mass of gentry, free peasants and villeins, and with scarcely any scale of ranks among the nobility.

However, it was not enough for him to write seminal works on the political and social structures of the High Middle Ages. Like Castro, he abandoned positivist documentation to move on to philosophical-anthropological interpretations of the 'being' of Spain. From his exile in Buenos Aires, he published his *España, un enigma histórico* in 1956, a work that in private he called his 'anti-Castro'. His central thesis was that a 'continuity' existed in the national identity, around a *Homo hispanus* who had taken shape in the distant past, and whose sober character was due to the 'physical setting' and the dryness of the land (of the *meseta*, naturally, since Sánchez Albornoz identified Spain with Castile). This, together with the moral inheritance derived from all the invasions that this group of humans had had to confront, would also explain its brusqueness, its violence, its exaggerated individualism. Although Sánchez Albornoz – a declared enemy, as a positivist, of romanticism – refused to call this set of features a *Volksgeist*, it was certainly the case that he considered it to have been a constant for millennia.

However, the fact that the Hispanic archetype had lasted did not mean that it had remained immutable. The 'river of history', wrote Sánchez Albornoz, had received constant fresh contributions from successive tributaries – with a relative weight, though, that was very different in each case. The Roman legacy united the Hispanic peoples around a single language and culture and softened their passionate nature, but did not lead to the emergence of a new 'vital structure', since the Romans in Iberia were eventually 'Hispanicized', as was demonstrated by the group of Hispano-Latin writers with clearly Spanish features, classically represented by Seneca. Not even Christianity, which added a crucial, and permanent, element to the Spanish personality, brought a decisive change of course in the formative process. As to the Visigoths, Sánchez Albornoz believed that their cultural contribution had been highly valuable, since it had been the origin of the 'sentimental intuition of the living unity of Hispania', as a singular and particular human community. However, they had ultimately been absorbed by the strong cultural personality of the indigenous Hispanic population.

In complete opposition to Castro's view, for Sánchez Albornoz the invasion of least importance had been that of the Muslims. This was so firstly because those who arrived in 711 were 'scarcely influenced by Islamic culture', he believed, and the level of cultural exchange between them and the Christians of the north was negligible. But, it was above all because as the *Reconquista* advanced southwards, the replacement of the population was almost total. The Hispanic populations subjected to Muslim rule were only Arabicized to an infinitely small degree. In terms of cultural contributions, the most notable aspect that remained was religious mysticism, which would confer upon the Spanish people that baroque, or romantic, element in their character that created difficulties in their adaptation to modern rationalism. The principal effect of this invasion had been negative, in the reaction it provoked, since the Spaniards had united to struggle against it. As to the Jews, for whom Sánchez Albornoz felt little sympathy, coexistence with them had been difficult, because they had dominated and exploited the people. Their principal legacy, he added malevolently, was the Inquisition, a 'Satanic invention' of Jewish converts to use against their own former coreligionists.

To sum up, then, one could not speak in any way of a 'symbiosis between cultures', but of antitheses, clashes, persecutions and massacres. The Christians became united thanks to the 'Reconquest', the joint enterprise that saved 'the being and the very essence of *Hispania*', and the Spanish identity thus became based on entirely Latin and Christian cultural pillars, a clear contrast to the ideas of Castro, who linked it to 'Semitic' or 'oriental' cultures.

The principal difference between Castro and Sánchez Albornoz lay therefore in the point that, for the former, Spanish identity emerged in the Middle Ages, thanks to the residues left by Jews and Muslims, while for the latter the process had begun much earlier, since it was anchored in permanent elements such as the race and the land, and had taken place more slowly and been nourished by a wider variety of cultural contributions. However, Sánchez Albornoz also added to these 'material' aspects one very conventional idea: the existence of a 'historic mission', the defence of religion, initiated in the long centuries of struggle with Islam and developed to its full vigour during the Counter-Reformation. A mission that in part was a question of destiny and in part a matter of collective will, since Spaniards had joyfully accepted this assignment from providence. 'In defence of the unity of the faith Spain gave everything. And it did so to the point of prostration and sterility', Sánchez Albornoz wrote, 'the Counter-Reformation was its glory and its tragedy', 'it was madness, the greatest in history, the sacrifice Spain made to maintain the Catholic unity of the West and to remain faithful to moral principles ... that were ridiculed by a world conquered by Machiavelli and Jean Bodin.'

These discrepancies between the arguments put forward by Castro and Sánchez Albornoz appear less important if we consider the conceptual framework against which they each unfolded their histories.

Both of them accepted that the object to be studied was the nation as an entity, and that the question to be answered was the definition of its identity. Even the basic outlines that they drew of that identity were substantially the same, since both found in the 'Spanish temperament' features such as pride, personal dignity, strength of will, a sense of honour, loyalty to people rather than to ideas, ethical rigour and a defence of ideal values instead of a concern for success and efficiency.

Despite the negative aspects that he detected, Sánchez Albornoz, overall, set out to vindicate Spain's cultural identity. Europe owed much more to Spain than Spain to Europe, since 'the discoveries and voyages of exploration of the Spaniards contributed decisively to the birth of modernity ... prompted the true free examination of nature and of life ... and prepared the way to the victory of reason and its philosophical and scientific promise'.

Like Castro, Sánchez Albornoz abandoned the field of concrete research to move into global interpretations and reach arbitrary conclusions on the 'temperamental constitution' of the country, a concept that was not too far distant from the *morada vital* of his antagonist. His providentialism, too, did not go well with his purported respect for facts; for example, the historical circumstances that had placed a people with 'particular psychic and tactical reactions' in the Cantabrian region of Spain, a place 'from which it was not possible to retreat', could not have been fortuitous, he claimed, but had been 'prepared by the divinity to serve as a decisive barrier to save Christianity'. In contrast to Menéndez Pidal, who had made the language the axis of Spanish identity, Sánchez Albornoz returned to religion, like nineteenth-century Catholic writers such as Jaime Balmes and Menéndez Pelayo.

If Castro was well accepted in North American Hispanics departments, Sánchez Albornoz was in contrast better received among Spanish historians. He was applauded by colleagues from fellow medievalist Luis García de Valdeavellano to Menéndez Pidal, and writers close to the Franco regime such as Pedro Sáinz Rodríguez or Gonzalo Fernández de la Mora. None of them liked the great weight that Castro had attributed to Jews and Muslims in the Hispanic past.

When this polemical exchange wore itself out, at the beginning of the 1960s, the essentialist debate on the 'Spanish character' came to a close. Critiques of the identity-based essay appeared, associated with the names of Francisco Ayala, Julio Caro Baroja, José Antonio Maravall and Jaume Vicens Vives, who deserve recognition for their work of intellectual cleansing.[12] They provoked angry reactions, above all from Sánchez Albornoz and the exiled republican historian Salvador de Madariaga, but these had no effect. Since the end of the Second

World War, the world of the social sciences had undergone a healthy reaction against primordialist approaches on the subject of nations.

The Last Great Paradigms

In the final stages of Francoism, at a time when society was changing at great speed, a previously unheard-of level of interest in history became visible in Spain, especially in the recent past, the turbulent nineteenth century, the republic and the Civil War, subjects on which huge numbers of books and articles were published as soon as access to sources and the censorship of the regime permitted it.

For young researchers, the most attractive field was the one that was referred to as 'social history', which in reality was identified with the 'history of the workers' movement'. Work had been going on in this field since the beginning of the century, with autobiographical writings by workers' leaders themselves or the pioneer works of Juan Díaz del Moral or Manuel Núñez de Arenas. It also received increasing attention in general histories, such as those of Antonio Ramos Oliveira or especially Pierre Vilar, who produced a *Histoire de l'Espagne* in 1947, which, despite its brief length, became a standard work of reference. The person who would exercise the greatest influence in this field was precisely the translator of this book into Spanish, the exiled historian and professor of the University of Pau Manuel Tuñón de Lara, who expressed as no one else the vision of the past accepted by those opposed to the Franco regime.

The most significant feature of Tuñón de Lara's historiographical approach was his use of information from press sources and concepts and methods of analysis drawn from sociology, economics and political science. His work was full of terms nonexistent in previous Spanish history books: 'power bloc', the 'apparatus of the state', 'social formation', 'contradictions', 'crisis', 'struggles for hegemony', 'elites', 'mentalities', 'pressure groups'. Although his basic roots were Marxist, he did not reduce his explanations to a rigid schema of class struggle. Socioeconomic structures were the basis of his thinking, but it was also evident that – in addition to a moralistic tone, dating back to Joaquín Costa – an added imprint had been left upon him by the *Annales* school and French structuralism, which opened him up to a more interdisciplinary approach.

Tuñón distinguished between three 'levels' or 'aspects' in historical structures, the socioeconomic, the political and the cultural, which, he insisted, were all 'interdependent'. He recommended that quantitative methods should preferably be used in analysing the deepest levels, but socioeconomic 'reality' could not be limited to them; the quantitative had to be combined with the qualitative, as structures had to be with *conjonctures* and long-term processes with short-term ones. A concept like that of 'social mentality' allowed him to give great attention to cultural themes, particularly literary subjects. However, he always sought to look at culture not 'as an enumeration of personalities and works in the style of the old histories', but with a focus on 'ideologies and their formation, as well as their dissemination through the varying apparatus of hegemony'.

One of his most widely repeated concepts was that of the 'power bloc' or 'hegemonic bloc', which evoked the 'historic bloc' put forward in the 1960s by the Greek sociologist Nikos Poulantzas and Italian Communists. A 'power bloc' was more than a simple alliance, more 'real' even – though less visible – than the mere formal or political powers. It consisted of a grouping of forces that 'directed' – not 'dominated', although the 'dominant' social classes did form part of it – the rest of society. The paradigmatic example of this situation was for Tuñón the Bourbon Restoration in Spain in the last quarter of the nineteenth century, the point at which the architect of the new regime, Cánovas del Castillo, based his system on the support of a 'bloc of oligarchical power', made up of the monarchy, the Church – its extreme supporters in Carlism having been defeated – the military hierarchy, the aristocracy, a large part of the 'political personnel' in the bureaucracy, the Catalan bourgeoisie – won over by protectionist tariffs for their industries – and their equivalents in the Basque Country, drawn in by tax concessions. Unlike Pierre Vilar, Tuñón believed that there had indeed been a 'bourgeois revolution' in Spain in the nineteenth century. After this had taken place, the new 'power bloc' adapted to liberal parliamentary conventions, but obstructed political participation by the popular classes and felt itself constrained by an 'ideological ceiling' inherited from the *ancien régime*. This situation created under Cánovas was maintained until the events of 1898 created a 'crisis of hegemony', or an 'ideological crisis'. From then on, the dominant bloc could only survive by relying on force and direct oppression, to withstand rising social tensions without reforming the system. This whole unstable construct eventually resulted in a 'crisis of the state', which led to the dictatorship of Primo de Rivera and, following the defection of part of the bourgeoisie – those who read the liberal newspaper *El Sol* – the collapse of the monarchy in 1931.[13]

As I write, near half a century has passed since the most important works by Tuñón de Lara appeared in print. And it shows. Cultural studies, relegated to a subordinate level by Tuñón, have dominated the scene since the 1980s. The political sphere has also been re-evaluated, although it is no longer dealt with at all as a mere sequence of struggles for and handovers of power, but through an analysis of the systems of decision-making, taking special care to maintain conceptual rigour and incorporating a comparative approach. The 'history of the workers' movement' has been replaced by another, more complex story, within an overall vision of 'social movements'. The schematic formula of bourgeois revolution / proletarian revolution as the central axis of contemporary history has come under very severe criticism and today has practically fallen out of use entirely, affected, like so many other concepts with their roots in Marxism, by the discrediting and collapse of so-called real socialism in the former Communist countries. As to Tuñón's vision of the Cánovas era, it was questioned from the mid-1970s by historians trained in Oxford by the British Hispanist Raymond Carr such as Juan Pablo Fusi or Joaquín Romero Maura, and later by others who, taking their cue from sociologists and political analysts who have studied clientelism, have stressed the difficulties in establishing a liberal parliamentary system and modernizing the economy in a primarily rural, fragmented society. As a mediator between this rural world and the urban centres of political power, it can be argued, *caciquismo* was a functional solution. Eliminating the ethical condemnation of the regime, inherited from Joaquín Costa in the 1900s, the Cánovas system is now analysed by comparing it with several other limited representative systems that existed in other countries nearby, and that in some cases evolved less traumatically towards higher levels of democratic participation. The conclusion, in short, tends to be that Spain was not such an exceptional country after all.

The success of Tuñón de Lara was no doubt influenced by his personal charisma, as a militant and political exile, and his agile, journalistic writing style. Aside from his role in greatly increasing general interest in recent history, and highlighting aspects of social conflict that had previously been left in the shadows, he should also be accorded the merit of having moved historical debate away from speculative essays on the national 'essence' and the 'problem of Spain'. A process to which a contribution was also undoubtedly made by Jaume Vicens Vives, from within the other historical vision in a pre-eminent position in the anti-Francoist world, that of Catalan nationalism.

The atmosphere of the 1950s did not, in principle, appear propitious for a resurgence of Catalanism, which in the previous decade had felt itself defeated and seen several of its leading politicians and intellectuals (Francesc Cambó, Josep Pla, Eugeni D'Ors) giving their support to the Franco regime. Still less could one have expected that such a thing would come from the hand of Vicens Vives, who had initiated his career in the 1930s by engaging in disputes with traditional Catalanist historiography, which he considered to be romantic, over-politicized and excessively weak in its scientific underpinnings. As a medievalist, he reassessed the figure of King Ferdinand the Catholic, classically demonized in Catalan history for having handed Catalonia over to Castile and implanting a system of royal absolutism that replaced indigenous institutions that were idealized as a form of democratic self-government. For Vicens, in contrast, Ferdinand represented the rationalism of the state and modernity against the exhausted, oligarchical and corrupt world of the Generalitat, the Catalan government and parliament that had survived from earlier centuries.

After spending the Civil War in Barcelona, Vicens Vives was purged from his university post in 1939, but managed to rebuild his relations with the regime, especially through his contacts with the group of writers known as the 'Generation of 1948', close to the influential Catholic organization the Opus Dei. At that time he was writing pieces on geopolitics and eulogies of the Spanish and Portuguese empires of the sixteenth century. He obtained a history professorship in Zaragoza, and soon managed to transfer to Barcelona. A crucial year in his life was 1950, when he attended the Congress of Historical Sciences in Paris, where Lucien Febvre and the *Annales* school convinced him of the need to centre the study of the past on the 'common man' and abandon the philosophy of history, imperial rhetoric and great abstract themes such as the 'Spanish being'. Seeking a new type of scientific history, removed from ideology, he took refuge in a form of history based on statistics, typical of one branch of the *Annalistes*.

His rapprochement with Catalanism came at the beginning of the 1950s. Following in the same line as Arnold Toynbee, he wrote that no culture could possibly exist without a select minority to give it structure. In the Catalan case, this had been the role of the nineteenth century bourgeoisie, which had had the ability to create a social consensus that overcame class conflicts and offer a political project that had only failed due to the exclusionary, inflexible nature of the Spanish State. That is, that in the Catalonia of the nineteenth century a minority had appeared that possessed a modernizing project, something that had been nonexistent in the fifteenth. Catalonia's decadence, therefore, had corresponded to the era of the Trastámara Kings of Aragon after 1412, and its 'recovery' to that of the nineteenth-century bourgeois. He thus presented the past in terms of Paradise-Fall-Redemption, a vision very acceptable for traditional Catalan nationalism. His closeness to

Catalanism grew with the publication of *Notícia de Cataluña* (News of Catalonia) in 1954, which gave high praise to the 'generation of giants' of 1901, headed by Enric Prat de la Riba, the effective founder of modern Catalan nationalism, a regenerationist who in Vicens's account had come up against the 'incomprehension of the state', incapable of seeing in his ideas anything more than separatism.

Through the means of socioeconomic history, with a historical apparatus and a language that were presented as modern and objective, Vicens Vives thus proposed a renovation of history that ultimately converged with Catalanist precepts. In the name of quantitative data, and by basing his arguments on documents found in archives, he had sidestepped the polemics on national essences. However, at the end of the book, and on the basis of differences in the pace of modernization and attitudes to modernity, he ultimately relaunched an essentialist counter-positioning of Catalonia to the rest of Spain. The former, thanks to industrialization, had become a bourgeois society, had acquired a sense of responsibility and structure and had proposed to Spain a 'redemption through labour'. However, in the rest of Spain a 'fossilization of an agrarian regime based on *latifundios* (great estates)' had predominated, which had made any understanding impossible. This point made, the Manichaean image was complete: there had been a 'basic clash' between the '"productive thinking" – the thinking that Catalonia has sustained since 1830, and in which they were later joined by the Basque iron-makers – and the "consumer thinking", which has prevailed throughout this same period of time in the mercantilist group of Cadiz and, hanging on to their coat-tails, the parliamentary and bureaucratic circles in Madrid'.

From his description, the Catalonia of the reactionary rural Carlists, that of the Virgin of Montserrat and the arch-traditionalist Cardinal Torras i Bages, Prat de la Riba's racism and imperialism, and the support given by some Catalans to Generals Weyler and Polavieja against the Cuban revolutionaries, to General Martínez Anido in repressing the labour movement, to Primo de Rivera and even to Franco, had all disappeared. The Catalonia of late-period Vicens Vives was solely modern, progressive and secular. In the same way that the liberal tradition, the ideas of the *Institución Libre de Enseñanza* and Manuel Azaña, or the Madrid that had resisted the Francoist siege, had all disappeared from Castile, converted, with no halftones, into somewhere archaic, reactionary and Catholic.[14]

With Vicens and Tuñón de Lara, the great paradigms came to an end. In democratic Spain, social history has ceded its position to the study of culture, economic history has become more technical and turned into an autonomous field and an inordinate interest has been unleashed in everything local. Above all, however, the reign of the 'grand narrative' has ended. Rather than any kind of historic paradigm with pretensions to hegemony, fragmentation, pluralism and methodological relativism now prevail. And debates have ended on *el ser español*, the 'Spanish being', at least among the young. The essences of identity have been left to the sub-state nationalisms, and the care of the Royal Academy of History.

José Álvarez Junco is professor of Modern History at the Complutense University of Madrid. From 1992 to 2000, he held the Prince of the Asturias Chair in Spanish Culture and Civilization at Tufts University, Boston, and between 2004 and 2008 he was director of the Centre for Political and Constitutional Studies in Madrid. Among his books are *The Emergence of Mass Politics in Spain. Populist Demagoguery and Republican Culture, 1890–1910* (2003), and *Spanish Identity in the Age of Nations* (2011).

Notes

1. Marichal (1995); Juliá (2004).
2. Unamuno (2005 [1895]); Ganivet (1897).
3. Morales Moya (1993). On Rafael Altamira y Crevea, see Altamira (1900–1911, 1998 [1902]).
4. On Menéndez Pidal, my account is based on García Isasti (2004), as well as Varela (1999).
5. Cf. the critique of Menéndez Pidal by his own grandson and former student, Diego Catalán, in his Introduction to Menéndez Pidal (1971).
6. Ortega y Gasset (1922).
7. The 'Council for the Extension of Studies and Scientific Research', established in 1907 under the strong influence of the *Institución Libre de Enseñanza*. Headed by the Nobel Prize winner for medicine Santiago Ramón y Cajal, it created a number of research institutes within Spain and provided grants for Spanish students to study abroad.
8. All quotes taken from Pasamar (2010).
9. See Pérez Bustamante (1939, 1940, 1941, 1942); Ballesteros Beretta (1919–41).
10. Cf. Álvarez Chillida (1996).
11. Castro (1948, 1954). On Castro, see Asensio (1976) and Varela (1999).
12. See Ayala (1944). A second extended edition was published in Mexico City (1962).
13. Tuñón de Lara (1960, 1966, 1967, 1969, 1970, 1973, 1980–91).
14. See Vicens Vives (1952, 1954, 1954–59); Vicens Vives and Llorens (1958).

Chapter 2

The Flag and the Anthem
The Disputed Official Symbols of Spain

Javier Moreno-Luzón and Xosé M. Núñez Seixas

Whenever we set out to explore and analyse nationalist imaginaries, symbols are of great importance. They serve to mould national identities, help with the creation of national feeling among the population at large and accord legitimacy to regimes and nationalist movements. Some, the ones that have had the status of official symbols, have been used to meld together the nation and the state, with mixed results: in Germany, for example, with a solid national identity but changing flags and national anthems, or Great Britain, where several nations have been grouped together in a single state with lasting emblems associated with the monarchy.[1] Whichever the case may be, the webs of meanings that are woven together by national symbols illustrate and condense the content of nationalist imaginaries, at the same time as they demonstrate their conflicts and peculiarities.

In this chapter, we will examine two symbols that were of fundamental importance for the Spanish nationalist imaginary throughout the twentieth century, the flag and the national anthem. We will do so from three points of view. Firstly, through their official use, as representations of the state and instruments for the creation of national feeling in the hands of the authorities, via institutions such as schools and the army, but also through rituals and commemorations. Secondly, through the social uses that were made of these icons, which endowed them with different meanings, transforming them and adding all sorts of other elements, in continual interaction with the actors who shaped the 'social space' or field, in Bourdieu's sense of the term, around these symbols.[2] And finally, through that of the conflicts that have arisen around them, both between different versions of Spanish nationalism and between Spanish nationalism and sub-state nationalisms.

The progress of Spain's flag and its national anthem were characterized by notable vagaries. This can be summed up in a paradox: they
were symbols that were disputed but resilient. Disputed because they
always aroused feelings of rejection in large sections of society that
were also politically mobilized. The sub-state nationalist movements
protested against them in different ways, from ignoring legal require-
ments to display or play them to burning flags and whistling down the
anthem. However, neither was there consensus in the Spanish-nationalist camp. A significant portion of this sector of opinion identified
flag and anthem with a specific political regime – the monarchy, the
republic, a dictatorship – and not the nation. And they were resilient
because, in spite of all the fluctuations of politics and these challenges,
two variants of flag and anthem remained as official symbols for the
greater part of the century. The red-and-yellow flag and the anthem the
Marcha Real (Royal March) survived as emblems of the Spanish state
for more than nine decades, and were only dispensed with during the
brief interval of the Second Republic (between 1931 and 1936 and, in
part of the country, from 1936 to 1939). We will seek to explain this
apparent contradiction.

National Regeneration and the Militarization of Symbols

Around 1900, these official symbols, flag and anthem, were those of
the constitutional monarchy, at a time when, as in other European monarchical states, the Crown sought to legitimize its position by linking
itself to the nation. This implied, in the first years of the new century,
an increasing effort to 'nationalize' its set of symbols and regulate their
use. The red, yellow and red flag, with the central yellow band twice
as wide as the two red ones, had been adopted by the Spanish Navy in
1785 and become established as an emblem of the state in the course
of the nineteenth century, with or without a coat of arms on the central stripe.[3] This flag and the *Marcha Real* were employed in official
ceremonies and in contacts with foreign countries. At the same time,
both symbols had also acquired established social uses. The flag appeared in local celebrations and bullrings, as well as in widely read
publications. After being constantly exhibited for a hundred years, red
and yellow had come to be seen as the national colours. The anthem,
granted official status as a march for the rendering of military hon-
ours in the eighteenth century, was subsequently employed not just to
acknowledge the presence of the king or other authorities, but also in
religious ceremonies. It was played at the most sacred point of Mass

and, by extension, in other solemn moments. This connection gave the 'Royal March' a content that was religious as well as monarchist.

The political scene at the turn of the century was marked by two closely connected phenomena that both strongly affected the use of national symbols. On the one hand, the 'Disaster', Spain's defeat in its war with the United States in 1898, discredited many expressions of patriotism that had been common during the recent colonial conflicts. In the early stages of the Cuban war, for example, the *Marcha de Cádiz* (Cádiz March), taken from a zarzuela opera, had been so popular that it had been raised to the status of an unofficial anthem. However, as the century began, it was universally disowned as the embodiment of a suicidal ostentatious patriotism, 'that profound thoughtlessness that, to the tune of the *Marcha de Cádiz*, led us to lose our colonies', as the poet Antonio Machado wrote in 1908.[4] Spanish patriotism clad itself in seriousness, since it had passed from the sublime to the ridiculous in just a few months.

Meanwhile, on the other hand, the appearance of sub-state nationalist movements in Catalonia and the Basque Country, and later in Galicia, gave rise to a political clash with the symbols of the nation-state. From a very early point in the rise of these movements, attacks on Spanish national symbols were seen in these territories. Examples were the loud whistling to swamp out the 'Royal March', first heard in Barcelona in 1899, or the burning of a national flag in the Basque town of Lekeitio in 1905.[5] This situation caused alarm in Spanish patriotic circles, and moreover coincided with a fresh entry into political life of the army – as a self-conscious, corporate body, rather than as the factionalized force of the previous century – which self-proclaimed itself the defender of the fatherland against its new enemies: the 'separatists' within the Iberian peninsula, who had taken the place of the Cuban nationalists and in some cases – such as that of the Catalan pro-independence flag, with a single white star on a blue triangle added to the traditional Catalan flag of four red-on-yellow stripes – had taken their inspiration from the Cubans when creating their own emblems. The military officers considered any disdainful gesture towards the official flag to be an insult against them. This hypersensivity was the driving force behind the militarization of Spanish national symbols during a large part of the twentieth century. Many senior and junior officers were convinced that, given the weakness of national feeling among Spaniards, it was they who needed to 'nationalize' them – what the school was failing to do should be taken up by the barracks. Military ideas of national regeneration, like other similar currents of ideas in the same era, assumed without question the necessity of strengthening Spain's national identity.

Consequently, there began a series of aggressive acts by the military against nationalist centres in Bilbao and Barcelona, in an escalation that culminated in the assault at the end of 1905 on the offices of the Catalanist satirical magazine *Cu-Cut!* and the newspaper *La Veu de Catalunya*. This illegal act was endorsed by expressions of solidarity from the rest of the officer corps and the king, which forced the government to negotiate with the unruly officers, who demanded that all 'crimes against the fatherland' should be punished, and judged by military courts.[6] This led to the 'Law of Jurisdictions' of 1906, a hammer-blow for the supremacy of the civil power in Spain, which established penalties for acts of aggression against national symbols. The law established that 'those who in word, in writing, by means of the printed word, engravings, printed images, allegories, caricatures, symbols, shouting or allusions, commit outrages against the Nation, its flag, national anthem or other representative emblems will be punished with imprisonment'. It went on also to mention the flags or coats-of-arms of the 'regions, provinces, cities and towns of Spain'.[7] The flag and the anthem were thus recognized and given protection as national symbols, not just as those of the monarchy and the state. We do not have many details on the application of this law, although it does seem that it was significant in Catalonia at certain times, and that there were several prosecutions of Basque nationalists for the same reasons. A few court cases were also initiated over acts that insulted the Catalan flag.[8]

This military, reactive variant of Spanish nationalism provoked in turn a strengthening of the Catalan movement. The response made by the central authorities to Catalanist defiance led too to the legal regulation of the usage of national symbols: with a decree of 25 January 1908, a Conservative government stipulated that the national flag had to be displayed outside public buildings on national holidays – both those from the religious calendar and those associated with the monarchy, like the king's birthday and his saint's day – and set down a new official arrangement for the *Marcha Real*. Previously the raising of flags on official buildings during holidays had already been common in many towns, but it now became obligatory.

The concern among the military for the work of raising national feeling could be seen in 1906 when the War Ministry proposed to sponsor a prize for a poem dedicated to the flag, which could then be recited by children in schools.[9] The *Salutación* (salute) that won the competition, by the nationalist writer Sinesio Delgado, was a warrior hymn ('Hail, Flag of my Fatherland, hail / and flying high may you always defy the wind'), and its public promotion was added to the other uses made of the Spanish national symbols in education. Much earlier, in 1893, a

Liberal government had already ordered that the national arms should be displayed and the flag flown in all schools. Teachers were expected to encourage the patriotism of their pupils with parades and salutes to the flag. For the same purpose, there was a proliferation of patriotic prayers and special children's festivals around the flag, and from time to time suggestions were made to establish something on a national scale similar to Empire Day in Great Britain.[10] Moreover, even in schools created by different civil society groups, such as those financed by remittances from associations of Spanish emigrants abroad, ceremonies paying homage to the flag – inspired by those already seen in Latin American countries – played a central role. With time, these habits spread, and schoolchildren became accustomed to this cult around the national flag.[11]

The army's determination to generate greater national feeling was also manifested in the new encouragement given to the patriotic education of its recruits and, above all, in the conversion of the ceremonies for swearing an oath to the flag, the *juras de bandera,* which soldiers undertook at the end of their basic training, into major public festivals. Taking as a model similar rituals in the German Empire, from 1903 these ceremonies, which had previously been held inside barracks, were transferred to the streets and squares of towns and cities, and included parades, a Mass (during which the Royal March was played) and the solemn act of each soldier kissing the flag (orders of 18 and 28 March 1903). The established formula for the oath itself, faithful to regulations first set down in the eighteenth century, obliged the soldier to swear by God and promise the king to follow his flag and standards and shed his blood for them. These ceremonies took on major proportions, and were attended by school groups and civil associations. From 1912, when a law was passed fully establishing compulsory military service, the *juras* almost gained the status of national holidays. To remember the day, the new recruits received souvenir booklets with texts exhorting them to show their love for the flag, which was thus sacralized to extremes.[12]

The exhibition of official symbols in public events was also associated with the figure of King Alfonso XIII, presented by monarchists as the champion of national regeneration ever since he swore an oath on the constitution on attaining his official majority and taking up his powers, at the age of sixteen, in 1902. Whenever he went by, in the many royal tours he made around different regions, the national colours were displayed in ornamental arches and garlands. The monarch and his family, always accompanied by the national anthem, took part in all sorts of ceremonies in homage to the flag, from the presentation of standards – supposedly embroidered by the queen and Queen Mother – to military units to *juras de bandera* ceremonies, the principal of which were presided over by the king in person. In commemorations of national myths, such as those which from 1908 to 1914 marked the centenaries of the anti-Napoleonic war against France (1808–14), known in Spain as the War of Independence, the broader social use of national symbols was linked with the royal family's attendance at acts of homage to the nation's heroes.[13]

In the face of this militarist and monarchist fervour for such symbols, republicanism rejected those that it considered emblems of the regime and not the nation. The issue was frequently debated in the press and in the Spanish parliament, with supporters of the dynasty determined to demonstrate that these were truly national symbols, and republicans placing this in doubt. Regarding the flag there were certain ambiguities. The republican tricolour – with horizontal stripes of red, yellow and purple – coexisted among anti-monarchists with the red-and-yellow flag, which had also been used during the First Republic of 1873, and appeared most especially when they sought to defend the fatherland from Catalanist attacks. The followers of the republican leader and focus of popular anti-Catalanism Alejandro Lerroux brandished both flags in Barcelona. Some republican centres in Madrid continued to display the red-and-yellow flag, and when the former President of the First Republic Nicolás Salmerón died in 1908, it was used to shroud his coffin.[14]

There were fewer doubts about the *Marcha Real*. Republicans rejected it as a piece of music identified with the Bourbon dynasty, as foreign as they were – since it was said to be of Prussian origin – and not even an anthem, since it did not have any words. For monarchists, in contrast, the *Marcha* was felt to have a solemn grandeur.[15] It was not the only national anthem in Europe without words, since there was also the Italian anthem of the House of Savoy, another military march. In addition, it was no doubt also well suited to the model of citizenship that was being put forward from the centres of power in the state: one based on obedience to authority and the fulfilment of obligations such as military service. In accordance with this hierarchical perspective, the anthem was to be heard with a respectful attitude, standing, bareheaded and in silence. Comparisons were inevitable with the *Marseillaise*, which, sung, we may suppose, with Spanish words, was the preferred anthem of Spanish republicanism, since the French anthem certainly did have a strongly emotional and participatory style. In second place among progressives was the *Himno de Riego* (Riego Hymn), written in homage to the liberal General Rafael de Riego, who led the revolt against the absolutist rule of Ferdinand VII in 1820, and which evoked the shared memories of nineteenth-century progressive liberalism. It was employed chiefly by republicans, but also by some pro-dynastic liberals.[16]

Nevertheless, some monarchists had already warned that the lack of singable verses for the national anthem represented a serious shortcoming in terms of its conversion into a vehicle for exciting patriotic emotions. Ever since those years at the beginning of the last century, over many decades and almost to the present day, the search for suitable lyrics for the *Marcha Real* has been a kind of intermittent obsession. Thus, at one point Delgado's salute to the flag was adapted to the tune. There were also discussions of possible alternative national anthems, such as one based on the traditional Aragonese dance the *jota,* a much-loved musical form.[17] This was not such an outlandish suggestion, if one considers that among the anthems of the sub-state nationalisms, a more 'serious' piece of music also commonly existed alongside another that was less solemn, as was the case in Galicia with the shared popularity of the formal anthem *Os Pinos* and the popular *Alborada* by Pascual Veiga.

Symbols of the Conservative
and Authoritarian Monarchy

The military and conservative connotations of the official symbols became more accentuated from the beginning of the First World War. Growing political tension exhausted liberal-monarchist Spanish patriotism, while giving strength to its reactionary equivalent. The continuing rise of the workers' movements and sub-state nationalisms provoked a proliferation of expressions of Spanish nationalism that did not restrict themselves to defending the centralized structure of the state but also associated Spain with Catholic monarchy and a counter-revolutionary social order. The republicans who celebrated the victory of the democracies in 1918 whistled during the *Marcha Real.*[18] However, the principal symbolic battle was fought around the campaigns for regional autonomy, which, heartened by what seemed to be a Europe-wide triumph for the principle of national self-determination, disrupted the accepted patterns of Spanish politics, above all from Catalonia, and prompted a massive display of national emblems.

At the end of 1918 and in the first months of 1919, Barcelona experienced a real street war of flags and anthems. On one side, the Catalanist anthem *Els Segadors* complemented the four-red-striped Catalan flag, the *Senyera*, while beside it the *Marseillaise* was also heard, an indication of the strength of Catalan republicanism. Their opponents vigorously brandished the Spanish flag, and some even tried to sing along – with what words, we do not know – to the 'Royal March'. Violent clashes occurred between Catalan separatists who held up the *Estelada* flag with added white-on-blue star and Spanish nationalists on the extreme right. Each side wore rosettes and ribbons with their respective combinations of colours. In the theatres, each of them listened to patriotic songs, and performances often ended in brawls and pistol shots. This went on until the distinctive emblems were banned.[19]

During the World War and the tumultuous period that followed it, there was a reduction in the number of royal ceremonies and similar rituals, and the military ceremonies of oath-swearing to the flag were returned to the barracks. However, both the authorities and a variety of civil associations were concerned to promote patriotism in connection with the colonial campaigns then underway in Morocco. Although it appeared difficult to overcome the public rejection of a war that the Left blamed on the illegitimate interests of the oligarchy and the military, these campaigns did attain some high points of popularity. One symptom of the spread of war-like nationalism was the impact made by songs that celebrated the cult of the flag; songs such as the famous *pasodoble Banderita* (Little Flag), from the musical comedy *Las Corsarias* (1919), dedicated to the soldiers who died in North Africa ('Little flag, you are red / Little flag, your are golden / you have blood and you have gold / in the depths of your soul'). It was an overwhelming success, and, whether adapted as a military march or as part of the repertoire of the stars of the distinctly Spanish style of popular music known as *canción española,* it has survived to the present day.[20]

The rightward drift of Spanish nationalism took solid form under the dictatorship of General Miguel Primo de Rivera, which from 1923 set out to force through a definitive consolidation of national feeling among the country's citizens via their indoctrination on the basis of Catholic, 'imperial' and anti-liberal values. The official emblems of the state were thus irredeemably fused with the religious and authoritarian variant of Spanish patriotism. Almost as soon as it had taken power, Primo de Rivera's 'Military Directorate' prohibited all flags other than the national red-and-yellow one on public buildings and ships and in 'places of any kind', according to a decree of 18 September 1923, which rather confusingly also authorized the display of 'traditional or historic banners'. Making a reality of the frustrated intentions expressed in the 'Law of Jurisdictions' of 1906, the regime transferred all offenses against national emblems to military jurisdiction, and subsequently incorporated them into the penal code. Henceforward, therefore, anyone accused of insulting the national flag could be submitted to a court martial.[21] To combat separatism in Catalonia, penalties were also established for any kind of disobedience of official regulations on the use of the Spanish language, the flag and the anthem.

With the dictatorship, the ceremonies of swearing an oath to the flag by army recruits once again took over streets and squares, the associated ceremonial was made more elaborate and they were officially given the status of national holidays. The relevant directive, of 21 March 1924, called for the observation of a minute's silence 'in memory of those who have died for the fatherland', one of the first manifestations in Spain of the cult of the fallen that had spread across Europe after the Great War. The ceremonial of the *jura* was subsequently perfected with the addition of a reference to the *patria,* the fatherland, which had previously been absent.[22] Beyond these pre-existing events, the army also fulfilled its responsibilities of heightening national feeling through the activities of the military 'delegates' that under Primo de Rivera were assigned to all municipalities, and oversaw a multiplication of patriotic celebrations throughout the country. Most notable among them were the ceremonies for the 'Day of the Race' – 12 October, the anniversary of Columbus's discovery of America, and a national holiday since 1918 – and those in which Church blessings were granted to the also red-and-yellow banners of the *Somatén,* an auxiliary armed militia recruited by the dictatorship to assist in the maintenance of order. These ceremonies also involved the participation of schoolchildren, whose text books highlighted the same nationalistic messages as those proclaimed by the dictator, and the *Exploradores de España,* the Spanish branch of the Boy Scouts, who also had their own rituals for showing respect for the flag.[23]

The monarchy once again took centre stage in royal tours and parades, as it had in the first years of King Alfonso's reign. In 1927, for the twenty-fifth anniversary of his Oath on the Constitution, Alfonso XIII did not wish for large-scale celebrations, but a variety of patriotic initiatives were put into effect. The writer Eduardo Marquina wrote twelve sets of possible lyrics for the *Marcha Real,* standing out among them one dedicated to the flag: 'Glory, glory, crown of the Fatherland / sovereign light / that is gold in your pennant ... / Purple and gold: immortal banner.' These words were publicized on radio and then on records issued in 1930, although, given the lateness of the date, they achieved scant popularity.[24] Acts of rejection of monarchist symbols came from the habitual sources, republicans and sub-state nationalists, albeit now in new settings. An example was the football crowd responsible for the resounding whistling of the 'Royal March' in the stadium of Barcelona Football Club in 1925, which led to the ground being closed for several months.[25]

The fall of Primo de Rivera in 1930 brought the disappearance of some of his controversial 'anti-separatist' measures. The government of General Dámaso Berenguer, charged with saving the monarchy by returning the country to constitutional normality, abrogated the famous decree of 1923 in June 1930 and authorized 'flags with characteristics that have been consecrated by usage with local and regional significance', so long as they always appeared together with the Spanish flag, which was to be given a position of preference. The Catalan *senyera* was immediately restored to the balconies of many town halls.[26]

The Symbolic Doubts of the Second Republic

The rapid politicization of public space following the fall of the dictatorship was accompanied by the eruption into the streets of the republican variant of the national flag. This was a tricolour, in accordance with the model established by the French Revolution, since it added below the two upper horizontal stripes in red and yellow a third in purple, normally of the same width as the others. It had been setting down roots among the Spanish Left for some fifty years. The colour purple was identified with Castile and, by extension, with the liberal myth of the Castilian *Comunero* rebels who in 1520 had risen up in defense of their civic liberties against the Emperor Charles V. It was not a very different flag, but one that complemented the previously pre-eminent flag with liberal and democratic references. The addition of the new stripe, one republican newspaper said, was 'the offering of a purple fringe to the unconquered banner of the Spanish fatherland'.[27]

The republican tidal wave of 14 April 1931, after the triumph of the republican-socialist candidates in Spain's cities in the municipal elections on the 12th, replaced one flag with another almost automatically. A few days later, on 27 April, a decree ratified the change with allusions to the history of the national colours, to the popular revolution that had brought the new regime and to Castile as the 'nerve of the nation'. Subsequently the flag was also included, for the first time, in the constitution: the republic's Constitution of 1931 concisely stated that 'the flag of the Spanish Republic is red, yellow and purple'. If the red-and-yellow flag had been bound up with a monarchy brought down by its authoritarian impulses, the tricolour would be the symbol of the new democracy, with the result that any possibilities of achieving a broad consensus on the subject of shared national symbols were derailed for a long time. The new government also revised the national coat of arms, displayed in the centre of the yellow stripe on the flag, eliminating the Bourbon fleurs-de-lis and restoring a simple mural crown, which represented the idea of collective authority in opposition to the sole power of the monarch.

The change in the national flag gave rise to some polemics. Conservative sectors expressed their opinion, naturally, that it would have been enough just to replace the specific dynastic elements in the coat of arms, as had happened in 1873.[28] However, the disappearance of red-and-yellow flags was abrupt and emphatic. Beginning with the army, which sent theirs to museums, an order from Minister of War Manuel Azaña of 6 May 1931 accelerated the flags' replacement. Azaña also secularized the manner in which soldiers declared their loyalty, since they no longer gave an oath but a promise, without any religious ceremony. Recruits were now asked to be 'faithful to the Nation' and 'loyal to the Government of the Republic'.[29] In schools, teachers were to explain the change in the flag with lessons on citizenship and the exemplary valour of the Spanish people, who had peacefully decided their destiny. The new flag and the coat of arms, frequently portrayed together with the female figure of the republic, were often reproduced in school text books, with the aim of cultivating respectful and patriotic attitudes among children. The republican colours, as was often pointed out in classrooms, had certain polysemic qualities: they symbolized freedom and human progress, but, at the same time, national unity.[30]

On the question of a national anthem, things progressed rather differently. There was no such resounding imposition of change as with the flag, perhaps because republicans themselves harboured doubts on the issue. From the first days of the republic, the old progressive anthem the *Himno de Riego* was employed, but opinions of the song varied within republicanism, and there were some who considered it of poor quality and even a little coarse and vulgar. In effect, several attempts were made during 1931 to find a new national anthem.[31] However, what had been merely provisional became definitive, and the use of the *Himno de Riego* was retained throughout the years of the republic, even though it was never given fully official status. Its original words spoke of the sons of *El Cid* being ready to die for the fatherland, although it became popular with a very well-known set of alternative, anti-clerical words that began, 'If the priest and friars knew / about the beating they're going to get'. In Spain, therefore, this Hispanic equivalent of the *Carmagnole* usurped the place occupied in France by the *Marseillaise,* and became confused with it.

The leaders of the republican government abolished the monarchist legislation that had protected official emblems, but approved other measures of their own that obstructed the use of symbols different from those of the new regime, in a manner that the constitutional monarchy had not done, but which had been seen under the Primo de Rivera dictatorship. The 'Law for the Defence of the Republic' of 21 October 1931 placed among the 'acts of agression' against the new state that were to be penalized any actions or statements 'in defence of the monarchist regime or persons who may be presented as representative of it, and the use of emblems, insignia or other devices alluding to one or the other'.[32] Consequently, in the following years the monarchist press highlighted reports of fines and orders for the closure of buildings imposed on anyone who played the *Marcha Real*. There were also arrests of military officers for writing articles in favour of the red-and-yellow flag, or for burning the Republican flag.[33] This persecution of the symbols of the monarchy reduced their public presence so much that they were effectively consigned to a clandestine existence.

In reality, the authorities of the recently inaugurated democracy lacked the effectiveness and time necessary to make the new official symbols take root in the non-republican sectors of the population. Spanish-nationalist demonstrations, such as those in opposition to the Statute of Autonomy for Catalonia, deployed the tricolour as the national flag.[34] And in 1934, with a centre-right government in power, a serious effort was made to infuse patriotic values into the national holiday for 14 April, the republic's anniversary. However, the emblems of the republic also had enemies in their own camp. On the one hand, there was the growth in expressions of sub-state nationalism, although Galician and Catalan nationalists showed greater acceptance of the tricolour flag and the *Himno de Riego* than did Basque nationalism, which almost stood apart from republican political culture. On the other, there was the competition of the emblems of the working-class left, which for the militants of mass parties like the Socialists were much more important than any national symbols. For them, the *Internationale* and the red flag had much greater emotive power.[35]

Civil War: 'Renationalization' and the New Meanings of Patriotic Symbols

The Civil War was presented by both sides as a struggle for national independence. The symbols of the nation, equally, constituted an essential ingredient in mobilization for war.[36] In the Republican zone, the fates of the flag and the anthem diverged. In theory, the flag of the republic was adopted by all the units of the popular army. However, many militias flew their own ensigns. Only those of non-Marxist or non-anarchist groups displayed the symbols of the republic in a prominent place and employed the swearing of an oath to the flag as a vehicle for the transmission of patriotic emotions. When several militia batallions paraded through Madrid in September 1936, they carried 'socialist and communist banners' and were accompanied by the *Internationale* and the *Himno de Riego*.[37] In mixed militias, the tricolour flag tended to be adopted as a lowest common denominator. During the parade of the First Division of the Republican Popular Army in Barcelona in March 1937, the preponderance of the tricolour flag among the troops, alongside Catalan ensigns and the banners of different political organizations, was more apparent.[38]

For the Republican Left and other sectors represented in the government, the symbols of the republic were without question those of the authentic fatherland, and the tricolor, 'the flag of Spanish independence'.[39] The efforts made to recentralize the administration and the more patriotic and Spanish-nationalist language developed under the government of Prime Minister Juan Negrín from May 1937 also implied a veneration of the tricolour flag. This was shown in some press reports from the front, such as this one, from 1938:

> Alfonso Galeote was the standard bearer of the batallion, and carried the banner of the republic in the advance.... Suddenly, a shot caused Alfonso to fall. He did not waver.... A third bullet then left him mortally wounded, but he still had sufficient spirit and courage to take the flag in both hands, raise it high and then, with a supreme effort, drive it into the ground, before falling for ever. The flag of Spain is never struck![40]

The *Himno de Riego*, however, met with a different outcome. Outside ceremonial events attended by the Republican authorities, it fell progressively into disuse in the face of the rise of the *Internationale*, the anarchist hymn *A las Barricadas* and other revolutionary songs.

In the insurgent zone, there was initially a degree of confusion on the question of symbols. Many of those who had risen against the republic still flew the tricolour flag and several of the insurgent generals were reluctant to raise that of the monarchy, since what they thought they were putting forward was an authoritarian solution within a republican system. Nevertheless, a few days before the coup, a pact had been signed by General Emilio Mola and the Carlist *Comunión Tradicionalista*, heirs to the partisans of the *ancien régime* in the previous century, which clearly implied the restoration of the red-and-yellow flag. This was put into effect in just a few weeks, and sanctioned by a decree of the Burgos National Defence Committee on 15 August 1936. In contrast to the partisan tricolour, it was argued, this had been the flag defended by generations of Spaniards. In communities controlled by the insurgents, solemn ceremonies were then held to mark the restitution of the flag.[41] However, many different hymns were sung to this same flag. While in some towns and villages the ceremonies concluded with the Falangist anthem *Cara al Sol* (Face to the Sun), in others religious music or a selection of 'patriotic hymns' predominated. The first Francoist school books included illustrations featuring national symbols, with text on the respect that had to be shown towards them. The liberal matron of the republic was replaced by *Madre España* (Mother Spain), holding up the national coat of arms and the flag.[42]

These new regulations did not do away with the multiplicity of flags. Together with the red-and-black banners of the Falange, and the white and red-and-yellow flags with different emblems of the Carlist militias, one also sporadically found regional standards and religious banners.[43] The Carlist Traditionalists saw in the red-and-yellow bicolour flag a symbol of the restoration of monarchy and Catholicism, as well as a patriotic emblem; the Falangists had no great problems in accepting it, since for them their own red-and-black flag symbolized the revolutionary sacrifice of a new generation for a fatherland that was represented by the traditional red-and-yellow flag. Some time later, in February 1938, the Republican coat of arms, decried as 'Frenchified', and also despised because of its mural crown, was replaced not by that of the Bourbon monarchy but with another different design, as a sign of the 'New State'. Inspired by the heraldic imagery of the Catholic Monarchs Ferdinand and Isabella and the Spanish Habsburgs, it incorporated imperial references (the Eagle of St John, from the Arms of Queen Isabella) together with the bundle of yoke and arrows – a motif that also dated back to the time of the Catholic Monarchs, as a symbol of the unity of their kingdoms, but had been revived as the badge of the Falange – and the Falangist motto that lauded Spain as *Una, Grande, Libre* (One, Great, Free).[44] The process through which this new crest was given fully institutional status was slow, and not completed until October 1945.[45]

The anthems sung in the insurgent zone were characterized by a high degree of inconsistency. In celebrations in the rearguard, the Carlist *Oriamendi* march, *Cara al Sol*, the marching song of the Spanish Legion and a variety of *pasodobles* were all sung, together with regional songs. If there was a consensus on the bicolour flag, initially even Carlists sheltered doubts over the value of the 'Royal March', due to its 'paltry and slipshod' character.[46] However, arguments for the restoration of the *Marcha* soon prevailed within traditionalism and other sectors of the insurgent coalition, since it was seen as a conciliatory anthem that could unite patriotic sensibilities together around a common denominator: history, religion and tradition. In the end, its supporters achieved their objective. The Royal March was restored as the national anthem by a decree of 27 February 1937. It was to be heard standing, in silence and with one arm raised in the fascist salute. *Cara al Sol, Oriamendi* and the Legionaries' hymn were all given the status of patriotic songs. Three months later, new words were published for the national anthem, the work of the writer José María Pemán. The commission had been given to him by Franco himself, who lamented that the *Marcha Real* lacked emotive force, but hoped to link his own leadership to the restoration of the anthem and the flag. Pemán's words revived with slight retouches some verses that he had already composed for the anthem in 1928, and combined a glorification of Spain's former overseas empire with the idea of a new beginning, a vague allusion to the Falangist salute ('Raise your arms, sons of the Spanish people') and references to the work of reconstruction, in an enterprise presided over by God. However, the fact that these words were never given official status by decree casts doubt on how much they were ever obligatory and how widely they were learnt.[47]

The conflicts that arose over the pre-eminence given to the *Marcha Real* did not disappear for many years. It was opposed above all by the Falangists, who identified it with an obsolete monarchy, and mounted numerous actions to show their boycott of the official anthem, such as remaining seated or singing their own *Cara al Sol* when it was played.[48] A fresh decree of August 1942 called for the 'Royal March' to be heard with due respect. For the Franco regime, this was not a matter of returning purely and simply to the symbols of the monarchy, but of connecting itself to an earlier tradition and interweaving its own emblems with an idea of a patriotic and authoritarian restoration of the national identity, intimately linked to the Catholic faith. The flag was never referred to as 'monarchist', but its restoration and public display reflected the same nationalist impulse.[49]

As well as being defined, the emblems of the state also had to be disseminated through a renovated system of education. In the first directives issued by the mayors and Civil Governors of Francoist Spain for the school year of 1936–37, no great attention was paid to this area, and priority was given to the restoration of crucifixes and morning prayers in classrooms. In 1938, the Ministry of National Education gave orders for the creation of a 'patriotic atmosphere' in schools. Nevertheless, in parallel, ever since the beginning of the war, traditional Spanish patriotic imagery had invaded every area of daily life, from commercial advertising to bullfights, as a spur to a pro-authoritarian social mobilization, which exhorted the population to listen respectfully to the anthem, salute the flag and wear red-and-yellow rosettes.[50]

Francoism: Official and Informal Symbols

The Francoism of the initial years after the war retrieved a large part of the official practices that had been ordained by the governments of the monarchy for the educational system, broadening their nationalist content. In the 'Norms for Primary Schools' of May 1939, it was declared obligatory to 'raise the flag before classes begin and lower it at the end of the day, while the National Anthem is played'. In October 1940, secondary schools were urged to 'celebrate national holidays with all possible splendour'.[51] The Falange was given responsibility for political, civic and physical education, so long as classes always conformed to Catholic orthodoxy, as well as for teaching the subject titled 'Formation of the National Spirit', which from 1945 brought together ideological indoctrination and preparation for military service. The new law on education of 17 July 1945, which enshrined the predominant position of Catholicism in teaching programmes, did not include any specific indications regarding flags and anthems; however, school books contained abundant references to the banner and arms of Spain.[52] During the 1950s, guidance issued to teachers stressed the importance of these symbols 'for bringing a basic idea of the fatherland into the mind of the child'.[53]

The interest in ceremonial that fostered the cult of the flag and the singing of anthems came above all from Falangism. For example, the instructions given to sections of the Falangist youth organization called on them to commemorate certain dates and educate the young in patriotism by means of particular rituals. In 1944, they were recommended to raise the Spanish flag and that of the Falange single party every day, accompanied by the singing in turn of *Cara al Sol*, *Oriamendi* and *Prietas las Filas* (Close Ranks), the specific marching song of the Youth Front. At the end of classes, the flags were to be ceremonially lowered accompanied by the singing of the national anthem. Ten years later, the relevant regulations were still similar, but the reference to the national anthem had been dropped. The application of these directives across schools was very irregular, and fell away very notably from the 1950s onwards. Many private schools – which often meant religious –

dispensed with Falangist ceremonies, flags and anthems. Even in state schools there was no consistent pattern of observance.[54]

The Falange continued to show no great enthusiasm for the official national anthem. In the mid-1950s, a textbook for political education asserted that there were two musical compositions that represented Spain, the 'Royal or Grenadiers' March and the *Cara al Sol*. Regarding the former, the writer went on to recall that it was incapable of gen-erating patriotic empathy. 'Since it has no words, the people does not feel itself embodied in it other than in a passive way', he wrote, so that 'the true popular anthem of Spain' was *Cara al Sol*, 'the song that is sung by Spaniards, whether Falangists or not, in glory and in peril'.[55] Perhaps for this reason *Cara al Sol* would go on to emerge as a kind of substitute national anthem among supporters of the regime in its dy-ing moments. To add to the confusion, in schools the Royal March was sung with as many as four different sets of words: those of Marquina, those by Pemán, another version titled ¡*Patria Mía!* (My Fatherland) and another that invoked the presence of the Virgin Mary.[56]

Some accounts given by people who were born in the 1950s and at-tended school at that time suggest that, in spite of everything, these na-tionalistic rituals did attain some of their objectives. The most widely remembered songs are those of the Falange. The martial nature of the music and the ceremonies created fellow feeling. One former pupil of a rural school recalled the 'tremendous enthusiasm' with which *Cara al Sol* was sung every morning: 'We fought to be the one charged with raising the flag. ... What it represented was beyond us. What we liked was the paraphernalia built up around it.'[57] Pupils in primary schools also rapidly interiorized two things: the map of Spain and the colours of the flag.[58]

The *Marcha Real* and the bicolour flag were never accepted in areas where alternative national symbols had deep roots in society, or wher-ever a conscious loyalty was maintained to the republic. However, the use of the red-and-yellow flag spread in public and, in part, in private settings irrespective of its political connotations, as was seen in the appearance of the colours in local *fiestas*, other celebrations and sports events. Another indicator of the fact that the educational system had succeeded in 'banalizing' – in the sense used by Michael Billig – the official emblems of the state can be seen in the attitudes of the thou-sands of migrants who left Spain between 1947 and 1970. Many of them accepted the red-and-yellow flag and the *Marcha Real* as their symbols, without further complications. Moreover, in the late 1960s, some popular pieces of music also helped in banalizing the national identity as an element in everyday life, becoming unofficial anthems. The best-known was *Que viva España* (1973), actually first written by a

Belgian, Leo Caerts, but most popular in Spain in the version by singer Manolo Escobar, the words of which were a blend of nostalgic reverie, a pseudo-Andalusian ambience and references to bullfighting with a catchy, multipurpose chorus.

In contrast, the *Himno de Riego* had become a relic of the past that was not even popular in anti-Francoist circles, where internationalist or party symbols were more prevalent. Attachment to the Republican flag survived primarily among those who had been socialized politically in the 1930s, but not in the new generations. While Basque nationalists clandestinely unfurled their flag whenever they had the opportunity to do so, it was much less common to see the republic's flag play a role in similar events. The tricolour was venerated above all in Republican circles in exile, as a symbol of the continued existence of the regime of 1931.[59] Even so, it enjoyed greater longevity than the *Himno de Riego*.

The symbols of the stateless nations, on the other hand, and other regional emblems that were not necessarily seen as quite so opposed to those of Spain acted as common denominators in their respective territories. Their national flags and anthems (*Els Segadors* in Catalonia, *Os Pinos* in Galicia) were shared by all sectors of opposition to the regime. For, ahead of other considerations, they represented solidarity with the victims of the political repression of the proscribed cultures. The Franco regime had not enacted such detailed legislation against these symbols as that of Primo de Rivera, but any reference to their existence could provoke incidents. One such occurred, for example, in the Palau de la Música Catalana concert hall in Barcelona in 1960, when, during a special performance attended by several government ministers, a section of the audience sang the Catalan patriotic song the *Cant de la Senyera* as an act of defiance, leading to several arrests and prison sentences. In the final years of the dictatorship, the public display of the symbols of sub-state nationalisms accelerated in an unstoppable manner. However, anti-Francoism still lacked any specifically Spanish national emblems that were sufficiently emotive, and among its sympathizers there was a notable discomfort with the official symbols of the state, a feeling closely related to the difficulties that would be encountered in giving them a positive civic content.

Transition and Democracy:
Consensual Symbols, Conflictive Practices

At the death of the dictator, the Republican flag briefly re-emerged as the emblem of the sections of the left opposed to a monarchy inherited from Francoism. On 14 April 1976, tricolour flags appeared in several cities, to be immediately pulled down by the authorities. The public exhibition of this flag was prohibited during the first years of the transition. While 'regional' flags were tolerated from the end of 1976, the Republican tricolour met with the ire of the monarchist governments of Carlos Arias Navarro and Adolfo Suárez, concerned to protect the Crown, seen as a guarantee of orderly democratization. The tricolour evoked memories of chaos. The principal parties of the Left were legalized in time for the first general election in June 1977, but those that were specifically republican had a further wait of several months. Despite its limitations, some radical groups did show a liking for the tricolour, such as the Patriotic and Anti-fascist Revolutionary Front (FRAP) and its political arm the Communist Party of Spain (Marxist-Leninist), a pro-Albanian, Maoist group. Similarly, the use of the tricolour was quite widespread in the workers' unions, both the Socialist Unión General de Trabajadores (General Workers' Union, UGT) and the more Communist-inclined Comisiones Obreras (Workers' Commissions, CCOO), perhaps as a means of reconciling the differing political sensibilities of their members.

The restoration of the republican symbols was soon revealed to be an unviable option for the majority of the Left. Renunciation of the flag and accepting a constitutional monarchy represented two essential tolls that had to be paid for their integration into the new democracy – as was done by the Spanish Communist Party (PCE), legalized in April 1977. In spite of the opposition of some of its militants, the Party's Central Committee agreed a week later to display the flag 'of the state that recognizes us' beside the red flag at all party events. The red-and-yellow flag, it went on, could not be be abandoned to those who 'wished to obstruct the peaceful path to democracy'. This position went together with an acceptance of the democratic monarchy and a defence of 'the unity of our common homeland', compatible with the recognition of its different nationalities and regions. The party's general secretary, Santiago Carrillo, now recalled, moreover, that 'the repression of October 1934 had been carried out under the flag with the colour purple'. The red-and-yellow banner was the flag of Spain, 'and the reactionaries are not Spain'.[60]

Nor did the mainstream socialists of the Spanish Socialist Workers Party (PSOE) consider the flag of the republic a *casus belli*. This was made clear in its Twenty-seventh Congress, held in Madrid in December 1976. During the closing session, one militant produced a tricolour flag and attempted to place it on the stage, to the discomfort of the leadership. The incident was defused when someone began to sing the

Internationale with a raised fist, and the Congress delegates joined in.[61] During the election campaign of March 1979, the Republican flag was still seen at some Socialist meetings. However, when leftist sympathizers celebrated their victories in many cities in the municipal elections of April that year, red flags clearly predominated.

The attitude of the mainstream leftist parties on these issues, highly sensitive as they were to the position of the reformists who had come from within Francoism, cleared the way to a lasting agreement on the question of national symbols. In its Article 4.1, the Spanish Constitution of 1978 lays down that 'the flag of Spain is composed of three horizontal stripes, red, yellow and red, the yellow stripe being double the width of the two red ones'. A combination that was considered to be legitimized by its own history, which went back much further than the Franco dictatorship. However, no similar measure defined the Spanish national anthem. By default, the *Marcha Real* continued to be used. The desirability of its being given words once again became a spasmodic cause for debate. In January 1982, a 'Commision for a Sung National Anthem' was formed with the backing of a music publisher and several concerned individuals, the objective of which was to provide some words that the Spanish football team could sing during the World Cup to be held in Spain that summer. The project was soon forgotten, as several other similar initiatives would be into the twenty-first century.[62]

It was above all the extreme Right, and in particular the overtly Francoist Fuerza Nueva (New Force) party, that made most public use of the red-and-yellow flag in its events and demonstrations. It went so far as to organize a major demonstration in Madrid on 11 May 1979 under the slogan *Día de la Patria Española* (Day of the Spanish Fatherland), to protest against the 'disintegration of the fatherland' and the 'continuous insults and outrages committed against the flag'.[63] In an attempt to avoid the identification of public displays of the red-and-yellow flag with nostalgia for Francoism, preventive measures had been taken even before the passing of the Constitution. A decree of 24 November 1978 prohibited parties, unions and associations from 'utilizing the flag of Spain or its colours' as 'distinctive symbols'. However, this did not prevent the flag question from continuing to be a source of discord.

The reality was that in the field of national symbols, the normalization of the democratic system proceeded slowly. In the beginning, it was assumed that the 'constitutional' flag would not include a coat of arms, but uncertainty reigned in public institutions as to whether or not they had to replace their old banners with others without the Francoist coat of arms. The redefinition of the coat of arms of Spain was not a matter of excessive concern for politicians for more than a year after the promulgation of the constitution. Then, in February 1980, the Socialist parliamentary group, with a fresh determination to construct new symbols, proposed adding to the flag a coat of arms that would properly represent the nation, one based on traditional designs, a motion that was accepted by the then ruling party, the Unión de Centro Democrático (Union of the Democratic Centre, UCD).[64] After fifteen months of debates, a law of 5 October 1981 established the definitive design of Spain's official arms, incorporating the fleur-de-lis escutcheon of the Bourbons and a royal crown. On either side of the shield, two more crowns were shown on top of the Pillars of Hercules, representing the kingdom and the empire.[65] Shortly afterwards, the shield was incorporated into the flag. Later the same month, another decree regulated the ways in which the national flag was to be displayed in public institutions, military establishments and on ships, proclaimed its prior status over the flags of autonomous communities and other local flags and prohibited its use in the symbols of parties, unions and private organizations. The flag was now an emblem of the 'sovereignty, independence, unity and integrity of the fatherland, as well as of 'the higher values expressed in the Constitution'.[66]

After the failed coup d'état of 23 February 1981, a more accentuated Spanish-nationalist tone became visible in the language and practice of the democratic political elites, conscious as they were of the need to give fresh legitimacy to the nation's symbols in order to avoid a situation in which the idea of Spanish national identity could continue to seem to be a monopoly of the extreme right. The mass demonstrations in defence of the constitutional order that were held in the capitals of nearly every Spanish province on 27 February all lined up behind the red-and-yellow flag as a common emblem. Senior ministerial officials received instructions to always be photographed with the flag behind them. This climate of patriotic and constitutional enthusiasm imposed respect for the symbols inherited from the past, even if they might now be given different meanings. Good examples of this atmosphere were the events held for the Armed Forces' Day, on 30 and 31 May 1981 in Barcelona, with the participation of the Catalan autonomous government. Its pragmatic president, Jordi Pujol, declared that the programme for the two days embodied the Catalan desire to construct a constitutional Spain. Barcelona was garlanded with both Spanish banners and Catalan *senyeras* and the presence of the king and queen was applauded by large crowds, associating together the parliamentary monarchy, the cultural diversity of Spain and the constitutional flag. The culmination of the celebrations was the performance of a giant ring of the Catalan folk dance the *sardana* around a flagpole with the Spanish flag.[67] On 6 December 1981, the anniversary of the referendum ratifying the Constitution, several newspapers gave away paper Spanish banners with the slogan *Viva la Constitución*. Except in Navarra and the Basque Country, municipal councils organized events in homage to the Constitution and the flag. Nevertheless, popular enthusiasm was limited. Some of the press complained the next day that few constitutional ensigns had been seen on balconies in Madrid, and pointed out ironically that anyone who had a Spanish flag at home was likely still to have a Francoist one, while anti-Francoists did not have them.[68]

The eulogizing of the national flag was joined by the PSOE, which saw its opportunity to gain access to power coming closer and moderated its gestures accordingly. In October 1981, the party held one of its regular conferences with the red-and-yellow flag on the main stage for the first time. Throughout the following year, too, Socialist leaders expressed their attachment to the bicolour emblem, since it embodied constitutional principles. In the 1982 election campaign, Felipe González made clear the party's claim to 'the flag of the Constitution', which 'we have conquered for everyone'.[69] With the PSOE in power from December 1982, the links were reinforced between the red-and-yellow flag and democratic Spain, at the same time as the flag began to be generally referred to as the 'constitutional flag'. However, insistence was still also placed on its historical legitimacy. One suitable opportunity was the two-hundredth anniversary of the creation of the flag in May 1985, an occasion principally marked by a ceremony in the Royal Palace at Aranjuez. All the principal speakers emphasized their commitment to the flag, albeit with certain variations. While the conservative Manuel Fraga Iribarne praised its value as the synthesis of a shared past, the representatives of the centrists and the PSOE asserted that the flag embodied, in addition to a common past, the civic values of the Constitution. The spokesman for the Catalan nationalist *Convergéncia i Unió* (Convergence and Union, CiU) reminded his listeners of the territorial diversity and pluralism that it comprehended, while the Communist Party representative added that the contention between the 'two Spains' had been concluded.[70]

Once the new national coat of arms had been approved in 1981, the process of gradually replacing the emblems displayed on or outside public buildings had begun, with ceremonies for the presentation and donation of flags to military regiments and Civil Guard barracks. In these events it was stressed that these symbols reflected the constitutional order, and in some regions much emphasis was also given to the connections between the flag and the variety of Spain, made up of nationalities and regions. Elected officials of the Basque Nationalist Party (PNV) played a prominent role in donating some of the flags, implying thereby that the army also accepted the symbols of the autonomous regions.

The despatch of new flags to town halls aroused a degree of resistance in different parts of the country, but the most frontal rejection came from radical Basque nationalism, whose militants frequently removed the red-and-yellow national emblems from town halls during local festivals, as in San Sebastián in 1979. The entry of 'anti-system' forces into municipal councils widened the range of available options for protesting against the flag. This pressure from the Basque nationalist left, at a time when it needed to reinforce its capacity for street mobilization, increased in the summer of 1983. Municipal councillors from Herri Batasuna, the party regarded as the political wing of violent Basque nationalism, presented motions proposing that the constitutional flag, seen in the Basque Country as a symbol of 'Spanish occupation' both before and since the death of Franco, should no longer be raised on their town halls. At the same time, there was a succession of street clashes and protests that often included the burning of the national flag. The Basque Nationalist Party and the regional government, which it controlled, sought intermediate solutions; one that was very widely used was the withdrawal of *all* flags from town hall balconies. After several years of confrontations, a new strategy was adopted that consisted of raising all the relevant ensigns (the Spanish flag, the Basque flag, a local town emblem) on balconies for a few minutes early in the morning on the main day of local *fiestas,* and then immediately lowering them.[71] Alongside this symbolic battle, one also began to see public demonstrations of rejection of the Spanish national anthem. The most notorious was in September 1989, when several Catalan pro-independence organizations staged a loud protest against the king and the *Marcha Real* during the ceremony to inaugurate the Olympic Stadium on the mountain of Montjuïc in Barcelona. Nevertheless, three years later the opening ceremony of the Olympic Games in the same stadium was characterized by the virtual absence of any gestures of rejection towards the king or the athletes of the Spanish team.[72]

The use made of the old republican flag, on a broader social level, underwent several highs and lows. Some small republican parties still combatted the idea that it should be identified only with 'utopian' positions of the extreme Left.[73] It was also still waved by the main labour unions during their demonstrations for the First of May. By the mid-1980s, however, only a few revolutionaries raised it regularly. Nevertheless, it re-emerged strongly in the demonstrations against Spain's entry into NATO during 1986. The tricolour also reappeared in the marches of conscientious objectors against military service, as well as in gatherings of the revolutionary Left during the 1990s, reflecting a new rereading of the republican legacy in revolutionary terms.

The fervour within the PSOE for the constitutional flag abated in the course of the 1980s. In Socialist meetings in the main regions, the flags of the respective autonomous community were far more visible, as they were in labour and union campaigns. Even on the Right, there was a certain burst of enthusiasm for regional flags. This was not always a matter of expressing an identity separate from that of Spain, but could also be a means of enlisting a symbol free of negative political connotations, and even of asserting a sense of Spanish identity threatened by a neighbouring sub-state nationalism. This was the explanation for the rise in popularity of the Valencian flag, with a blue band to differentiate it from that of Catalonia, among substantial anti-Catalanist sectors of society in Valencia from the end of the 1970s.[74] Even in the mid-1990s, any profusion of red-and-yellow flags at a political event was still associated with the Far Right. Alianza Popular (Popular Alliance, AP), the conservative party founded by Manuel Fraga Iribarne in 1976, which in 1989 renamed itself the Partido Popular (Popular Party, PP), had also made constant use of the national flag in its early years. Nevertheless, from the mid-1980s this symbolic imagery also gave way to regional flags and the party's own banners, above all in Galicia and the Balearics, while in the Basque Country and Catalonia the AP and later the PP performed a kind of symbolic high-wire act. During election campaigns in 1993, 1995 and 1996, meetings held by the Popular Party in Barcelona were marked by a proliferation of Catalan flags and a scarcity of national ones.

Once it had gained power in the central government in 1996, the PP, by this time headed by José María Aznar, set out to apply a programme of Spanish-patriotic 'renationalization'. One of its central axes was the reinforcement of national symbols and commemorations in order to stimulate patriotic feelings, the necessary glue, in the party's judgement, for social cohesion. In October 1997, regulations were issued to establish that the Spanish national anthem took precedence over those of the autonomous regions, and to assert that it was obligatory for it to be played whenever the king or the prime minister were present. Another initiative was the installation of a gigantic Spanish flag in a central square in Madrid, the Plaza de Colón. It was initially suggested that it would be associated with military parades, but subsequently a proposal was made to stage ceremonies in homage to the flag around it every month. In the ceremony held when the ensign was raised for the first time, in October 2002, Defence Minister Federico Trillo declared that the flag evoked an 'inspiring project of life in common', but also a past and a culture, and the 'pride in possessing a language, in belonging to a land, in sharing blood, dreams and historic memories'. In the face of the controversy this unleashed, the PP came to an agreement with the PSOE to limit ceremonies in homage to the flag in the square to a few specific occasions.[75]

At the end of the twentieth century, the official symbols of the Spanish nation continued to suffer from certain problems in terms of public acceptance. In 1998, the majority of Spanish citizens claimed they felt 'some emotion' when they heard the national anthem, with a higher percentage among voters of the PP and much less among those of Izquierda Unida (United Left, the coalition formed by the Communist Party and other smaller groups in 1986), a quarter of whom said they felt nothing special, as did 62 per cent of supporters of the Basque Nationalist Party and 50 per cent of the Catalanist CiU.[76] Levels of emotional identification were highest when associated with informal emblems without obvious political connections. Nevertheless, from the 1990s onwards, and in areas other than those with strong sub-state nationalisms, one can also see an increase in the social use of the Spanish flag, to celebrate local festivals or sporting successes. In this regard there has been a progressive normalization of the situation, which has continued into the twenty-first century. New iconic objects have also arisen, such as the Osborne Bulls – giant black silhouettes of bulls originally placed by roadsides as advertising for Osborne sherry – which from their origins as a commercial image have emerged forth to be added to the red-and-yellow flag as an unofficial 'coat of arms'. Today the colours of the flag are applied to all kinds of objects, from T-shirts to caps. The Spanish nation thus becomes an item of consumption and the content of its symbols is trivialized, which in turn produces accentuated reactions to them among sub-state nationalists.

Conclusion

The symbols were disputed but resilient. Throughout the twentieth century Spain's national symbols suffered the effects of the politicial conflicts that surrounded the question of the identity and national feelings of Spaniards with constant polemics. Sub-state nationalist movements, primarily in Catalonia and the Basque Country, encountered the response of a wave of reactive Spanish patriotism that eventually imposed itself, in its most reactionary and intolerant forms, during the two dictatorships. Ever since the regenerationist era at the turn of the century, the army had taken the lead in the drive to give sacred status to patriotic emblems, as seen, for example, in the ceremonies of swearing the oath to the flag undertaken by military recruits. Schools, in turn, sought to implant a cult around these symbols, and their presence multiplied in commemorations and other public ceremonies. All these efforts, even when they had the absolute support of the state under authoritarian centralist regimes, produced very uneven results. This was the case in part because an inefficient administrative apparatus could not guarantee a successful outcome, but also because any kind of opposition to the dictators then inevitably led to a complete rejection of their symbols of identity as well, which were at the same time those of Spain. The brief Republican interlude, which sought to replace the insignia of the monarchy with others rooted in democracy, adopted similarly repressive measures against its enemies, and fared no better. Hence, between 1923 and 1977 official emblems were imposed by force, and those who defied the established order were persecuted, which prevented the attainment of any consensus on the question of symbols. Only with the establishment of democracy in the final quarter of the twentieth century has it been possible at least partly to overcome these obstacles.

Nevertheless, the continued existence as official symbols of the red-and-yellow flag and the Royal March has always been accompanied by conflict. In the absence of anything better, these emblems, first established in the eighteenth century and spread around the country in the nineteenth, identified with the monarchy but also with the nation, acquired a range of connotations that enabled them to be adapted successfully to different circumstances. While the flag has received more attention from governments and been more widely accepted as an element consubstantial with Spanish identity, the anthem has been less fortunate. Red and yellow have functioned, almost without discussion, as national colours, and republicans limited themselves to adding purple because of its progressive associations. It is true that the bicolour flag, associated with the aggressively Spanish-nationalist forces of Francoism, was consigned to the circles of the extreme Right for some years, but this stigma was overcome to a large extent, if not everywhere, by the change of coat of arms and its subsequent presentation as the 'constitutional flag' after 1981. Only the 'renationalizing' zeal of the central governments at the end of the century have put this level of agreement in danger.

The *Marcha Real*, in contrast, the object of much less care from the authorities, has aroused adverse reactions far more frequently, from a multicoloured range of political tendencies; from republicans under the constitutional monarchy to Falangists under Francoism, not to mention the Catalan nationalists. According to its supporters, its notes instilled sublime emotions in its listeners; however, the absence of any accepted lyrics reduced its possibilities of being considered a genuine national anthem. But, even though the need to establish some lyrics was discussed repeatedly, none of those that were proposed, not even the ones that had the approval of Alfonso XIII or Franco, had been made official. The *Himno de Riego* of the nineteenth-century progressive liberals, little used and soon forgotten, had not been a lasting rival; *Cara al Sol*, though it had threatened the anthem's hegemony during Francoism, rapidly evaporated in the transition to democracy. As substitutes for the official anthem in the role of patriotic songs, other pieces of music appeared with more staying power, such as *Banderita* or *Que viva España*.

The conflicts around these symbols and their continued survival were, however, combined with their growing use across society, aided by the steady drip-drip that came not just through the army or the educational system, but also through informal channels that stimulated national identification. By the 1930s, the bulk of Spaniards had been 'nationalized', in that they felt part of the Spanish nation, which did not mean that they all agreed on a single version of Spanish nationalism or, in some regions, were unaffected by alternative nationalist imaginaries. Nationalization, integration into the nation, did not mean uniformity. Not even Francoism was able to send into reverse processes of national construction that had taken root strongly and have continued to the present day. However, some of Spain's national emblems, in a more or less trivialized form, are now employed ever more visibly in all kinds of contexts. This popularization has above all affected the red-and-yellow flag in all its manifestations, with or without a coat of arms, in local *fiestas* or crowds at a sports match. It is in these informal settings that the transformation of the official symbols into real symbols of the nation has actually been possible.

Notes

1. Geisler (2005).
2. Bourdieu (1997).
3. Serrano (1999).
4. A. Machado, 'Nuestro patriotismo y la marcha de Cádiz, quoted in Romero Ferrer (2012: 199).
5. *Blanco y Negro*, 29 July 1899; *El Año Político*, 5 September 1905.

6. J. Romero Maura, 'El Ejército español y Cataluña. El incidente del *Cu-Cut!* y la Ley de Jurisdicciones, 1905–1906', in Romero Maura (2000: 111–42).
7. Law of 23 April 1906, in *Gaceta de Madrid*, 24 April 1906.
8. *ABC*, 9 May 1908 and 11 September 1915.
9. 30 April 1906, published in *Gaceta de Madrid*, 1 May 1906.
10. R. Vergés, *La Bandera Española en las Escuelas*, Tortosa, 1906. *ABC*, 26 June 1914.
11. Pozo Andrés (2000).
12. Cf. for example F. Redondo, *Patria y Bandera*, San Sebastián, 1907.
13. Moreno-Luzón (2004).
14. P. Rico López, *Roja, Amarilla y Morada*, A Coruña, 2006, p. 13.
15. *El Motín*, 24 August 1901; *Heraldo de Madrid*, 4 February 1915.
16. *ABC*, 5 October 1908.
17. *La Época*, 2 February 1915.
18. *El País*, 28 November 1918.
19. Moreno-Luzón (2006).
20. Serrano (1999); Salaün (1990).
21. *ABC*, 14 March and 24 July 1925.
22. Pinto Cebrián (1999: 108–9).
23. Quiroga Fernández de Soto (2008).
24. Real Biblioteca MUS/MSS/1581. See also *La Voz*, 17 May 1927, and *Blanco y Negro*, 22 May 1927.
25. *El Imparcial*, 25 June 1925.
26. *ABC*, 11 and 12 June 1930.
27. *La Libertad*, 19 April 1931.
28. *ABC*, 18 August 1931.
29. Pinto Cebrián (1999: 111).
30. Campos Pérez (2010: 87–95); Pozo Andrés (2007).
31. *Crisol*, 30 April 1931.
32. *Ley de Defensa de la República*, Article 1.6, *Gaceta de Madrid*, 22 October 1931.
33. *ABC*, 2 September 1931 and 20 May 1933; *Informaciones*, 12 July 1934; and *Luz*, 6 August 1932.
34. *El Sol*, 28 July 1932.
35. Radcliff (1997).
36. See Núñez Seixas (2006); Cruz (2005).
37. *ABC*, 5 September 1936.
38. *ABC*, 1 May 1937.
39. Manuel Azaña, speech given at Valencia city hall on 21 January 1937, in Azaña (1966, vol. III: 329–41).
40. From the *Ejército del Ebro* trench newspaper, quoted in Núñez Seixas (2006: 150).
41. Box (2010: 287–90).
42. Campos Pérez (2010: 137–38, 146–48).
43. Peña López and Alonso González (2004).
44. Account given by Joaquín Satrústegui, in *ABC*, 28 February 1980; Menéndez Pidal (1999: 219–20).

45. *Boletín Oficial del Estado,* 12 October 1945.
46. R. Oyarzun, 'La Bandera y el Himno de España', *La Voz de España,* 8 October 1936.
47. For Pemán's lyrics to the *Marcha Real,* see *ABC,* 2 May 1937; on the commission, see J. M. Pemán, *Mis encuentros con Franco,* Barcelona: Mundo Actual de Ediciones, 1976, 66–67.
48. Box (2010: 302–03).
49. For example, the new text for the blessing of flags approved in July 1941 referred to the flag as the 'sacred symbol of the immortal homeland'; see Pinto Cebrián (1999: 58–59).
50. Cf. for example Rodríguez Centeno (2003) and Zenobi (2011: 307–9).
51. Mayordomo and Fernández Soria (1993: 146–49).
52. Cf. for example *Enciclopedia escolar en dibujos. Grado Superior,* Madrid: Afrodisio Aguado, 1941, and A. Fernández, *Enciclopedia Práctica. Grado Medio,* Barcelona: Miguel A. Salvatella, 1948.
53. Cf. for example F. Izquierdo, 'Iniciación político-social. De los símbolos', *Vida Escolar,* 2 (1958): 32–33.
54. Mayordomo and Fernández Soria (1993: 188–89); Cruz Orozco (2001: 181–82 and 222–24).
55. *Formación Política. Lecciones para las Flechas,* Madrid: Sección Femenina de FET y de las JONS, 6ª ed., pp. 36–37.
56. Sopeña Monsalvo (1994: 221–22).
57. Fuertes Muñoz (2012), and J. L. Rodríguez Mera, *Recuerdos escolares (I),* unpublished manuscript, 2012.
58. Carrión (1976).
59. Duarte (2009: 303–31).
60. *El País,* 16 and 24 April 1977; F. Melchor, 'De la política responsable', *Mundo Obrero,* 17, 29 April 1977.
61. *ABC,* 9 September 1976.
62. *ABC,* 21 March 1982.
63. *ABC,* 12 May 1979; 'España unida, en pie', *Fuerza Nueva,* 19 May 1979, and 'España, en la calle', *Fuerza Nueva,* 26 May 1979.
64. *Diario de Sesiones. Congreso de los Diputados,* 68/1980, pp. 4565–69; 166/1981, pp. 10163–66; and 183/1981, pp. 10952–88.
65. Menéndez Pidal (1999: 221–25).
66. *Ley de 28 Octubre 1981,* in *Boletín Oficial del Estado,* 12 November 1981.
67. *ABC,* 30 and 31 May and 4 June 1981; 'El seny y la Bandera' and 'Barcelona: Una explosión de españolismo', *Reconquista,* 373, June 1981.
68. *El País,* 8 December 1981; *ABC,* 8 December 1981; *Ya,* 8 December 1981; 'La Bandera, símbolo de unidad', *La Vanguardia,* 8 December 1981. Criticisms in E. Romero, 'Después del baile', *Ya,* 9 December 1981, and C. Tobías Rodríguez, 'La bandera de España', *Ya,* 13 January 1982.
69. *El País,* 27 October 1982; J. Bernárdez, 'En la Universitaria ... frente a la Moncloa', *El Socialista,* 3–9 November 1982.
70. *ABC,* 28 and 29 May 1985; *La Vanguardia,* 29 May 1985.
71. Casquete and De la Granja (2012: 528–29).
72. Hargreaves (2000: 68–69, 90–92, 98–101, 110–111).

73. 'Repudio de la violencia y defensa de nuestra bandera', *Acción Republicana*, IV (30), March 1981.
74. Flor (2012: 127–40, 296–301).
75. *El Mundo*, 14 October 2002: *ABC*, 4 October, 26 October and 27 November 2002.
76. Moral (1998: 52–53).

Chapter 3

The Republic,
or Spain Freed from Itself

Àngel Duarte

The slogans 'Spain', 'tomorrow' and 'republic' have, throughout the twentieth century, formed a conceptual trio that has been desirable for some and inadvisable for others. At times, the three concepts, grouped together, have been yelled out by crowds in public squares. Most of the time, however, they have reflected a silent yearning of many platonic republicans. Republican Spain has been a metaphor for the possibility of another Spain, different from the one we have always known, and better.

The rhyming slogan *España, mañana, será republicana* (Spain, tomorrow, will be republican) has been used to express a diversity of horizons, but all of them have extended further than simply the particular institutional form of the state. This was the hope that was contained in the phrase proclaimed in November 1872 by Nicolás Estévanez, one of the patriarchs of Spanish republicanism: 'Everybody happy, and Spain prosperous, under the free government of the federal democratic Republic.'[1] Happiness for the citizenry and a Spain that was liberated in the spheres of culture, economics, politics, social affairs and administration – this was, for its supporters, the republic. It was a desire that had originated in the times of revolutionary liberalism and retained its place as an aspiration for two centuries. The exceptional periods when it took institutional shape, were few and short: a few months in 1873, and a brief interval of time between April 1931 and the spring of 1939.

In other words, Spanish republicanism – from its origins in the mid-nineteenth century to the defeat of the Second Republic in the Spanish Civil War – was also a nationalist project. Liberal and democratic nationalism formed the nucleus of the diverse traditions that constituted republicanism. This was the case for the unitary and socially moderate variants of republicanism, which placed their faith in the electoral participation of educated and progressive citizens or, alternatively, in the intervention of a liberal general of the armed forces. The same can be said for the more radical and popular expressions of republicanism, which favoured an advanced form of federalism and collective action on the part of the populace, now freed from fear and oppression. These groups saw either legal intervention or revolution as the mechanisms by which traditional loyalties could be eroded, and the process of na-tionalization could be strengthened. Ultimately, the republic was per-ceived as the setting in which the nation could fulfil its potential.[2]

In the central decades of the twentieth century, during the nearly forty years of the Franco dictatorship, the republic was cast into the corner of things that were seen as abominable. It lived on in the mem-ory of a few of the defeated, condemned to exile or to invisibility within the country, and a few rather distant, and cold, approaches were made to the subject by those who evaluated Spain's national history as a trauma from which recovery was necessary by means of some kind of exercise in reconciliation between Spaniards.[3] In the mid-1970s, during the transition to democracy, the 'republic' factor did not re-appear with the strength that some had feared and others wished for. Then, when everything seemed lost, around the time of the changeover from the twentieth to the twenty-first centuries, republicanism once again regained its place in the landscape of national hypotheses.

The interest in the subject among the new generations is evident, generations that have been politicized by the discovery of the Second Republic and the Civil War in a context of the 'emergence of memory', by the changeover of generations in the Spanish political elites and, lastly, by the success of civic republicanism in an atmosphere domi-nated by the need to rethink the cultural baggage of that sector of the Left that is rooted in the socialist tradition. Equally, these factors can in no way be disassociated from the fact that Spain has been one of the few countries in which, without there actually being a republic in place, the actions of a government of the centre Left have been given a thorough evaluation from the point of view of a republican political philosophy, as happened with the Socialist government of Rodríguez Zapatero in 2004–10 through its association with Philip Pettit.[4] Nor, equally, from its having been the only country in which social protest movements have given rise to debates on themes as diverse as the potential for par-ticipatory and deliberative democracy implied by the *15-M* (15 May) occupy movement that took over city squares across Spain in 2011, the existence of a legacy of local democracy at municipal level and whether or not all these phenomena together indicate the continuing survival of a residue of republican sentiment in Spanish culture.[5]

Due perhaps to all these factors, added to the many errors made in handling the image of the Crown, opinion polls by 2010 demonstrated a reduction in monarchist preferences among the population. At the end of 2011, the sociologist José Juan Toharia pointed out that 'what is perhaps most striking is that, at present, among the youngest age groups (aged 18–35) preferences for one form or other of the state (monarchy or republic) are equally divided'.[6] This was in no way definitive, for subsequently the abdication of Juan Carlos I and the proclamation of his son as Felipe VI in June 2014 restored some buoyancy to the monarchy's popularity. Nevertheless, all these references to a generation of young people in which republican leanings have reappeared has once again given the republic the status of a viable hypothesis.[7]

One of the singular features of this rebirth of republican conceptions among the young lies in the fact that this attraction for the republic refers to a republicanism without any transmission between generations – this was lost in the exile of 1939 – and characterized by the drawing of only a weak, fragmentary link between the country's history and ideals expressed for the future. The foundations of republican sentiment among modern youth have been, in the first place, the anachronistic nature of monarchist practices, and how expensive, and inefficient, it could be to maintain the Royal Household. Added to this among left-wing militants is the conviction that a republic would necessarily bring with it a general raising of the ethical tone, an unfurling of reforming initiatives in every area of society, and even in all of the individuals of which it is composed. There is also, similarly, a presumption that a republic will ensure the continuation of a cycle of politicization and the assumption of new responsibilities by a citizenry that will be vigilant and attentive to the common good, a body of citizens who will put an end to the degradation of the practices of representative democracy, and, most daring of all, put into action the fresh practices and mechanisms typical of deliberative democracies.

Some readings of this republican rebirth apply to it the concept of 'republican legitimism', the faith in the unbroken legitimacy of the republic founded on 14 April 1931 that had been cultivated in exile, in order to disparage it.[8] Chained to a past of failure, this argument goes, the new republicans relativize the role of the constitutional monarchy in the construction of representative democracy in Spain and face backwards to seek the roots of their project for the future in a conflictive past that ultimately exhausted itself in a civil war. It is the case that the impression given by the republicans of the twenty-first century that they have reinvented the wheel would have disconcerted their coreligionists of the first third of the previous one, those who continued to venerate the bust of the federalist and president of the First Republic of 1873, Francisco Pi y Margall. However, those of today also have the advantage, precisely because of the fading away of any culture transmitted from the past, of being able to connect with the classical conception of republicanism – that which associates the idea of liberty with a guarantee of the right to exist – while leaving behind in the fog of family nostalgia the specific liberal practices and institutions with which the term *republican* had been associated in the formative period of contemporary society, so that they can make their own way, and respond to fresh dilemmas.[9]

All in all, then, it is quite possible today that the republic may again figure among the future prospects that are imagined, with more or less precision, by and for Spaniards. However, we will not continue to discuss these expectations.[10] We will turn our focus towards clarifying the meaning that the republic possessed in the national and patriotic imaginary during the twentieth century, most especially among its partisans.

Today we know a great deal about this republicanism – perhaps not everything, but a lot, in any case. In the last few decades, historians have meticulously reconstructed the pieces of a puzzle that leads us back to a dynamic that was set in motion in the era of the first political socialization in the country, and the precarious establishment of the practical foundations of liberal democracy and municipal administration. It was, equally, the time of a first extension of nation-building, and of a national feeling that was similarly precarious and weak, especially at the bottom, among the poor and working classes, and in those of Spain's outer regions with marked cultural differences. Some of the republican men and women distributed around every corner of the Kingdom of Spain were actively militant in support of their ideal, others were simply loyal to the republic as an idealized vision of what their homeland could have become; a land that was more just, more European, more open to the participation of its men and women in setting forth common national objectives and determining the means necessary to attain them. Republicanism was, in both the nineteenth and twentieth centuries, a democratic form, banal or otherwise depending on the circumstances, of nationalism.[11]

The Republic of 1900

What did the Spaniards of 1900 understand by a 'republic'? The term had reached the first year of the new century with particular connotations. Whichever ideological tendency a republican identified with, whether it was the federalist strand or a unitary state, whether they declared themselves supporters of economic liberalism or gave first priority to the mass of the people, republicans knew that the modern Spanish nation, as it had been forged in the time of the liberal revolution of the early nineteenth century, had virtually always been ruled by a monarchy. And the cornerstone of the structure that underpinned this regime was tradition. Whether as a standard unfurled on a battlefield or as an ultimate justification for their institutional logic, the supporters of the dynasty, as republicans saw it, always, always hid behind tradition in order to impose the administrative architecture of the monarchy as the only possible means of state construction. The continuing transmission of both the syntagm *Reino de España* (Kingdom of Spain) and the obsequiousness that was inherent within it towards the person who incarnated the phrase simultaneously reinforced the authority of the Crown, its links with the Catholic Church and the principles of respect for property and public order. Tradition gave continuity to the nation and acted as a barrier to the possibility of revolution. For the social groups that enjoyed a hegemonic position in Spanish life, the republic, as the antinomic opposite of monarchy, represented in contrast something entirely hazardous: a violent break with the past, the danger of ceasing to exist, the anti-Spain.

This characterization of the republic was not born with the new century. During the previous decades, the progress made by the term *republic* had already been countered by its assumed identification with chaos and misrule. Republicans were ungodly, libertines, Freemasons, traitors to the fatherland, copyists of the French Revolution. Spanish reactionaries and conservatives saw 1789 and 1793 as not just dates of foreign significance, but the point of departure for a whole cycle of subversion that had put into question the fatherland, the powers of the state, the very foundations of social order. Ultimately, too, one can see that the first of Spain's Republics, that of 1873, with its many vicissitudes, only provided republicanism's opponents with a whole host of fresh reasons for their hostility. Republicans of both the federalist and unitary varieties, with separatism exploding around them in Spain's Cuban colony and the radical 'cantonalist' movement that declared towns across Spain semi-independent 'cantons', had put at risk two things that were both equally dear to the elites who went on to forge the regime of the Bourbon monarchy after its 1874 restoration: the integrity of the nation and the stability of a social order founded upon the modern concept of property.

On the other side of political life, in contrast, in 1900 the republic also filled the imaginations of a not insignificant number of individuals for whom it represented a space in which to project their expectations, a goal to achieve and a symbol of identity.[12] For them, the republic continued to be the land of redemption, a realm of liberty and the location of a possible utopia. It also represented at the same time something that as a nation we perhaps had not been but could have become, if not for the others, if not, perhaps, for ourselves, incapable of dragging ourselves out from under the influence of superstition and the domination of a few in the making of decisions. The republic was the terrain on which Spaniards would fight their battles against ignorance and privilege.

If the republic offered a prospect of national plenitude, material progress and social justice, being a republican was also a specific way of being Spanish. The most advanced, complete and ambitious way of being so; that of the individual who ceased to be a subject in order to attain the status of citizen in a community of free human beings who paid attention to the common good; that of men and women who by means of the suffrage and other forms of participation in the public sphere gave expression to national sovereignty and the popular will; that of the militia member or volunteer who fought, first against the reactionary Carlists in the nineteenth century and then against the army of the rebel generals in 1936; that of the mothers and wives who made their homes a seedbed of free compatriots while at the same time winning their own autonomy in public life; that of the audacious radical journalists; that of the lawyers who defended the needy; that of the doctors who struggled equally against tuberculosis and the monarchy; that of the skilled workers who were proud of their status; that of the agricultural labourer or tenant farmer who challenged landowners over wages or the use they made of the land; that of the teachers who freed the people from ignorance; that of the citizens who sought to form juries to administer justice; even, in some cases, that of the few exceptional members of the clergy who rebelled against the Church hierarchy and took up the cause of profane love.

In opposition to the vision proclaimed by monarchists, republicans were convinced, at least until 1939, that the republic, as a project or an institutional framework, would create 'Spaniards'. It was a patriotic ideal that associated the 'nation' with liberty, equality and fraternity. This was no impediment to it also nourishing, particularly among those of its followers most inclined to popular democratic radicalism, a certain cosmopolitan outlook. This would be so in the twentieth century, just as it had been in the previous hundred years.

The new century, moreover, had begun with an environment that seemed to favour the belief that republic and nation were, in their fullest expression, the same thing. After a quarter of a century of severe limitations whenever it came to offering republican solutions, favourable circumstances had arrived. The long-standing collision between Spain's past status as an imperial power and its complicated present had become evident in 1898 with the war against the United States, and the loss of its last colonies in the Antilles and the Pacific. Colonial projects in North Africa, which arose frequently in the following years, did not prevent anyone from realizing the extent of this change of fortune. At the same time, public opinion had witnessed the passing away not only of the figures responsible for the First Republic, but also of the leaders who had made possible the consolidation of the Restoration monarchy under Alfonso XII between 1874 and 1881. The resulting vacuum in the leadership of the pro-dynastic Conservatives and Liberals coincided with the arrival on the throne of a young monarch, Alfonso XIII. His youth generated sympathy, but also uncertainty.

In these years, the counterposition of the 'real' country to the official one created the conditions required for the reappearance of the republic as a possible way of being Spanish, as a means of reconciling legality with existing reality. This was recalled in the new liberal newspaper *Crisol* shortly after the proclamation of the Second Republic in 1931 by Azorín (José Martínez Ruiz), one of the intellectuals who had come to the fore with the turn of the century. 'The Republic has taken shape slowly in the consciousness of Spain,' he wrote, 'over the course of thirty years, since 1898.'[13] Everything had begun with the educational projects of the positivist circles influenced by the ideas of Karl C. F. Krause and associated with the hugely influential school they founded in Madrid, the Institución Libre de Enseñanza, and with the success of the diagnoses of the state of the nation made by Joaquín Costa, who joined the broad electoral coalition the Unión Republicana in 1903. As an alternative to oligarchical rule and *caciquismo*, the domination of politics by local bosses, Costa proposed an executive republic, opposed to sterile parliamentarism, that would be prepared to carry forward the restoration of a sense of community, make the benefits of schooling universal and promote new infrastructure. Republicanism, by one route or another, left behind the squabbles of the years between 1868 and 1874 and the early stages of the Restoration to modernize its language, its ways of taking part in social life and its forms of political action. It was attentive and receptive to almost any kind of intellectual model, to the point where, in its most libertarian fringes, it could even assimilate the attractions of the vitalism and spiritualism in fashion at the time. Republicans and republicanism seemed once again, as they had in the 1870s, to be the enzyme that would Europeanize the nation and 'nationalize' the new airs, charged with electricity, that were blow-ing in from across the Pyrenees. Both European and national, that was the position of a republican during the hostilities with the Yankees in 1898; part of a movement, a project and a way of life that did not stand apart from the mobilization in the main cities of thousands of students and shop and office workers, journalists and lawyers, who demonstrated their discontent with institutions that had put the nation's treasures up for sale.

This republican patriotism would soon discover that a pair of powerful obstacles to its possible development had emerged within it, or in the ambience around it. The general strike in Barcelona in 1902, the bloody riots of the *Semana Trágica* (Tragic Week) against conscription for the war in Morocco that exploded in the same city seven years later, the foundation of the anarcho-syndicalist labour confederation the Confederación Nacional del Trabajo (CNT) in 1911, the coming together of republicans and socialists after decades of confrontations, misunderstandings and hostility and the rift that appeared within republicanism during the First World War between the pro-Allied *aliadó-filos* and those who followed the pacifist teachings of Romain Rolland, all brought into profile the extent to which ideas of national unanimity could be overshadowed by the logic of class, dialectics of social confrontation and arguments that had split the Left in Europe apart by 1917. The problem of the question of property, as a central condition for allowing any possibility of liberty, became intensely controversial within Spanish republicanism, and competed for attention with all the problems associated with creating national feeling among the masses. Populist leaderships sought to sew both elements together, that of identification with the nation and a sense of distributive justice in the treatment of wealth. In the first part of his career, in 1901, the future republican prime minister Alejandro Lerroux called as insistently for a leading role for the proletariat as he did for the nation, appealing both to patriotic pride and to the masculine strength of the wage-earning masses gathered in the outskirts of Spain's cities, who, he implied, would burst into the urban centres to clear the air and make the cities fruitful, and demand the part of their material wealth that they were due. For a few years, this operation did not appear entirely impossible – not in Barcelona, nor Valencia, nor in Madrid.

A second obstacle also appeared in the way of a full identification of the different, plural republicanisms with the Spanish nation, with the republic as an instrument for the creation of national feeling: the formation and success of mass sub-state nationalisms. They offered significant competition from the middle of the first decade of the century. The creation of a specific system of political parties in Catalonia, which included some republican tendencies, and their inclination to set up a 'sacred union' of their own – as seen in the cross-party *Solidaritat Catalana* (Catalan Solidarity) movement of 1906–9, or the campaign for a *Mancomunitat* or administrative union of the four Catalan provinces in 1911–14 – as an alternative to a Spanish one placed conditions on the maintenance of this equivalence between the republic and the Spanish nation. Catalan republicans neutralized it or, at the very least, obliged it to pass through the filter of a form of federalism that was more (Catalan) nationalist than localist. In contrast to the pattern seen, for example, in the Valencian provinces, Andalusia or several other regions, Catalan nationalism created problems both for the idea of a republican Spain – in the federal sense – and for the prospect of a Catalonia in which the axis of political debate might centre on a republic rather than autonomy.

The process that took place across Spain during the Second Republic of 1931–36, which was contradictory in the extent to which it combined acts of complicity and cooperation, notably between Catalan and other sub-state nationalisms and Spanish republicanism, with open fissures, in the resistance to autonomy from the right, meant that from this point on the republic came to be identified with the imaginary of a Spain that was plural, complex and respectful, beyond the point of mere rhetoric, of the diversity of its peoples. This was so before October 1934, when large sections of the Left across Spain launched a revolutionary movement in opposition to the inclusion in the government of members of the rightist Confederación Española de Derechas Autónomas (CEDA), which they considered as tantamount to surrendering the republic to fascism, and equally after 6 October of that year, when Lluís Companys, head of the leftist Catalan autonomous government, joined the rebellion and proclaimed the 'Catalan State within the Spanish Federal Republic', doing so in order to 're-establish and fortify relations with the leaders of the general protest against fascism' and invited these leaders to 'establish in Catalonia the Provisional Government of the Republic, which will find in our Catalan people the most generous feeling of fraternity in the common desire to build a free and magnificent Federal Republic'.[14]

As in the time of Estévanez? Not exactly; not in the reference to fascism – which places us in a context in which the republic appeared as a dam holding back totalitarian barbarism – nor in the plurality of nations that could now be discovered beneath the formula of the federal republic.

The Republic, the People, the Nation
and the Historical Substrata of Them All

The republic also had to compete, with unequal success, with the monarchy in an effort to be identified not just with the decisions made by individuals in the present or expectations for the future, as we have examined so far, but with a readiness to preserve the essence of a community built up over centuries. Although the republic, as could be seen on the day of its proclamation on 14 April 1931, always had a certain character of being a new dawn for the nation, it also needed to mark out some merits for itself at the level of the primordial nation, the one that pre-existed before the decisions of the citizens that composed it as a political community. It had to observe the limits of a given field of play, those of the nation as a geological reality. Since, unlike the monarchy, it did not have the option of arguing on the basis of any connection with a hereditary lineage, republicanism resorted to popular national features and idiosyncrasies. Thus, in the nineteenth century, republicans took as a given the existence of a thousand-year-old Spanish *Volksgeist* characterized by rebelliousness, a will to independence and a sense of political justice and moral economy. Historicism allowed them to present themselves as heirs to all the country's heterodoxies: victims of invaders, of the powerful, of the Inquisition and clerical intolerance, and all those who had suffered the disastrous effects inflicted on their homeland by the separation of its national development from the spirit of modernity, the Enlightenment and scientific progress. Every shade of rebelliousness could find room for itself in this model. As the century progressed, this kind of argument became more problematic, but did not cease to be useful. After all, the crowds who attended the act of homage in Madrid in May 1931 for Mariana Pineda – condemned to death in Granada in 1831 after a liberal banner had been found in her house – felt that the same blood ran in their veins as in the democratic heroine when she had been executed by the reactionaries a hundred years earlier.

Nevertheless, the republicans of the twentieth century, and Spaniards in general whether leftist or conservative, had become men and women who were moving a little away from the taste for legendary means of defining the nation, most particularly when they saw political intervention as a practical possibility. Even when they defined themselves as conservative, they preferred to see themselves as individuals creating their own destiny rather than heirs to some national genetic code with deep popular roots. They might appeal to such an idea when in trouble – as, for example, during the Civil War[15] – but in normal times they opted for a political patriotism, even when they wished to disparage sub-state nationalisms, ahead of a nationalism that turned back to the essences found in the vessels of the past. This would be most clearly but not solely visible in the 'new republicans', liberals who had grown hostile to the monarchy because the regime itself had decided to break with parliamentarism and representative government, and who wished to rid themselves of the reminders of a past of disputes and civil wars.

In the days following 14 April, the philosopher José Ortega y Gasset, a republican of the kind that had become so in 1931 on the basis of his liberalism, assured his readers that the republic could have a seminal effect on the nation, that it could 'anticipate the future, creating it!' and construct a 'nation for generations'.[16] Ortega accorded the republic the responsibility of giving rise to a modern way of being Spanish as yet unseen, a collective way of being that would break with stereotypes. A few weeks later, however, the philosopher, who had placed himself at the service of the republic, demanded that it rectify the course it had chosen. In his view, rebelliousness, anti-clericalism, the social reform agenda, the prominence of the labour unions, the revival of old disputes and stale forms of political language and the stress inflicted on the nation by the demand for Catalan autonomy all represented deviations and causes for concern touching on the very being of Spain.

Niceto Alcalá-Zamora, first prime minister and later first president of the republic and an archetype of the monarchists who had gone over to the republican side in 1930, put things a different way. He understood that Spanish national continuity was not sustainable under Alfonso XIII and that its cause had to be taken up by himself and his colleagues, the signatories of the revolutionary pact of San Sebastián in August 1930, the members of the provisional government who on 14 April went from prisons to the centres of power in the state. He had recalled, before this happened, that in other situations – in France – 'men from monarchist backgrounds had given an example of serving and reinforcing republican institutions'. For the problem of the nation was that of its institutions, of a series of institutions that needed to be placed at the service of 'of a *patria* [fatherland] that we have to preserve' and bring about 'the daily exercise of republican virtue', and which, while they might be open to progress and social improvements, would initially act 'in the most prudent manner possible'.[17]

This reference to virtue was not a casual one. It demonstrates the extent to which liberals disillusioned with the monarchy were prepared to take up the nucleus of republican philosophy, in a manner that was also conceived in national terms. The point made by Alcalá-Zamora was that, in the same way that the citizens needed to acquire good habits, so too institutions needed to be designed that would have as their aim the public good and political justice. The *patria* had existed before the republic, and the latter could and should be placed at the service of the nation. In reality, these institutions, as was stated in the preamble to the decree that appointed Alcalá-Zamora president of the republic, would stem from the power of the people, 'without procedural interference nor resistance nor protocolary opposition of any kind'. It was from the people, heart and core of the political nation, that all authority proceeded.

The echoing words of the radical republican Roque Barcía in the constituent assembly of 1868 – 'We republicans are not a party, we are not a "part" of anything, but the entire people; all the living, healthy, beating energies of the country, with no exception other than the privileged classes' – resounded once again in 1931.[18] The only elements left outside the republic were the enemies of the people, and consequently of the nation. There was no republic without the people, who were the expression of the fatherland, of the political nation. On this point there was full agreement, which extended to include a republican Left who only wished to see excluded from the republic the 'parasites', those who since time immemorial had lived not *for* the body of the nation but *off* it. The matter in hand, in short, was to leave behind a time-worn Spain bound to a feudal world, an *ancien régime* that had still not lain down and died.

The fragility of the republic, of which neither Ortega nor of course Alcalá-Zamora could have had certain evidence in the autumn of 1931, could, however, lead us into confusion on certain issues. In opposition to the instability of 'what there is' (the monarchy that had provided the background to the whole host of constituent processes throughout the nineteenth century and, with the exception of the one in which Ortega was involved, into the twentieth), in contemporary times the republic had come to embody the 'stability of what has not yet been put into effect': the forever-delayed task of liquidating the remnants of an obdurate past that was continually determined to show its presence.

This effort to create a bright new nation, based upon the mutual assimilation of people, fatherland and republic, would fail yet again due to the central role of social conflict in all its multiple variations. Social discipline and a sense of republican austerity, as called for by the recent recruits to the ranks of republicanism, were lacking. The republican revolution, by putting into question social relations based on deference, aided the creation of a situation in which collective action took on powerful dimensions. The progress of the Second Republic, which we shall scarcely enter into here, was marked by the presence of antagonistic social programmes that collided with each other, gravely threatened the existing order and eventually plunged the nation into conflict. At the same time, the republic's course was also affected by the loss of the high patriotic esteem that had been attributed to republicans, and the reappearance, in the words of its most prominent politician and second prime minister, Manuel Azaña, of the old politics, those of 'prior obligations' and the 'duties of a party man'.[19]

If the elections of autumn 1933, in which conservative republicans and overtly rightist parties won a majority following the collapse of the Left Republican-Socialist coalition headed by Azaña, ended the hegemony of the reformist project, the events that followed the entry of right-wing CEDA ministers into the government in 1934 – the revolutionary uprising in Asturias, the attempted General Strike, Companys's proclamation in Barcelona – signified the starting point for a reconstruction of the republic's founding logic; with the republic effectively under constraint, a demonstrative democracy emerged. During 1935, Azaña, at the head of the republican nation and by means of the classic republican instrument – the human voice – addressed massive crowds in open-air meetings. These would be the men and women who would add their support to the plan for a Popular Front. These mass meetings were followed by a fresh process of meetings, communication and negotiation between republican and Left leaders, which, due to the sheer weight of the hopes that went together with the ongoing faith in the republic itself, adopted proposals of a kind unheard of in 1931. The first manifestation of the renewed popular and national hopes attached to the republic was seen in the polling stations in February 1936, when fresh elections were won by the Popular Front. The second came in July 1936, in streets and in fields, in the popular resistance to the military uprising against the republican government that led to civil war. Neither the multiplicity of options that was contained within the Popular Front, nor the dissolution of a shared outlook that accompanied the dislocation of the republican state, prevented the defence of the republic from being associated, even at the cost of restricting the social revolution, with the defence of legality. A legality that had liberated Spaniards, and that now offered them the opportunity to defend themselves against their historic oppressors, and would always guarantee them a conviction of their own moral superiority.[20]

As a bulwark against fascism, for its adherents the republic preserved national independence in a time of European confrontations and foreign interference. Up until the last agonies of its institutions on Spanish soil, the republic represented the people and the nation, both in the past and in its capacity for autonomous decision-making in the present. And, when its defenders left to cross the frontier or board ships from Mediterranean ports in the face of Franco's final victory in early 1939, an entire nation departed. Although it may have been experienced as such in personal terms, this was not an exclusively in-dividual or family exile. For republicans, the nation's knowledge, its creative efforts, the progress made in education, the advances it had made in the liberation of workers, the secularization of public space, all these areas of its social life, even its sense of political decency, had gone abroad. In other words, the entity that had escaped from Spanish territory was the political nation.

Consequently, the reintegration of the republic could only come about with the return of all the expatriates as a body and, most im-portantly, of the institutions erected with the support of the citizens and by popular will in the spring of 1931. The drip-drip of returning exiles that was seen from the first months, whether from France or from different parts of Latin America, did not change this diagnosis. The nation continued to be somewhere else. Francoist Spain was not a nation in the extent that it was purely the expression of a tyranny with no sense of a homeland.

The Republican Spains

The republic's defeat condemned it as a national ideal. Inside Spain, its image was reviled ad nauseam. *Reespañolizar,* the process of re-educating the country in patriotism, meant, for the fascist Spain of 1939, de-republicanizing it down to the roots. To do so it was necessary to maintain, in the same way that an official state of war was main-tained until 1948, a war culture, with the logic of violence applied to political cleansing, and the transubstantiation of anything 'republican' into 'red'.[21] The republican rearguard, meanwhile, continued to culti-vate a positive imaginary. The problem, however, was that this rear-guard had been confined abroad, in an endless exile; as a 'wandering' Spain that, as the years went by, appeared increasingly disconnected from the dynamics that were developing inside the country. The out-come could not be anything other than a growing sense of uselessness around the republic as a national imaginary – clandestine, in a state of stagnation, but, nevertheless, still possessed of beauty; a gratitude towards this set of images remained, in a latent state.

Francoism carried its work of stigmatizing the republic to manic ex-tremes. It did so with the collaboration of historians, essayists, teachers and propagandists. The republic was nothing less than the final milestone in the anti-national course that certain local elites had set out to follow ever since the end of the reign of King Philip II, in 1598. In collusion with foreign interests, the republic had sunk the nation into ruin, brought about chaos and made inevitable a 'national uprising', or *Alzamiento Nacional*, to avoid the disintegration that was so desired by the enemies of the fatherland and its thousand-year history. Restorative, counter-revolutionary and fascistic violence had risen up against democratic reasoning. At the same time, beyond all these anti-republican narratives, the hardships of the war and a long postwar period in which violence remained ever-present and living conditions deteriorated to levels unforeseen even by the most imaginative did establish in the minds of a not insignificant proportion of a population deprived of any rights a causal connection between the republic and the miseries of the postwar years.

The republic meant politics, and politics was pernicious for every individual and, naturally, for the nation. The fatigue generated in broad sectors of society by the long cycle of politicization leading up to 1936 contributed to the articulation of an alternative consensus to that of the republican years, one based now on the political inactivity of the populace. Tradition recovered its role of guarantor of the continuity of the nation, and with this the question of the form of the state was also resolved. In 1947, the Spanish state once again acquired the status, as had virtually been the case, of a kingdom. 'Spain, as a political unit', the relevant decree stated, 'is a Catholic, social and representative state which, in accordance with its tradition, is declared to constitute a Kingdom.'[22]

The republic certainly continued to represent one idea of Spain – a Spain seen as the legitimate one – an idea that was silently transmitted from generation to generation, from that of 1927–36, those with direct experience, to that of 1956–68, the children and younger brothers.[23] It was expressed too in the titles of the exile press ('Republican Spain', 'New Spain'), as an idea that intellectual circles sought to modernize from the cultural institutions abroad that had welcomed them. Magazines like *Las Españas*, published in Mexico from 1946 to 1963, become laboratories in which the notion of a Spanish republic was brought up to date, efforts were made to associate it with the constructive dynamic of the democracies after their victory over the Nazis and fascists in the world war, and it was put forward as an interlocutor for the Spanish nation before an international community that was becoming polarized – like republican Spain in exile itself – by the question of communism. This republican Spain ceased to be paid any attention within

Spain, and subsequently became a forgotten Spain. Nevertheless, the activities of the exiles were in no way insignificant, and it should be remembered that some states, such as Mexico, continued to consider the republic the real Spain. And that, in another sphere, committed intellectuals of the 1950s, perhaps most importantly Albert Camus, still reimagined republican Spain as an experience that resisted being devoured by the binary logic of the Cold War, taking them back to the experience of anti-fascism in a land of free human beings and solidarity.

Meanwhile, inside Spain, Francoism continued its work of denigrating the image of the republic. The efficacy with which this was done, and the need to break with a conception of republican democracy that, it seemed, could not be evoked without simultaneously raising the spectre of a fratricidal war, led the new circles of dissident intellectuals of the 1950s and early 1960s, as well as the new social and labour movements that protested against living and working conditions, to distance themselves from republican imagery.[24] The strength of the system, and the need to develop contacts with monarchist circles, made the politicized elements among the internal dissidents move away from any cultivation of the republican myth. In June 1956, on the verge of the twentieth anniversary of the outbreak of the Civil War, the Spanish Communist Party (PCE) announced that, in the interests of national reconciliation, democracy, not the republic, would be its first priority.[25]

For those that did not give up the cause, what could be done? How could they give concrete form, in exile if not inside Spain, to the task of cultivating and maintaining a republican patriotic imaginary? First of all, by examining the present experience of their compatriots. Current news from Spain would always be a cause of anguish. Anguish over the continuing repression, the nonexistence of civil liberties and the material shortages of all kinds, stemming from the collapse of the economy and the isolation and moral inanity of the regime. 'Abducted' Spain was characterized by starvation wages, chaos in its public services, irregularities in the application of law and corruption. There was also the domination of a Catholicism that was first vengeful and obscurantist, and then later technocratic and hypocritical, but which mutilated consciences at all times.

Republicans looked on with great distress, due both to the prolongation of a regime that destroyed liberties and to their very early realization of the lack of interest that had grown among Spaniards in politics and, consequently, in the republic. As early as August 1946, a report appeared in one of the Paris exile magazines that set out to give a portrait of 'The Francoist Paradise' and dealt graphically with the world of bullfighting, modifying a traditional cliché on what was needed to keep ordinary Spaniards happy – *pan y toros* (bread and bullfights), obviously based on the Roman 'bread and circuses' – with the title *Hambre y Toros* (Hunger and Bullfights). The anonymous author recorded that Spain was in the midst of a moment of great excitement over bullfighting. 'We will not go so far as to say that the Franco regime has organized this recrudescence of bullfighting', the article argued, 'but it does look upon it sympathetically and encourages it, because it instinctively understands that everything that distracts and excites the public works in its favour, turning their attention away from political topics.' The parallel drawn with Roman circuses and the carnivals of the Venice of the Doges or Buenos Aires under the dictator Juan Manuel de Rosas were impossible to miss. What was most lamentable, the article concluded, was that the other half of the traditional duo (bread) never became reality. 'The rule of Franco is one of *fiestas* for the beneficiaries and black-marketeers of the regime, and a hunger diet for common citizens, who make up the rest of all Spaniards.'[26]

Alongside the gaze that examined Spain's present, there was another that turned to the past. If the leading circles of republicanism had conceived their future projects by drawing on the lessons of the past when they were inside the country, they were not going to give them up when they were far from the landscapes of their childhood and early maturity. The republican intellectual community prolonged the debate on Spain and the causes of its national tragedy. Heirs to an Enlightenment vision that presented the path of humanity as one of perpetual progress, but traumatized by their own experience of defeat and forced emigration, the exiles believed that by deciphering the causes of Spain's 'exceptionality' they would give back to the nation its possibilities of a future.[27]

The visions of the Spain of the past that were cultivated by the exiles in Latin America or France were complex. Alongside all the themes that can be related to a recent past – the achievements of the republic, the heroic feats of the war – one detects a huge passion for going deeper into the distant roots of Spain's national identity as a people. The efforts made in this field were enhanced by the great intellectual prestige of many of the expatriates. Academic historians such as Rafael Altamira, Claudio Sánchez Albornoz and Américo Castro or the Catalan archaeologist Pere Bosch-Gimpera provided these narratives of the remote past. Particularly noticeable in the contributions of Bosch-Gimpera in the 1940s and Anselmo Carretero in the 1950s and 1960s is their acceptance of the complexity of Spanish-ness and what is Spanish.[28] For Bosch or Carretero, a republican analysis of the past had to take as its starting point a preliminary question, namely 'Where is, then, the true Spain and its true tradition, in which everyone, Castilians, Andalusians, Galicians, Basques and Catalans, can come together as brothers? Where is the Spain in which the free nations of America – a melting pot of peoples – can recognize and love the mother country of one part of their ancestry and their civilization? The blood of the ancestors of Bolívar, Hidalgo, Sucre and San Martín could not be the same as that of Torquemada, or the executioners of their own fatherland.'[29]

The Spain that the republicans wished to embrace and put forward to those inside the country was a nation in which both the countries that it had created and which had since gained their independence as well as all the different peoples within its own borders could see themselves reflected and so identify with a common homeland, from a position of pluralism. It also had to be a country that renounced reactionary attitudes and obscurantism. What needed to be rescued from the past was a living, complex reality that for centuries had been shackled by a structure of Catholic and monarchist domination, to which the Falangists were heirs.

From the Absent Republic to the Republic as a Missing Necessity

In the political mobilizations of the 1970s, in which the anti-Francoist opposition sought to build a certain degree of strength that would permit them to make their presence felt in the transition from dictatorship to democracy, the shouted rhyme of 'Spain, tomorrow, will be Republican' did not go missing. On occasion it infiltrated its way in alongside the canonical slogan 'Liberty and Amnesty', and calls for a Statute of Autonomy in the Catalan, Basque, Galician, Andalusian, Valencian and, very soon, other communities. However, while there were those who had it in mind in the streets, when it came to offices and other arenas of negotiation, the republic vanished. The reformist elements that had emerged from Francoism were perhaps willing to omit references to 18 July 1936 or the foundational nature for the state of the 'National Uprising' and the Civil War, but they would not give up the delegitimization of the Second Republic.[30] It provided the exact contrast they needed to invoke to justify their links with the 'second Francoism', the one that was committed to development, and had celebrated '35 Years of Peace' in 1971. Democracy was possible, it was maintained, because the growth and economic and social modernization that had followed the stabilization programme introduced by the regime at the end of the

1950s had eventually made it so that Spaniards as individuals could possibly coexist in freedom. In the face of this kind of argument, as regards the republic, a degree of renunciation became the accepted norm in an opposition that was now being called upon to take part in dialogue.

Those who managed Spain's transition took great care to veto any possibility that the concept of the 'republic' could interfere in its dynamics. The Socialist and Communist parties renounced their republican identities for the sake of consensus.[31] Celebrations of the republic's proclamation on 14 April, which after all had been a day of 'national' dimensions, were banned until the end of the 1970s. Those parties that defined themselves as republican, from the historic Esquerra Republicana de Catalunya (Catalan Republican Left, ERC) to Acción Republicana Democrática Española (ARDE), created in 1960, were not allowed to stand for election as such in the first democratic elections of 1977, which had constituent status, since the resulting *Cortes* (parliament) oversaw and approved the creation of Spain's new constitution. By cooperating in an ad hoc electoral alliance with a similarly barred Marxist-Leninist organization, the Partido de Trabajo de España (Spanish Labour Party, PTE), the ERC did succeed in winning a seat in the *Cortes* for its leader, Heribert Barrera, who, together with the deputy from the Basque radical-nationalist Left, Francisco Letamendia, continued to defend the validity of the republican idea, associating it with the right to self-determination.

Beyond these minor episodes, the truth is that the republic seemed to have given way to democracy, even though the latter was administrated by a monarchy. At the start of the final decade of the twentieth century, the republic appeared to lack any precise content: 'A form [of government] of great historical weight, which lacks clear content in the present time', as one dictionary of political terminology put it.[32] Moreover, the young, lacking in historical memory and attracted by different horizons, seemed uninterested in the republic.[33] In 2001, it was asserted that the republican spirit was 'blurred' and confined to 'the realm of melancholy'.[34] Nevertheless, only a short time later, the republic was reactivated, as a valuable inheritance and as a project for the future.

The continuity in time of the republican ideal, its prolonged role in the history of contemporary Spain, thus appears to be revealing itself once again in the twenty-first century, and probably for the same reasons as ever: individuals who share the same experiences of domination believe they see in the ideal of the republic a set of resources with which they can act collectively, and hope for a free future as a nation.

Àngel Duarte is professor of Modern History at the University of Girona. His main research interests relate the analysis of Republican cultures in modern Spain. His latest books include *El otoño de un ideal* (Madrid, 2009) and *El republicanismo: una pasión política* (Madrid, 2013).

Notes

1. La Igualdad, 1 December 1872.
2. De Blas (1991).
3. Aróstegui (2006).
4. Traverso (2007). On historical memory, see Juliá (2003). For the evaluation of the Zapatero government, see Martín and Petit (2010).
5. E. Botella-Ordinas et al., *La Vie des idées*. http://www.laviedesidees.fr/Re publicanisme-et-participation.html (last accessed (8 June 2015).
6. http://blogs.elpais.com/metroscopia/2011/12/monarquia-republica.html.
7. http://elpais.com/diario/2011/04/14/espana/1302732018_850215.html; http://www.publico.es/espana/354248/es-posible-la-tercera-republica; http://www.elmundo.es/elmundo/2005/11/20/espana/1132456951.html (last accesed 16 June 2015)
8. Romero Samper (2005: 161ff.).
9. Ovejero, Martí and Gargarella (2003); De Francisco (2012).
10. Duarte (2008).
11. M. P. Salomón Chéliz (2009).
12. Duarte (1997).
13. Azorín, 'Un momento decisivo', *Crisol*, 12 May 1931, quoted in Zamora Bonilla (2011: 530).
14. Speech by Lluís Companys reproduced in Coste i Deu and Sabaté (2006: 1567–59).
15. Núñez Seixas (2006).
16. Ortega y Gasset (1931: 10, 17).
17. Alcalá Zamora (1930: 54–56).
18. E. Rodríguez Solís, *La Ilustración Republicana Federal*, 15 June 1871.
19. Azaña (1998: 355).
20. Ucelay Da Cal (1994: 194–98).
21. Sevillano (2007); Rodrigo (2008).
22. *Boletín Oficial del Estado*, 208, 27 July 1947.
23. Cuesta (2006).
24. Muñoz Soro (2003); González (2009).
25. Partido Comunista de España, 'Por la Reconciliación Nacional, por una solución democrática y pacífica del problema español', *Boletín de Información*, Prague, 1 July 1956. http://www.filosofia.org/his/h1956rn.htm (last accessed 2 July 2015).
26. *La Nouvelle Espagne*, Paris, 22 August 1946.
27. Pérez Garzón (2000: 104–5); *España Republicana*, Buenos Aires, 4, 1955.
28. Carretero y Nieva (1952).

29. P. Bosch Gimpera. 'Dos Españas', *Las Españas, Revista Literaria*, 29 November 1946, 1–12.
30. Gallego (2008: 23).
31. Andrade Blanco (2012).
32. Haro Tecglen (1997: 377).
33. Fernández (2000: 307–08); Casares (1981); Dreyfus-Armand (2000: 325–27, 333–34).
34. Villares (2001: 51).

Chapter 4

'The King of All Spaniards'?
Monarchy and Nation

Javier Moreno-Luzón

◦━━━━━◦

'I am the King of all Spaniards, and also a Spaniard.' – Alfonso XIII,
'To the Country', statement on his departure, 14 April 1931

'The institution that I personify integrates all Spaniards, and
today, in this momentous hour, I call upon you because the duty
of serving Spain falls to us all, equally.' – Juan Carlos I, 'Message
of His Majesty the King to all Spaniards on his Proclamation',
speech to the *Cortes*, 22 November 1975

When the twentieth century began, Europe was a monarchical continent in which there were only three republics: France, Switzerland
and San Marino. When it ended, the great majority of European states
had republican constitutions. A few monarchies survived: those in the
United Kingdom, the Netherlands, Belgium, Luxembourg, Sweden,
Norway, Denmark and Spain, as well as the micro-states of Liech-
tenstein and Monaco. Virtually all of them, too, could be described
as parliamentary monarchies. That is, even where thrones had been
maintained, the monarchs had lost the bulk of their powers – whether
because of a constitutional ordinance, or as a consequence of political
practice – and governments were formed from parliaments elected by
the citizens of the country. Kings and princes did retain symbolic and
representative functions, as heads of their respective states.

Nevertheless, the European monarchies should not be considered
mere leftovers from the past. Historians, jurists and social scientists,
intrigued by the continuation of such ancient institutions in contemporary political systems, have inquired into their meaning and legitimacy. In so doing, they have often found them in the links between the

monarchies and national identities. The states that the monarchs once represented eventually reconfigured themselves as nation-states, and at different times and in different contexts their Crowns managed to acquire a significant positions in their respective nationalist imaginaries. Michael Billig, for example, has revealed the extent to which British people were unable to conceive their country without the presence of the royal family, during the 1980s.[1] Monarchies, faced with the rise of popular nationalisms and the ever more influential exercise of public opinion, transformed themselves into 'performing monarchies' that projected their image through the mass media. In the same process, monarchical regimes associated themselves with the dominant forms of nationalist discourse, presenting kings and queens as symbols of the homeland, its long history and its inherent values, as defenders of its unity and greatness.[2]

The Spanish case presents certain peculiarities. The most striking is the return journey undertaken by the monarchy in the course of the century. It had fallen in 1931, but not because of a war, like a large proportion of those that disappeared in the rest of Europe, but rather following some local elections. It returned in 1975, with a king designated by a dictator who had held power for nearly four decades. In total, during the twentieth century, Spain lived under a monarchical regime for slightly more than five and a half decades. At the same time, in the field of identities, acute conflicts had developed between those who saw the state as coinciding exactly with the Spanish nation and those who, from within sub-state nationalist movements, rejected this equivalence. Accordingly, the various nationalist movements and policies mutated, clashed with each other – sometimes violently – and also reached agreements. The question arises, therefore, of what role was played by the monarchy in this context, whether it attempted to incorporate itself into the imaginary of Spanish nationalism and to what extent it succeeded, and what kind of relations it maintained with the other nationalisms – overall, whether the monarchy effectively became an ingredient in Spanish identity and an element that aided the integration of diverse nations, and whether these factors played an influence in its consolidation. In this chapter we will seek to respond to these questions by means of a comparison between the two reigns of the century: that of Alfonso XIII (1902–31) and Juan Carlos I (1975–2014).

At the start of their reigns, the original sources of legitimacy for each monarch were very different. Alfonso XIII, the posthumous son of Alfonso XII, had been king ever since his birth in 1886, and assumed his powers upon reaching his official majority at the age of sixteen in 1902. His position on the throne resided on the Constitution of 1876, which defined his prerogatives in accordance with the principle of shared sovereignty between the parliament or *Cortes* and the Crown, a habitual precept in liberal constitutions, and one that had been accepted by the principal political forces in Spain, despite the criticisms of extremist minorities. In contrast, Juan Carlos I – the grandson of Alfonso XIII and son of the latter's heir, Don Juan de Borbón, who in 1975 was still alive – was proclaimed king by virtue of laws enacted by the dictatorship of Francisco Franco, who had named him as his successor after supervising his education in accordance with the authoritarian ideology of the victors of the Civil War of 1936–39. A rarity, almost an anachronism, in the midst of a Western Europe governed by constitutional and democratic systems. Lacking the support of the greater part of the broad opposition movement against Francoism, Juan Carlos had to gain legitimacy by means of exercising the powers left to him by Franco in order to ultimately cast them off. The new king did not encounter a solid basis for his throne until he sanctioned the Constitution of 1978, after it had been approved by a parliament elected by universal suffrage and ratified by a referendum. In this constitution, national sovereignty was assigned to the Spanish people, the source of all powers, and a parliamentary monarchy was established as the political form of the state.

In the same way, the political atmospheres that were felt across Spain in 1902 and 1975 were not especially similar. Prospects at the turn of the century, in a country that was poor and had a regime that was questioned but stable, had little to do in common with those of the 1970s, when a developed society demanded the replacement of tyranny with democracy. Nor could the health of Spanish nationalism be considered the same in both contexts. In the early 1900s, Spanish citizens with an interest in public affairs were still feeling the consequences of the so-called Disaster of 1898 – the defeat in a colonial war with the United States – as a profound humiliation for national pride. In this climate, different forms of broadly 'regenerationist' ideas spread that, saturated with nationalism, sought to breathe new life into Spain, drag it out of backwardness and make it a part of the international scene. Seventy years later, the uses and abuses that the dictatorship had made of the nationalist imaginary got in the way of any employment of patriotic language by the Left, who associated the main national symbols with Francoism. The old Spanish nationalist language only found a refuge on the extreme right, which thereby imposed certain conditions on the responses that would be made to the rise of sub-state nationalisms. The initial appearance of these movements around 1900 in Catalonia and the Basque Country had prompted very energetic reactions at the time, which extended across the whole parliamentary spectrum, into the army's barracks and out into the streets. By 1975, the descendents of these early nationalists had broadened their activities and, given new legitimacy by their prestige as centres of anti-Francoist resistance, they met with more flexible responses. Reinforcing Spanish identity did not seem a priority in the political agenda, while bolstering other territorial identities did indeed appear to be so. In effect, the final quarter of the twentieth century witnessed a real new springtime for the peoples that occupied a good part of the map of Spain. The monarchy had to adapt to these changes.

Performing Monarchies

In contrast to some other monarchies such as that in Britain, the Spanish monarchy has lost much of the courtly ceremonial that had surrounded it at the turn of the century. In the time of Alfonso XIII, the principal protagonists of life in the palace were the aristocracy, and the king used the awarding of titles and palace appointments as tools for gaining loyalty. Major ceremonies, such as the periodic opening of parliament, were occasions for the carriages of the royal household to emerge out into the streets, accompanied during the most solemn events – such as the king's swearing of an oath on the constitution on attaining his majority in 1902, or his wedding in 1906 – by the Grandees of Spain, the highest rank of the nobility. The royal family conformed to a rigid calendar in which religious ceremonies occupied the place of honour, a routine that had virtually disappeared by the time of Juan Carlos I, whose decision not to re-create a full-scale court was seen by his supporters as a sign of dynastic modernization. Aristocratic titles had lost much of their attraction in the society of the last decades of the century. Some celebrations with a Catholic-nationalist flavour were retained, such as the annual ceremony in honour of Santiago, Saint James, the patron saint of Spain. However, many of the more ostentatious privileges were abandoned, such as the right to enter churches beneath a baldachin or ornamental canopy, a practice very closely associated with images of Franco. In general, the idea of a monarchy that was functional, professionalized and cheaper than many others in the world took precedence over the propaganda possibilities of traditional rituals.

During Alfonso's reign, particular dates such as the birthdays or the *onomástica* (saint's day) of the king were considered national holidays, and marked by public celebrations throughout the country. Those for

23 January, San Ildefonso and so the king's saint's day, were the most visible, in an attempt to connect the institution of monarchy with the country, as in Great Britain or the Netherlands. In 1976, this custom was revived and the king's saint's day began to be celebrated each 24 June, the Feast of Saint John the Baptist. During the time that the holiday calendar of the democratic regime remained to be clarified, this date served as an official celebration. Later it survived as a grand reception in the Royal Palace in Madrid, when the king and queen took the opportunity to greet thousands of invited guests. In 1987, the king declared that with this event he wished to 'bring the Crown closer to Spaniards'.[3] However, the event went into a decline in the 1990s, and was reduced to a much smaller reception in the Zarzuela, the monarch's modest residence in the capital. There were no jubilee celebrations of any kind to mark the king having completed twenty-five years of his reign in 2000, in the same way that there had been no major commemorations for Alfonso XIII in 1927. The most important new ceremony consisted of the swearing of an oath to the constitution by the heir to the throne, Prince Felipe, when he reached his majority in 1986.

Both kings made use of a fundamental instrument in creating national identification with the monarchy: royal visits. Immediately following their respective arrivals on the throne, each undertook a tour of the Spanish regions. This was especially intense in the case of Alfonso XIII, who by 1906 had already visited every province in the country. The object of these visits was to enable the citizens to come into contact with their monarchs, and so feel part of a political community headed by them. They were very repetitive rituals, which nearly always followed the same pattern. At the beginning of the century, religious and military elements predominated. They did not disappear under Juan Carlos, but the religious connotations were diluted. In all such tours, there was an abundance of speeches that appealed to the population of each locality with paeans of praise for their history and patriotism. The heads of state visited all sorts of institutions, inspected industries and public works and received a variety of acclamations, while the local authorities informed them of each area's aspirations. The messages that emerged most frequently from these occasions, first in the press and later on television, highlighted the ease of communication between the monarchs and their people; young, friendly and accessible, they were prepared to break with protocol to get closer to the crowds. In the process, they revived old connections between the Crown and particular regions, as when they visited the Sanctuary of Covadonga, in Asturias, to recall the near-legendary initiation there of the medieval Christian 'Reconquest' of Spain from Muslim rule. On his visit, Juan

Carlos spoke of a region where 'one day Spain raised its head, never to bow it down again'.[4] Overall, these initiatives obtained positive results, although it was difficult to distinguish between the curiosity provoked by the spectacle and genuine support for the regime.

Official visits by the monarchs acquired a crucial political dimension when they involved Catalonia or the Basque Country. In these regions, they confronted nationalist movements that had placed in doubt the identification between the state and the nation, and therefore also the conversion of the Crown into a national symbol. Different governments encouraged the presence of the Crown and royalty as a means of confirming the Spanish-ness of these areas. At the same time, however, the references that were made during each tour to the history of the Spanish monarchy, as the head of a composite monarchy in the modern era, permitted the introduction of ambiguities and an interplay of identities that could serve to reinforce the Crown itself as an institution and the unity of the state – in the same way as similar complexities had done in older empires, and still do today in the United Kingdom and Belgium. Basing themselves on such historical precedents, the conservative sectors of Catalan and Basque nationalism looked for ways to move closer to a confederal model, in which each region's relationship with the Crown would be more important than any other link with the state.

Alfonso XIII's visits to Catalonia in 1904 and 1908 coincided with the rise of the conservative brand of Catalan nationalism headed by the Lliga Regionalista (Regionalist League), which occupied a central position in the Spanish political scene. In his expeditions, the king connected with a monarchist, Catholic and bourgeois audience that trusted in the protection of the regime against revolution. Alfonso also made gestures of recognition towards Catalan culture; he listened happily to speeches in Catalan, although – a decisive factor for nationalists – he never went so far as to speak it. Catalanist circles dreamt of a monarchy in the style of Austria-Hungary, in which the sovereign would protect indigenous political structures. If the emperor of Austria could also rule as king of Hungary, the king of Castile could also act as count of Barcelona. These aspirations were not fulfilled. In 1914, the *Mancomunitat* was created, which brought together the four Catalan provinces for administrative purposes, but a Statute of Autonomy was never approved. During the pro-autonomy campaign of 1918–19, the king tried unsuccessfully to win over Francesc Cambó, the leader of moderate Catalanism. In the end, the dictatorship of Primo de Rivera, established in 1923, put a stop to any notions of decentralization.

The first official tour undertaken by Juan Carlos I, only two months after his coronation, was of Catalonia. He wished to gain the goodwill of Catalanism, by this time much more inclined to the left, and his gestures of recognition towards the cultural singularity of Catalonia were emphatic: from the beginning, his speeches included paragraphs in Catalan, a fact that was interpreted as support for the official use of the language. Shortly afterwards, and before discussions on the constitution had really begun, the king accepted the restoration of the *Generalitat* – the autonomous Catalan government established under the Second Republic – and the return from exile of its president, Josep Tarradellas. Juan Carlos thus became a kind of anti-Philip V, the Bourbon who had taken away Catalan liberties in 1714. Once the constitutional situation had been normalized, the main centre of initiative within Catalanism became the conservative movement led by Jordi Pujol, a liberal who sought to cultivate the trust of the Crown. Heir to the attitudes of Cambó, Pujol wished to see the monarch as a safeguard for Catalan interests in Madrid. In 1985, a fresh royal visit confirmed the Crown's explicit recognition of the personality of Catalonia, and three years later Pujol declared that Catalonia was a nation integrated within the framework of Spain, so that 'therefore, the King is our King'.[5] There were still some less harmonious moments, such as when nationalist youth booed the king in 1989, but concord was soon re-established. The following year Prince Felipe visited the various Catalan localities whose titles he held – prince of Girona, count of Cervera and lord of Balaguer – and his sister Princess Cristina moved to live in Barcelona.

Relations between the Crown and the Basque Country were quite different. The development of nationalism there proceeded more slowly than in Catalonia, and at the beginning of the twentieth century had less impact on the political life of the state. The royal family visited frequently, since they spent part of their summer holidays on the Cantabrian coast every year, and Alfonso XIII, who was also lord of the Basque province of Vizcaya, got on well with the moderate wing of the nationalists. In the 1970s, the situation was far more problematic. The terrorist violence of ETA (the separatist group called Euskadi ta Askatasuna, or 'Basque Homeland and Freedom") and its sympathizers in the *Abertzale* (nationalist) Left that had been radicalized under Francoism limited the scope of any approach between the Crown and Basque nationalism. The Basque Nationalist Party (PNV), the hegemonic political force in the region, called in the debates on the constitution for a renewal of the old pact with the monarchy based on its recognition of the *fueros* (historic laws) and rights of the Basque provinces, which had been broken at the end of the Carlist Wars in the nineteenth century. 'For us', explained the party's spokesman Xabier Arzalluz, 'the special and specific value of the Crown at this point is precisely that it constitutes the point of convergence and common bond between free peoples who have limited their sovereignty by their own decision.'[6] They were not successful, although the constitution did refer to the historic rights of the Basques, and the Basque Country, *Euskadi*, and Navarre did separately gain their autonomy. Particularly significant on a symbolic level was the visit made by King Juan Carlos at the beginning of February 1981, when he visited Gernika, site of the most famous of the historic Basque assemblies, and, standing next to the tree where Castilian kings had sworn to respect the *fueros* of Vizcaya, reiterated the monarchy's commitment to Basque freedoms. The members of the Basque parliament closest to ETA interrupted the king's speech and created an uproar, but the position of the king, who remained calm, emerged strengthened from the incident. Nevertheless, the threat of terrorism and the fluctuations in the understanding between the central government and the PNV postponed any further royal visits to the Basque provinces until 1991. Ultimately, too, the Crown's flexibility as a symbol came up against serious limits; within the constitutional framework, it was conceivable to associate it with a variety of cultural nationalities with their own institutions, but not with a series of sovereign nations.

In the process of identifying the monarchy with the Spanish nation, foreign affairs took on considerable importance. Both monarchs presented themselves as the personifications of a new Spain that was re-emerging after different periods of isolation and seeking a recognizable position in the international arena. Its national interests came into play above all in two, complementary, areas, Europe and Latin America. In the European context, the objective in both reigns consisted of integrating the Spanish state in Western alliances. Alfonso XIII, who was very active – like other sovereigns of his era – in diplomatic negotiations, placed himself at the head of government plans to situate Spain in the orbit of the Franco-British *entente*. His frequent visits to Paris and London between 1904 and 1913 reflected this intention, which in its fundamentals was achieved. However, the king's image suffered a fall as a consequence of the repressive measures taken following the anti-clerical riots of the 'Tragic Week' of 1909 in Barcelona, which set progressive Europe against him. During the Great War, the king moved from an initial pro-Allied stance to a position of strict neutrality, full of apprehension about the dangers of revolution. The role he chose to pursue consisted of promoting the dedication shown by Spanish diplomacy to humanitarian tasks associated with the conflict, with the object of then being able to act as an arbiter in a future negotiated peace. This never happened, but his efforts consolidated his

image as a charitable monarch. Juan Carlos, though with less influence in international affairs than his grandfather, travelled more, and
also contributed to the insertion of Spain into European structures.
Once doubts had been dispelled over his potential behaviour as the
heir of Franco, the regard in which he was held abroad increased. His
role in the transition to democracy buttressed his image as a modern
king, comfortably at home with the liberal values of NATO and the
European institutions.

An American dimension, a preoccupation of different kinds with
the countries of Hispanic America, was an integral part of Spanish
nationalism, in which a sense of history was intermixed with political projects and concerns over identity. The discovery and conquest
of a continent were seen by Spanish nationalists of a range of tendencies as the greatest thing that Spain had ever done, an inspiration for
the pursuit of ambitious goals in the present. It was imagined that by
establishing tighter links with the Spanish-speaking countries of the
Americas, a gigantic cultural community could be created, a kind of
transatlantic super-nation that would give its head – peninsular Spain,
the 'mother country' – a prominence in the world that it would be impossible to achieve by any other means. In this scheme of things, its
monarchs, patrons of that far-off overseas expansion, could be seen as
the patriarchs of the whole entity, whether it was called *la Raza* (the
race), *Hispanidad* or the Ibero-American Community of Nations.

The Hispano-Americanist movement was still in its infancy in 1902,
but it rapidly gained momentum. Commercial interests and cultural
associations from civil society played an influence in foreign policy
in this regard, and obtained the support of the Crown. The symbolic
capacity of the monarchy came to the fore in 1910, when a Spanish
delegation headed by Princess Isabel, the king's aunt, attended the celebrations for the centenary of Argentinian independence. The royal
emissary, loudly applauded in Buenos Aires by Spanish emigrants, initiated a series of similar gestures that would continue for several years,
with more rhetorical impact than economic or strategic results. Alfonso
XIII never fulfilled his promise to travel to the Americas, but he participated enthusiastically in outbursts of Hispano-Americanist verbosity,
which reached their zenith under the Primo dictatorship. In a speech
broadcast by radio, the king addressed the Spanish-American nations
as 'the most living testimony of the greatness of Spain ... appointed by
God as the agent to share his creation and as a missionary of the Christian faith'.[7] The Ibero-American Exhibition in Seville in 1929 served
as a showcase for a monarchist Spain that was acknowledged as the
progenitor of the countries with which it shared ties of blood.

Juan Carlos, unlike his predecessor, travelled ceaselessly around the American continent to speak of shared historical and cultural roots. The same messages that were put forward each 12 October, the Day of *Hispanidad* on the anniversary of Columbus's first landing in America, which in the 1980s was officially renamed the 'Spanish National Day'. It was no longer a matter of evoking memories of the *Conquistadores* or the Catholic faith. Traditional rhetoric, discredited by its associations with Francoism, was abandoned in favour of a language in which concepts such as justice and solidarity played the most conspicuous role. Even so, Hispano-Americanism – now rechristened Ibero-Americanism – continued to be at the heart of national identity. Official policy in this field was focussed on the preparations for the *Quinto Centenario*, the five-hundredth anniversary of the discovery of America, which King Juan Carlos called upon his audiences to celebrate without allowing national pride to be diminished by the denunciations of colonization made by indigenous peoples and their supporters. The Universal Exposition, or Expo '92, in Seville in 1992 renewed the commitment to Hispanic America seen in 1929, although it was now spoken of as an 'encounter of two worlds'. A year earlier, the first Ibero-American Summit of Heads of State and Governments had taken place, in which Juan Carlos acted as a *primus inter pares*. Through these subsequently annual gatherings, Spanish diplomacy hoped to forge a form of 'common-wealth' that – without a formal position such as that occupied by the queen of Great Britain, head of the organization and head of state of sixteen of its member nations – would at least make use of the charisma of the king of Spain. When it came to defining the nature of transoceanic bonds, under Juan Carlos the Spanish language recovered the pre-eminent position it had enjoyed among politicians and intellectuals at the turn of the century. Following Miguel de Unamuno, the king asserted that 'the language is our spiritual blood, and establishes the external frontier of our peoples in the world'.[8] From 1976, similarly, he presented the Miguel de Cervantes Prize for literature in the Spanish language, which was promoted as a kind of Hispanic Nobel, and the *Quinto Centenario* provided the occasion for the foundation of the Cervantes Institute, the official government organization for spreading knowledge of Spanish language and culture abroad.

The nationalization of the Spanish monarchy proceeded through many other channels as well. On postage stamps, coins and bank notes, images of the monarchs were associated with Spain. Their portraits were present in every government office. Public and private institutions – hospitals, universities, theatres, museums, hotels – were baptized with the names of the monarchs or members of their families. In the time of Alfonso XIII, this tendency was generally limited to institutions or places that had some direct relationship with the royal household. In the era of Juan Carlos I, the phenomenon became generalized, and dozens of towns and cities had a street, avenue or square dedicated to the king, sometimes in the local language. The links between monarchy and nation were similarly underlined in centres of education. Alfonso XIII appeared in school books as the key figure in the destiny of the nation, and as an authority to whom children, future soldiers, owed loyalty. The king himself cultivated patriotic feelings among the young, through pseudo-military organizations such as the Batallones Escolares (school battalions), groups of boys given physical and military training, or the Exploradores de España, the Spanish branch of the boy scouts. The image of Juan Carlos given in text books was initially closely linked to that of Franco, and children saw him as an all-powerful ruler whose task was to resolve all the problems of the country. When the journalist Ignacio Carrión suggested to several thousand children that they should write letters to the king, among the responses were, for example, 'I hope you do well with the job of Governing Spain, and that you Govern well' (José, aged nine), or, as something of a warning, 'If you do not govern with justice we Spaniards will take you off your throne and choose another king' (Rafa, also aged nine).[9] Within a short time, however, he would be associated with the performance of his official functions in the constitutional system.

The image of the monarchs was carefully cosseted by the media. Surprisingly, one cannot trace substantial differences in this regard between the two periods, aside from the obvious development of new communications channels like radio and television. Appearances by the monarchs occurred in two spheres: the official arena, and that of the family. Within the former, they appeared at formal events as representatives of the state, often in military uniform, and accounts were also given of their political activities. There was very little criticism or reports of any protests or demonstrations against them. In the era of Alfonso XIII, judgements about the king in the main media were predominantly positive and the information given about him was anodyne, although from time to time articles appeared in republican newspapers that led to their prosecution. Freedom of the press reigned until the Primo dictatorship imposed censorship prior to publication, which did not of course prevent the circulation of pamphlets attacking the monarch. The cinema made Alfonso's activities very widely known, since films of his wedding or various royal tours were shown on screens throughout the country.[10] In the case of Juan Carlos, it was widely claimed that there was a degree of complicity between the press and the royal household, above all during the years of the transition, and for almost thirty years, except at the two extremes of the political spectrum, there was a basic agreement not to harm the figure of the monarch.[11]

In the family sphere, the lives of the kings and queens were scrutinized by a growing public. As was already the case with other European monarchies, the Spanish royal family reflected the values of the middle classes, in magazines mostly directed at women. Thus, the family behaved in these magazine reports as people who were affectionate towards their children and grief-stricken at funerals. Family events became mass spectacles. A prime example was the wedding of King Alfonso to Victoria Eugenie of Battenberg, granddaughter of Queen Victoria, in 1906, which over and above the political considerations that made a greater closeness to Great Britain advisable was presented as a fairy tale between the bride and groom, given a tragic tone by the terrorist attack, a failed attempt to assassinate the king and new queen, that left fifteen bystanders dead. Similarly, there were the weddings of the daughters of Juan Carlos, Elena and Cristina, in 1995 and 1997 respectively, which gave a fresh shine to the banal side of a monarchy that had shed the obligation to marry only with other royal houses. As in other countries, the respective queens adopted roles in the social field, giving their support to charitable works and cultural activities. If Victoria Eugenia distinguished herself by her dedication to the Spanish Red Cross, Queen Sofía preferred artistic or scientific patronage.

Lastly, both Alfonso and Juan Carlos and their children took an interest in sport. Both kings presented themselves as sportsmen, in a manner that had rather ambivalent effects. On the one hand, it associated them with modernity and healthy living. On the other, the elitist nature of their preferred activities – polo, sailing – situated them in a frivolous aristocratic world, permanently on holiday. In terms of the national identity, sport acquired a crucial importance as the century went on, so that consequently the royal cultivation of sporting connections favoured the fusion between the monarchy and patriotic feelings. In this regard, the constant presence of the king, queen and their children in the Barcelona Olympic Games in 1992 summed up, better than any other image, the successes obtained by this association. A modern royal family for a modern country.

The Exercise of Power and Royal Myths

The effective conversion of a contemporary monarchy into a national symbol depends not only on images such as these, but also on the man-

ner in which each monarch exercises his powers. The British writer
Walter Bagehot laid down in his *The English Constitution* of 1867 that
the monarchy 'seems to order, but it never seems to struggle.... Its
apparent separation from business is that which removes it both from
enmities and from desecration, which preserves its mystery, which en-
ables it to combine the affection of conflicting parties – to be a visible
symbol of unity to those still so imperfectly educated as to need a symbol.'[12] That is, it was easier to attribute national status to the monarchy
when a king remained above partisan struggles, as an independent arbiter, and more difficult when he took part in public affairs as a leading
actor who took sides to benefit one sector and prejudice others. In this
regard, the differences between Alfonso XIII and Juan Carlos I could
not be greater.

In the first place, the powers that were accorded them in the Constitutions of 1876 and 1978 were very different, since they corresponded
to those of a constitutional monarchy and a parliamentary monarchy
respectively. According to the 1876 constitution, the king held executive power and shared legislative powers with the *Cortes*. He could ap-
point and dismiss his ministers freely, even if none of his actions could
enter law without the ratification of at least one member of the government, and could dissolve the parliament, although he was then obliged
to convoke a new one within a space of three months. He similarly
had the power to direct diplomatic relations, declare war and make
peace. According to that of 1978, the European constitution that most
reduced the functions of the Crown after the Swedish example of 1975,
the monarch lacked all legislative powers or any substantial executive ones, which were exercised by the *Cortes* and the government that
could command a majority within them, headed by the prime minister.
Neither head of state, under the 1876 or the 1978 constitutions, could
be held responsible before the law – only ministers could be called to
answer for the actions of a government – and both held the status of
supreme commander of the armed forces. The 1978 constitution also
accorded the monarch the capacity to act as a moderator in certain
circumstances, and the status of being a symbol of the unity and permanence of the state. This latter point prompted arguments, because
the Right insisted that the king be declared representative of the Spanish nation, 'as the living and existentially active body of the community
of persons and peoples that constitute Spain', as Carlos Ollero put it.[13]
No such statement was accepted, but the question remained in the air.

As a result, from this point on there was much discussion of the
constitutional implications of considering the monarch an emblem of
the homeland. In the view of intellectuals such as the influential phi-

losopher Julián Marías, the king was its head, and his constitutional role consisted of 'the representation of the nation, in being a symbol of it, in regulating and moderating the course of its historic progress'.[14] It was also possible to link the throne with the controversial second article of the 1978 Constitution, which affirmed the indissoluble unity of the indivisible Spanish nation. If the king symbolized the unity of the state, and the state was a nation-state, then it could be deduced that some responsibilities fell to him in the defence of a single united *patria*. Some jurists alluded to the integrative function of the Crown in bringing together all the elements of the nation. The moderate conservative Miguel Herrero-Rodríguez de Miñón went so far as to defend the special suitability of the monarchy for accommodating complex, asymmetrical political arrangements, in accordance with the 'historical poly-territoriality' of Spain, ideas close to those of sub-state nationalists.[15] However, it was always difficult to ignore the fact that the constitution spoke only of one sovereign nation, the Spanish one. The king himself, in his crucial address to the nation in the early morning of 24 February 1981, after the failed attempt to derail the constitutional process through a military coup, spoke of the Crown as the 'symbol of the permanence and unity of the homeland'.[16]

Nevertheless, the constitution was one thing, and political practice another. In reality, many of Europe's parliamentary monarchies can be defined as such because they function accordingly, not because this is set down in constitutional precepts, which continue to accord powers to the Crown that it can no longer exercise. Alfonso XIII intervened intensely in the political affairs of his time. His prerogatives made him the arbiter of parliamentary disputes and, amid a climate that called for national 'regeneration', he embraced his role as the saviour of Spain. Nevertheless, certain unwritten rules imposed limits on his freedom of action. The system set up following the restoration of his father in the 1870s established that two large political groupings, the Conservative and Liberal parties, would alternate in power, and, since the sitting government always won elections – thanks to the enormous level of electoral fraud – it fell to the king to decide which of the two should govern, according to the cohesion and leadership qualities of each party. During his effective reign from 1902, the two major parties engaged in near-constant splits and internal divisions, leaving ample space for interference by the king, who in each situation was able to choose between various options. By the time of the last years of the First World War, these divisions had become irretrievable and attempts were made to create a range of coalitions, in which Alfonso was also fully involved. His decisions were challenged in public, and even in parliamentary debates, so that he could not be considered a consensual symbol.[17] He would not have accepted such a position, in any case. 'We modern kings are not like those of old', he said in 1921, 'we are the first citizens of the fatherland, and instead of remaining immobile upon the throne, we guide our nations on the path of progress.'[18] This monarchy, far from approaching the ideal outlined by Bagehot, became mired in all the dangers that the eminent essayist had feared.

The case of Juan Carlos was very different. When he enjoyed wide powers, those left to him by Franco, he agreed, with the aid of reformists from within the authoritarian regime and some members of the opposition, to articulate a constituent process that led to democracy and, therefore, the loss of nearly all his prerogatives. He had come to the conclusion that the only way to establish the monarchy on a secure footing in Spain was to bring it in line with other parliamentary monarchies. Not all his decisions were greeted with applause by the majority of political tendencies. However, from 1978, and with greater foundation after the failed coup of 1981, he began to be seen as someone endowed with the prestige of his success in democratization and as a symbolic figure safe from partisan squabbles. He respected the results of free elections and, even though he might not have been equally in harmony with all his prime ministers, he coexisted with governments of different colours, and his political actions were not disputed in the press or in parliament.

Nevertheless, the decisive difference between these two individuals was in their behaviour in the face of specific coups d'état, those of 1923 and 1981. Both monarchs had had a military education and conceived their duties as a patriotic mission in military terms. Alfonso shared in the version of Spanish nationalism cultivated by the officer class, who, following the 1898 'Disaster', distrusted politicians and claimed the role of champions of the fatherland against its external and internal enemies – sub-state nationalists and the workers' movement. The king, who was nearly always seen in uniform, shared the officers' providentialist rhetoric on the sacred role of the army in saving the nation, and made the overseeing of appointments in the army and most especially in the Moroccan campaign his personal preserve. Each time a conflict arose between the military authorities and the civil powers, he did not act as a mediator between the two, but took the side of the former. In 1921, these inclinations led him to be suspected of culpability in a new military 'disaster' that left over ten thousand Spanish soldiers dead at Annual, in Morocco. The shadow of the 'responsibilities' for Annual pursued the king until Primo de Rivera's military intervention brought an abrupt end to parliamentary inquiries into the matter. Juan

Carlos was also surrounded by military officers, whose mentality had been formed by that of the victorious side in the Civil War of 1936–39. Educated in the same military academies, the king also shared with them the same language, which glorified the heroic acts of the past and made the intangible unity of the homeland a supreme value. The majority of them were loyal to him after the death of Franco, and this loyalty facilitated the democratic transition.

However, the close bonds between each king and their armies did not lead to similar responses when each of them had to confront military challenges to the constitutional order. It was not that the respective monarchs were indifferent to the critical opinions of their companions-in-arms regarding the political situation. Alfonso XIII was in favour of armed intervention and the use of force to finish with governments that seemed to him to be weak and ineffective, and even threatened to lead a coup himself. The same cannot be said of Juan Carlos, even though in 1980 he disapproved of the attitude of his government towards terrorist attacks and the demands of regional nationalists, and toyed with the idea of endorsing a government of national unity headed by a military officer. Both were aware of the preparations for military intervention, which involved senior officers in which they had had complete confidence. The dynamics of the two coup attempts presented other common features as well, since in each case they initially involved only a minority in the army, while the majority of the forces awaited orders from their supreme commander, the king. However, the attitudes of the two monarchs could not have been more different. Alfonso XIII allowed the situation to deteriorate and then, after a tense waiting period, called upon the leader of the coup, General Miguel Primo de Rivera, to form a government. As in the case of other monarchs who consented to the establishment of dictatorial regimes in interwar Europe, from Italy to Yugoslavia, for Alfonso this was a fatal embrace that would cost him the throne. In contrast, Juan Carlos, a few hours after the violent attack upon democratic institutions, rendered an authoritarian solution non-viable by defending the constitutional order. He may perhaps have been thinking of the destiny of his grandfather, or of his in-laws in the Greek royal family, who had been through a similar situation nearly twenty years earlier; he may also have been influenced by an unfavourable international context. Whichever it was, the fact is that he decided the issue against the coup, and Spanish democracy remained intact.

In both official statements and the messages disseminated by the mass media, the political careers of both kings were accompanied by certain narratives that gave meaning to their actions and created myths that moulded the relationship between the monarchy and national identity. Alfonso XIII was presented, from the moment of his oath on the constitution in 1902, as the standard-bearer of national regeneration. Monarchists assigned him a primordial role in this task, which involved the moral and material reconstruction of Spain. That is, the effective 'nationalization' of the people, and economic progress. In public and in private, the king nearly always spoke the language of the nation, ahead of other factors such as the dynasty or the constitutional system. He also justified all his actions, even those that were most controversial, such as his support for the coup in 1923 or his departure into exile in 1931, with patriotic pretexts. He was an active and committed monarch: the first student, the first soldier, the first agriculturalist in the country – in short, the first Spaniard. If at the beginning of his reign this activism appeared compatible with the liberal foundations of the constitution, from the years of the Great War onwards it took on a clearly reactionary tone, which identified Spain with its Catholic essence and committed the Crown to the maintenance of order in the face of threats of revolution. With the result that the monarchy as an institution became integrated into the Spanish-nationalist rhetoric of the Primo de Rivera dictatorship, which took as its motto 'fatherland, religion and monarchy' (*patria, religión y monarquía*). The curious point was that, under the new authoritarian system, Alfonso found himself confined to the representative and ceremonial role that he had previously rejected.

Juan Carlos had behind him the long domination of Francoist national-Catholicism, which identified Spain with the faith of the Church, evoked the imperial monarchy of the sixteenth-century Habsburgs and regarded the military uprising of 1936 as the initiation of a crusade. It was no accident that the first place he visited when he arrived in the country as a ten-year-old boy in 1948 was the Cerro de los Ángeles outside Madrid, where he had to repeat the same words with which Alfonso XIII had dedicated Spain to the Sacred Heart of Jesus on the same site in 1919. Against this background, however, an image of the monarchy would later be created that presented it as an aid to the integration of all Spaniards, not just the victors in the war. In addition, during his proclamation as king before the *Cortes*, in November 1975, the new monarch referred to the desires that had been repeatedly expressed by his father, Don Juan, from exile, which clearly implied an effort for national reconciliation, an effort that was given concrete form during the process of democratization, and which led to such significant gestures as the meeting between the king and queen and the widow of Manuel Azaña, the president of the Second Republic during the Civil War, during the royal visit to Mexico in 1978.

In the official messages presented since that time, Juan Carlos distilled a concept of the nation quite different from that of Francoism. In
the broadcasts he made each Christmas Eve on television, for example,
the royal broadcasts with the greatest audience, Spain was understood
as a collective enterprise forged by history and focussed on the future.
Elements that could suggest any kind of exclusion were blurred in favour of an insistence on the unity of all Spaniards, compatible with
their diversity. The homeland was equated with a family, indissoluble
and all the stronger the more united it became. The Crown was at
the head of and aided the coalescence of this coexistence, this shared
destiny of a people who felt proud of what they were achieving under democracy. In other words, the hegemony of a nationalism based
on religion and ideas of a national essence, inspired by the works of
Marcelino Menéndez Pelayo or Ramiro de Maeztu, was replaced by a
Spanish nationalism that looked to the writings of José Ortega y Gasset. 'We have', the king said in 1979, 'a common project for life together, which is called Spain.'[19]

Together with the image of Juan Carlos as the king of all Spaniards,
the other grand narrative that ran through his reign was the one that
pointed to him as the engine of the transition to democracy and, subsequently, a guarantee of its continuation. Politicians, journalists and
historians have stressed the point that not only would the transition
from Francoism to a constitutional regime have been much more complicated without the monarch, but he himself also became the leading actor in the process, the 'pilot of change'. In the words of Charles
Powell, this was because he 'evaded the icebergs represented as much
by the immobilism of the "continuists" as by the impatience of those
who sought a clear break with the past'.[20] Some hagiographic accounts
go further and recount his life in teleological form, as if from the very
beginning it had been directed towards a single end, the installation
of democracy in Spain. In any case, the pre-eminent role given to the
king has left other significant figures and events consigned to the background, which has prompted criticism of the manufacture of Juan
Carlos as the *rey taumaturgo* (king-miracle worker).[21] His image as a
bulwark of democracy was definitively sealed after 23 February 1981,
when the entire political spectrum recognized the service he had made
to constitutional freedoms.

One last point is that some monarchist circles have promoted the
idea that the monarchy should be considered an essential element in
Spanish identity. Hagiographers of Alfonso XIII customarily emphasized the 'Spanishness' of his personality, whose virtues corresponded
to those of the stereotypes then current regarding the national char-

acter – warm, passionate, courageous – and whose errors could be forgiven as an excess of patriotism. With Juan Carlos, this sort of argument was more scarce, although the writer Camilo José Cela did not refrain from describing him as 'the archetype of Spanishness', in the line of Miguel de Cervantes or Francisco de Goya.[22] More frequent were the assertions of the essentially monarchist nature of Spain made on the basis of historical reasoning. The monarchy had made Spain, it was said, and the history of Spain was equivalent in its main outlines to the history of the Spanish monarchy. This was the conviction of conservative politicians and intellectuals, who saw Spain as the oldest nation in Europe, and the monarchy the key element in its integration – 'the conscience and the voice of the centuries, which has always brought integration in the face of dispersion', according to the historian Carlos Seco Serrano.[23]

Conclusion

Overall, then, did the kings of Spain manage, like other European monarchs, to turn themselves into national symbols and consolidate the monarchy as an integral element in Spanish identity in the course of the twentieth century? Alfonso XIII had substantial success in the first part of his reign, when broad sectors of political opinion accepted his role as the promoter of national regeneration. This was a time when nearly all the European monarchies still enjoyed considerable powers, and he could be seen as a young *Kaiser* at the service of the fatherland. After 1913, and above all from 1917, royal interventionism unleashed interminable polemics which involved sectors of the pro-dynastic parties themselves. The king was perceived as a participant who was heavily implicated in partisan politics, not as an arbiter standing above them, an active participant who moreover was inclined towards conservative and militarist factions. Added to this was a certain image of frivolity, of being over-fond of the luxuries of international high society, which combined with the parliamentary criticisms he received after the new colonial disaster at Annual. From 1923, the Crown bound its fate to that of the Primo dictatorship, and after the fall of the latter suffered the reaction of a rapidly mobilized public opinion for whom democracy was equivalent to a republic. Hence it cannot of course be said that Alfonso XIII had made himself a national emblem accepted by the majority of the country's citizens.

Unlike his grandfather, Juan Carlos I consolidated his position during the final quarter of the century as quite a solid national symbol, albeit with some ups and downs. He experienced his best moments between 1981 and 1993, reaching a peak in 1992. In that *annus horribilis* for the queen of Great Britain, her Spanish colleague emerged as the embodiment of a modern country, as European as it was Ibero-American, which was making a collection of political and sporting triumphs. In accordance with this positive image, republicanism was virtually insignificant as a political force, except in a few groups of the extreme Left. The available surveys and polls traced this evolution, which placed the monarchy among the most highly valued institutions in the country up until the first years of the twenty-first century. In reality, its high reputation was very closely linked to the figure of King Juan Carlos, more than to the monarchy in general, since a majority were of the opinion that 'everything depends on what the king is like'.[24] It became commonplace to say that in Spain there were more 'Juancarlists' than monarchists, so that it seemed improbable that a situation could be reached in which the bulk of citizens would refuse to consider their country without a king or queen, as has happened in the United Kingdom. Although the conversion of the Crown into a national emblem had progressed much further during the reign of Juan Carlos than in that of Alfonso, at the end of the century this fusion was still not complete. Even so, one can still say that for some decades the monarchy operated as the symbol of the Spanish nation that was least frequently challenged.

Beyond the period examined here, however, in the first fifteen years of this century such challenges to the monarchy have grown very visibly. In part this has been due to the strengthening of nationalist sectors who combat the monarch simply as a symbol of the Spanish state. However, other factors have also played an influence, such as the deterioration of the benevolent attitude previously conceded to the royal family by the media, and the many errors in terms of their image and their own behaviour made by the family themselves since 2006. The Spanish monarchy has at last received the same treatment as its European fellows, always under the spotlight. Some newspapers and radio stations of the Right have even complained of a supposed royal preference for left-wing governments. In the most recent times, the Crown has been bespattered by matrimonial crises and major corruption scandals, and the degree of public confidence in the institution as detected in surveys has plummeted. The deterioration in Juan Carlos's public image was accompanied by his physical decline and led, in June 2014, to his abdication in favour of his son and heir, who since then has reigned as Felipe VI. The future of the monarchy will depend upon whether it can manage to remain outside party conflicts and – much more difficult in present conditions – to reinvent itself as a national symbol.

Notes

1. See Billig (1992).
2. Cannadine (1983); Deploige and Deneckere (2006).
3. *ABC,* 25 June 1987.
4. 'Palabras de Su Majestad el rey con motivo del homenaje al Príncipe Felipe como Príncipe de Asturias en agradecimiento al pueblo asturiano', Covadonga, 1 November 1977. http://www.casareal.es/ES/actividades/Paginas/actividades_discursos_detalle.aspx?data=3613
5. Antich (1994: 174).
6. Quote from *Cortes Generales de España,* 1980, I: 679.
7. *Saludo a las Repúblicas Americanas; Alocución al pueblo español por S.M. El Rey Don Alfonso XIII,* Camden, N.J.: Victor Talking Machine Co., 1924.
8. Galvani (1982: 32).
9. Carrión (1976: 73, 114, 45 and 69).
10. Montero Díaz, Paz and Sánchez Aranda (2001).
11. Zugasti (2007).
12. Bagehot (2010: 56).
13. *Constitución Española,* 1980, III: 3547.
14. J. Marías, 'La identificación con España', in Marías (2000: 198).
15. Herrero Rodríguez de Miñón (2004: 153).
16. See 'Palabras de Su Majestad el Rey al pueblo español en la noche del 23 al 24 de febrero de 1981' http://www.casareal.es/ES/ArchivoMultimedia/Paginas/archivo-multimedia_archivos-audios.aspx
17. Moreno-Luzón (2012).
18. 'Discurso pronunciado con motivo de la apertura del curso académico de 1921 a 1922 en la Universidad Central de Madrid', quoted in Gutérrez-Ravé (1955: 215).
19. *Con España,* 2001. The quotation from "Mensaje de Navidad de Su Majestad el Rey, 24 de diciembre de 1979", http://www.casareal.es/ES/Actividades/Paginas/actividades_discursos_detalle.aspx?data=2823. See also Maddens and Vanden Berghe (2003).
20. Powell (1991: 20).
21. González Cuevas (1997).
22. C. J. Cela Trulock, 'La persona del Rey', in Real Academia de la Historia (2003: 66).
23. Seco Serrano (1988: 10).
24. Centro de Investigaciones Sociológicas (CIS), '25 años después. Estudio n° 2401. Diciembre de 2000'. http://www.cis.es/cis/export/sites/default/-Archivos/Marginales/2400_2419/2401/Es2401mar.pdf.

Chapter 5

Gender and the Spanish Nation

Inmaculada Blasco Herranz

A few decades ago, female scholars of French, German and Italian modern history insisted on the need to link two key processes in the configuration of the contemporary world: nationalization and the consolidation of the modern sexual difference.[1] In other words, the construction of modern nations (and their myths) in Europe since the late eighteenth and early nineteenth centuries and the configuration of a model of relations between the sexes based on sexual difference have been shown to be mutually influencing phenomena. As a result, men and women were integrated into the nation in different ways. While men acquired national identity through their commitment as citizens of the state or as defenders of the homeland by carrying weapons into war, women did so in the capacity of wives and mothers, making use of virtues considered inherent to their sex, such as charity and piety. In Spain, though historical research in this area is still in its infancy, the scant work available indicates that something similar occurred in the construction of the Spanish national identity, and consequently in the process of nationalization.[2] Thus, it could be said that the definition of national identity in the nineteenth century was articulated around the operative gender attributions, which assumed that men and women were different by nature. Their assigned and complementary social roles derived from differentiated physical and psychological attributes that were considered inherent to their sexual condition.

The entrenchment of sexual difference during the nineteenth century (and the discourse of domesticity that it generated) led to the initial and theoretical exclusion of women from mechanisms – such as schooling and military service – that the liberal state under construction provided to socialize in a specific national culture even those men who were formally marginalized from political decision-making processes. However, this did not mean that liberalism disregarded the integration of women into the national community. Xavier Andreu has demonstrated how several mechanisms in nineteenth-century Spanish liberal discourse already linked national and gender identities. Alongside their symbolic function (gender metaphors served to make novel or abstract concepts comprehensible to a sizeable portion of the population), liberal discourse attributed to women other roles as participants in liberal movements, guardians of the national honour, signs of modernity, benefactresses, civilizers of manners, reproducers of culture and educators of patriots. Certainly, though, Spanish women configured their national identity outside direct state channels and spaces throughout the nineteenth century.[3]

With the exception of state-sponsored education, the early decades of the twentieth century inherited this predominance of informal channels for female acquisition of Spanish national identity. The strong discursive imprint of the sexual difference also carried over, deeply affecting what it meant to be a Spanish woman. The purpose of this contribution to collective and general reflection on issues surrounding Spanish national identity in the twentieth century is two-fold. First, it seeks to identify the characteristic features of Spanish nationalization of women during the twentieth century. Second, it analyses how definitions of gender (mainly, though not exclusively, femininity) were articulated within the different ideas of Spain that inhabited that century.

Gender and National Regeneration: From Fin-De-Siècle to the Restoration Crisis

Gender images constituted a suggestive channel for reflecting the national identity crisis that Spain and other European countries experienced at the end of the nineteenth century. Defeat in the Spanish-American War (1898) translated into concern for a 'weak' and 'effeminate' nation, which in the political language of the time indicated physical and moral debilitation. An image emerged of a Spain that had lost the virility associated with its former experience as an empire. Similarly, frustration regarding national weakness was explained as a deterioration of masculinity. The discourse of many regenerationists attributed national weakness to the loss of the attributes that defined the authentic Spanish man: valour, manliness, virility and strength.[4]

This crisis led to harsh criticism of the fin-de-siècle masculine ideal, reflected in the Don Juan stereotype of promiscuity, paternal irresponsibility, lack of self-control and disdain for work. When Miguel de Unamuno stated that the 'cause of liberty would not prosper in Spain until its rulers went to bed at ten o'clock, drank only water, stopped gambling and kept no mistresses', he was unseating the Don Juan stereotype as pernicious to the progress of the nation and replacing it with a model of masculine respectability linked to Protestantism. For regenerationism in general, the Don Juan stereotype had to be eliminated; such a lifestyle was unproductive, as its activity revolved entirely around sexual conquest.[5]

Militant-confessional Catholicism also articulated a critique of the prevailing masculinity, though in different terms than those of the regenerationists. Among clerics and the laity, the decline of the prototypical Spanish man, the 'favourite son of misnamed modern civilization', was linked to the effects of modernity, such as materialism and sensuality, which had distanced him from deep faith and left him vulnerable to his basest passions. In practice, the moral weakness of the modern man eroded the family as the enemies of the correct masculine ideal – the tavern and the casino, among others – facilitated his abandonment of the home. The Catholic proposal defined its version of national masculinity as that of 'an irreproachable, hard-working and diligent father, steadfastly faithful to his wife, who helps educate his children with rectitude tempered by prudence and love, who carefully tends to the family economy'. As such, it did not stand too far off from the regenerationist proposal.[6] During the first third of the twentieth century, a national ideal of masculinity took shape in reaction to the Don Juan model and gradually attained social consensus in the 1930s, thanks to a receptive political atmosphere. Some considered this model of the faithful husband – austere, industrious, self-controlled and devoted to the home – very necessary for transforming Spain into a dignified and respectable country.

The prevailing feminine ideal also played a core symbolic role in the turn-of-the-century debate over what it meant to be Spanish, which revolved around the definition and expression of the authentic essence(s) of the nation. Without going further afield, the narratives of modernist writers such as Unamuno, Azorín and Pío Baroja – who contributed enormously to that debate – identified women, the family and marriage as representative microcosms of the nation and the measure of its health. In other words, the role of women and the discourse of domesticity prevailed as a metaphor of the authentic Spanish essence. However, the gender discourse was most actively involved in the national regeneration projects that flourished in all Spanish political cultures at the turn of the century. If the men were passive and spineless, then hope of regeneration was placed in the 'other half of humanity'. As Joaquin Costa affirmed, 'the only men left in Spain are the women'.[7]

Concepción Gimeno, a writer, journalist and defender of a 'sensible feminism', complained that 'in the conflicts of Spain ... when the atmosphere seems charged with regenerationist content and words like *redemption, regeneration* escape from our lips ... Spaniards have completely overlooked the influence of women'. For her, the contribution of women to national redemption was undeniable for two reasons. First, because they were mothers and, therefore, 'how can you not count on the collaboration of women for the regeneration of the homeland, if they carry out the most transcendental, sacrosanct ministry in this life, that of motherhood?' Spanish women also safeguarded an entire rosary of virtues ('vigour, heroism, feminine enthusiasm') that 'are not yet spent, it is the only healthy thing about Spain'. Accordingly, she advised that feminine action be put to good use, since its influence could constitute 'in the national life an antiseptic against corruption, a beneficent north wind that blows away the deleterious vapours that envelop us'.[8] Underlying this assignation of different tasks in the national recovery was a vision of the human being that consisted of two irreducible and complementary essences: men and women, whose attributes and virtues derived from nature and were equally necessary for social life.

All political cultures on the ideological spectrum shared a similar discourse of regeneration of the nation by women. Krausists, with their liberal-Christian discourse that considered women as rational beings who should be educated to advance Spanish society, Republicans and Catholics alike emphasized the central role of women (in fact, women attributed it to themselves) in their respective projects for national rehabilitation, whether imagined as Republican-secular or monarchic-confessional. Within the broader objectives of contributing to the liberation of the people and counteracting what they understood as conservative and traditionalist manipulation of patriotism, the Republicans demanded improvements in the education of women. For social and national regeneration, the highly relevant role assigned to women as mothers, educators of their sons and wives devoted to their husbands required training: they would transmit secular, Republican values to the future citizens of Spain.[9]

Confronted with the dominant belief, some Republican women sought to prove that Spanish females were moving away from obscurantism and clerical domination, which was understood as a symbol of national backwardness. This pursuit gradually shaped a Spanish identity for women that was detached from religious influence. A good example is seen in the feminist anti-clerical street and press campaign in favour of the 1906 Law of Associations, in response to the protest of

Catholic women over the law. However, defence of the law was eclipsed by the resolve to construct and disseminate a Spanish national identity for women that repudiated the prevailing image of their devotion to the confessional booth. This identity was articulated around notions of progress, secularism, anti-clericalism and the emancipation of female workers.[10]

For Catholics, the salvation of Spain depended on the recovery of what they felt was a threatened Catholic tradition in the homeland. As with Republicanism, women were central to this project. Based on their natural condition as mothers, they were attributed with the incarnation and perpetuation of the values and moral principles of tradition and Catholicism. The Catholic press routinely published articles that elevated Spanish women as the natural guardians of the similarly natural religiosity of the country in the face of secularizing threats. According to the Catholic weekly *El Pilar* in Zaragoza, the 'Spanish homeland' had 'without equal, great women who honoured and elevated it, whose example is always a powerful incentive for every great and noble undertaking. The woman, with her mother instinct, sees clearly the danger of the project that threatens us and thinks of her young son, her older son, her husband and her father. To see them brought up without God terrifies her.'[11]

Clearly, the various political cultures produced their own versions of a discourse of the regeneration of the nation through women, based on the conceptualization of women as mother-educators who possessed a strength not yet corrupted. This strength would counteract the deterioration and degeneration of men, who were responsible for the colonial disaster and for the eventual failure of the rotating parliamentary system. The intense associative and educational activity of Krausists, Catholics, Republicans, Socialists and anarchists during the first two decades of the twentieth century involved the development of more or less systematic projects for Spanish national regeneration. Their activities created an informal channel for diverse formulations of Spanish national identity, which spread among sectors of the population – such as women – that until that point had been excluded from top-down nationalization mechanisms.

The interest exhibited by early twentieth-century political cultures in the education of women as socializers of future citizens in the values associated with the Spanish national essence also seems to have guided similar initiatives by the Restoration governments. In the end, the liberal-positivist *institucionistas* were behind the most relevant governmental reforms in educational content, while the Catholic imprint, with its solid nationalist repertoire, could be felt in the conservative governments.

The significant increase of females in primary and secondary schools between 1900 and 1930, and the subsequent decrease in female illiteracy (from 71.4 per cent in 1900 to 50.1 per cent in 1930) should be attributed to both feminist and nationalist regenerationist drives. Thus, state schools could become channels for the nationalization of an increasing number of Spanish women, in spite of deficient actual attendance, especially in rural hubs. There, women left school early, attended more intermittently or faced the resistance of their parents. Nonetheless, by 1910 girls accounted for 47.1 per cent (and boys the remaining 52.9 per cent) of school populations and the total number of girls in national schools had increased by 57 per cent as of 1930. Female students in high school increased significantly from 14.7 per cent in 1910 to 26.7 per cent in 1930. The obstacles to women accessing higher education were also eliminated in 1910.[12] The action of church-run schools was especially significant in women's education. They captured a considerable female public and, as Maitane Ostolaza demonstrated for the Basque Country, they had a nationalizing function modelled around a national-Catholic vision of the history of Spain.[13]

Feminism, Nation and Top-Down Nationalization: From the Great War to the Primo de Rivera Dictatorship

In the 1920s, feminine ideals underwent a series of significant transformations that had been forged earlier and were consolidated by the First World War. The Great War and the intensification of the feminist debate facilitated modifications in the social roles carried out by women (work, politics, etc.) and in the conventional images of femininity, represented by the 'new woman'. This also had its impact in the Spanish nationalist imaginary. Along with a blurring of the lines that separated sexual attributes and spaces by gender, some perceived an erosion of the foundations of Spanish society in the new feminine roles and definitions of a woman (incarnated in the minds of many by the members of the Lyceum Club, an international network that defended the interests and educational, cultural and professional development of women). Such forces would undermine the family, and national integrity by extension. Others, however, saw it as a sign of modernity and of Spain's ascent to the level of European countries.

The maturing of the feminist debate and the proliferation of self-proclaimed feminist associations in defence of 'women's rights' from 1913 on helped to reshape the early twentieth-century regenerationist discourse that assigned to women a role in national regeneration based on their role as mothers. This was accomplished as two lesser lines of argument, developed in the first two decades of the twentieth century, became generalized. The first asserted that the demand for female education was aimed at both the well being of the nation and improvement of the situation of women, individually and collectively. The second argument affirmed that women could contribute to national regeneration (and improve the female condition) not only from the home or through beneficence, but politically, through exercising the right to representation and the right to vote. Public intervention would contribute to the progress of Spain and also serve to improve the social condition of women.

The global context after the Great War was marked by intense feminist debate. In Spain, feminist associations pushed to establish their feminism as the best and most appropriate for Spanish women. Other European historiographies have looked at feminists before and after the Great War in different nation-states, and how 'adherence to liberal-feminist objectives in Europe included a meaningful enthusiasm for patriotism'.[14] Though Spanish historiography has not addressed the intensification of the relationship between feminism and Spanish nationalism in the 1920s, it is abundantly clear that a certain nationalist Spanish identity guided the actions of feminists (though not all understood Spain in the same way) and converted these associations into channels for spreading the Spanish national identity.

A vivid, though not singular, example of this was the Asociación Nacional de Mujeres Españolas (National Association of Spanish Women, ANME), which began in 1919 and was presided by María Espinosa de los Monteros. Considered above all a feminist association, the first two articles of their programme in defence of women's rights surprisingly sought 'to oppose, by any means available to the Association, any purpose, act or manifestation that threatens the national territory' and 'procure that every Spanish mother, in perfect parallel with the teacher, instils in the child, from earliest infancy, love for the single and indivisible motherland'.[15] This pre-eminence of the defence of the nation in the objectives of what was – and still is – considered the foremost feminist association in Spain can be explained as part of an immediate response to a specific situation: the Catalanist push that took place from late 1918 to early 1919. Javier Moreno-Luzón has interpreted it in this light, very correctly including the position of the ANME among the numerous responses to the Catalan nationalist demand for the approval of a statute of autonomy. The ANME encouraged rejection of separatism by recurring to the deeply rooted attribution of the maternal role to women as educators of future Spanish and *pro-Spain* citizens.[16]

The crisis that ended the Restoration system brought the critique of *caciquismo* to the forefront as a national evil. With it, the feminine discourse regarding the regeneration of the nation was re-edited in light of the failure of men in their political tasks. Unlike what had been argued earlier in the century, it was accepted (and considered necessary) that women participate in national regeneration through the exercise of public office, 'that was not incompatible with the well-being of the family and their exalted condition as mothers and as queen of the home'.[17] However, even though they were asked to transfer outside the home those qualities they were accustomed to cultivating in the domestic environment, the contribution of women to national rehabilitation again rested on the axiom of sexual difference.

The Primo de Rivera dictatorship strongly encouraged a language of projecting the home into society. His authoritarian nationalization project marked a pivotal moment in the Spanish nationalization of women, which until then had been carried out through informal mechanisms of associationism, press, celebrations, rituals, etc. Within a broad state project to nationalize the masses, General Primo de Rivera also sought to integrate women into the national community by appropriating a programme of social Catholicism, and its model of women with domestic and political responsibility in equal measure, as a patriotic duty. The most representative and nationally structured organization was the women's branch of Catholic Action, known as Acción Católica de la Mujer (ACM). This association became the primary representative of 'state feminism', and its leaders and directors the beneficiaries of the dictator's concessions of political rights to women.[18] The first attempt to channel the nationalization of women through a State-controlled single political party took the form of women's branches within the Unión Patriótica (Spanish Patriotic Union, UP). They engaged in propagandistic, altruistic and pedagogical activities, according to their guiding vision of patriotic maternity.[19] To sum up, the nationalizing project of Primo de Rivera introduced a novel element into the relationship between women and the Spanish nation. It constituted a state attempt to nationalize the female population through authoritarian means. The regime gave institutional backing to the idea that the contribution of women to the homeland was not defined on the basis of physical, private maternity alone (educators of sons as future citizens), but also included social maternity. This could be exercised through political offices that did not place their femininity in question.

The dictator also converted masculinity, as Nerea Aresti has demonstrated, into an axis of his nationalizing project. He set out to renovate the classic prototype of the Spanish male, who had supposedly fallen into decadence, a symptom and cause of moral laxity and the degeneration of good habits. He imposed a model of masculine behaviour that could serve as a patriotic symbol within the national regeneration project. As with the women, it seems that Primo de Rivera made recourse to the renovating tendencies of social Catholicism, within the Catholic tradition, to formulate a new male prototype: an authentic Spanish gentleman, though enhanced with paternal responsibility and moral rectitude.[20] The prohibition of flirtatious comments reflects the model of masculinity he was fighting against.

Meanwhile, in the 1920s, decisive steps were also taken in the construction of a 'new ideal of masculinity [that] took shape and gained popularity through literature, be it fiction, non-fiction or scientific'. In Republican, Socialist and Progressive liberal ranks, doctors, lawyers, journalists, secular moralists and writers created new identitary references. These began to generate a significant social echo in the 1920s, but were not politically supported until the Second Spanish Republic. Unlike Primo de Rivera, they sought to change rather than refurbish what was there. The prototype of the Spanish man that took hold in the climate of the Second Republic was grounded in values and qualities such as work, reason, self-control, austerity, responsibility and respect for the other sex.[21]

Between Rights and Obligations: Spanish Women-Mothers in the Second Republic

With the proclamation of the Second Republic in April 1931, a Republican-Socialist coalition formed the first government and popularized the notion that Spain was rooted in a Republican and Socialist tradition (a secular, egalitarian and populist nation, the 'Republic of the workers'). The citizenry, which had played a central role in that tradition, now came to the forefront with full rights. Rafael Cruz affirms that the republic deployed a wide range of cultural policies that mainly took the path of educational reform to 'nationalize' the citizens and 'republicanize' the nation: to unify the people by making them Spaniards.[22] If the essence of the new Republican regime was 'a people become Spain'; Spanish Republicans imagined something similar must be true for Spanish women and the republic. This image spread, favoured by a new element introduced by the governments of the Second Republic: the institutionalization of the relationship of women to the nation-state, which contemplated rights as well as duties. The Constitution of 1931 extended to women full civil and political citizenship, the latter after an intense and well-known dispute during the parliamentary proceedings for the constitution. Article 25 of Title III stated that 'nature, parentage, sex, social class, wealth, political ideas or religious beliefs may not be the basis of legal privilege'. Likewise, Article 36 of the same title stated that the 'citizens of either sex, aged twenty-three or older would have the same electoral rights as determined by law'.

In February of 1932, divorce was also legalized; this long-awaited 'redemptive' alternative for 'women in unhappy marriages' had been a demand of secular feminism since the beginning of the century. Grateful women exalted the new regime. On 18 November 1932, the Unión Femenina Republicana (Feminine Republican Union, UFR) rendered tribute to the constituent parliament 'for having recognized in the current Constitution all the civil and political rights of women, thereby remedying their absence from prior legislation'. By extending rights to women, Spain had finally reached what many – informed by the maxim that the best symbol of a country's progress was the dignity of its women – perceived as the civilizing benchmark of other nations. It was no surprise, then, that this new homeland, which extended full rights to women thanks to the republic, was symbolized as a young woman freed from her bonds, carrying the Republican flag and holding the scales of justice, accompanied by the people (represented as a lion). The Republican regime was projected not only as that which had most benefitted women and contributed to their 'redemption', but also as that which opened the door to hope for the implementation of a series of legislative changes that had been demanded since the beginning of the century. Thus, a symbolic interchange was easily established between women and the Spanish nation (both historically subjected to control by monarchy-marriage and clergy-Church).

However, this did not mean that the duties of women to Spain, now symbiotic with the republic, were perceived as secondary (except in cases such as that of Clara Campoamor), and less that they should in any way cease to be articulated around their identity as mothers. Quite to the contrary, in most ideological discourse, Spanish women continued to be presented as 'aware of their duties as citizens', which derived from their maternal 'nature'. The UFR itself, immediately after expressing its appreciation for the rights ceded, encouraged women to commit themselves 'with all the strength that their sensitive and noble hearts are capable of … to freely give days of glory to our beloved Republic, labouring ceaselessly for its good and educating its sons, the men of tomorrow, in the most austere principles of rectitude and justice, making them an asset to their motherland'. It launched the message to females that the homeland meant different things to men and women: for men it was a mother, for women a son. Only this could explain 'the great love with which we carry out our duties as citizens and how our new and great Spain will be happily attended and defended by us [women]'.[23]

The UFR formulated the contribution of women to Republican Spain in the same way that female patriotic work had been generically configured since the nineteenth century: based on their role as mother-educators of future citizens (now Republicans) and as maternal-workers that could 'take the home to the world, or, if they want to, turn the world into a home.' They again recurred to social maternity, or the projection of maternal qualities into social and public spheres, to mobilize feminine efforts in favour of the Spanish – and now Republican – nation. Alongside the image of Republican Spain as a young woman liberated from every (legal, political, religious) yoke, many Republican women imagined the republic – the government of the national community that was Spain – as a son they must protect.[24]

Meanwhile, the political Right mobilized the female population with great success around the motto 'religion, family, homeland, order, work and private property'. From their perspective, the Republican-Socialist legislation that forbade religious education and public worship constituted a great threat to the permanence of all those elements, which for them defined the Spanish nation. The conservative newspaper *La Unión* affirmed in 1931 that 'the Spanish woman' had always been distinguished by 'her faith, her religiosity, love for family and home'. The new legislation was thus perceived as 'an attack on women'. They felt another 'turn of the screw' with the legalization of divorce in March 1932 (one year after the encyclical *Casti Connubii* by Pope Pious XI regarding Christian marriage), which reinforced the opinion that Republican legislation offended Spanish women. In light of what the patriotic Republican imaginary suggested, the magazine *Ellas* stated in August 1933 that with the approval of the law on divorce, the republic had consummated a real, effective and undeniable 'divorce' between 'the Spanish Catholic woman' – the real 'Spanish woman' – and the revolution, legislating for an illusory and inexistent 'revolutionary woman' (who was not, nor had been, nor would be the Spanish woman) in a parliament where 'not a single deputy had been elected by female votes'.[25]

The feminine sections of all the Spanish right-wing parties contributed in this way to strengthen a Spanish identity for women that was consubstantial with Catholicism and distanced from the secularism

that the Republican regime represented to them. In other words, being Spanish meant being fervently Catholic; the two were inseparable.
Acción Popular very clearly expressed this in a pamphlet encouraging
women to vote for the Catholic cause: 'If you are a Spanish woman, we
would offend you BY ASKING IF YOU ARE CATHOLIC'.[26] Little by little, they
turned the republic into the enemy of the true Spanish woman.

Virtuous Mothers for the Homeland:
Civil War and the Francoist Dictatorship

During the Spanish Civil War (1936–39), patriotic discourse intensified in defence of what were presented as irreconcilable ideas regarding Spain. Though female mobilization activated different models of
the Spanish nation and society in the Rebel and Republican camps,
Spanish women on both sides of the conflict based their participation
on the attributes and virtues assigned to them by modern ideas of sexual difference. Specifically, maternity acted as the motor of female involvement in the rearguard on both sides. Perhaps mothers felt that
they bore the great responsibility of educating sons to fight against enemies, whether under the umbrella of fascism or the revolution; perhaps maternity was associated with the capacity to relieve pain, raise
morale among soldiers and comfort the injured. In any case, the sphere
of action outside the home increased in an unprecedented manner for
women in the rearguard on both sides.

On the Republican side, as Mary Nash has studied, combative, sacrificial mothers constituted the dominant model. Dolores Ibárruri *Pasionaria* incarnated this to perfection: 'the epitome of the valiant and
impetuous, but demanding, Spanish mother who enfolds all Spanish
men in her embrace'. As defence of the republic hardened into anti-
fascism, war and fascism became associated with destruction and hate
and were presented as the antithesis of what the Agrupación de Mujeres Antifascistas (Antifascist Women's Group) referred to as 'a woman's
nature', defined by 'her constructive spirit and her love'. Spanish mothers could not permit their sons to live in the society fascism seemed
to be creating; it was not only foreign but hostile to feminine values.
Furthermore, they perceived the Rebel side as a foreign enemy, an in-
vading force in the homeland. For women, this struggle 'to annihilate
the foreign invader' and secure for their sons 'a homeland that will be
yours' involved sacrificing them on the front.[27]

In the Rebel camp, sacrificial maternity (giving their sons for the
true homeland) also became the reference of patriotic behaviour for

women, though the sacrifice was aimed at achieving a different model of national community and society. Mothers were praised as 'one hundred per cent Spaniards', because they raised their sons 'for the homeland without a thought for the day when they would give them up'. Newspapers such as *La Información* in Cadiz (1938) published letters from mothers who, though devastated 'over the irreparable loss of my only son', were proud to proclaim that their sons had given 'their lives for the Spain we all dream of'.[28]

This discourse of maternal sacrifice to save the homeland from Soviet meddling as well as everything the 'revolution' represented to the Rebels (secularism, immorality, separatism) formed part of the foundation that sustained the relationship between women and the Spanish nation under Franco. Though Francoist Spain rested on the ideological bases of the diverse political cultures of the Spanish Right, which had taken shape during the first third of the twentieth century, the Civil War and its outcomes introduced new elements. What we are most interested in highlighting here is the fact that the result of the war allowed the political project for the nation (even with its internal differences) to erase every trace of the other Spanish identity (the losers) and impose itself as a recovery of the true Spanish identity that had deteriorated or been lost during – and even prior to – the Republican years. Gender was a crucial element in the enterprise of recovering the supposedly lost national identity, and accounts for the politics of recovering Spanishness.[29] The official diagnosis read that with the republic, women had lost their true identity – their innate religiosity, maternal qualities, devotion and homemaker spirit – in a Spain that contemplated the possibility of women having rights along with obligations. The idea was to recover women and make them serviceable in reconstructing the nation, based on a reference subject with attributes grounded in obedience, service, self-denial and sacrifice for a dilapidated homeland, an image the Civil War had helped to naturalize.

To this end, the Spanish nationalist project sought to include women collectively and from the top-down. Without contest, the most intense and systematic nationalization of Spanish women in the twentieth century was carried out by the Women's Section of the Falange, the Sección Femenina (SF), which officially served the Francoist State from 1939–75 (though it was created in 1934 and dismantled in 1978). The SF introduced a new dimension in the nationalization of Spanish women, which was clearly reflected in their Servicio Social (Social Service). Originally conceived in 1937 for civil recruitment and to alleviate the effects of the war among all single Spanish women between seventeen and thirty-five years of age, it became a dual nationalization channel by which the organization discharged the duty of national reconstruction of the homeland while indoctrinating women in the ideas of the Francoist State regarding Spanish Catholic femininity. The unprecedented feminine mobilization achieved by the Social Service would have been unimaginable ten years earlier. It can only be explained by the Civil War and fascistization of the Rebel side, which led to the adoption of totalitarian modes of service to the national community.

The contribution of women to the national project was initially defined by a conciliation of the domestic and public woman, of femininity and intellect, of political power and maternity. This combination of features was deeply rooted in the model that the political Right had been creating (and re-creating) throughout the first half of the twentieth century. Thus, the historical figures presented as references for Spanish women included heroines and patriots such as Isabella of Castile or Teresa of Avila, who, alongside femininity and domesticity, exemplified patriotism, courage and incessant public activity.[30]

However, in Francoist nationalist projects, the emphasis on maternity as the national mission of women in the new Spain displaced the idea that participation in the public sphere constituted an appropriate and necessary channel by which women could contribute to the national good. Accordingly, messages such as 'the real mission of the woman is to provide sons for the homeland. And this is therefore her supreme aspiration' filled the pages of the Falangist female press during the 1940s and into the 1950s.[31] Into this patriotic discourse, Francoism introduced novel elements that assigned unparalleled significance to maternity. This reflected the pro-natality eagerness of a state with totalitarian designs and increasing powers, one that linked national strength to number of inhabitants. Similarly, it figured in the formulation of the eugenic aim to obtain human beings that 'would biologically and morally be the pride of Spain', as affirmed by Doctor Luque, a regular collaborator with the national syndicalist women's magazine *Y, Revista de las Mujeres Nacional-Sindicalistas*. This way of thinking became the practical application of the Francoist pro-natality policy and transformed mothers – particularly strong, healthy mothers – into the centrepiece, the 'most important citizen'.[32] The statist conception of the mother was reinforced by the role assigned to the family in the symbolic nation-state imaginary and in the social policies of the Francoist State.

Clearly, the novelties introduced by an authoritarian state with totalitarian ambitions scarcely hesitated to invade the private sphere. It was the only way to bring the politicization of maternity to its climax,

and it favoured the intensification of the nationalization of the female population. However, the most 'fascist' elements of this feminine
model soon found themselves tempered by female traits recovered
from a long Catholic tradition. Authentic Spanish women were defined
not only by their reproductive capacity and the patriotic sense they
assigned to it, but also by their religious and moral sentiments emanat-
ing from the concept of virtue. Not all real maternities were assigned
the same weight in the national reconstruction project. In fact, true
Spanish maternity was based on the exclusion from the Spanish nation
(and its imaginary) of other maternities (and femininities) that were
considered aberrant, threatening and strange from the perspective of
correct sexual and national criteria. All this abject national femininity
was incarnated by the other women, the 'Reds'. According to studies
by Ricard Vinyes and others,[33] they were first stigmatized in order to
attempt their later regeneration through cleansing and purification.

From the early 1950s, this national model of the woman as the basis
of the family as well as the spinal column of the nation itself and the
Francoist regime was reformulated in consonance with the sociocultural transformations occurring in Spanish society. Modernization of
mass consumption, tourism and emigration (outside of Spain or to
the cities) facilitated the imitation of American habits and lifestyles
as seen on film. These had important repercussions in what until then
had been a highly homogeneous model of ideal Spanish femininity
and the perception of the family upon which it was based. Though it
remained operative during the 1950s, the virginal feminine model of
patriotic maternity began to coexist with others. New advertising called
on women to configure their sense of worth on physical appearance
and capacity for consumption of new products more than on spiritual
value. Mechanization also reached the private sphere and rationalized
domestic work.[34] The image of the Spanish woman as seductress and
consumer aggressively established itself as the new national identity
reference for women.

Even Francoist legislation (the 1958 Law to Reform the Civil Code
and the 1961 Law on Political Rights, etc.) might have unwittingly contributed to the decline of the hegemonic model by sanctioning socioeconomic changes. The SF, which had backed such legislation, sought
to preserve the Catholic model of the Spanish woman by reconciling
modernity with Catholicism, but the Francoist model broke down definitively in the 1960s. This crisis certainly contributed to the demise of
national discourse in broad intellectual and political sectors during the
same decade. Spain was 'fed up', even with symbols and pillars such
as the maternal woman and the Catholic family, which had saturated

public and private discourse for more than two decades.[35] This weariness, however, did not translate into national disassociation. During the transition to democracy, the projects of democratic Spain rested theoretically on the general principle of legal equality that would make it possible for the country to 'rise to the level of the most advanced societies in the world'. Once again, the socio-legal condition of women became the indicator of national (this time democratic) health. Once again, exactly as in the 1931 debate on female suffrage, feminist claims were debated in the context of the Spanish national identity.[36]

Inmaculada Blasco Herranz is an associate professor of Modern History at the University of La Laguna. Her work focuses on the relationship between gender and religion in late modern Spanish history, with a focus on the discursive basis of women's mobilization during the first decades of the twentieth century. She is currently working on questions of gender and Spanish modern identities, as well as the gendered dimension of social reform.

Notes

1. Schaser (2007); Landes (2001); Banti (2005).
2. Andreu (2009).
3. Archilés (2008) defends a focus that is neither exclusively statist nor instrumentalist in the analysis of nationalization processes.
4. Cleminson and Vázquez (2011: 171–230) and Aresti (2014) study the links between the crisis of hegemonic masculinity and the fin-de-siècle crisis.
5. Unamuno, in Aresti (2010: 266).
6. Bilbao (1916: 18).
7. Cited by Munson (2000: 43).
8. Gimeno (1900: 262–68).
9. Salomón (2005).
10. *El País*, 13 December 1906.
11. *El Pilar*, 15 March 1913.
12. Capel (1986: 326–96).
13. Ostolaza (2007).
14. Caine and Sluga (2000: 179).
15. Espinosa de los Monteros (1920: 23).
16. Moreno-Luzón (2006: 130–31).
17. *La Voz de la Mujer*, 30 July 1925.
18. Blasco (2003).
19. Quiroga (2008: 301). No monographic study has been done on this topic.
20. Aresti (2010: 121–77).
21. Aresti (2010: 165).
22. Cruz (2006).

23. Fagoaga (1986: 282).
24. Bussy-Genevois (1995) analyses the repertoire of feminine images representing the Spanish nation.
25. *Ellas. Semanario de las mujeres españolas,* 6 August 1933; prior quote in *La Unión. Revista de la Unión de Damas del Sagrado Corazón,* July 1931.
26. Monge and Bernal (1936: 213).
27. Quoted in Nash (2006: 100, 102). For the Agrupación de Mujeres Antifascistas and La Pasionaria, see Nash (2006: 100–03). Núñez Seixas (2006) analyses the role of nationalism as a mobilizing factor during the Civil War.
28. Quoted by Narváez (2009: 93).
29. As suggested by Morcillo (2000).
30. Sanz Bachiller (1940). This question has formed the axis of one of the most interesting debates on women and Francoism (Cenarro 2006: 77–80; Ofer 2009).
31. Quote in *Medina. Semanario de la Sección Femenina de Falange,* July 1942.
32. See Doctor Luque, Luque, 'Futuras madres', *Y, Revista de las Mujeres Nacional-Sindicalistas,* April 1938.
33. Vinyes (2002).
34. Morcillo (2000: 56; 2010).
35. Saz (2003: 52).
36. Radcliff (2009: 56).

Chapter 6

Religion

The Idea of Catholic Spain

Mary Vincent

The history of religion in twentieth-century Spain is the history of both public presence and individual belief. The former is easy to chart, the latter much less so. As surveys of religious values and beliefs show, religious identities are complex. Spain is still overwhelmingly a Catholic country: in 2002, 79.7 per cent of respondents identified themselves as Catholic, with a mere 1.7 per cent belonging to another religion. Intriguingly, only 72.9 per cent said they believed in God, either firmly (41.7 per cent) or with reservations (31.2 per cent).[1] This suggests a higher level of identity with the institution than with the faith, a similar pattern to Greece and other countries with a strong historical confessional identity. There is no doubt that this is the case in Spain, nor that it has been so since the early modern period. There still seems to be a clear correlation between national and religious identity, particularly if religion is defined as a series of practices in which one participates rather than as a set of beliefs to which one adheres.

This identification of what it is to be Spanish, and what it is to be Catholic, is reinforced by the finding in the 2002 survey that virtually all respondents with children had had them baptized (94.5 per cent) and expected them to make their first communion (90.7 per cent). This suggests a strong desire to transmit a Catholic identity to future generations, though it also illustrates the difficulty of studying religious identities, which may crystallize around a series of rarely considered beliefs. Clearly, though, Catholicism still monopolized the rites of passage through an individual lifetime, contributing to the shared identity that people understood as 'Spanish'. Hence, perhaps, there is a sense of these as formative experiences, expressed by those who saw baptism and first communion as essential stages of childhood, even if they had themselves dispensed with religious marriage or mass-attendance.

Historically, however, Spanish Catholicism has been a divisive rather than a cohesive identity. Catholicism may have been ubiquitous in twentieth-century Spain, but it was never uncontested. In France and Germany, the 'culture wars' were broadly resolved in favour of a secular or religiously neutral state, but in Spain a chronically impoverished state continued to bolster its authority by retaining a public and official presence for Catholicism that was fast fading elsewhere in Europe.[2] This acute concern with the Church's public position symbolized its contested role in questions of national identity. Spain had been defined as Catholic in the same way – and more firmly – as England had been as Protestant. By the early twentieth century, however, there was profound uncertainty as to how the nation should be defined in religious terms, or if it should be defined in such terms at all. This was manifested in the struggles over urban space that in Spain, as elsewhere, pitted liberals and 'progressives' against Catholicism and tradition.[3] The desire to sacralize did not always come from official quarters. Antoni Gaudí's Casa Milà (La Pedrera), built on Barcelona's Passeig de Gracià (1906–10), was originally intended to be topped by a twelve-metre high statue of the Virgin of the Rosary – a pious conceit on Milà's wife's name, Roser – which would have converted the building into a plinth.

Such forms of devotional practice were concrete attempts at Christian witness, derived from the contemporary cult of the Sacred Heart, which 'enthroned' images in domestic and municipal space as expiation for the sins of a faithless world. This symbolic context was hard-fought. An increasingly politicized Catholic mobilization took the religious habits of centuries and employed them in modern contexts.[4] At the same time, secularists and freethinkers claimed ownership of public space and communal ritual. If there were various ways of being Spanish, then there should, for example, be various ways of being buried in Spanish soil. These opposing moods – clericalism and anticlericalism – existed in symbiosis; they defined themselves against each other and their actions were patterned by the others.

A typical confrontation was that of a 'kidnapped' corpse recounted by the Communist leader Dolores Ibárruri. In 1903, a man in Vizcaya who wanted civil burial for his young daughter insisted on going to the cemetery 'by the usual route', with her coffin carried by 'four workers'. However, the Civil Guard intercepted the procession and, accompanied by various pious ladies or *beatas,* took the coffin to the cemetery, where the priest was waiting to bury it.[5] The story is archetypical – there are many similar accounts, usually with the same gendered tropes – but such confrontations were real. The Church claimed right of burial over all the baptized, whether believers or not. As late as 1947, a Protestant pastor in Leon was unable to bury one woman, despite her certified wish for a civil burial, as the parish priest 'refused to give up the Key of the Cemetery'. She was eventually buried 'outside ... where they dared not to have buried a dog or a donkey'.[6]

These tussles over funerals – complete with allegations of kidnapping and occasional violent assaults – conformed to a pattern recognizable from other 'culture wars'. Elsewhere in western Europe, however, the Church came to an accommodation with secular liberalism, as in France after 1905. In contrast, in Spain, positions hardened. A key point of cleavage came with the Barcelona Tragic Week of July 1909 when a general strike called as a protest against colonial war in Morocco war spiralled into anticlerical rioting. Fifty-two churches and thirty convents – among them hospitals and schools – went up in flames. According to one socialist organizer, maintaining control of the strike proved impossible given the accusations, even within the organizing committee, of 'defending the priests'.[7] Two days of intense rioting clearly showed that the prime object of attack was religious rather than political or financial.

The Tragic Week was the earliest outbreak of mass anticlerical violence in the twentieth century, antedating both the Mexican and Russian revolutions. It set Spain on a path in which political and class divisions were increasingly refracted through the prism of religion. Anticlericalism provided a 'common currency' on a Left divided between Republicans, socialists and anarchosyndicalists, though what they understood by anticlericalism was not necessarily the same. Anarchists in particular saw religion as both the symbol and the source of injustice, and combined this with a belief in the transformative power of violence in particularly potent ways. The Tragic Week was a notable failure for organized labour, but it led to the foundation of Europe's only mass anarchosyndicalist trade union in 1912, Confederación Nacional del Trabajo (CNT), which was to give a distinctive – and distinctively anticlerical – focus to the broader labour movement in Spain.

There was no sense in early twentieth-century Spain that religion was irrelevant, the 'out-worn creed' of Malcolm Arnold that, if left alone, would simply decay. On both left and right, religion occupied an imaginative space that made it omnipresent, even if not everyone adhered to it as a set of spiritual beliefs. Catholicism coalesced sharply as a *political* identity in Spain, a process that often had little direct connection with customary practice – whether baptizing children, ringing the angelus or celebrating *fiestas* in the pueblo – but which was, in turn, to politicize all of these. The reasons for this political recreation of religious identities lay with the Right as much as with the Left, and the symbiotic tension between them developed apace.

For the Right, the defining moment came in September 1923 with General Miguel Primo de Rivera's coup d'état, the first in Spain to lead to a military dictatorship. The coup was generally welcomed: conservatives saw it as firm action against disorder and revolt and even some on the left felt it could be no worse than what had gone before. Primo's programme of regeneration was, however, both to nationalize and divide Spain. The regime attempted to achieve political modernity on the basis of mobilization and patriotic display, a national project that firmly excluded the 'mob'.[8] The language of nation was conflated with the language of the Right as the panoply of monarchism continued to symbolize the nation in a specific, hierarchical conception of social order. The ecclesiastical hierarchy was clear in its support for Primo de Rivera, unsurprisingly given that CNT gunmen assassinated Cardinal Soldevila, archbishop of Zaragoza in June 1923. Even the cardinal archbishop of Tarragona, Francesc Vidal i Barraquer – who would later be exiled by the Franco regime – applauded the 'honourable general' who would, at last, regenerate Spain.

The regime's continued monarchism was also much to the taste of Catholic activists. Primo's chosen agent of political mobilization was a new mass party – or 'anti-party' – in which all members were required to be practising Catholics. The Unión Patriótica (UP) attracted younger Catholic men, many of them from provincial cities and active in agrarian politics. This Catholic prominence was repeated at a symbolic level that articulated National-Catholicism in a dictatorial context. What had been a clearly defined intellectual current in the nineteenth century now became an accessible, everyday feature of political life.[9] Primo's national militia, the Somatén, held ceremonies to bless its flag, with military parades and open-air masses, making explicit the connection the conservative Right saw between nationalism and religion. Good Spanish citizens were also dutiful Catholics; their duties were harmonious: that which they owed to Caesar, they also owed to God.

As a national identity, Catholicism claimed to be inclusive, common to all Spaniards regardless of social class or cultural background. But, paradoxically, Primo's attempt at a legitimating National-Catholic identity definitively established the Left/Right dichotomy that characterized the history of religion in twentieth-century Spain. Some groups, for example the Castilian peasantry, were brought into the National-Catholic fold. Others were left outside. Despite sustained attempts to use Catholicism to unite the regions of Spain – for example proclaiming the Catalan Virgin of Montserrat, patron of the Somatén, as a national symbol – the dictatorship's insistence on a unitary, centralizing nationalism quickly created conflict with the Catalan Church, where local clergy used the language their congregations understood best for liturgies and catechesis. Now, preaching in Catalan was banned and Vidal i Barraquer was forced to work hard both locally and with Rome to protect his priests against a regime that expelled 'separatist' students from seminaries and, after 1926, insisted on non-Catalan episcopal appointments.

Similar predations occurred in the Basque Country, where the first fine was levied on a Basque-speaking priest in December 1923. Here, though, the episcopacy was less prepared to take on the regime, even after the Basque-speaking Mateo Múgica was appointed bishop of Vitoria in 1928. But, even so, the Basque and Catalan Churches occupied similar positions. The use of local vernaculars symbolized a wider acceptance of cultural pluralism that made it clear that, even under a nationalizing, dictatorial regime, there was still more than one way of being Catholic. The men who led these Churches were not radical – both Catalonia and the Basque Country had political parties that combined social conservatism, religion and regional nationalism – but they were aware of, and often sympathized with, wider and more diverse cultural positions than were represented in the regime. Even the traditional, monarchist Múgica worked behind the scenes to allow the use of Basque in certain circumstances.

During the 1920s and 1930s, most official Catholic voices insisted on the unity and orthodoxy of the Church. There was only one path to salvation: dissidence was heterodox if not heretical or blasphemous. Yet, there were dissident voices, some of which would be heard more vociferously during the Second Republic. The Basque priest identified in Arturo Barea's memoirs as Father Joaquín – 'the only person with whom I could talk and have discussions' – trusted the young Arturo enough to introduce him to his wife and son even though their existence had to remain hidden from the world.[10] This rare glimpse of social and sexual unorthodoxy in a man who was, according to Barea, an exceptional priest serves as a reminder that regionalism was not the only form of pluralism to exist within the Spanish Church. Even in unpropitious times, there were various ways of being Catholic. They could not, though, alter the fact that, by 1930, religion had become hopelessly entwined in ways of being *político*.

The Primo de Rivera regime hardened the association between conservatism and Catholicism. This was accentuated after its fall, during the election campaigns of 1930–31, when defence of the monarchy was widely presented as defence of the Church. The primate of Spain, Cardinal Segura, announced that 'the moral, religious and social order' was imperilled while Múgica instructed his flock to vote for those who offered 'solid guarantees' of the preservation of order and religion.[11] Theirs were not the only voices – the Catalan Catholic daily *El Matí* announced itself to be completely indifferent to the electoral result – but they were loud and would grow louder as the Second Republic progressed. The clamorous insistence that the defence of religion was also the defence of order, property, the family, and the fatherland – which may be traced through all elections from April 1931 to February 1936 – would eventually drown out other Catholic political options, with the notable exception of the Basque Nationalist Party.

In 1931, however, Catholic Republicanism was a real presence at the polls. Primo de Rivera had left power utterly discredited, with many conservatives disillusioned. The size of the Republican victory in the municipal elections that ushered in the new regime made it quite clear that not all Spanish Catholics had voted monarchist. Angel Ossorio y Gallardo, a convinced Catholic, who styled himself a 'monarchist without a king', produced the first, rejected, draft of a Republican Constitution, during a brief moment when Catholic Republicanism seemed poised for prominence. Miguel Maura was minister of the interior and Niceto Alcalá-Zamora president of the republic. Conflict with the Church soon erupted – notably with the expulsion of Segura in May – but the forced exile of the cardinal primate meant that the much more accommodating Vidal i Barraquer was left as the key ecclesiastical figure mediating relations between the republic and Rome. In terms of positions of influence, those who identified with a politically moderate Catholicism – Vidal, for example, voted for the conservative Catalanist party Lliga – were very well placed.

The eclipse of Catholic Republicanism thus needs to be explained; in 1931, the religious outcomes of the Second Republic were by no means a foregone conclusion. What, then, were the processes by which a monolithic, authoritarian Catholicism came to present itself – with relatively little challenge – as the authentic voice of Spanish religion? The answer lies partly in the way in which the republic rapidly became an arena for a polarized politics of Left and Right. The very structures of the Second Republic encouraged this. Parliament was established as a unicameral legislature: the new regime – the new nation – would be legislated into existence through laws debated on the floor of the chamber. More technical forms of governance – the remittance of leg-islation to committees, for example, or the use of fiscal instruments – went unused. The politics of the republic would be defined by con-frontation, first in the parliament, then in the press and finally in the streets.

This was clearly the case with the 1931 Constitution, a relatively short and distinctive document, which was debated for weeks in the Cortes, quickly revealing that religion was a fundamental political cleavage. Deputies lined up to adumbrate the faults or the virtues of the Church, the iniquitous behaviour of the popes or the moral virtues of Cathol-icism. Moderate voices were few, neutral ones silent. But the debates gave a specious clarity to positions that were often imprecise. Catho-lics looking to work with the republic accepted Article 3 that separated Church and State; erstwhile monarchists did not. Among Republicans, there were tensions between those for whom a secular republic was an end in itself and those looking to extirpate Catholicism from Spanish society. The final compromise was steered through by Manuel Azaña, who famously declared that 'Spain has ceased to be Catholic' at the same time as he persuaded the Cortes to preserve Catholic welfare ser-vices and all religious orders, save the Jesuits.

For all the parliamentary furore, these were not the articles of the constitution that caused most public concern. Popular outrage was reserved for infringements on everyday religious practices that had been part of Spanish life for centuries. The removal of crucifixes from schoolrooms and municipal injunctions against bell ringing affected the material culture of everyday life. Bells would no longer call people to mass, toll for the dead or, in rural areas, mark the agricultural day with the angelus. The disappearance of Holy Week processions from the streets of Seville, or Corpus from Toledo, was another affront to traditional ways of being Spanish, a process that, in the words of the bishop of Salamanca, amounted to 'expelling God'.[12] The dangers had been pointed out in the Cortes, when the ordained priest and indepen-dent deputy, Jerónimo García Gallego, warned: 'Removing a crucifix from an office ... you create disquiet and disturbance and you alienate many people from the Republic.'[13]

The anticlerical clauses of the constitution proved to be the best re-cruiting issues the Right could have had. They were a consequence of Spain's deep politico-religious divide, but led to a further hardening of positions as a new generation of Catholic activists presented the con-stitution as an assault on the religious practice of centuries. These men had cut their political teeth in Primo de Rivera's Unión Patriótica and they were quite prepared to follow the rules of the democratic game –

at least until such a time that they could be rewritten. Under the leadership of José María Gil Robles, a new political party took shape, first as Acción Popular and then, after 1933, as the CEDA, developing a language of social defence that struck a chord among many, particularly the peasant farmers of Castile. As Primo de Rivera's regime had shown, the Right already claimed a monopoly over the language of patriotism, indelibly associated with that of religion. The self-defined defenders of the faith were also the paladins of the patria. During the 1933 election campaign, when women voted for the first time, Catholic women represented themselves as an apolitical constituency and the moral health of the nation. Forced into action by the onslaughts of a left-wing government – 'the revolution and its accomplices' – they quickly adopted a public role. Despite her diehard monarchist beliefs, the Carlist orator María Rosa Urraca Pastor ran for election in Guipúzcoa. Even though, as women, 'we are content with our home and our Mass', 'if you don't vote ... who will save your Mass and your home for you?'[14] The language of Spain and anti-Spain was developing fast.

Religion had become one element in a raft of conservative – in some cases reactionary – social values the Right identified with 'Spain'. As the republic wore on, the idea of Catholicism as a component of 'true' Spanish identity became more pronounced. On left and right, radical options were becoming more commonplace, as both the Asturias revolt of October 1934 and the repression that followed it showed.[15] The CEDA was by now overtly corporatist and its youth movement, the JAP, visibly affected by what Stanley Payne has termed the 'vertigo of fascism'. Yet, Catholicism remained definitional to the political Right, even in its most radical forms. Spain's fascist party, Falange Española de las JONS, was established in 1933 from the merger of Onésimo Redondo's radically Catholic group and Ramiro Ledesma Ramos's National Socialist–oriented JONS.[16] Although Falangists insisted on the primacy of the (totalitarian) State even if this led to conflict with the Church, the new party retained Redondo's religious ethos. Falange Española saw Catholicism as integral to Spain's identity. The hyper-nationalism of fascism was translated into a hyper-Catholicism, threatened not only by anti-Spain but also by anti-Christ.

Under the Second Republic, the Church became both a political actor and a political target. The emergence of a mass Catholic party, and the lack of circumspection evident in many CEDA activists – not least its leader – had the effect of making anti-Republicanism appear to be the *only* Catholic political option. Indeed, the CEDA went to some lengths to insist that it was. Individual members of the party – notably Luis Lúcia and Manuel Giménez Fernández – were genuinely

Republican. But, while they made contact with other centrist figures, including Miguel Maura, in the wake of the Popular Front elections in February 1936, they could not save either the republic or the CEDA. Lúcia's Derecha Regional Valenciana (DRV) – whose youth movement was perhaps the most radical of any branch of the JAP – was even the first CEDA branch to espouse direct rebellion, making contact with the conspirators from May.[17]

Despite the involvement of individual Catholics in the military conspiracy, the institutional Church played no role in the coup of July 1936. Yet, the Second Republic had 'fixed' the Church as the ideological enemy of the Left. Once the generals had risen, the Church's guilt was assumed. A massive outpouring of anticlerical violence erupted in the 'hot summer' of 1936 and would, over the course of the Civil War, claim the lives of over six thousand clergy, and nearly three hundred nuns.[18] Still more widespread was the destruction of churches, shrines, images and liturgical objects, which were burnt and attacked, often in violent burlesques of religious rituals. In 1936, priests were not simply killed as class enemies. Rather, they were seen as responsible for the suffering of the people and so singled out to bear the sins of the old order. The visceral nature of much of the anticlerical violence – which saw bodies mutilated after death and victims stripped and tortured – reveals the rage and hatred that the Church now inspired.[19] Popular ire is, of course, only a partial explanation: much of the violence was organized and carried out by militiamen or revolutionary committees. But, throughout Republican Spain, they found townsfolk prepared to identify victims or participate in the assaults. The cleavage of the Civil War was understood in religious as well as in class terms.

'Spain' and 'anti-Spain' thus took physical form during the Civil War. Positions hardened as a result of the anticlerical violence. To the Church, those done to death were martyrs for the faith, and their blood baptized the Civil War as a Crusade. The language of martyrdom was emblazoned in the bishops' collective pastoral of 1 July 1937, where Cardinal Isidro Gomá – who wrote the letter – proclaimed the 'marvellous phenomenon of martyrdom', as a 'testimony of blood'.[20] In the eyes of the hierarchy, Catholicism was consubstantial with the history, people and nation that Franco's Crusade now claimed. A very few Catholics continued to struggle for a religion that was not identified with Francoism or the political Right – notably José Bergamín, whose reservations about the Crusade were echoed outside Spain by Jacques Maritain – but most priests who had once supported the republic now found such a position impossible, particularly those in Catalonia, where Barcelona was now the epicentre of anarchist revolution. The killing of their fellow clergy seemed proof of the nefarious purpose of those who would 'expel God'.[21]

Only in the Basque Country did a widespread Catholic pluralism persist throughout the war. Here, the dominant PNV had gradually separated itself from other Catholic groups in the Cortes. Though always both Catholic and socially conservative, the PNV's Republicanism strengthened, as that of other Catholic parties became more and more contingent on electoral success that would transform the republic along corporatist lines. The PNV fought the 1936 elections alone, aligned neither with the Popular Front nor the conservative and corporatist blocs. Once war broke out, the new Basque government stayed loyal, the only significant religious element on the Republican side. Basque *gudariak* fought with chaplains, the area experienced no social revolution and anticlericalism was scarcely in evidence. Separated from the rest of the republic both geographically and culturally, the Basque autonomous region fought for its own Catholic, Republican identity, distinguished from the rest of the Republican side, though not as sharply as from the Nationalists. It was no coincidence that the only two bishops who refused to sign Gomá's collective pastoral on principled, rather than technical, grounds were Múgica and Vidal i Barraquer.

The Basque Country was, with Carlist Navarra, the area of the highest religious practice in Spain. Elsewhere there was no such Catholic consensus. Those who burnt churches and detained priests were most likely to be young, male and working class, which would have come as no surprise to those priests immersed in social catholic projects, as these were exactly the Spaniards who were least likely to attend church.[22] Greater awareness of the pastoral difficulties that faced the Church did not, though, afford reforming priests any protection in 1936. The Dominican father, José Gafo, had a long career as a social reformer, but his bitter critiques of a Church devoted to 'legal recognitions and official acts of religiosity' did not save him, just as their ordination did not save the Basque Nationalist priests executed after the fall of Bilbao. The divisions and bitterness of the Civil War brought with them an immense pastoral task. Catholic practice had long varied by age, sex and social class, though this was seldom alluded to in either pastoral pronouncements or official rhetoric. The crushing victory of 'the Catholic arms of Franco' reinforced this silence after 1939. God had given victory to the 'Crusade', proof – should any be needed – that the interests of Spain and the Church were one and the same.

After April 1939, the Church hymned Franco's victory even as it encouraged penitence and the return of Spaniards to the Catholic fold.

This language of reparation and reconversion provided a theological framework for the repression and 'purification' carried out by the New State, about which the Church was silent. The liturgical language was that of spiritual cleansing, as the Church now reclaimed Republican Spain as its own. Congregations that had met in secret returned to their parishes; priests who had worked clandestinely now openly wore their soutanes. The Civil War was declared at an end on 1 April 1939, Palm Sunday. Reinstituting the street drama of Holy Week was thus a powerful imperative, returning religion to its rightful, public, role. In Madrid, the Good Friday procession left from the newly reconsecrated church of San José – used to store potatoes during the war – crossing the streets to the Puerta de Alcalá, where mass was to be said on Easter Sunday. Stations of the cross lined the route, a temporary Calvary thronged with people who knelt, wept or genuflected as 'the brutally pounded and broken' image of Christ of the Miracles passed by.[23] At its destination, though, the image was greeted with Roman salutes, and placed at the foot of the gigantic 'Cross of the Fallen', the base of which was formed by the Falangist yoke and arrows.

In the context of Franco's victory, the reassertion of Holy Week was a restitution as well as a victory, re-establishing not only the religious order but also a supposedly natural social hierarchy. This was the 'true' Spain, the Spain of history and tradition, and its permanent existence was articulated through the series of cultural values that came together as National-Catholicism, an idea that reached its zenith under Franco's dictatorship. Redefined during the Civil War as a discourse of victory that – heightened by the hyper-nationalism of fascism – reworked the idea of 'Catholic unity' through a process of spiritual cleansing and redemption, National-Catholicism depended on the physical repression and excision of the anti-Spain. This was exemplified by the dictator's gargantuan mausoleum, the Valle de los Caídos, which recreated the Crusade in stone, served as a final resting place for many who died 'for God and Spain' and was built, in part, by the forced labour of Republican prisoners. It is no coincidence that National-Catholicism originated in the same circumstances as the mass Spanish fascist movement. The internal 'other' combined notions of dissidence and violence in the blanket term Reds, within which a variety of creeds – communism, socialism, republicanism, Protestantism, masonry – were equally anathematized. The rhetorical power of National-Catholicism thus derived in a very direct sense from the Civil War, while its capacity to mobilize owed much to the experience of fascism.

As an official ideology, National-Catholicism provided a performative discourse of patriotism and reconstruction. Public cult was its defining characteristic, encouraged not only as testimony to individual faith but also as an expression of strength, loyalty and submission. Spain, true Spain, was Catholic; it did not have to become so. A demonstration of this fact was all that was required. In the aftermath of Franco's victory, public liturgies allowed citizens to display their fidelity to the true faith and the true Spain. Mission priests visited the pueblos of rural Spain, staying for two or three days filled with masses, dawn rosaries, stations of the cross and spiritual exercises, with confessors on hand to encourage repentance. This intensive period of spiritual renewal took the form of an immersive religious experience that emphasized communal, public adhesion. In an urban context, missions became vehicles for proselytizing campaigns that united and displayed the National-Catholic nation. In 1942, for example, a mission in Vigo saw eighty thousand gather for the 'rosary of the sea' said as a small flotilla accompanied a statue of Mary through the harbour.[24] These totalizing emotional events became emblematic of the postwar era, and were noted for their fervour, if not for any lasting effect.

Martial imagery and militant rhetoric brought the values of the Crusade to a new generation, now mobilized for the spiritual struggle of National-Catholicism rather than the physical fight of fascism and war. Spanish youth would be a spiritual army, battling against secularism as the country recreated itself as the 'spiritual reserve of the West'. New cults appeared, most significantly that of the Virgin of Fátima, who had appeared in Portugal in 1917, and which grew rapidly in popularity during the 1940s, its explicitly anti-communist tone both reflecting and reinforcing the logic of the Cold War. Many post-1945 apparitions – including those in the northern Spanish village of Garabandal in 1961 – followed the Fátima pattern of apocalyptic messages and revealed 'secrets'. The emphasis on the reparation of an unfaithful world clearly struck a chord in National-Catholic Spain.[25] A key stage in the globalization of the Fátima cult came in 1947 when the Virgin set out on a 'world tour' that that took her through Spain. The reception the image received was tumultuous, with crowds vying with each other to touch or carry the image. Famously, wherever the Fátima statue went, it was accompanied by doves, which were taken as a sign of divine presence. God's power was demonstrated by miracles: when the image reached Madrid in spring 1948, observers saw 'the sick getting up off their beds, doves taking turns in a guard of honour … sinners confessing' as the nation came together in a performance of Catholic unanimity.[26]

In some places, visits of the Fátima image seem to have been associated with attacks on Protestant chapels. Certainly, it is hard to see

Acción Católica's announcement of the discovery of a 'Protestant offensive against Spain' during the Fátima tour as entirely coincidental,
though this anti-Protestant campaign actually demonstrated the limits
of National-Catholicism as it proved hard to convince many people
that law-abiding Protestants were a real threat. In Girona in 1958, for
example, a police investigation into the local Baptist minister's 'illegal'
'anti-Catholic and consequently anti-Spanish' activities found him to
be 'of good moral conduct, public and private' with no political affil-
iations.[27] The cultural tropes of National-Catholicism ran very deep
in Francoist Spain, but they interacted with community mores and
accepted social practice.

National-Catholicism – powerful and omnipresent as it was – never
represented the totality of Spanish Catholicism, let alone the whole
of the nation. The Church presented itself as a monolithic institution
within which dissident opinions were heretical or heterodox; the regime
insisted that good Spaniards were good Catholics but only in so far as
they conformed to certain sociopolitical norms. Even here, though, the
monolith was more apparent than real. It proved impossible to maintain the dynamic of National-Catholicism, as the different treatment
meted out to religious enemies (Protestants, Freemasons) and political
enemies (communists, socialists, and anarchists) showed. Protestant
ministers, for example, insisted on their status as law-abiding citizens,
a status that, as we have seen, their neighbours often confirmed.

As the Franco regime lasted for nearly forty years, its weighty presence tends to dominate the religious history of twentieth-century Spain.
However, as the regime moved into economic growth in the 1960s and
so from poverty to affluence, more and more people within the Church
were questioning the old certainties. This was not simply a question
of secularization. A sustained rise in the number of people attending
mass meant that religion was thriving in Francoist Spain. According to
a 1969 survey, 98 per cent of housewives and 86 per cent of workers saw
themselves as Catholic.[28] At governmental level, Opus Dei introduced a
new understanding of capitalism and a Spain 'open for business' alongside a new emphasis on the educated, and spiritually honed, individual.
The canopy of the confessional state also meant that, in marked contrast to the 1930s, there was now some co-operation between spiritual
and secular. This was given physical form in contemporary church architecture, which abandoned the Baroque – for centuries the defining
cultural idiom of Spanish Catholicism – in favour of the modern. The
sanctuary of Our Lady of Aránzazu was begun in 1949, ten years before
the Valle de los Caídos was opened. In contrast, Aránzazu was uncom-
promising and modern, even brutal, in its construction, which drew on

the radical artistic talents of Eduardo Chillida and Jorge Oteiza. More muted versions of this spiritual modernism were to be seen in the new parish churches erected in all Spanish cities during the 1950s.

The architecture reflected a movement within the church, away from the external, 'totalizing' cults of the 1940s, towards a greater awareness of Catholicism as a global, rather than a national, Church. The process of dialogue – which became emblematic of the cultural transition to democracy during the 1970s – began with an increasing disjuncture between pastoral and dogmatic theology. The realities of social privation – particularly when the country was becoming wealthier – brought some parish clergy to question the Church's response to the poor. A new kind of activism developed with the foundation of 'specialist' branches of Acción Católica. The Juventudes Obreras Cristianas (JOC) and Hermandades Obreras de Acción Católica (HOAC) developed their own pastoral method of 'see, judge, act': they would identify a problem, investigate it, and try to redress it. Participation replaced passivity, taking these young activists into areas that many saw as political rather than religious, particularly in the industrial dioceses of northern Spain, where HOAC and JOC activists co-operated with illegal strikes and worked with underground communist unions. Seven Comisiones Obreras (Workers' Commissions, CCOO) leaders were tried for illegal association in Vizcaya in 1964; six of them were also members of HOAC.[29]

As these activists stood trial, the Second Vatican Council (1962–65) was taking place in Rome. From its very beginnings, Vatican II signalled a period of profound change for the universal Church. It is often depicted as a *deus ex machina*, an unforeseen, external event that finally introduced – or even imposed – pluralism on the Spanish Church.[30] But, while abandoning the certainties of National-Catholicism was difficult for those who had experienced the Civil War – Joaquín Ruíz-Giménez, for example, only resolved this 'crisis of conscience' as an observer at the council – the roots of doubt were already apparent.[31] Indeed, change could not have happened so readily had there not been a process of renewal within the Spanish Church, notably at level of pastoral practice and theological exchange. For, despite the hermetic certainties of National-Catholicism, the Spanish Church existed within the universal one. Diocesan priests and seminarians travelling to study in noted theological centres such as Munich or Innsbruck, often found themselves intellectually ill equipped for the journey.[32] Outside Spain, many discovered that the 'spiritual reserve of the West' was stuck in a by-water. During the council itself, Spain's bishops went to Rome only to find a worldwide Church they barely recognized. With the conciliar declaration on religious freedom, the discrepancy became apparent to the whole world. The Spanish Church's 'delusions of grandeur' collapsed.

It is tempting to posit the impact of Vatican II as a conflict: the old 'Spanish' Church against the 'new' universal one. But those involved in the currents of reform during the 1960s did not think of themselves as any less Spanish. In 1962, when the council opened, Spain had the oldest hierarchy and the youngest parish clergy in Europe. The stage was set for a period of both profound renewal and disquieting change as various constituencies struggled to reform the Spanish Church, retaining what was good, renewing and modernizing that which would no longer serve. The clearest break came when the declaration of religious freedom, promulgated by Paul VI in 1965, insisted that no-one should be forced to behave in ways contrary to their conscience. This re-evaluation of the role of individual conscience permanently separated the conciliar period from everything that had gone before. In Spain, this meant an end to the Church of the Crusade, which had fought a war in the 1930s against the cultural pluralism on which democracy is based. In the 1960s, the Roman Church had recognized this same pluralism as a universal human right.

The scale of the change is illustrated by John XXIII's definition of peace in *Pacem in Terris* (1963) as 'an order that is founded on truth, built up on justice, nurtured and animated by charity, and brought into effect under the auspices of freedom'. In contrast, the collective pastoral of the Spanish bishops in 1937 had defined peace as 'the tranquillity of divine order, national, social and individual, which assigns a place to everyone and gives him what he is due'. The earlier statement is static and hierarchical, the later dynamic. John XXIII's encyclical saw peace as universal and transnational, just like the Church itself. The Franco regime's notion of Catholicism in one country could no longer be sustained. The edifice of National-Catholicism cracked, revealing a pluralist Church with many members who had no difficulty in reconciling Catholicism and democracy or even Catholicism and socialism. But greater engagement with the secular world took its toll. An emphasis on Christian commitment rather than piety led many young priests and religious to question their vocation, although celibacy was often the defining issue for those applying to be secularized. Around four hundred priests left the Church each year between 1966 and 1971, as did a third of Spain's Jesuits in the ten years after 1966. The religious revival of the post–Civil War period was definitively at an end.

Some responded by retreating. The hiatus of the 1930s meant that the priesthood was broadly grouped into those over age sixty and those

under forty, both of whom found the searching examination of conscience instigated by Vatican II discomforting. Many – though by no
means all – of the older generation retreated to an ideological bunker defined by the certainties of the Caudillo's confessional state. In
marked contrast to the conciliar Church, such priests remained reso-
lute in their separation from the world, faithful to the political and religious values of the crusade. Reservations about the impact of Vatican
II were, however, not confined to the 'bunker' as the career of Joseph
Ratzinger – later Pope Benedict XV – showed. Concern about radicalism and disrespect for clerical authority, as well the haemorrhaging of
vocations, was increasingly common.

Young Catholic activists – both clerical and lay – were already moving outside the Church as pressing human rights issues seemed to re-
quire a political rather than a pastoral solution. The issues, and the
activists, were being secularized; Vatican II had destroyed the sense
of hierarchy that underpinned religious and social order in Franco's
Spain and introduced conscious individual choice. Nowhere was this
change more profoundly felt than in the Basque Country. The suppression of all manifestations of Basque nationalism after the Civil
War had led to a disjuncture between the parish clergy and the hierarchy, specifically over the use of Basque in church. Well aware that
their congregations were more fluent in Basque, village priests would
preach in the vernacular, switching quickly into Spanish if an outsider
entered the church. Unlike in Catalonia, where the abbey of Monserrat
had emerged as a focus for Catalan cultural and religious activism, the
Basque Country had endured non-Basque bishops and Basque sees
subordinated to Spanish archdioceses. But Vatican II's recognition of
the political and linguistic rights of ethnic minorities now fuelled the
claims of those who – like the 339 Basque clergy who petitioned their
bishops in 1960 – protested at the repression of 'the ethnic, linguistic
and social characteristics that God gave to the Basques'.

Euzkadi Ta Askatasuna (ETA) was the first Basque political organization to declare its aconfessionality in terms of religion, marking a
new stage in the secularization of Spain. Yet, many of its first members
came from Catholic youth organizations; in the village of Itziar, for
example, the first ETA militants had all been altar boys.[33] Few Basques
were involved in ETA terrorism and, for many Christians, the fight for
justice was fatally compromised by lethal violence. But many, including
churchmen, were provoked into tacit support by the fierce repression
unleashed upon their homeland. Few mourned Melitón Manzanas,
widely believed to be a police torturer, when ETA killed him in 1968.
The subsequent trials in the Castilian city of Burgos – where the de-

fendants spoke Basque, giving eloquent testimony of torture – raised sympathies further, particularly when, despite an effective defence by a young Catholic lawyer, Gregorio Peces-Barba, five death sentences were passed. Two of the defendants were priests and successful campaigns, first to have the trial held in public and then for clemency, were led by bishops. It was clear that significant sections of the Church had moved into outright political opposition.

There were few in Spain who had no contact with the Church during the 1970s. Opposition activists cut their political teeth in Church-sponsored circles; neighbourhood groups co-operated with parish bodies. But the old absolutes were gone for good. Aware that sincerely religious men and women were to be found across the political spectrum, Spanish Catholics abandoned the attempt to define a particular political space for the Church. Change was coming and, as General Franco's health declined, a clear consensus developed that the political role of the Church would have to change. The future did not lie with the confessional state but with confessional neutrality. This was the view espoused – and ably steered through after Franco's death in 1975 – by Cardinal Vicente Enrique y Tarancón, who, with Ruíz-Jiménez and Gregorio Peces-Barba, was instrumental in shaping the Church's new constitutional position.

The 1978 constitution guaranteed both freedom of conscience and the aconfessionality of the State. In marked contrast to 1931, the place of religion was relatively uncontentious; the old clerical/anticlerical divide had at last been superseded. Article 16 mentions only recognition of the 'religious beliefs of Spanish society' and 'co-operation with the Catholic Church and other confessions'. No defined Christian Democrat option emerged during or after the transition to democracy, in marked contrast to countries such as Italy or Austria. Rúiz Giménez consistently refused to use the term; he was, he said, simply 'a Christian and a democrat'. These new, democratic Catholics had no particular view of Spanish unity and many, including Tarancón, were wary of any direct political involvement. During the transition, various small Christian Democrat groupings coalesced briefly in Adolfo Suárez's Unión de Centro Democrático (UCD), but though the party governed from 1977, it was always a highly contingent political force and disbanded in 1982, when the Socialist party took office for the first time since the 1930s.

Even now, there was no perceived need for a Catholic political party, and understandable disquiet around the idea of a single political position. For the Catholic anti-Franco opposition, the implementation of democracy had been enough. A genuinely democratic Spain would have religious liberty at its heart. The architects of the constitution – including Peces-Barba – had looked to ensure that freedom of worship would extend to the Catholic Church but not be dominated or monopolized by it. For those marked by the profound changes of the 1960s, democracy was essential to true religiosity as, in contrast to other political systems, it respected the primacy of the individual conscience. The new regime, like the new monarch, should be for 'all Spaniards'. These constitutional aspirations were, to a great extent, realized. However, the Church retained an aspiration for profound spiritual renewal and here it was to be deeply disappointed.

Religious practice fell rapidly from the 1970s and, while Catholicism retained a cultural prominence – demonstrated most conspicuously by the revival of Holy Week and the continued popularity of first holy communions – the country was secularizing faster than ever before. During the 1980s, the numbers leaving the Church were highest in regions such as the Basque Country and Navarra that had historically been most Catholic while the proportion of non-believers was highest among the young.[34] Much to the disappointment of many Catholics, democratic Spain appeared to be seeing very similar processes of secularization – at least as measured by mass-attendance – as was occurring in the rest of western Europe. And, to the disappointment of many democrats, any belief in the Church's apoliticism was soon shown to be naïve. The Church expected to continue to play a public role, lobbying on particular areas of interest, notably education, family life and reproductive policy. It often assumed the voice of moral authority – a trend that was enhanced under the increasingly conservative pontificate of John Paul II – even if it now acted as a pressure group, one lobby among many.

To use the sociological terminology of Max Weber and Ernst Troeltsch, the Spanish Catholic Church had tried for most of the twentieth century – and certainly through the first two decades of the Franco regime – to maintain a church-type presence in national society. But this, much-vaunted, idea of Catholic unity had failed and, by the end of the century, the Church was reduced to a sect-type presence, a role that some adopted with enthusiasm – the church of true believers – others with regret or trepidation. New avenues have developed: the presence of non-Christian immigrants has, for example, led to a shared desire to see more respect for faith groups. In general, however, Catholicism has had to accept a reduced and even circumscribed presence within wider Spanish society. Increasingly, people understand the primacy of conscience in an essentially consumerist way, with even the most devout cherry-picking Church teachings. Those who attend mass are, for example, much more likely to receive communion regularly than they are to go to confession, while prohibitions around birth control and premarital sex are widely ignored. What Catholicism means has changed in twenty-first century Spain, but it is proving to be resilient, a long-established confessional identity that many (albeit fewer) Spaniards still share.

Mary Vincent is professor of Modern History at the University of Sheffield. Her main research interests lie in the history of modern Spain, particularly in the period of the Civil War and the Franco dictatorship, with a special interest in the social basis of Franco's support, particularly that provided by the Catholic Church, and the history of gender. Her most recent book is *Modern Spain 1833–2002: People and State* (2007). She is working on a book on religious violence in the Spanish Civil War.

Notes

1. Sociological data from the Centro de Estudios Sociológicos, Banco de Datos, particularly *Religión I* (1998), http://www.cis.es/cis/opencm/ES/2_bancodatos/estudios/ver.jsp?estudio=1290 (accessed 11 July 2012); and *Actitudes y creencias religiosas* (2002), http://www.cis.es/cis/opencm/ES/2_bancodatos/estudios/ver.jsp?estudio=2170 (accessed 11 July 2012).
2. On the modern Spanish state, see Vincent (2007).
3. Clark and Kaiser (2003).
4. See De la Cueva Merino (1994, 2000)
5. Ibárruri (1979: 46–51). See further Cruz (2009).
6. John Rylands Library, *Echoes of Service* correspondence: Grace Turrell to Mr Vine, 1/7/1947; Thornton (Eduardo) Turrell to Mr Vine 30/6/1947.
7. Fabra Ribas (1975: 45).
8. Quiroga (2007).
9. For the nineteenth century, see Alvarez Junco (2001: 305–498).
10. Barea (2002: 193, 216).
11. Both quoted in Vincent (1996: 136, 143).
12. *Boletín Eclesiástico del Obispado de Salamanca* (1932), 338.
13. *Diario de Sesiones de las Cortes Constituyentes de la República Español* (Madrid, 1931–33), 1575.
14. *El Pensamiento Navarro*, 1 November 1933.
15. In a large and often partisan historiography, Preston (1978) still holds its own.
16. See Payne (1999).
17. Tusell and Calvo (1990); Valls Montes (1992); Lowe (2012).
18. Montero Moreno (1961).
19. Vincent (2005); Thomas (2013: 100–72).
20. 'Sobre la Guerra de España', in Iribarren (1974: 235–6).

21. Raguer (2001: 275–320).
22. On the perpetrators, see Thomas (2013), 74–99.
23. *Madrid,* 8 April 1939; Vincent (2009).
24. Orensanz (1974: 9–21); *Ecclesia,* 18 April 1942.
25. Christian Jnr (1999); Zimdars-Swartz (1991: 190–219).
26. *Ecclesia,* 5 June 1948; *Signo,* 29 May 1948
27. Clara (2001).
28. See Hermet (1985: 72, 29).
29. Montero García (2000).
30. E.g. Casanova (2005).
31. See Vilar (1976: 399–419, at 409).
32. Pérez-Díaz (1993: 161–83).
33. Zulaika (1988).
34. González-Anelo (1999); Fundación Santa María (1992).

Chapter 7

The Language(s) of the Spanish Nation

Xosé M. Núñez Seixas

Language is implicit and ever-present in the discourse and praxis of Spanish nationalism, as a policy for nation-building or as political and cultural discourse; but it has seldom been treated as a topic in its own right.[1] This is partially due to the paradoxically late emergence of explicit linguistic concerns in Spanish national discourse. Until the beginning of the twentieth century, no real menace to the hegemonic Castilian language had been perceived. The other Iberian languages and dialects posed no serious threat and a practical tolerance of their instrumental use in education was common in mid- and late-nineteenth-century Spain. However, they were not generally included in political demands, subjected to grammatical modernization or regarded as culturally appropriated instruments for defining a sub-state public sphere.

Any true linguistic concern at that time could be found in the Americas. The independence of American colonies from the Spanish monarchy between 1810 and 1826 and the nation-building processes implemented by the intellectual and political elites of the new Latin American states fostered a debate that would last until the beginning of the twentieth century regarding the linguistic variants that should be adopted as new national languages. Debates centred around the purity of the Castilian language and on where it had been best preserved, as well as on its national appropriation by these new republics, implying that the language would no longer belong exclusively to Spain.[2]

In Spain, however, linguistic issues were of no great importance even in civil legislation. Some exceptions began to emerge in the 1860s, and soon after it was mandated that official documents should be written in Castilian or include a translation into Castilian if written in a foreign language or 'dialect of the country' (*Ley de Registro Civil*, 1870).

The main theorists of nineteenth-century Spanish nationalism were not excessively concerned with the role of language in national identity. The conservative premier Antonio Cánovas del Castillo stated in his 1882 *Discourse on the Nation* that language in itself was insufficient for defining a nation.[3] Marcelino Menéndez y Pelayo, the main theorist of traditionalist Spanish nationalism, assigned the Castilian language no significant role as a marker of the nation: for him the Catholic religion, the Monarchy and Spanish history were the true unifying factors. The linguistic question occupied almost no space in the reform movement (*Regeneracionismo*) that emerged after 1898; nor was it relevant in publications reflecting on Spanish identity at the end of the nineteenth century, such as *Idearium español* (1898), by the philosopher Angel Ganivet.[4]

Language as a nationality marker entered the scene in the late 1880s, when other Iberian languages began to be promoted as markers of ethnic distinctiveness. At that time, the first polemics arose regarding the feasibility of encouraging the rise of the 'dialects', a discussion aimed mainly against the Catalan and Galician languages. In 1888, the Spanish public sphere reacted with astonishment to the first demands that Catalan be given co-official status with Castilian. In 1896, a Valencian Carlist representative to the Spanish Parliament presented a motion requiring schoolteachers to have knowledge of the regional language in the place where they taught. This was rejected in light of the risk that large areas of Spain would continue to remain ignorant of Castilian and therefore not integrate into civilization. While the diverse languages, dialects and local forms of speech should be preserved and included in a heritage of rich diversity that even enhanced Spanish identity, *civilized people* had to speak Castilian.

From 1900 on, state legislation became more explicit in prescribing that Castilian be the exclusive language for education, state administration and public life.[5] In 1916, the *Mancomunitat* of Catalonia presented a bill in the Spanish Parliament to make Catalan a co-official language in its territory. Though the bill received the support of several traditionalist representatives, it was rejected. In the parliamentary debates that began in 1916, a clear reaction to Catalanist demands emerged throughout the political spectrum, from liberal conservatives to reformists, for two main reasons. First, it was seen as a 'serious issue' that a nation-state have its corresponding language. Second, linguistic diversity at the administrative and official levels would create difficulties for the free circulation of goods and persons within Spanish borders. Moreover, concern regarding the real state of schooling in Castilian also became evident. A 1916 memorandum of the Academy of the Castilian Language recognized that in many schools Castilian was not used for teaching and many local government edicts were not written in the national language.[6]

The linguistic debate gathered strength in the parliament and the Spanish public sphere, fed by increasingly intense discussion of the value that should be assigned to the common language and the regional languages. Opposition to the Catalan goal of becoming a co-official language in the governmental, legal and educational spheres rapidly congealed and was expressed in the popular mobilizations that took place in several Castilian towns between November 1918 and February 1919. The main accusations against Catalanism were its lack of solidarity with the rest of Spain and its attempt to gain privileges for Catalan manufacturers. Several outspoken anti-Catalanists, such as the Aragonese politician Antonio Royo Villanova, berated Catalan for lacking the universality of Castilian; only the latter could provide a spiritual nexus for unity and the expression of elevated thoughts.[7]

The Spanish Language as Symbol and Expression of the National Character

Defeat by the United States and the loss of Cuba in the war of 1898 marked the definitive end of the Spanish overseas empire, making it necessary to reformulate the constitutive elements of a Spanish national identity. Association of Castilian Spanish with the national character became more frequent as concern over strengthening ties with the young Latin American republics increased and the greater visibility of Catalanist proposals within the national territory, as seen above, brought language to the forefront as a symbol and key ethnic marker of the nation past and present.

Examples of this include historian Rafael Altamira, a great theorist of the collective psychology of the Spanish people, who wrote, 'the spirit of a people is found in its language'.[8] The Basque writer Miguel de Unamuno considered race, national spirit and language to be intrinsically linked: 'language creates the spiritual and psychological race, which is the blood of the spirit'. Though projected from a Hispanic-American angle, this sense of race could also be understood from the perspective of internal national integration. Paradoxically, Unamuno denied for vernacular languages what he defended for Castilian: that language was intrinsic to the collective genius of a people. Linguistic substitution – such as having Basques speak Castilian – in no way weakened the collective personality of those Spaniards whose original native tongue was not Castilian. In a 1902 speech, Unamuno stated that the Basque language was dying a natural death, but that this would make it possible for its soul to live on. All the languages of Spain had merged or would merge into Castilian, the only language that should receive official protection.[9] Castilian was not only the most extensively used language, but had the most consolidated high literature. It was also considered ontologically superior to the other peninsular languages, including Portuguese. Melded with its land of origin (Castile), its sober and audacious phonetics were incomparable in the family of romance languages. It reflected the rugged, austere, adventure-loving Castilian spirit. For much of the literary *Generation of 1898,* Castile had forged the soul of Spain.

In the early twentieth century, modernized philology emerged in Spain as an academic discipline with ambitious research to establish the bases for the prestige and universality of Castilian. This was aimed at Spain itself and the Americas, in an attempt to avoid creolization of the language and fragmentation of linguistic norms. Much research was carried out on the history of the language, particularly between 1910 and 1936, by the Centro de Estudios Históricos under the direction of historian and philologist Ramón Menéndez Pidal. He laid the groundwork for intertwining history, language and race or cultural community, considering the evolution of languages to be somewhat dependent on political factors.[10] Menéndez Pidal was attempting to demonstrate one key idea: that from the unifying reconquest of Spain from the Muslims and throughout the Middle Ages, Castilian had progressively established its hegemony over the other Iberian languages to become the language of the culture. Castilian included elements adopted from all the other peninsular languages. Centuries of interaction between them had indirectly consolidated the propensity towards political unity and expressed certain similar national character traits throughout the Iberian Peninsula. Castilian had established itself among both high and low classes throughout the Spanish territory, while Castile had provided a stable context in which this language could mature. A literary variant of superior prestige had evolved thanks to an expansionist will, yet at the same time it maintained its essence. Thus, Castilian had become *the* Spanish language by excellence.[11] In his 1925 work *Orígenes del español* (The Origins of Spanish), Menéndez Pidal went on to describe how Castilian was morphologically, phonetically and syntactically a more audacious language, the expression of a 'rebellious and discordant force that had arisen in and around the Cantabric valleys', reflected in its radical departure from vulgar Latin. Castilian also showcased a 'more correct artistic taste, having adopted early on the most euphonic forms of the vowel sounds'. The entrepreneurial and universalizing spirit of Castile, the character of its inhabitants and its promising future as the vehicle of a superior civilization had guaranteed the consolidation and expansion of its language.[12]

The work of Menéndez Pidal and his school of thought also involved reaffirming the role of Spanish in the world and the prestige of Spain as the civilization responsible for the linguistic unity of Hispanic America. The Iberian convergence of language and dialects into Castilian was a prelude to the subsequent fusion and harmonization of American dialects of Castilian. The Spanish nation therefore was predestined.

These basic concepts fed all the subsequent Spanish nationalist discourse on the supremacy of the Castilian language in the decades that followed. Nuances were imposed by the strategic need for Spanish Republicans to reach an agreement with Republican Catalanists. Also, between 1900 and 1936, sub-state nationalist movements began actively promoting, strengthening and defending their own languages, which were gradually becoming standardized, particularly in Catalonia. From 1917–18 on, Spanish nationalist opposition to demands for autonomy reinforced the symbolism of the defence of the Spanish language, primarily against Catalanism and later against Galician and Basque nationalism. After 1931, the linguistic rights of the Castilian speakers living in the autonomous bilingual territories were incorporated into the debate.

As the traditional arguments to justify Castilian hegemony became radicalized, the focus of public debate shifted to the introduction of sub-state languages into the educational system. During the 1923–30 dictatorship of General Primo de Rivera, tough and repressive legislation prohibited the use of languages other than Castilian in school (but not, paradoxically, in literature, advertising or the press).[13] Well-known Spanish linguists and intellectuals participated in the heated 1931 parliamentary debates on the new Republican Constitution, as well as the debates surrounding the ratification of the Statutes of Autonomy of Catalonia (1932), the Basque Country (1933) and Galicia (1936), which were approved during the short-lived Second Spanish Republic.[14]

The Castilian Right of Conquest and the Other Languages of Spain (1936–50)

The *New* Spain that emerged in the areas controlled by Franco's rebel army during the Spanish Civil War (1936–39) sought the complete authoritarian renationalization of Spain and eradication of sub-state nationalisms. This included a policy of linguistic uniformity. It is true that the war period gave rise to a variety of different attitudes regarding the political structuring of the new Francoist State. However, the other languages were generally regarded as connotative of folkloric peculiarities and relegated to marginal and subordinate roles. In prior years, Spanish fascism had proclaimed its tolerance (in theory) towards regional languages and cultures, so long as they remained within the sphere of literature on customs and folklore. However, this 'openness' was quickly swept away by the desire to subdue the vanquished.

Public criticism for speaking languages other than Castilian, at least outside the home, was frequent in the insurgent rearguard. The Falangist press and Francoist broadcast stations insisted on the need to speak exclusively in Castilian in the public arena. Some journalists and politicians argued that the Catholic tradition was linked to the vernacular and timidly defended the recognition of regional languages and their reintroduction as an auxiliary language in primary education. This was overpowered by the conviction that linguistic homogenization was a safer bet for the construction of the New Spain. Any official recognition of regional differences might be counterproductive. Spain was hence considered a single nation with a single official language; but one that included several dialects and incomplete languages. In reserving the public sphere exclusively for Castilian, these other vernaculars became diglossic and were condemned to extinction in the mid-range.[15]

The legal framework for enforcing monolingualism tended to be fairly lax and circumstantial, not overly imposing. There were several military edicts expressly prohibiting the use of languages other than Castilian in the public sphere and dispositions banning anything but Castilian for titles, regulations and statutes, but there was no law to establish a general framework for prohibiting the use of minority languages. Linguistic repression was primarily an intertwined network of suspicions, pressures, fear of informants and arbitrary interpretations by agents in authority.

The official creed imposed during the first years of the Franco regime insisted that all other national languages were nothing but dialects and inappropriate for modern use. Vernacular languages could be tolerated in minor literary genres, such as satire, burlesque theatre for popular consumption or folkloric poetry.[16] Clergymen Albino and Ignacio Menéndez-Reigada wrote in 1937 that the Castilian language was the only educated language for Spain, and therefore *the* language of the nation. Yet they noted the existence of the Galician, Valencian, Majorcan and Catalan *dialects*; as well as the Basque language, which was 'unique but limited to the functions of a dialect' due to its 'philological poverty'.[17]

The intensity of daily linguistic repression varied from one region to another, corresponding in part to how threatening to the political unity of Spain the particular vernacular was perceived. In the midst of this, an academic, scholarly, folkloric and ethnographic revival of interest in sub-national languages and dialects emerged, not without a certain propagandistic function.[18] This was manifest in the journal *Revista de Dialectología y Tradiciones Populares*, which was founded in 1944. Research and monographs published by several provincial institutions also helped spark interest, for example, in the Asturian dialect. Some books and brochures on peasants and folklore were published in Galician. By 1949, around twenty books on religious themes had been published in the Basque language. In Catalonia, several children's and religious theatre pieces were performed and select works were re-edited in the vernacular. The various academies of the vernacular languages survived under Francoism in spite of staffing with members loyal to the regime. The message was clear: regional languages could survive in a premodern and prestandardized state, and texts could be published in minor literary genres, folklore and ethnography, but without defining any written standard norm. This was regarded as another way of re-creating the entire range of Spanish traditions, as illustrated by the use of the Valencian variant of Catalan during local festivities, particularly the *Fallas* and the literary contests.[19]

In the late 1940s, the Francoist elites began to 'clean up' the image of the regime in order to gain favour with the Western world. This did not extend to changes in the legal framework; it was deemed sufficient to reduce the intensity of linguistic repression practices. Peripheral languages did not regain any legal status and education remained exclusively in Castilian. And the regime continued to intervene very intensely in controlling *what* was published in sub-state languages through the mid-1960s.

Francoist Spanish Nationalism: The Supremacy of Castilian over the 'Other' Languages (1950–75)

The Franco dictatorship made a radical turn back towards a traditional understanding of Iberian languages and their *natural* hierarchies. The first objective of the Francoist linguistic policy was to place Castilian on the throne of linguistic supremacy, to which it was 'inherently entitled'. Pre-1936 arguments of intrinsic superiority, greater usefulness, a universal dimension, intellectual prestige and association with the soul of Castile and the national spirit of Spain were resurrected to crown Castilian as the only official language. The semantic association between minority languages, rural backwardness and localism was also revived.

Yet a paradox arose during Francoism. On the one hand, there was accelerated cultural assimilation of the allophone peripheries into the Castilian-speaking mainstream of Spain, fostered by compulsory education in Castilian for the entire population The extension of mass media, primarily radio and later television, also contributed to extending its standardized knowledge and use. In addition to this, urban Catalonia, the Basque Provinces, the Balearic Islands and Valencia were strongly affected by internal migration from the rest of Spain, which greatly increased the number of monolingual Castilian speakers.

On the other hand, however, the minority languages did not disappear. From the late 1940s on, clandestine nationalist movements increased initiatives to defend their peripheral languages as the banner of their cause. Each of these languages had its own rhythm of recovery in public spheres. As soon as certain official dispositions were relaxed, new publishing initiatives began in Catalonia. Both the quantity and variety of books published in Catalan increased after the 1950s.[20] The Catholic Church was the main guardian of the Basque language until well into the 1960s. After 1950, a quiet rebirth was evident in the lesser genres of poetry and theatre. In Galicia, publishing in the vernacular was virtually monopolized by *Galaxia,* a publishing house created in 1950 by a group composed of survivors of the prewar nationalist movement. Its impact was qualitatively noteworthy, though quantitatively limited to some segments of the Galician middle class.[21]

Throughout the 1950s and 1960s, the belligerent position of the regime against vernacular languages became more moderated and nuanced. Catalan, Galician and Basque came to be considered as languages that had contributed to the Spanish cultural heritage and enjoyed a certain literary tradition. Though forbidden in public or educational spheres, they were tolerated for literary expression and the limited use they were allowed in festivities and commemorations increased. The regime shifted towards a permissive stance regarding the publication of books in regional languages. Literary censorship served as the filter of what was acceptable to publish or disseminate in minority languages. Until 1958, translations from foreign languages to vernacular languages were generally denied license and the genres of greatest intellectual and literary prestige tended to be those most rigorously censored.

However, exiled Catalanist and Galicianist groups periodically launched initiatives from France or the Americas to denounce the linguistic repression of the Franco regime, which was seeking to improve its standing with international public opinion. Prior to the 1954 UNE-SCO 8th General Conference in Montevideo, there were bitter words in the Argentine press between journalists close to the Franco regime and exiled intellectuals. A Francoist literary critic stated that the dictatorship was not persecuting the Galician language and that it was not officially prohibited. He argued that the triumph of Castilian was simply a case of 'a mental horizon that had broadened in Galicia', where writers now aspired to something more than 'outdated ruminating and nostalgia'. 'Local languages tend to merge into the national language. This is a law of culture.'[22]

The most widely used school handbooks in Francoist Spain clearly minimized the value of regional languages, arguing that they were adequate for literature and intimate communication within a limited scope but not for modern life, science or essay due to their lack of contemporary vocabulary. The exceptional linguistic nature of Basque was recognized as a unique part of the national heritage, but also considered poor for the functions of modern life. However, ambiguity regarding what value to assign the vernacular languages increased as the regime matured. The 1944 handbook *Enciclopedia Práctica* defined a language as 'the special manner of speaking of each country. The language of Spain is Castilian, or Spanish.' No mention was made of the other languages of Spain.[23] In the 1950s, classical arguments of the universality, intrinsic phonetic, grammatical and orthographical perfection of Castilian, along with its rich literary heritage, were recommissioned to bolster its superiority. The existence of other languages and dialects was recognized, but considered historically inferior. The 1957 *Enciclopedia elemental*, published by the Female Section of the *Falange*, stated the following:

> *The Spanish language* is the language of the countries that constitute the *Hispanidad*, that is, our Homeland and the nations that it formed in its civilizing work throughout History.... It is estimated that more than 100 million human beings have the privilege afforded by destiny and race to express themselves in Spanish, the most opulent and beautiful of all modern languages due to its harmonious phonetics, the most rational orthography of all existing languages, the richness and infinite delicate nuances of its vocabulary, its flexibility and elegance....

> The first romance language or language derived from Latin that was spoken in the Peninsula was not Spanish but rather the more archaic Galician-Catalan, which gave rise to both these languages as well as Portuguese. Then ... arose the more mature and perfect Spanish, which was first known as *Castilian*, ... and then, with the Reconquest

[of Spain from the Moors], this language gradually permeated the entire Peninsula until it became the emblematic Spanish language in the imperial sense.... The Basque language is not a romance language, but an aggregate existing from the times of the Iberian [tribes], and has remained intact largely due to its geographic isolation.... Later on, Castilian or Spanish for various reasons formed its own dialects such as Andalusian, Canarian or Extremeño ... along with the Spanish of the Americas and the Philippines.[24]

Nine years after this, a commonly used school handbook escalated the imprecision with a definition that established a political hierarchy between language (spoken by a nation) and dialect (spoken in a region). It then proceeded to confuse matters by referring to Galician, Catalan and Basque as *languages*, in contrast with other dialects:

Language. – Language is the manner of speaking of a people or nation. In Spain we speak Spanish or Castilian; in France, French is spoken....

Dialect. – A dialect refers to the specific manner of writing and speaking the official language of a country in certain regions. Dialects lack a literary tradition.... In Spain dialects include *Bable* or Asturian, *Extremeño* and *Andalusian*. In contrast, Catalan, Galician and Basque are categorized as languages and Valencian is a dialectical variant of Catalan.[25]

In addition to this, the democratic opposition movement began to equate democracy with political decentralization and the delegitimization of Spanish national discourse and symbolism; which increased the osmosis between the cultural, linguistic and even political tenets of the peripheral nationalists and the Spanish national left wing. The demand for full co-official status for the regional languages became the banner that was symbolically waved by many who opposed Francoism. This foreshadowed a change in attitude among many Spanish democratic nationalists, in which the vernacular languages came to be seen as part of the heritage and richness of Spain. They were neither subordinate nor hierarchically inferior. However, most left-wing parties did not embrace the equality or symmetry of all the other languages of Spain, except in Catalonia. Castilian was still pragmatically assumed to be the language of common communication, though it was no longer symbolically exalted as such.

With the 1970 General Law on Education, history textbooks moderated and covered over the most generic, organic, historicist and idealist features of classical Spanish nationalism. However, the stereotypes and values that associated language with national character or collective psychology lingered on in Spanish literature and language textbooks, most of which were produced by disciples of Menéndez Pidal, such as Rafael Lapesa and Fernando Lázaro Carreter. Thus their decisive influence on banal perceptions regarding the coexistence of several languages in Spain endured. Even after 1975, when Francoism died with its dictator, statements in textbooks still claimed that 'Castile, restless and ambitious in politics, revolutionary in law, heroic in its epic achievements, was linguistically the most innovative region. Just as its prodigious vitality destined it to be the axis of national enterprises, its dialect would become the language of the entire Hispanic community'; Castilian was the reflection of the 'particular temperament of a country'.[26]

Language and Spanish Nationalism since 1975

The monopolization of Spanish nationalist discourse by Francoism and the anti-democratic Right influenced the entire spectrum of Spanish nationalists or 'patriots', particularly during the final years of Francoism and the transition to democracy. Any explicit affirmation of Spanish patriotism was automatically delegitimized and identified with old-school National-Catholic tenets. This was particularly noticeable in liberal and left-wing circles as well as in the awkwardness that most democratic parties experienced concerning public use of the word _Spain_. Until the mid-1990s, the social and organizational expression of Spanish nationalism was disjointed at best; but it quietly survived in both the right and left wings of the political spectrum. Its broad internal diversity is characteristic of all nationalist ideologies, with a mix of civic tenets and ethnocultural elements.[27] All manner of political and social actors with their multifarious worldviews and ideological programs can be found rallying round the flag of Spain as the sole and sovereign entity with collective political rights.

With the new territorial framework set forth in the 1978 Constitution, Spanish nationalist discourse had to be reinvented. Explicit Spanish nationalism disappeared from the statements of most political parties and leaders, with the exception of the Far Right and post-Francoist conservatives. Defence of the territorial integrity of the Spanish nation by left-wing leaders was never defined as nationalism but rather 'patriotism' or 'loyalty to the Constitution' of 1978. Not until the mid-1990s did conservatives begin to wave the banner of explicit Spanish patriotism, which was sometimes equated with 'good nationalism'.

Spanish patriotic discourse has been present in the public sphere since the 1990s, particularly through mass media, books and pamphlets. The rearticulation of Spanish nationalism springs from confrontations with stateless nationalisms and is primarily concerned with supporting Spain as a nation. This is the fruit of a slow process in which the main ideological currents within Spanish patriotic discourse have adapted to the new circumstances of democratic Spain. It includes three elements.

First, adaptation to the new political/institutional framework established by the 1978 Constitution and the State of the Autonomous Communities. Renewed Spanish nationalist discourse had to recognize the institutional plurality that had resulted from the pressure of the stateless nationalisms, while also adjusting to political decentralization.

Second, the reinvention of a new political and historical legitimacy that side-steps the legacy of Francoism to make a fresh start at the most basic symbolic level. The need to 'forget' the Civil War and the Franco regime in order to coexist with the main actors of the democratic transition made it difficult for many Spanish democratic nationalists to unite around common issues; but one of which was most definitely the defence of the Spanish language.

Third, reaction to ongoing challenges by sub-state nationalisms. The continual demands of the latter for increased self-government reaffirm political goals that clearly exceed the boundaries of the 1978 Constitution. Certain persistent ethnocentric tenets in the discourse and praxis of minority nationalisms, along with the terrorist violence that continued throughout the first decade of the twenty-first century have encouraged the resurgence of Spanish patriotic discourse as an ongoing reaction to stateless nationalisms, particularly Basque nationalism.

Spanish nationalism has also had to adapt to the new legal framework that regulates the linguistic question. However, while this legislation recognizes the full co-official status of the regional languages in their respective territories, it also houses a clear legal asymmetry: every Spanish citizen has the duty to know Castilian, but only the right to use and know the sub-state languages. The statutes of several Autonomous Communities tend to symbolically reinforce the vernacular as *the* language of the area, which has facilitated a variety of positive discrimination measures in an effort to give the vernacular clear symbolic primacy. Linguistic quotas for primary and secondary education were not established by the central state; they were instead left to be regulated by the Autonomous Communities. Each of the bilingual autonomous communities has developed its own linguistic policies. The results have also been quite diverse but can be summarized as a notable increase in the vernacular linguistic competence of the population along with increased public presence and symbolic dominance of the minority languages in several fields. However, social use of vernacular languages has not advanced as notably vis-à-vis Castilian as it was expected.

The linguistic question has become one of the most effective symbolic arguments of Spanish nationalism, since its use by the Far Right and a portion of the post-Francoist right wing as a topic of opposition to the 1978 Constitution. It was present in the reticence of the conservative Popular Alliance to full bilingualism in the Autonomous Communities and the use of the term *nationality* throughout much of the 1980s. However, in some places the conservative right adopted until the beginning of twenty-first century a neo-regionalist discourse and practice that actually incorporated a number of sub-state nationalist demands regarding language, particularly in Galicia and the Balearic Islands. However, the patriotic discourse of the Spanish right wing in the Basque Country and Catalonia has criticized the objectives and methods of the linguistic policies implemented by the autonomic governments. During the 1980s and 1990s, some spokespersons insisted on the discriminatory nature of these linguistic and cultural normalization policies, denouncing the purported persecution of Castilian as a first step in the Balkanization of the Spanish nation. The frequency, intensity and aggressiveness of this issue in the Spanish press increased most notably after 1993–94. Sub-state nationalisms were portrayed as tending towards intrinsically totalitarian positions by emphasizing collective rights and seeking to impose a monolithic culture on citizens. Some journalists and right-wing leaders spoke against the linguistic policies of Catalonia's autonomous government in the 1980s.[28] Fairly similar reactions have occurred in Galicia, particularly within fringe groups since the beginning of the twenty-first century.[29]

Although sub-state languages are no longer reduced to dialects, in Spanish conservative nationalism there is still the idea that Castilian is intrinsically superior. While it is no longer based on historicist arguments, the discourse of Spanish neo-patriotism centers around: (a) the greater diffusion and universality of Castilian and; (b) thus its greater usefulness; (c) the de facto universal knowledge of Castilian by the Spanish population, accompanied by the imbedded notion of it being the natural language of all Spaniards; and (d) the defence of the linguistic rights of Castilian speakers in bilingual territories, giving priority to individual rights over collective ones and the freedom of choice of language in administration and education for all citizens. This provides Spanish neo-patriotism with a coating of democratic legitimacy vis-à-vis the sub-state nationalisms.

Spanish conservative thinking has also resurrected the old triumphalist argument regarding the invented and artificial nature of the standardized linguistic norms of the minority languages; an argument that has always been leveled against the unified norm of Basque (*euskara batua*), and has begun to affect Galician as well.[30] The new frame of meaning that is being subliminally distilled in these two regions considers the 'modern' (middle class, professional, urban) speaker of minority languages as a peripheral nationalist but not a traditional (rural, working class) and natural speaker of the vernacular. Such individuals are seen as conscious deserters of the Castilian language, possibly because they hope to advance in the regional public administration and education system. The defence of minority languages 'overburdens' identity politics and thus the speakers should be left to choose their language of expression. Again we encounter resistance to positive discrimination in favor of minority languages, mainly from the right though occasionally from the left, as classic liberal arguments are combined with other unscientific rationales such as the supposed incompatibility of simultaneously learning minority languages as opposed and more *useful* foreign languages.

Much of Spanish nationalist or patriotic discourse still venerates Castilian as the defining Spanish national and cultural identity marker and even the greatest contribution of Spain to universal culture, especially through its rich literary legacy.[31] The traditional role of language comes packaged with a sense of economic utility in an era of globalization,[32] a tool for economic and commercial progress thanks especially to the fact that Spanish has become the de facto second language in the United States. This overrides the traditional reticence towards 'Spanglish', which had been considered an unacceptable deformation of the language, and has had an additional meaning in terms of domestic Spanish politics. In a July 2003 speech in New Mexico, José María Aznar, the conservative president of the Spanish government, described North American Hispanics as people with multiple identities, in contrast with 'societies that exclude' and use languages as weapons.[33]

Though the discourse on the linguistic question deployed by Spanish democratic nationalism generically recognizes and condemns the repression of minority languages by the Franco regime and the Spanish nation-state in prior periods, there is an underlying conviction that loss of the minority languages was the necessary sacrifice for modernity; therefore it is not necessary for the speakers of the majority language to continue expressing remorse. The vice president of the

Royal Academy of the Spanish Language, Gregorio Salvador, created no small polemic in May 2007 when he stated that the linguistic imposition of Castilian by the Francoist State was wrong yet forgivable, since it resulted in all Spaniards learning and becoming proficient in a universal language. However, the inverse process of imposing minority languages, which are thought useless for relating to a larger world, would be seen as much less forgivable from a normative perspective.[34] A similar argument was proposed in response to the accusations of cultural genocide that are periodically expressed by some Latin American leaders: Castilian was not imposed on the Americas by right of conquest, but as a consequence of its natural superiority and as a vehicle for communication between peoples.

Since 2005, conservative nationalism has renewed its offensive. Bilingualism is accepted only within certain limits, accompanied by express symbolic recognition of the dominance of Castilian. However, there is still room for pragmatic nuancing of discourse and positions by conservatives, especially when addressing the Catalan and Galician electorates. Some of these tenets have also mobilized part of the Left. The centre-left party Unión Progreso y Democracia (UPyD) managed for some years to find a niche within the political space between the most secular-liberal segments of the conservative electorate and the disenchanted left-wing voters who are tired of the pseudo-confederate tendencies of the State of the Autonomies. Thus, this party has unabashedly fed the polemics regarding the policies of linguistic normalization in the bilingual regions, defending the rights of Castilian speakers who are discriminated against when choosing a language in the spheres of education or citizen interaction with public administrations. This question was especially prominent in the foundational manifesto of UPyD: 'A State under the Rule of Law needs a common language, and its use is not only a matter of personal choice but also and especially a political instrument for the linguistic structuring of the democracy itself. All the languages of our nation are respectable and worthy of support, but Castilian is also essential as a vehicle for understanding one another and debating questions.'[35] A common language thus becomes a necessary instrument for articulating the large spheres of democratic deliberation and socioeconomic solidarity and cohesion. To possess and privilege a common language therefore becomes a progressive demand to the extent that it is thought to be linked to equal rights for all citizens inhabiting the Spanish State.

The Spanish left wing has oscillated between a conception of Spain as a nation of nations, which is a specific reading of the concept of constitutional patriotism, and the idea of a 'plural Spain' proposed early in the millennium by President José Luis Rodríguez-Zapatero. Within this idea, the multicultural nature of Spain as a nation that is a sum of cultures, languages and diverse yet complementary identities has been reaffirmed. These matters are felt differently in Catalonia, Galicia and the Basque Country than in the rest of Spain. In linguistic matters, the left wing in Spain has generally followed the principles of the constitution, with very diverse local and regional expressions: from adamantly Castilianist mayors to leaders thoroughly identified with linguistic normalization for peripheral languages. Rodríguez-Zapatero's central idea appeared in the 2002–3 manifestos projecting Spain as 'a plural and integrating Nation, proud of its diversity and its linguistic and cultural pluralism'.[36] He described Spain as a nation, not a pluri-national state; but it was a multicultural nation based on civic values and democratic deliberation, including diverse languages, capable of hosting multiple versions of collective identities with variable intensity and a legacy of shared historic and cultural roots. Belief in the existence of these roots and the need to bring them to the forefront became patent in the initiatives of the first Rodríguez-Zapatero government (2004–8), which included celebrating the 400th anniversary of the publication of *Don Quixote* in 2005 and promoting the international efforts of the Cervantes Institute (Instituto Cervantes), founded in 1991, to establish a commemorative day for the Spanish language. The date of 23 April was suggested for the Commemorative Day for the Spanish Language to honor the death of Cervantes, rather than 12 October, or the Day of *Hispanidad*. More recently, 18 June was proposed as 'E Day' (*Español* Day) in several cities; commemorative acts have taken place between 2009 and 2011 on that day and a Castilian word is voted by internet.

The greatest value and essential richness of the identity of Spain would reside precisely in the internal plurality of cultures and languages as expressed in the Declaration of Santillana del Mar, signed by the territorial leaders of the Socialist Party in August 2003. Their definition of Spain as a 'shared project of coexistence' echoed words expressed long ago by Ernest Renan and José Ortega y Gasset. It was essentially a more radical reading of the concept of constitutional patriotism and the idea of a *nation of nations,* combined with an anti-centralist view of the history of Spain and manifest in a symbolic policy of recognition of linguistic diversity with no debate on the constitutional status of languages. The motto was reframed in April 2008, when in his inaugural speech before the Spanish Parliament, President Rodríguez-Zapatero described Spain as a 'united and diverse' nation that 'distills its richness from its diversity.... A country united by its past but especially by its future.'[37] Though this discourse appeared to integrate vernacular languages symmetrically and without hierarchy, only one language was supposed to have universal projection and symbolize the role and contribution of Spain to world culture. In fact, some socialist intellectuals and leaders openly rejected the plural Spain formula for lacking a precise statement of elements common to all Spaniards. Thus, the jurist Luis Fajardo stated in 2009 that the State of the Autonomies needed functional reform in order to complete its development while retaining the 'representation of what is common' – in other words, the Spanish Nation, one of whose most prominent elements is 'the common language'.[38]

Conclusion

In the final years of the Franco regime, Spanish nationalism began to rather visibly incorporate an acceptance of internal ethnocultural diversity, with variable tolerance towards the co-official nature of the peripheral languages. However, problems arose when absolute symmetry of rights and duties among the various languages of Spain was postulated. Although plurality was recognized in the concept of the Spanish nation that democratic Spanish nationalism has integrated more or less ambitiously since the transition to democracy, the actual limits of that recognition in the linguistic sphere were imprecise and ambiguous. It has had to adjust to the central role of linguistic demands in the sub-state nationalisms, whose maximum objective was no longer co-official status but the full social normalization or even (in some cases) official exclusivity of their languages in their territories, on the legitimizing basis of having been persecuted under Francoism. The enduring reluctance of sub-state nationalisms towards accepting Castilian as a sociolinguistic reality in their territories, where it is in most cases the native tongue of the majority of citizens, and as part of their own cultural legacy as a language that was not only seen as something foreign or imposed in the past, constantly interacted with the Spanish nationalist tendency to not consider the vernacular languages as having full and equal rights and duties.

Does democratic Spanish nationalism today cherish and symbolically integrate the vernacular languages, embracing them as part of the Spanish cultural heritage? It does not, or at least not yet. It coexists with them because it must, to maintain the integrity of the Nation. This position reflects some of the nostalgia expressed by Manuel Azaña, the president of the Spanish Second Republic, who wished for a homogenizing past like that of France, which might have simplified the governance of Spain. To him, the monarchy and the nineteenth-century liberal state had not finished their work in this area, leaving no alternative but to pragmatically cope with ethnolinguistic diversity.[39] Such reticence is also symbolically influenced by the fact that the non-Castilian languages in their current social configuration largely involve processes of standardization and policies of social normalization that have been mostly fostered by sub-state nationalist movements. This explains the persistent differences in the value assigned by Spanish nationalists to 'our' *regional* languages: as Castilianized and more or less rural dialects, they would express diversity within unity, rather than the elaborate 'inventions' of sub-state nationalists.

Notes

1. An exception in Mar-Molinero (1996).
2. See Sepúlveda (2005: 210–16), as well as several contributions in Del Valle (2013).
3. Cánovas del Castillo (1997: 70–73).
4. See Alvarez Junco (2011).
5. See Ferrer i Gironés (1985: 82–90).
6. See the report reproduced in *Estudios Gallegos*, 18 (1916).
7. See Moreno-Luzón (2006).
8. See Altamira (1998: 79–80; 1900: 28–29).
9. See Zabaltza (2003: 249–51).
10. See García Isasti (2004).
11. Menéndez Pidal (1941: 2).
12. Menéndez Pidal (1971: 144–52).
13. See Quiroga (2008: 239–58).
14. See Monteagudo (2013).
15. Núñez Seixas (2006: 306–20).
16. See Massot i Muntaner (1996: 429–33).
17. See Menéndez Reigada (2003: 39–41).
18. Extensively on this aspect, see Núñez Seixas (2014).
19. See de Pablo (2007); Freitas (2008); Gallofré (1991) and Ballester (1992).
20. See Crexell (1998: 35–47).
21. See Tejerina (1992: 119–21); Sarasola (1976); Núñez Seixas (1994).
22. B. Mostaza, 'El gallego no es un idioma prohibido', *Criterio*, Buenos Aires, 12 August 1954.
23. Fernández (1948: 112).
24. *Enciclopedia Elemental* (Madrid: Sección Femenina, 1957), pp. 176–78.
25. Álvarez Pérez (1966: 89).
26. López Facal (2000).
27. See Balfour and Quiroga (2007); Núñez Seixas (2001, 2010).
28. See Jiménez Losantos (1995); Vidal-Quadras (1993).
29. See Jardón (1993).

30. See e.g. Freire (2009).
31. See Salvador (1999); Lodares (1999, 2002); López García (1985, 2006); Bueno (1996, 2005).
32. Del Valle and Gabriel-Steehman (2004).
33. *El País,* 12 July 2003.
34. See *El País,* 11 May 2007.
35. See the founding manifesto of UPyD, http://www.upyd.es/servlets/VerFic hero?id=11223 (last accessed June 15, 2015).
36. See PSOE, *Manifiesto socialista para la España autonómica del siglo XXI,* 14 April 2003.
37. See http://www.abc.es/gestordocumental/uploads/nacional/discurso-inves tidura-zapatero.pdf.
38. Fajardo Spínola (2009: 217–18).
39. Azaña (1990: 511–13).

Chapter 8

The Americas and
the Celebration of 12 October

Marcela García Sebastiani and David Marcilhacy

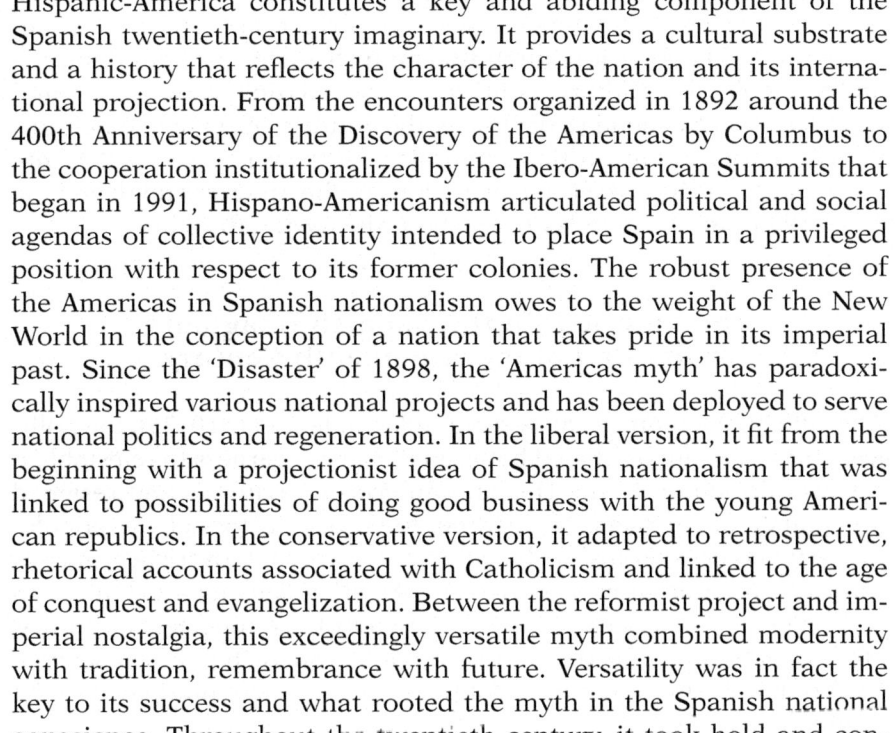

Hispanic-America constitutes a key and abiding component of the Spanish twentieth-century imaginary. It provides a cultural substrate and a history that reflects the character of the nation and its international projection. From the encounters organized in 1892 around the 400th Anniversary of the Discovery of the Americas by Columbus to the cooperation institutionalized by the Ibero-American Summits that began in 1991, Hispano-Americanism articulated political and social agendas of collective identity intended to place Spain in a privileged position with respect to its former colonies. The robust presence of the Americas in Spanish nationalism owes to the weight of the New World in the conception of a nation that takes pride in its imperial past. Since the 'Disaster' of 1898, the 'Americas myth' has paradoxically inspired various national projects and has been deployed to serve national politics and regeneration. In the liberal version, it fit from the beginning with a projectionist idea of Spanish nationalism that was linked to possibilities of doing good business with the young American republics. In the conservative version, it adapted to retrospective, rhetorical accounts associated with Catholicism and linked to the age of conquest and evangelization. Between the reformist project and imperial nostalgia, this exceedingly versatile myth combined modernity with tradition, remembrance with future. Versatility was in fact the key to its success and what rooted the myth in the Spanish national conscience. Throughout the twentieth century, it took hold and constructed an imagined pan-Hispanic, transatlantic community based on cultural affinity. Condensing both memory and project, the Americas myth served the power structure and international appraisal of it, forming part of every twentieth-century Spanish diplomatic offensive, including the democratization process and integration into Europe.

Without a doubt, the National Holiday of 12 October provides the most crystalline manifestation of the Americas myth and its rooting within the Spanish national imaginary. Though the commemoration has undergone several transformations since its establishment in 1918, it has endured on the holiday calendar throughout the twentieth century until the present day. What began as the *Día de la Raza*, or Day of the (Hispanic) Race, later became the Day of *Hispanidad*, and finally, from 1987, a national holiday. The day commemorated the empire as the foundation stone of the nation. With multiple historical and cultural references, 12 October was adapted by a diverse set of regimes, and moulded to suit changing territorial and national contexts. The celebration of the very existence of Spaniards was imbued with different meanings, in which America became the integrating component of national unity. The day fostered the development of Hispano-Americanism, and portrayed successes in foreign policy as confirmation of collective Spanish identity. The Americas myth was an instrument for both domestic and foreign policy. Culture, politics, power and diplomacy swirled and mixed around the holiday, deploying the entire propaganda apparatus, with its actors and institutions, in projecting the very essence of Spain. This chapter reviews the transformations of the Americas myth and the 12 October national holiday throughout the twentieth century.

The Americas in the Spanish Imaginary at the End of the Nineteenth Century

After the Spanish American wars of independence (1810–25), the political elites in Spain oscillated between illusory eagerness to re-establish Spanish dominion in the Hispano-American territories and resigned acceptance of the facts. Meanwhile, for broad sectors of the population – whether veterans of the colonial wars or impoverished masses drawn to the migratory experience – America became a key piece in the collective imaginary. Towards the end of the nineteenth century, affairs in the Americas rose to the top of the Spanish political agenda. Lack of reform in the colonial politics of the Antilles culminated in the dramatic defeat of 1898.

Paradoxically, with the collapse of the overseas empire America, emerged as an essential component of the Spanish identity and the seedbed of a propagandist nationalist offensive. The Bourbon Restoration period offered an opportunity to consolidate a new sociopolitical

order based on conservative-tinted liberalism of a persistently oligar-
chic nature. Regime elites recurred to history to construct a legitimizing national narrative, with the past in the Americas as a central
element. This inspired the commemorative fever that began in 1892
with the 400th Anniversary of the Discovery of the Americas. With support from top authorities and across the political spectrum, the Columbus Day Anniversary was organized by the recently created Unión
Ibero-Americana (Ibero-American Union, UIA), the primary agency
for promoting Hispano-Americanism, in collaboration with the Real
Academia de la Historia (Royal Academy of History, RAH). The cream
of the Spanish Restoration gathered for the celebrations in Madrid and
Huelva, alongside ample delegations from all over Latin America. In
addition to historical lectures, inaugurations of monuments and other
commemorative acts, the Regent María Cristina signed a decree in
1892 establishing 12 October as a national holiday: the anniversary of
the discovery of the 'New World'.[1] For the first time, institutional backing was provided for the idea of making this date an annual commemoration for all of Spain, Portugal and Ibero-America. The festivities
centred on the great achievements of Columbus and his distinguished
travelling companions, emphatically exalting a glorious, common past
and the unbreakable bonds that united the Iberian lion with its cubs in
the Americas. Beyond the rhetoric, the anniversary helped to promote
intellectual exchanges on both shores and favoured better mutual understanding – a precondition for reconciliation and overcoming accu-
mulated mistrust.

The Cuban uprising of 1895 and the subsequent intervention of the
United States in the conflict brought the Spanish overseas empire to
an end in 1898. The humiliating Treaty of Paris stripped Spain of its
American possessions in Cuba, Puerto Rico, the Philippines and other
Pacific islands. The defeat seemed to confirm the views of decaden-
tism, which was flourishing in fin-de-siècle Spain. Influenced by social
Darwinism, this current contemplated a supposed Anglo-Saxon supe-
riority and an irremediable Latin decline, especially in the Americas.[2]
Declarations such as that of British Premier Lord Salisbury regarding
Finis Hispaniae fed the prevalent pessimism and resignation in the face
of the unavoidable Hispanic retreat in the West.

While the authorities remained undecided and divided regarding the
colonial question, Spanish Americanist circles emerged with a vocation to strengthen transatlantic cooperation, especially in cultural and
academic spheres. Groups and publications sprang up in peripheral
parts of Spain as well as in Madrid, dedicated to creating favourable
public opinion and revitalizing Hispano-American relations. Examples

include the Sociedad Colombina (Columbus Society) of Huelva in 1880 or the already-mentioned UIA, which had been founded in Madrid in 1885 by a group of writers, diplomats and politicians. These initiatives peaked with the 'cultural embassy' of the historian Rafael Altamira, who visited seven American republics in 1910–11 in order to establish solid academic exchanges, study grants and Americanist teaching chairs.

Hispano-Americanism and Power in the First Third of the Twentieth Century

During the decade that opened in 1910, the Americanist campaign intensified and expanded its sphere of action. The peripheral elites created new associations – such as the Casa de America (America's House) in Barcelona – that were keen to revitalize Spanish commerce and modernize the sociopolitical structures of the monarchy. Along with plans to promote transatlantic business, proposals proliferated to reinforce the cultural and diplomatic presence of Spain in the Americas, disseminate the Spanish language and literature or channel the waves of immigrants that were crossing the Atlantic. Little by little, the heterodox regenerationist current outlined an Americanist action programme of national interest, which its ardent promoters submitted to the governing political parties.[3]

The young King Alfonso XIII quickly expressed his sympathies with Hispano-Americanism. The monarch and his elites were anxious to recover a bit of prestige for a rather tarnished monarchy beleaguered with concerns over worker protests, the rise of disintegrating tendencies among peripheral nationalisms and growing military insubordination. They opted to combat internal political tensions by insufflating patriotic ideals and extolling the modern history of the nation alongside the glories of its imperial past. Americanism was seized upon as an ideal antidote for the blundering colonial campaign that had been going on in Morocco since 1909. It would restore the lustre of the ancient Hispanic monarchy and distract public opinion from the more pressing issues of the day.

In this way, an Americanist myth established itself in the national imaginary, constructed from emigrant stories, bilateral cooperation projects and a politics of memory manifest in monuments, anniversaries and other expressions. The myth combined two currents: the projectionist and practical approach of liberal regenerationism and a conservative, retrospective project associated with the imperial past. This second, nostalgic dimension asserted the legacy and weight of

Catholicism, which explained the widespread intellectual and political admiration for the conquest and evangelization of the Indies. It also fed the conservative ideology of future authoritarian regimes.

The nationalist campaign celebrated anniversaries to counteract the much reviled, anti-Spanish black legend and reinterpret national history to the tune of rehabilitating the imperial legacy. Commemorative fever channelled Hispano-Americanism and subordinated its development to serve domestic politics. During the first three decades of the century, several 400th anniversaries were recorded in association with the heroic conquest of the Americas. In 1914, the RAH and the Real Sociedad Geográfica (Royal Geographical Society) celebrated the 400th anniversary of the discovery of the Pacific Ocean by Vasco Núñez de Balboa as a glorious milestone in Spanish maritime exploration. Similarly, the 400th anniversary of the first circumnavigation of the earth, by Ferdinand Magellan and Juan Sebastián Elcano, was celebrated from 1919 to 1922. For the occasion, the king placed the first stone of an allegorical monument in Elcano's hometown of Getaria (Guipúzcoa), to commemorate the great feats accomplished through the 'genius' of the 'Spanish race'.

Such anniversaries not only remembered and exalted the illustrious chapters of Spanish colonization, they also permitted a revised interpretation of the painful episodes of the Spanish American independence movements as the natural emancipation of children who had reached adulthood. With glittering diplomacy, the Spanish monarchy associated itself with independence centenaries in the Americas. This began in 1910 with the popular Princess Infanta Isabel's trip to Argentina, followed by the visit of the Marquis of Polavieja to Mexico.

Of all the manifestations of pride for the Spanish work in the Americas, 12 October stood pre-eminent and was eventually established as the national holiday. Since the Revolution of 1808–14, those partial to liberalism had fought to consolidate a new regime by constructing national narratives capable of articulating the community, presenting a common past and offering a project for the future. Throughout much of the nineteenth century, the Spanish Anti-Napoleonic War was considered a founding event, with its highest symbolic expression in the popular uprising of the Second of May. Converted into a liberal patriotic myth, it was celebrated every year as a national holiday until its centenary in 1908. However, during the Democratic Sexennium (1868–74) – the turbulent six-year period of democratic experimentation that preceded the Bourbon Restoration – the anniversary became a source of division and entered a time of crisis. Subsequently, the Restoration elites looked for a patriotic commemoration day that was synonymous with national regeneration and capable of inspiring the popular masses, but with an ideological background that did not question the bases of the political regime.

With its regenerationist associations, 12 October convinced progressives and conservatives alike. It also connected with emigrant colonies across the ocean who claimed Spanish parentage. The date presented several advantages: it appealed to the most illustrious aspect of Spain's past – the discovery of the New World – while providing a religious backdrop by coinciding with the Feast of the Virgin of Pilar in Zaragoza. Thus, two essential ingredients of Spanish nationalism were bound together in a single symbolic bundle: the patriotic cult to conquering through *Plus Ultra* Spain and the Catholic cult to missionary Spain with its universal destiny.

Between 1912 and 1929, all the Hispano-American republics established 12 October as a holiday, a symbol of peace and brotherhood with the former colonizer, Spain. In 1917, when both nations coincided in their position of neutrality during the First World War, Argentine President Hipólito Yrigoyen instituted 12 October 'in honour of Spain, the progenitor of nations'. King Alfonso XIII himself reciprocated by supporting the holiday, and the following year the national unity government presided by Antonio Maura officially adopted 12 October as a new national holiday, baptizing it the *Fiesta de la Raza* (the Day of the Race), in reference to the 'racial' community of Spanish-speaking peoples.[4] Confronted with severe institutional crisis, Maura found in this new patriotic national ritual the ideal means for nationalizing the masses and giving structure to a deeply divided national community.

From that time on, the 12 October celebration extended throughout the Spanish territory and became a patriotic rite that served the power structure. Once institutionalized, the symbol escaped the control of the reformist sectors and private interest groups that had originally promoted it. Organization of the acts now corresponded to the political, ecclesiastical and military authorities. Accordingly, the ceremonies became pompous, protocolistic stages for a univocal, discriminatory reading of the symbol. Progressively, the content of the 12 October holiday shifted away from the celebration of peace and solidarity oriented towards a modern, pan-Hispanic ideal based on commerce and culture. Instead, it came to represent a family of chauvinistic peoples intent on preserving the values of the past.

During the dictatorship of Miguel Primo de Rivera, the Day of the Race reached its full propagandistic strength in domestic as well as foreign politics. The 'Iron Surgeon' assumed power in 1923 to resolve the political and social crisis generated by the rupture between the political elites who were weakened by internal strife and broad sectors of the population that were seduced by contentious discourse from socialism, anarcho-syndicalism and Catalan or Basque nationalisms. With the consent of Alfonso XIII, the general sought to revitalize the country by re-establishing domestic order and reaffirming Spain's international vocation.

As the military fiasco in the protectorate of Morocco was exposed with the Disaster of Annual in 1921, Hispanic America appeared as an alternative horizon for frustrated Spanish attempts at projection. Along with more decisive military action in Morocco, the dictatorship relaunched Spanish foreign involvement towards the Americas. When the Ministry of State was reorganized in 1926, it promoted the 'Americas area' through specific budgets and agencies such as the Junta de Relaciones Culturales (Cultural Relations Council). Parallel to this, the authorities took advantage of the possibilities that the Americanist project offered for domestic consumption. The same year, military officials completed an unprecedented transatlantic flight between the Andalusian port of Palos and Buenos Aires aboard the hydroplane *Plus Ultra*. That extraordinary aeronautic feat – piloted by Commander Ramón Franco, brother of the future dictator – created a popular fervour that the press on both shores celebrated as a modern rendition of the explorations of years past. The aerial resurrection of Columbus's achievements fuelled the nostalgic cult to the intrepid Spain of the fifteenth century and the splendour of a lost Hispanic empire. As apologetics and reinterpretations of colonial history flourished, the 12 October celebrations were fully integrated in the campaign to recover Spanish pride. From 1923 on, the Day of the Race represented a privileged space in which the dictatorship could embed in the national conscience the values it embodied: order, hierarchy, militarism, unity and patriotism.

With the ritual established, those in power staged their own vision of the national body and the Hispanic community. Besides opening with a solemn mass and closing with a military parade, the ceremonies usually included a showy civic procession down major avenues and past power centres and symbolic monuments (such as those dedicated to Columbus in Madrid, Barcelona, Salamanca, Valladolid, etc.). As a space for patriotic socialization and nationalization of the masses, ample delegations of school children starred in the civic parade, wearing the red and yellow flag. Diverse civic associations and institutions

– their steps marked by the bands that lined the route – also paraded with their respective banners, waving to the authorities, dignitaries and diplomats gathered on the official grandstand. These highly formal, ostentatious and ceremonial acts lacked the popular fervour that characterized the Aragonese feasts of the Virgin of Pilar on the same day.

As a Hispano-American 'family' holiday, 12 October also served to reinforce Hispanic solidarity through the deployment of bronze and marble diplomacy: with inaugurations of streets, plaques or monuments to commemorate the former empire. The relevant speeches consecrated a nostalgic, conservative reading of the relations that should prevail in a Hispanic 'family', casting Spain as an elderly mother surrounded by her grateful daughters. Incongruity with the reality of the Americas could not have been greater; numerous Hispano-American intellectuals and leaders maintained a prudent distance from the mother country. When they did lay claim to their Iberian heritage, it was expressly to distinguish them from their North American neighbour.

Strong propagandistic use of 12 October by the Primo de Rivera dictatorship idealized the content and form of the holiday, awakening criticism and dissent in social groups not aligned with the regime. In Catalonia as well as in republican or socialist circles, a degree of disregard for the celebration could be observed in the 1920s. Some intellectuals declared it openly, such as exiled philosopher Miguel de Unamuno, who repeatedly denounced the racist, intolerant and conservative hijacking of the holiday. Far from uniting the dispersed members of the national (Spanish) and linguistic (pan-Hispanic) community, 12 October became a patriotic-military festival that served the dictatorial regime and brought the divisions that encumbered adherence to the symbol into sharp relief.

The Ibero-American Exposition in Seville (1929–30) constituted a paradoxical success in a context of growing social tension in the waning years of the dictatorship. It represented the apex of Americanism as a pillar of the national narrative – filled with nostalgia, pride and projection into the future – that had been crafted by politically diverse governments and elites in Spain since the loss of its overseas empire. In the midst of a world crisis and a dictatorship without support, this clearly historicist, conservative and paternalistic exposition could not carry off the anticipated double role. It failed to unite the masses in a single cult combining the 'Great Spain' of the sixteenth century with the contemporary Spain envisioned by the post-regenerationist ruling classes, and was unsuccessful in sealing the desired and rather chimerical political union of Hispanic nations.

From Hispano-Americanism to *Hispanidad*: The Republic and Civil War

During the Second Republic (1931–36), the Americanist myth fed ambitious plans for foreign politics, but eventually shipwrecked among the different interpretations of *españolismo* – what it means to be Spanish – that erupted with the Civil War and affected the observance of 12 October. The Americanism of the first republican governments connected with the early twentieth-century liberal version and was then updated to invent a modern national identity based on culture. Americanist policy drove state projects for scientific exchange and others for the wider public, which were cut short by political ups and downs. For its part, conservative nationalism revived the Spanish imaginary with Ramiro de Maetzu's ideas regarding *Hispanidad*, which associated America with Spanish ingenuity, Catholicism and imperial nostalgia. The idea was not new, but in those years it managed to articulate universal values that sank deep into the political right and would later find their place in Francoism.

The Day of the Race survived on the holiday calendar of the new regime and responded to the enthusiasm that accompanied the political change. The commemoration was adorned with the new official symbols of the republic (the tricolour flag and the *Himno de Riego* anthem), but did not break with the traditional rites that civic observance had acquired during the Primo de Rivera dictatorship. To reinforce the new republican myths, Americanism was at the centre of all symbolic disputes concerned with renovating the nationalist project. The Americas myth starred in the republican anniversaries of 14 April, stirring up in the public feelings of national unity and codifying the festivities with universal messages. In harmony with liberal secular nationalism, eulogies abounded for Spain's expansion in the world and the civilizing nature of the Spanish language. Meanwhile, conservative republicanism opted for military parades and solemn literary, diplomatic and religious acts to reconstruct the idea of *Hispanidad* and counteract the vague Hispanic-American internationalism of the radical republicans.

During the Spanish Civil War, 12 October continued to be celebrated as the Day of the Race in both loyalist-controlled and rebel territories, becoming an object of propagandistic dispute between the two. Each side used the commemoration to reaffirm itself in its representation of the national past and future as well as to mobilize wills against the enemy, even on the other side of the Atlantic. Both sides made use of the holiday to gain the support of the American republics and the Spaniards residing there. In the Republican zone, the holiday was reinterpreted with epic popular and libertarian overtones and the Americanist ritual rallied the people to resist the invader. It was stripped of all Catholic rhetoric and sweetened with the personified feats of Columbus and of the Catholic Monarchs Isabel and Ferdinand, who were equally exalted by the other side. Conquest and colonization were portrayed as the great heroic epic of anonymous Spaniards. In some places, parallels were contrived between the struggle against the rebels and the wars of Spanish American independence. Great feats in favour of liberty served as a connecting point between Spain and Ibero-America; the Americanism symbolized in the Day of the Race also served as propaganda for a republic abandoned by European democracies.

The rebel side celebrated Americanism in its territory from the beginning of the war, utilizing the 12 October holiday to implicate a divided society in a national project with renovated ranks, values and symbols. Those who attended were fascinated by the presence of military, political and ecclesiastical authorities in a liturgy that fitted religious traditions into civic holidays. For the military, the Civil War had rectified the symbolism of the festival. Since the nineteenth century, the Virgin of Pilar had provided a religious aspect to the national holiday. However, from August 1936, belief spread that this Virgin had saved the Francoist army from the failed Republican bombardment of the Plaza de Pilar in Zaragoza. This gave rise to pilgrimages, Masses and adherence to Catholicism and the rebel cause.

From that point on, different interpretations regarding _Hispanidad_ emerged within the nationalist ranks. The Catholics insisted on the missionary nature of the Spanish nation, predestined to propagate its faith in the Americas and occupy an elevated place in history. The Day of the Race was fundamentally – though unofficially – the Festival of _Hispanidad,_ because it commemorated the consecration of the Hispanic empire that the Church and the Catholic Monarchs had transplanted in the Americas. The Falangists emphasized this imperial vocation of Spain more than the spiritual dimension: every 12 October they celebrated the heroic nature of the Conquest, with melancholy allusion to the raw power of an empire and menacing undertones of expansionist policy.

Francoism and the Imperial Dream of _Hispanidad_

Francoism utilized the Americas myth as never before in Spain. _Hispanidad_ became the official doctrine of the regime and a reference point in the Catholic imaginary that revived during the forty years of dictatorship. *Hispanidad* articulated collective identity projects associated with the idea of a Catholic, ecumenical Spain: the civilizer of the Americas. It was used as a propagandistic offensive to construct the symbolic framework of the regime, legitimize itself and project itself outward, sometimes with the help of Spanish emigrants. The dictatorship reinvigorated the idea of Hispanic America as an extension of Spanish identity in the world. Foreign policy was constructed accordingly, as Francoism was confronted with fascist Europe, the Second World War, the postwar period and the unification of Europe.

The myth of *Hispanidad* reaffirmed the essentially Catholic nature of Spanish conservative nationalism. More significantly, it re-created the dream of an imperial, eternal Spain as an explanatory key to the past, present and future of the nation. Imperial nostalgia shaped the idea of a Great Spain, united and centralized by an absolute Catholic monarch. Earlier conquests and colonization by the Castilian *hidalgos* (lower nobility) was relived in the 'crusade' of the winners of the Civil War against the 'enemies' of Spain. As such, it augured a magnificent future. Imperial fantasy permeated Spanish nationalism just after the Civil War and became disputed territory between Catholics and Falangists. In the late 1940s, the latter group created the Council of *Hispanidad* as an ideological, political and cultural platform for the new state. It imagined Spain as the privileged interlocutor between Hispanic America and the new Europe, and the alternative to North American imperialist intent in the region. After it came into Catholic hands, the organism was renamed the Instituto de Cultura Hispánica (Institute of Hispanic Culture, ICH) in 1945 and constituted an early institutional attempt of the regime to exalt the Spanish identity with the Americas myth.

The 12 October holiday was already a tradition in Spanish history and remained as the national holiday on the new Francoist calendar, along with other dates such as 18 July and 19 April. Francoism incorporated the pre-existing elements of the Catholic nationalist imaginary into the observance of the holiday. The date alluded to the 1492 conquest of the Americas thanks to the Catholic Monarchs, who that same year reconquered and unified Spain, initiating the Golden Age of the civilizing nation and its Castilian language. The holiday extolled the myth of *Hispanidad,* and with it the evangelizing mission of the Spanish nation in American territories. The regime and the commemoration passed through several different stages. In 1958, it was renamed *Día de la Hispanidad* (Day of *Hispanidad*) and became an itinerant festival throughout Spain, organized by the state with the participation of diverse consulting institutions.

The ritual and discourses of the central acts of the first post–Civil War observances celebrated in Zaragoza and Madrid linked the victory of the *national* side with religion to symbolize the idealized empire of the Falangists. Later, the demise of fascism during the Second World War attenuated the pomp that the state had lent to the Catholic nationalist reading of the holiday. Falangist triumphalist excesses became ill-advised in public and references to empire were avoided. Being a spiritual bridge with the Americas was codified as an integral part of the Spanish personality; it also served as a convenient strategy to overcome international isolation. Accordingly, every 12 October the regime promoted the prestige of the nation outside its borders. Its shining political-cultural offensive aimed at the Americas was entrusted to the Catholic Church and to young university students: the radiating core of Hispanic thinking. From 1947 on, the ICH began to celebrate the opening of the academic year on 'its most important holiday, 12 October every year, Day of *Hispanidad*. Eventually, it made room for political and diplomatic participation.[5] As the institution gained notoriety, the discourses for this day reviewed the annual labour of promoting culture and reported on Spanish international standing. During the 1950s, the international image of Spain began to improve through the agreements reached with Peronist Argentina, the United States and the United Nations. Observance of 12 October fit with economic development projects; it gave impetus to tourism during the last phase of the regime and to a foreign policy featuring Spain as interlocutor between the Americas and Europe.

In 1958, the 'Day of the Race' was renamed the 'Day of *Hispanidad*'[6] by a decree that with a stroke of the pen obliterated the Falangist commemoration and placed it in pragmatic Catholic hands. The ICH was charged with the formal acts related to the discovery of the Americas. Diplomatic Spanish representations had to find their place alongside events organized by governments as well as social and cultural institutions outside of Spain.[7] Without renouncing the past or deeply anticommunist Catholic values, the celebration adjusted to the times to better suit future projection and Spanish commerce.

From the Civil War on, the Church was fully involved in enacting every 12 October the privilege of Hispanic heritage and religious conservatism in service to power. The coincidence of this day with the religious feast of the Virgin of Pilar, which had revived during the conflict, contributed to this. There was no Day of *Hispanidad* celebration without a *Te Deum* Mass. However, devotion to *la Pilarica* (Pilar) competed with that of Our Lady of Guadalupe, patron saint of Extremadura and 'Queen of the Spains' since 1928. Her monastery was a symbol of empire and evangelization of the New World: there Columbus had received the order from the Catholic Monarchs commissioning his voyage of discovery; there he returned in 1493 to give thanks for the Virgin's protection. The ICH divided its attention between the Virgin of Pilar and the Virgin of Guadalupe, opting for the latter when it came to dedicating buildings and monuments as symbols of cultural exchange between Spain and the Americas.[8] The prominence of the ICH ended the exclusive dedication of the antecedent Day of the Race to the Virgin of Pilar. In fact, the first official celebration of the Day of *Hispanidad* in 1958 was meant to take place in the Extremadura monastery to commemorate the 400th anniversary of the death of Charles V, but was moved to Madrid due to unforeseen circumstances.

Finally, from 1951 on, the festivities became itinerant in nature, though they returned to Madrid every few years. The state organized the principal celebration of 12 October in different Spanish cities that vied to host it. Since the early twentieth century, 12 October had taken root in places with important administrative functions, migratory traditions or lively associative cultural or economic Americanism. In the celebrations, the different actors annually renewed local and regional ties with the holiday calendar and the nation by extension. The progress of the main observance throughout Spain began during the Civil War and continued under Francoism, which entrusted organizational aspects of the holiday to the ICH and the Ministry of Foreign Affairs' Directorate of Cultural Relations. With the passing years, other areas of the state were integrated into the celebration and centrality was ceded to local, provincial, military and ecclesiastical authorities, as well as those of single party, the Falange.

The festival itinerary throughout the Spanish geography over the years was not random; the places chosen had a symbolic meaning related to the discovery of the Americas or the Hispanic monarchy. The intent was to re-create the empire of the Catholic Monarchs and their Habsburg descendants, while acknowledging the diversity of Spain. Thus, for example, in 1952 the day was celebrated in Granada to commemorate the Reconquest of Spain. In 1967, Barcelona hosted the celebration in remembrance of the reception of Columbus – and ratification of his titles and privileges – by the Monarchs in 1493, along with the Regulation on Free Commerce sanctioned by Carlos III, who had opened up trading among several ports in the Peninsula and the Americas.[9] In 1968, the day was observed in Alcalá de Henares, where Columbus had been given royal audience in 1486. Burgos hosted the holiday in 1971, based on its relevance during the empire and association with the 'crusade' of 1936–39. The Canary Islands got a turn in

1957 and again in 1972, because all early expeditions into the Atlantic had put into port there and the islanders boasted a solid tradition of Americanism.

Through all these travelling observances, local and regional identities associated themselves with the national identity. Cities such as Oviedo, Toledo, Valencia, San Sebastian or A Coruña did not host the festivities, but everyone liked the itinerant nature of the holiday. It responded to the myth of Spanish nationalism – which was traditionally conservative and had been updated by the Falangists – that gave Castile a foundational role in the construction of the national identity. It also fit with the idea of a unitary Spain that integrated regional diversity. The itinerant Day of *Hispanidad* served as a cohesive element in the periphery and placated anti-Francoism in certain regions along the way. From the 1960s on, the travelling holiday was incorporated into the promotion of places and regions by the new Ministry of Information and Tourism. Towards the end of Francoism, tradition and modernity melded together on 12 October.

Hispanic America and Democratic Spain

During the years of transition to democracy in Spain, links to the Americas were intertwined with the political determination to project to the world a democratic and modern Spain. The arrival of democracy updated the liberal, forward-looking version of Americanism. The ideological weight of *Hispanidad* was abandoned as the notion of an Ibero-American Community of Nations took hold, after King Juan Carlos I declared himself in favour of it during the 12 October 1976 festivities he attended in Cartagena de Indias (Colombia). Embedded in the Spanish identity, the Americas myth moved amidst the erratic foreign policy and the pursuit of internal consensus that marked those years.

With the death of Franco, the new regime encountered difficulties finding symbols that would consensually represent the nation. The legitimacy of the monarchy, which had been established by the dictator, was also in question. In 1976 and 1977, Francoist symbols persisted and 12 October was observed as a national holiday alongside 18 July and 1 May. In the new holiday calendar that was published towards the end of 1978, any festivity recalling the dictatorship had been decisively eliminated, but others had not been introduced to commemorate the fledgling democracy. The government of Adolfo Suarez avoided discussion of Spanish national symbols such as the flag, the hymn, the national holiday or the coat of arms. The ICH was renamed the Centro Iberoamericano de Cooperación (Centre for Ibero-American Cooperation, CIC) to distance itself from the dictatorship and promote renewed international action towards the Americas. In its hands, 12 October was preserved without generating debate, thus perpetuating Americanism in the Spanish national identity.

From the beginning of the transition to democracy, retrospective exaltation of Hispanic America constituted a key reference for the projects of the restored monarchy in the late twentieth century. The king and queen became involved in the celebrations of the Day of *Hispanidad*, which recovered their itinerancy after the death of Franco. In 1976, the institutional acts of observance took place in Salamanca. The official mood had begun a week before when the king and the minister of education and science opened the academic year, pushing education to the centre of national affairs. On 12 October 1977, Las Palmas de Gran Canaria hosted the main festivities and made good use of Iberia Airlines to project a modern, democratic Spain to the world. Additionally, the celebration incorporated the official visit of Mexican President José López Portillo to Spain as a sign of the renewed relations – severed since the Civil War – between the two countries.

Because Spanish nationalism had a strong Catholic component, during the transition to democracy it was difficult to remove the religious weight from the holiday. Out of the sectarian disputes over the holy throne of *Hispanidad* in those years emerged regional identities associated with the construction of the constitutional state. In 1978, the Day of *Hispanidad* took place in the Monastery of Guadalupe. There a modern Spain did not shine through, but rather a Catholic offensive in the midst of the autonomic and territorial challenges of the early transition years. In 1979, Madrid closed the Fourth Ibero-American Congress on Education on 12 October. Without parade, popular presence or a dominant presence of the Church, it unveiled forward-looking public and private initiatives linked to the Instituto de Cooperación Iberoamericana (ICI, formerly CIC). Valladolid hosted the 1980 festivities with a program of regional interests tied to both the autonomic challenge and Columbus's enterprise under the auspices of the Crown and the Catholic Church. In the new democracy, commemoration did not disassociate itself from the rites of Francoist imperial rhetoric.

The failed military coup d'état on 23 February 1981 revived the debate over the national symbols of Spain. The 12 October holiday was tangled between commemorative rivalries and the difficulties of articulating a holiday calendar for the Spanish democracy. The parliamentary Left wanted to break all ties with Francoist symbols and strengthen democratic Spanish nationalism by proposing 6 December – the day the new constitution was approved by popular referendum in 1978 – as the national holiday. In the end, it acknowledged the overseas enterprise as the greatest historical achievement of the Spanish nation. Without other foundational references, Spain would continue to celebrate its international exploits in order to affirm its collective identity. The debate ended in April 1981 when the government of Calvo Sotelo created the National Commission for the 1992 celebration of the 500th Anniversary of the Discovery of the Americas. In November 1981, 12 October was decreed the national holiday of Spain and Day of *Hispanidad*, and was justified by holding that it was the beginning 'of a period of linguistic and cultural projection beyond European borders'.[10] This decision assimilated the burden of the original ambiguity surrounding 12 October and reflected the intent of the UCD governments to renew relations between Spain and Ibero-America. In fact, the 1981 festivities took place between Seville and the port of Palos de la Frontera, with an impressive array of recourse and symbol intended to recall the relevant role of those Andalusian places in the overseas empire. For the occasion, and in order to prepare the 500th anniversary, in the presence of the king and queen the ICI created a high council that included prominent Spanish and American personalities from the cultural, scientific, political and financial spheres. In 1982, Cadiz hosted the celebrations and the rites were coupled to new policies. During the final UCD governments, the 12 October festivities represented the unity of Spain, but also recognized its plurality and readiness for renewed projects. The Americanism of the Spanish identity blended modernity and tradition in democracy.

When the Socialist Party came to power in late 1982, the American dimension of the Spanish identity reoriented itself towards affirming democracy, European integration and an optimistic future for the nation. The state recurred to Americanism for social cohesion and the design of a foreign policy articulated on new pillars of reciprocity and cooperation, human rights, economic development, peace and solidarity. The political offensive took hold with renewed initiatives to construct an Ibero-American Community of Nations and support for democratization processes in Latin America. During the socialist governments, commemoration of 12 October underwent yet another transformation, becoming the founding symbol of the Spanish nation in its progress towards political normalization, for lack of other symbols. The main celebration continued its touring – with royalty, diplomats and authorities – to Granada and Palma de Mallorca before settling in Madrid in 1985. A change of ritual was being prepared, which came with the definitive law that in 1987 declared 12 October the pre-eminent national holiday. Without references to *Hispanidad,* Columbus, the Discovery or the New World, the Americas myth was recycled for the third time since the Spanish democracy began. The law expressly mentioned 1492, alluding to two references embedded in the idea of *Hispanidad.* The first was the reconquest and unification of the kingdoms of Spain. The second was the Discovery, though without references to epic achievements or the evangelization of the Americas. It only alluded to a vague linguistic and cultural projection beyond Europe. Emptied of content, the new discourse left the observance without memories of solemn moments in national history and referred to others that had occurred in distant lands: an empire.[11]

With the new decree, the 12 October holiday split into two official acts. The first consists of a public ceremony in which the king places a floral offering on the Monument to the Fallen for Spain and later presides over the military parade down the Paseo del Prado in Madrid. The celebration concludes with a reception for foreign diplomats in the Royal Palace. The second was a formal act in the ICI and its successor the Spanish Agency for International Cooperation, which lasted until 1991.

The new ritual of Spanish nationalism in the national holiday sought to combine older commemorative dates. The tribute to the fallen recalled the Second of May 1808, while the military parade recovered the liturgy of Francoism. Americanism was relegated to a peripheral place from which the king could evoke the Spanish intention of constituting both bridge and nexus between two worlds, thereby reinforcing its international prestige once political normalization and European integration were complete. The proposal fit neatly within the preparations for the commemoration of the 500th Anniversary of the Discovery of the Americas.

The ostentatious commemoration of 1992 was linked to the World Exhibition in Seville, the Olympic Games in Barcelona and the II Ibero-American Summit in Madrid. For the occasion, the Cervantes Institute and the Casa de América were inaugurated in Madrid. The idea of Hispanic America in the national imaginary enjoyed citizen participation and was vigorously deployed for the benefit of future enterprise. Similarly, the 1992 commemorations managed to blend the myth of Cervantes – symbol of the regional and cultural contribution of Castile to the civilizing role of Spain – with an international aspect that situated the Spanish language as the guardian of transatlantic ties, without especially upsetting National-Catholic Spanish nationalism. In the end, the Socialists were satisfied with the results of their ambitious image campaign to present a modern, democratic and promising Spain to the world.[12]

When the conservative Popular Party came to power, the ritual of the national holiday was reactivated and the symbols of the nation returned to the political arena. With a 1997 Royal Decree that expanded 12 October to Armed Forces Day and to include an 'Act of Tribute to the Flag', the military became responsible for regulating the acts of the national holiday. That year, in the presence of the monarchs and all the presidents of the Autonomous Communities – a gathering that would not occur again for several years – the military parade along the Paseo de la Castellana in Madrid displayed the contribution of the armed forces to the nation like never before in the democracy. Madrid assumed control of a holiday no longer associated with the Americas. Without discourse, the celebration became a public rehearsal for assessing the state of national politics. During the second government of the Popular Party, the dispute revived over the emblems of Hispanity that were implied by the 12 October holiday. A remodel of the Columbus Square in Madrid gave occasion to place an immense red and gold Spanish flag in the Jardines del Descubrimiento (Discovery Gardens) for the 2002 festivities, awakening the symbolism of militant Spanish nationalism.

The commemoration dragged its polemic tradition into the twenty-first century, as representation of the nation every 12 October became the barometer for assessing Spanish political polarization. From 2005 on, Americanism recovered a place in the acts of the day, with the participation of troops from diverse Latin American countries in the military parade. Since then, the Americas flavour has intensified with the presence of the families of those receiving tribute and those central to the military parade, many of whom are children of Latin American immigrants parading their Spanish identity in public. Outside the official celebration, the Americas folklore is represented in colourful, popular festivities that acknowledge the cultural diversity of cities such as Madrid or Barcelona.

Conclusion

The idea of Hispanic America in Spanish nationalism stems from its particular colonial history, linguistic community and the important colonies of Spanish emigrants. From the late nineteenth century on, Hispanic America was incorporated into the construction of the national collective identity. During the Bourbon Restoration, the political elites shaped a politics of memory that assigned a place of honour to the former empire. Undoubtedly, the 12 October commemoration has since been the most meaningful and lasting symbol of deep-rooted Americanism in the national imaginary. Consecrated as a national holiday in Spain and a civic holiday throughout Ibero-America, this anniversary brings together multiple historical references for the national narrative: the Discovery of the Americas, the Catholic monarchs, evangelization, empire, language. All of them help construct the myth of a Spain entrusted with a universal mission. The 12 October holiday also contains contradictory ideological trajectories of Spanish nationalism: the reformism of the liberal-republican project in contrast with neocolonial conservativism; the secular cult to Columbus as opposed to the Marianist cult to the Virgin of Pilar and Our Lady of Guadalupe; obsession for unity versus recognition of Hispanic diversity. Hispanic America forms part of the founding myth of Spanish unity and generates values that reinforce patriotic traditions and social cohesion.

From the reign of Alfonso XIII to present-day democracy, the idea of the Americas in Spanish nationalism underwent important changes throughout the twentieth century. Significantly, the Americas myth became stronger in moments of institutional crisis. Burdened by internal weakness or lack of legitimacy, successive regimes made use of the Americas to strengthen their image and unite the national body. Throughout the century, Americanism was subordinated to domestic policy, which reinforced its ideological functionality. It also proved useful in Spanish foreign affairs and as a diplomatic propaganda instrument. Events from the flight of the *Plus Ultra* to the Seville World Exhibition and the 500th anniversary have served as resonance chambers for Spanish foreign policy and a safeguard to power. The persistence of the Americas myth in Spanish nationalism through the political and cultural changes of the entire twentieth century is striking to contemplate. Once again, 12 October clarifies things. Its pliable nature and association with a plural imaginary allowed the holiday to conform to political fashions as it rooted itself in the collective imaginary. In spite of the ideological divergence that accompanies any historical narrative or political project, the idea of Hispanic America – alongside other founding myths such as the Reconquest or the War of Independence against Napoleon – constitutes the mortar of Spanish nationalism.

Marcela García Sebastiani is a tenured lecturer of History of Political Thought and Social Movements at Complutense University, Madrid. Her research focuses on Argentine and Spanish political history in the twentieth century, paying special attention to identity politics, cultural transfers and commemorations. She has published several books and chapters and edited the volume *Patriotas entre naciones* (Madrid, 2010).

David Marcilhacy is a tenured lecturer of Iberian and Latin American Studies at the University of Paris-Sorbonne. His areas of research include the sociopolitical history of the contemporary Hispanic countries, particularly national and transnational imaginaries, as well as global history and the cultural dimension of international relations. He has edited several books and a monographical volume, *Raza hispana: Hispanoamericanismo e imaginario nacional en la España de la Restauración* (Madrid, CEPC, 2010).

Notes

1. Royal Decree of 23 September 1892 (*Gaceta de Madrid*, 25 September 1892).
2. Demolins (1899).
3. Altamira (1917).
4. Law of 15 June 1918 (*Gaceta de Madrid*, 16 June 1918).
5. Organic Regulation of the ICH. Decree of 18 April 1947 (BOE, 25 April 1947).
6. BOE, 8 February 1958.
7. Dirección General de Política Exterior, *Supresión de fiestas españolas*, 1958 (Archive of the Ministerio de Asuntos Exteriores y Cooperación, Madrid, Exp. 5013/2).
8. Article 3 of the Organic Regulations of the ICH. Decree of 18 April 1947 (BOE, 25 April 1947).
9. *Día de la Hispanidad*, Barcelona, 12 October 1967. Speech by the director of the ICH, Gregorio Marañón, Madrid, Ediciones de Cultura Hispánica, 1967, pp. 9–13.
10. R.D. 3217/1981, BOE, 1 January 1982.
11. Santos Juliá, 'Vieja nación, fiesta imperial', *El País*, 19 July 1990.
12. 'Los deberes están cumplidos', *El País*, 13 September 1992.

Chapter 9

Bullfights as a National Festivity

Rafael Núñez Florencio

'The splendid, wild festival / of terror and joy / of this fierce and ancient people / Gold, silk, blood and sun!'[1] Here we find festivity and tragedy, fear and jubilation, blood and bold defiance, life and death all united in supreme art: as delicate as silk, as valuable as gold, as vital as flowing blood. The artist's palette fills with yellows and reds, the distinctive colours of the national flag. It is no accident that these hues symbolize the Spaniard throughout the world; for many, sun and blood distil the sentiment and the essence of a nation.[2]

Here, without going into the pros and cons of the festivity itself, we attempt to discern how and why bullfighting has permeated all cultural manifestations of Spain – its art, literature, language, architecture, politics and philosophy – to become a representative element of the country. The insistent presence of the bull in the Spanish countryside is more than a mere recurring shadow, it serves as an easy identity marker and signifies a specifically Spanish trait outside national borders. Innumerable books underscore, even in their titles, the character of the bullfight as a *fiesta nacional* (national festivity).[3]

Though the scope of this work remains within the chronological frame of the twentieth century, it is important to recall that the post-1898 anti-taurine discourse that opened the century was in fact the exacerbated continuation of much earlier Enlightenment rationality. The accommodating mood of the generations that followed can therefore be interpreted as an updating of nineteenth-century populism. The second half of the twentieth century was marked by the longevity of Francoism and a crude manipulation of the festivity that persisted beyond the death of the dictator, to some degree. The reactionary flank of militant anti-Francoism associated bullfighting with the dictator

himself and everything related to the regime. Henry Kamen suggests
that the heightened anti-taurine stance of Catalan nationalism should
be understood in this way.[4]

Bullfights as a 'Modern' Spectacle

Some researchers hold that 'bullfights as we know them today developed in the eighteenth century.... They are, undoubtedly, the irrational response to a pretended – only pretended – rationality. They were
born in a nation incapable of loosing its moorings with the past, still
clinging longingly to former glories. They form part of this suicidal
authenticity, this masochistic self-affirmation in the irrational.'[5] This
assessment emerged out of enlightened reformism and endures to the
present; it considers the taurine spectacle a clear indicator of 'Spanish
backwardness'. By including the 'barbaric festivity' in what is known
as the 'problem of Spain', it blamed *casticismo*, the insistence on traditional authenticity, for the 'maladies of the country' and prescribed
incorporation into more advanced Europe as the cure.

As in other historiographic spheres, critique 'from the outside' has
been more benign than from the inside and has mitigated the fero-
ciously pessimistic tendency of Spanish intellectualism throughout the
twentieth century.[6] A good sample of this is found in the research of
Adrian Shubert on bullfights as a 'modern festivity'. Shubert proposes
that the national festivity was not an expression of a supposedly timeless Spanishness, but an entertainment created by specific beings at
a precise moment in history. Following this anti-essentialist proposal
would deny bullfights their specificity as an Iberian product on the one
hand and reject their use as an indicator of the Spanish incapacity to
modernize on the other.

Thus, Shubert's perspective digresses from those of both traditional
enthusiasts and detractors by locating the festivity in the context of
the great mass spectacles of the modern world. The aesthetic and ethical assessment – supreme art for some, barbarism for others – is set
aside in favour of the simple consideration of the festivity as a modern cultural industry. According to Shubert, *tauromachy*, or the art of
bullfighting, stands out as one of the most precocious phenomena in
this category of social entertainment. Even if the bullfights stop being
considered an expression of the genius and character of a community
and come to be seen as a collective pastime, the survival of the festivity
throughout the centuries indicates two things: first, that it is widely
accepted by the popular masses, and second, that it constitutes a prof-

itable business for some sectors of society (cattle farmers, entrepreneurs, bullfighters, agents) as well as for the state.[7]

This contribution comes as a breath of fresh air in a context stagnant with sterile debates. However, one wonders if the break might not be excessive: whether it goes to the opposite extreme. In other words, rather than the archetype of Spanish backwardness, in this assessment the bullfight might be construed as a precociously modern phenomenon. Specifically, four arguments can be presented from this interpretation, not so much as rebuttals, but as areas for further research. First, Spaniards have not perceived bullfighting in this way during these many centuries; second, and parallel to the first, foreigners attempting to describe the national festivity have not represented to it in this way; third, this analysis does not clarify why bullfighting emerged, developed and continued so successfully for so long as a popular pastime in Spain; and fourth, it fails to explain the core issue of bullfights as a national festivity as they are understood to be by defenders and detractors alike.

Although bullfights similar to those we see today emerged in the eighteenth century, they did not acquire the features of a national festivity until the first half of the following century. The Enlightenment stigmatized the bullfights by transforming them into something paradigmatically working-class, according to Xavier Andreu. However, nineteenth-century elites used the same trait to make *los toros* (bullfighting) an important factor in the nation-building process: a complex passage marked by progress, regression and contradiction. For example, the contrast between the eighteenth and nineteenth centuries need not muffle the presence of notable voices that were discordant with the predominant current in both centuries. However, it can be said that with the War of Independence (1808–14) and the political shift from the Ancien Régime to the new liberal order, Spain and other European countries entered a new era in which 'the people' took centre stage. Liberal elites could no longer look down on popular customs, as the Enlightenment elites had, without falling into an uncomfortable critique of the constitutive elements of the nation itself.

In spite of this, the attitude of early Spanish liberalism towards bullfighting oscillated between perplexity and criticism, ambivalence and indifference, in constant dissonance with the passion the topic awoke in foreign visitors. Reticent or openly critical attitudes regarding bullfights (Mariano José de Larra, Ramón Mesonero Romanos) argued in the name of progress: the anathema was not directed so much against the people as against the desensitizing effect of the festivity, which was precisely what impeded the collective progress of the Spanish nation. In practise, however, the liberals could not ignore the importance of this mass spectacle in the process of popular mobilization. Invocation of 'the people', no matter how rhetorical or demagogical, required the payment of certain 'dues'. This confluence of interests between respectable liberalism and taurine enthusiasm is mirrored in Paquiro's (pseudonym of Francisco Montes) *Tauromaquia* (1836), which regulated the festivity according to a model considered respectable and acceptable by all. Even the intellectuals succumbed to the power of the spectacle as aesthetic manifestation and national expression.

In these terms, bullfights became completely acceptable to the liberal current, as they demonstrated the 'democratic spirit' of the 'authentic Spanish people'. They no longer constituted a 'barbarian spectacle, but the triumph of reason over the beast. It was no simple game, but a consummate art.'[8] From that perspective, the bullfight gained social acceptance and enjoyed overwhelming success. In the context of greater sociopolitical stability during the second half of the nineteenth century, bullrings were constructed around the country according to local economic possibilities and numbered more than one hundred by the 1860s. Though centred in Andalusia and Madrid at first, the pastime extended throughout the national territory, including Catalonia prior to the mass migrations from the southern provinces. The festivals increased from around 400 per year in 1860 to 700 by 1870 and to 800 at the beginning of the twentieth century.

For nineteenth-century foreign travellers, particularly those with romantic sensibilities, Spain was, above all, Andalusia. Within this, bullfighting epitomized not only Spanish entertainment, but rather, and more importantly, a way of life and profound sense of 'national being'. Despite its reductive and simplifying nature, the synonymity between Andalusia and bullfighting was not entirely unfounded. Indeed, bullfighting was more popular in Andalusia than the rest of Spain put together, and many of the most famous and popular bullfighters came from the south of the country. In addition, some of the most emblematic bullrings, such as those in Seville and Ronda, were located on Andalusian soil. Furthermore, this fusion of bullfighting with Andalusian idiosyncrasy was also reproduced in perennially important works from the romantic tradition – beginning with *Carmen*, by Prosper Mérimée and Georges Bizet (1847).

Bullfights as an 'Authentic' Liability

The Disaster of 1898 marked the peak of criticism for the festivity, which was cast as the prototype of national backwardness, the epitome of barbarism and a manifestation of atavistic cruelty in the writings of reformist and progressive minorities. For critics and intellectuals of the time, the 'Spanish malady' was severe and profound. Exploring the reasons behind the country's decadence became a pet topic in which national bullfighting festivities appeared as both cause and consequence of Spanish decline.

One of the most representative samples of this attitude is found in the book *Hacia otra España* (1899), by Ramiro de Maeztu. On the topic of who was responsible for national backwardness, he wrote: 'Responsibility! Look to our indolence, our laziness, our *zarzuela* operetta, the bullfights, our national diet of chickpeas, the ground we walk on and the water we drink.'[9] Some chronicles of the time indicate that on the same day the Spanish navy was crushed by the Americans in Cavite (Philippines), one could see Alcalá Street in Madrid full of men in their finest suits and women in elegant dresses on their way to enjoy a bullfighting spectacle. The inevitable conclusion: this frivolous and thoughtless society concerned itself with its traditional amusements while the nation suffered one of the most dramatic moments in its history.

Joaquín Costa, one of the most active and influential voices of regenerationism, protested loudly that the country was languishing and a once vigorous race had become a herd of steers, or eunuchs. He contended that this brutal and stupid country with its marked perversion of public sentiment was the Spain of the Iberian bullring and its malady, the 'national festivity'. The country was debasing itself, wallowing in contemptible traditions while losing the respect of neighbouring nations and earning a reputation as an abject and despicable people. 'Only Spain appears on the world stage with dishevelled hair, arms steaming with blood, and an awful, coarse voice still shouting, "Blood, blood, more horses for the bulls!"'[10] When the national body was in greatest need of fighting blood, more blood was spilled in obscene entertainment. Weighed down by ignorance and corruption, Spain had gone into a massive breakdown from which it could only recover by burying its past and its traditions – from *El Cid* to the bullfights – forever.

Although Costa's apocalyptic tone constitutes an exception, many of his contemporaries shared the substance of his ideas regarding the taurine festivities. The majority opinion among intellectuals associated the national festivity of bullfighting with a traditionalism that must be overcome in the name of progress, modernization or what the philosopher José Ortega y Gasset roundly referred to as 'Europeanization'. This coarse and perverse pastime had to be abandoned, along with so many other things. One of the most important literary figures of the period, Pío Baroja, illustrates this attitude. In one of his most celebrated novels, *El árbol de la ciencia* (1911), the doctor Juan Sánchez is labelled a 'brute' on the sole basis of his fondness for the bullring. Later, the main character – and alter ego of the author – remarks that the brutish public leaving the bullfights deserved to be mowed down with machine guns: 'Sundays especially, when he encountered people returning from the bullfights, he thought of the pleasure it would give him to place a half-dozen machine guns on every street corner and not let a single one escape on their return from the stupid, bloody festivity.'[11]

Another step in this direction placed bullfights in the category of *España negra* (Black Spain). At the turn of the century, this image of Spain revived and gained new strength: it had never completely disappeared in the first place and it provided an opportunity to indulge in the most tragic aspects of this romantic 'lithograph print'. Some of these elements – passion, ferocity, valour, cruelty, primitivism, fiery blood, spilled blood, the contest between life and death – seemed to find a natural stage in the crude but exhilarating ceremony of the bullring. Both the romantic print and the creation of Black Spain were partial (elements were chosen in a biased, arbitrary manner, rejecting those that did not fit with an aprioristic tendency), largely projected and above all ambivalent: revealing rejection and fascination at the same time. All in all, the most noteworthy novelty at this point was that the Spaniards themselves embraced, assimilated and re-created this Spanish 'blackness' as an essential component of their own idiosyncrasy.

The painter Darío de Regoyos was one of the main people responsible for propagating this image in his pictorial and literary representations of the country. He travelled in the north of the Peninsula at the end of the nineteenth century with his friend, the Belgian poet Emile Verhaeren. Their experiences led to the publication of their seminal book *Viaje a la España negra* (A Trip to Black Spain, 1899): a surprising fresco of a country they deemed to be obsessed with death and things macabre.[12] Regoyos took it upon himself to transmit this conception in his distinctively black paintings of religious processions, Masses, funeral processions, burials, mourning, and so on. He was not alone: in the sombre aesthetics of the first third of the twentieth century – from Ricardo Baroja to Julio Romero de Torres, from Ignacio Zuloaga to José Gutiérrez Solana – the gloomiest and bloodiest aspects of the taurine festivity find a place of their own right.

Here, the national festivity lost its epic qualities and became a lacerating masquerade along the ethical and aesthetic lines of Goya at his most lugubrious. The attention shifted from artistic merit or even the balanced struggle between human and beast to the most sordid details:

giving preference to blood, cruelty and suffering. Regoyos and Zuloaga turned their attention to the humble horses, giving them virtually identical titles as 'victims of the festivity' in their paintings. Solana takes it a step further in *El desolladero* (The Slaughterhouse, 1924), a painting of cold, blood-curdling cruelty. He accompanies the title with some shocking pages describing the horrifying death of those poor horses, the darkest and most overlooked participants in the festivity. Gored mercilessly by the ferocious bulls, the pitiful animals died in a dirty, obscene way, their entrails spilling out through immense lacerations in their stomachs, their eyes bulging and rolling, necks outstretched, agonizing between stiff terror and dreadful convulsions.

Solana again turns his attention to the less splendid aspects of the festivity – and therefore the most revealing of its essence – in an article entitled 'Corrida de toros en Tetuán' (The Bullfight in Tetuán, 1913). More than the particular bullfights themselves, it addressed popular entertainment featuring the bull as a propitiatory sacrifice. He describes these amusements, these *charlotadas*, as 'burlesque and repugnant bullfights that surpass all barbarism'. From this perspective, when such festivities were stripped of the glitter of grand occasion, the sadist and bestial condition of the taurine ritual was revealed. In the case Solana described, the objective was none other than to pierce the calf everywhere imaginable until it perished in terrible agony. 'The public, with every pass or stab laughs wildly and enjoys this spectacle a great deal and they have to hold their sides from laughing. Some, very few, leave the bullring as though ashamed of such vile behaviour.'[13]

Criticism of tauromachy reached its zenith with Eugenio Noel, a writer who made the fight against this spectacle one of his leitmotivs, along with anti-flamencoism. In his opinion, bullfighting and this genre of folksong constituted two sides of the same coin. With visceral rejection and vehement tone,[14] Noel both condemned bullfighting for its cruelty and attacked its status as a national festivity. Ultimately, he came to see them as the epitome of Spanish defects. Noel's crusade was received well – even enthusiastically – among many intellectuals. Miguel de Unamuno, for example, dedicated to Noel one of his articles against bullfighting. In another, 'The Work of Eugenio Noel', he expounded on the deleterious effects of the festivity on Spanish society.[15] Much more recently, the novelist Manuel Vicent worthily continued the anti-taurine crusade, deploying arguments similar to those we have seen (brutality, cruelty, primitivism, symbol of the darkest and most reactionary aspects of the country, etc.).[16] The tendency towards reproach persists in the present day, normally along the same lines of associating bullfighting with Black Spain.[17]

Bullfighting as an Expression of the National Essence

During the twentieth century, detractors and enthusiasts of the national festivity coincided in their perception of it as a genuine expression of the Spanish people. This was one of the arguments in Rosario Cambria's thorough work on bullfighting in the twentieth century.[18] Ortega y Gasset held that the taurine festivity was an essential element for understanding Spain and *that which is Spanish*. In his usual bombastic style, the Madrid thinker exclaimed: 'I affirm, in the most emphatic way possible, that no one can properly understand the history of Spain since 1650 who has not rigorously constructed the history of bullfighting in the strictest sense of the word.' A few lines later he insists: 'The history of bullfighting reveals some of the most hidden secrets of the life of the Spanish nation during almost three centuries.'[19]

Here it seems fitting to expand on the classification of bullfights as a national festivity. They appear as such in multiple titles of the period under analysis and clearly identify this as a fundamental category rather than mere rhetoric. Critics and devotees – and the entire range of attitudes in between – converge in linking bullfighting with *that which is Spanish* as parts of one same reality. 'The Spanish festivity is the shadow projected by the body of the nation', wrote the Count of Navas in a book entitled *El espectáculo más nacional* (1899). From a broader perspective, the abundant bibliography of the early twentieth century regarding the national psychology, the Spanish soul and the Spanish essence insists on tauromachy as a Spanish identity marker, for better or for worse. The anarchist Diego Abad de Santillán, for example, exhibited the habitual manic-depressive syndrome of that literature, with deep lamentations regarding the disproportionate prostration and exaltation of the national spirit. Bullfighting appears in this context – alongside a full array of clichés: Don Quixote, Castilian austerity, Andalusian idleness and even the Inquisition – as an essential element of a people at once valiant and fanatic, intelligent and ignorant, passionate and apathetic.[20]

Let us return to Ortega y Gasset as the person clearly in the best position to offer a detailed examination and assessment of bullfighting as a national festivity. Like few of his time, he was both devotee and fine analyst of 'things Spanish', an intellectual critic and a passionate expert on national enigmas. However, in spite of the fact that he is often quoted whenever this subject is addressed, the pages that this philosopher dedicates to bullfights constitute little more than a series of rhetorical digressions full of hollow generalizations, with an occasional 'pearl', such as the affirmation that in Spain nobody – except him, supposedly – truly understands bullfighting. As in so many other aspects of his thinking, Ortega periodically promised a complete book on the topic (he even had a title for it: *Paquiro o de las corridas de toros*), which never materialized.

In contrast, another contemporary intellectual, Ramón Pérez de Ayala, expressed some very interesting views regarding tauromachy as a national festivity. He started with the decisive declaration that bullfighting is without a doubt 'one of the fundamental Spanish institutions', to the point that 'the birth of bullfighting coincides with the very birth of Spanish nationality'. Perez de Ayala was especially interested in the how the Spanish essence works itself out in tauromachy, as though the 'Iberian soul' and the 'festivity' were two sides of the same coin. Thus, he emphasized how 'the bullfights did not rain down on us, nor were they left to us, nor were they brought from elsewhere. They are something so very ours, as compulsory to our nature and history as the language we speak. They were born with Spain and one senses that they will not cease until she [Spain] ceases to be.'

These opinions were especially meaningful because the author, though an enthusiast, acknowledged several negative aspects of bullfighting. Though he admittedly enjoyed them as a private individual, he stated that as a regenerationist dictator he would abolish them with the stroke of a pen. This responded less to their being a cause of decadence (an argument he considered exaggerated) as to the fact that they constituted a compendium of Spanish shortcomings. Specifically, Pérez de Ayala concluded that Spaniards demonstrated in public life all the defects of the enthusiast in the bullring: they were voluble, submissive to the tyrant and tyrannical to the weak, arguing over every conceivable topic, stupid or dogmatic. In other words, he saw 'taurine psychology spread throughout all of Spanish life'.[21]

This eclectic or ambivalent line of reflection persisted throughout the century in Spanish writing. One sample of its endurance was the psycho-sociological approach of the law professor, and later socialist major of Madrid, Enrique Tierno Galván, once again under the revealing title, 'Bullfighting as a National Event'. He insisted that 'when the taurine event becomes for the Spanish people a simple spectacle, the foundations of Spain as a nation will have been altered'. This conviction seems so entrenched that it is repeated with similar formulations, such as 'bullfighting is the event that has most educated the Spanish people socially and politically'. In other words, Spanish society attended bullfights in order to see itself reflected there. From the outside, bullfights constituted a mirror of the national community.

According to Tierno Galván, three main features of the Spanish people as a collective manifest themselves unambiguously in the bull-ring. First, a plebeian penchant, or the tendency of the upper classes to imitate the ordinary people. Second, a deep egalitarianism that was evident outside as well as inside the bullring. Third, a profoundly passionate attitude or philosophy of living life as a drunken ecstasy or an intense outburst. Thus, the taurine event reverberated in the most intimate spaces of Spanish life, including sexual relations: 'the Spanish man sees the erotic exchange with a woman in close relation with the attitude of the bullfighter confronting the bull. In erotic relations, the woman sees herself as the rebellious, fierce entity that must be subdued by the same methods and techniques used in the taurine struggle.' It correlates, then, that the *torero* would evolve into a Don Juan, a type of Casanova. Both the bullfighter and the seducer coincide in seeing life as a game: a contest with life or love – and both are profoundly Spanish. Tierno Galvan reiterated this: 'existence, for the Spaniard, only seems authentic when it is lived as a one-night stand'.[22]

It could be affirmed, then, that writers and essayists interpreted with greater or lesser success what was essentially a vibrant social and cultural phenomenon. Obviously, Spanish society – or at least a considerable part of it – enjoyed the bullfighting spectacles. Bullrings became an indispensable element of the urban landscape in the large Spanish cities, and at times in midsize or smaller towns. Going to the bullfights was not a mere pastime, but a very important social event. As such, they inevitably became a political space. Prior to the construction of large arenas in the twentieth century, the bullrings were the only venues capable of holding thousands of spectators. This feature became central to every initiative that involved 'the people'. What better place than the great bullrings for a meeting, for making a claim, for a protest, a tribute, a commemoration or a fundraiser? Unsurprisingly, the bullrings became stages for the most diverse political events.

The temptation has always existed to instrumentalize taurine interest for the benefit of certain sectors or to serve different factions. In fact, such political manipulation was an incontrovertible reality on numerous occasions and even over long periods, especially during the Franco era. However, political manipulation of the bullfights cannot be limited to that dictatorship; many prior cases existed. During the twentieth century, political power of every tendency succumbed to the impulse to use the popularity of the bullfights for their diverse initiatives. Around 1898, several 'patriotic' bullfights took place to raise money for the army and the war. This tendency was repeated later when the Spanish army went through dramatic moments in northern

Africa during the colonial war. The Primo de Rivera dictatorship also indulged in the use of the bullring for political objectives. The temptation persisted and intensified throughout the stormy republic years and even during the Civil War.[23]

Without question, however, political instrumentalization of everything related to tauromachy (bulls, bullfighters, the events themselves, the bullring, posters, costumes, etc.) reached its zenith during the Franco era. Bullfighting came to represent the antithesis of political commitment for both adherents and detractors of the regime. In the bleak context of late Francoist economic development policies (*desarrollismo*), bullfights and football constituted the 'bread and circuses' of the day. The link between the two spectacles was masterfully synthesized for the Spanish public in a caricature by the ingenious humourist Antonio Mingote, which appeared on the cover of his book *Las fiestas nacionales*. In the foreground, a bullfighter with his cape extended looks on, stupefied, as the bull enters the ring kicking a football.[24] Even today, bullfights remain an expression of the national – Francoist – spirit in certain political or ideological currents.

Bullfighting as the Supreme Art

'A good bullfight releases emotion, it transports us to the essence of life itself. It is the sublimation, the synthesis of life.'[25] 'The bullfight, then, as art, is sentiment', adds the writer Carlos Marzal in an interesting compilation of what poets, novelists, singer-songwriters, essayists, painters, journalists and intellectuals – united in their core enthusiasm and admiration for tauromachy – have said about the festivity. It includes writings by José M. Caballero Bonald, Miquel Barceló, Mario Vargas Llosa, Joaquín Vidal, Andrés Trapiello and others.[26] For most of them, bullfighting is not only art, but the supreme art: a perfect synthesis of the Apollonian and the Dionysian.

Spanish artists and intellectuals demonstrated an increasingly benevolent attitude towards bullfighting as the twentieth century progressed. With unavoidable exceptions, the literary disdain of the generation of 1898 was replaced by a critical but understanding attitude in the authors of 1914. An increasingly favourable tone can be detected in the literary currents of 1927 and 1936; the tone that intensified in the enthusiasm and lyrical effusion of great poets such as Federico García Lorca and Rafael Alberti. Intellectuals were drawn to the bullring, finding 'many points of union'[27] between thinkers and the skilful *toreros*. Juan Belmonte, for example, was admired by the great writers of the time, from Ramón del Valle-Inclán to Julio Camba. Bergamín proclaimed himself a devoted admirer of *Joselito,* Belmonte's rival. Ignacio Sánchez Mejías mixed with artists and intellectuals before he was immortalized in García Lorca's celebrated verse *Lament for Ignacio Sánchez Mejías* (1935). Support from intellectual spheres was decisive in elevating the ritual of the bullring and its consummate *matadores* to prestige in Spanish society.

Far from being considered a mere popular entertainment, tauromachy achieved literary status as a serious affair, a theme for contemplation, an important cultural event and a genuine expression of the Spanish people as a collective. This is best corroborated in the mammoth undertaking of José María de Cossío – incited by Ortega y Gasset – to write a monumental thirty-volume work that would cover every aspect of the taurine festivity. His work was first published in 1943 and underwent multiple revisions, expansions and adaptations in the years that followed.[28]

In a complementary manner, the *torero* became an indisputable 'literary hero' to inspired writers who had developed a fondness for the world of bullfighting.[29] Production ranged from popular literature (*Currito de la Cruz,* by Alejandro Pérez Lugín, 1921) to successful, more literary works such as the novels of Vicente Blasco Ibáñez (*Sangre y arena,* 1908) or – to a lesser extent – the work of Ángel María de Lera (*Los clarines del miedo,* 1958). In his distinctive hyper-realistic and intensely graphic style, Nobel laureate in literature Camilo José Cela also dedicated some of his works to bullfighting. Foreign appraisals of the Spanish festivity were also a key to its intellectual dignification. We have only to think of the decisive role of the avid bullfighting enthusiast Ernest Hemingway and some of his most renowned novels, such as *The Sun Also Rises* (1926) or *Death in the Afternoon* (1932).

As a consequence, tauromachy enjoyed great cultural approbation. The bull itself became a recurrent theme in artistic production during the middle decades of the twentieth century. It occupied a privileged place in the work of Pablo Picasso as a mythical animal, an expression of vital strength and raw sexuality. Apart from its universal connotations, in all these manifestations the noble animal was above all a genuine representation of the Iberian essence. The lyrical poetry of the period adopted the bull as the incarnation of Spain and everything Spanish, as the verse of Miguel Hernández illustrates: 'Rise up, *toro de España*: rouse yourself, wake up. / Awaken fully, foaming black bull, / that breathes in light and exudes shadow, / distilling oceans beneath your unpierced skin' ('Llamo al toro de España'). This poet symbolizes in the tragedy of the bull the tortuous history of Spain – the drama of

Spain – and ends by identifying with the energy and black fortune of the bull: 'Like the bull I was born for mourning / and pain, like the bull I am marked / by a hellish sword in my side / and as a man by the fruit in my groin.'[30] In Spanish culture, bullfighting came to be considered authentic art, even the supreme art, but above all an original Spanish art form, as José Bergamín argued.[31]

This type of analysis continued as a constant feature in twentieth-century Spanish art, literature, essay and thought. One of the most tenacious defenders of the festivity from the cultural perspective, Andrés Amorós, inserted it naturally in the Spanish worldview. He echoed the emphatic statements of García Lorca, that bullfighting 'is probably the greatest poetic and vital treasure of Spain', and 'the most cultured festivity in the world today'. For Amorós, to speak of bullfighting was tantamount to speaking of Spanish culture: 'The bullfights are culture in many senses: they are bound up in the history of Spain at every instant and serve as an exceptional way of understanding our collective psychology.... They also constitute a myth, a rite, one of the highest Spanish symbols.' According to this author, myth and rite are two fundamental elements in explaining the origins of the festivity: 'The cultural reality of the bull cannot be reduced to what thousands of spectators see in the ring. A long history culminates there, of course, but the myth, the rite, the sacred ceremony, existed long before. This is one of the reasons why the bullfight is given pre-eminence over other mass spectacles.' History, culture, festivity and language meld into a harmonious whole in the bullring: 'Yes, in spite of what the detractors say, the culture of the bullfight is our great national festivity. That is how our people have lived it down through the centuries, on the *skin of the bull*, in this *Iberian bullring*.'[32]

Bullfighting from Yesterday to Tomorrow

For most of the modern era, for better or worse, tauromachy has been a consubstantial element with Spain and *that which is Spanish*, for natives and foreigners alike. It has significant ramifications in the most diverse contexts, from art to literature to politics to language to music to cuisine. As such, the taurine festivity has been considered a 'national expression', though this classification remains problematic for broad sectors of Spanish society. Bullfighting awakens conflicting passions, heated debate and visceral reactions on both sides of the issue.

Picking up one of the threads we alluded to earlier will assist in a summary of what has been discussed. The romantic 'lithograph' of the bullfight, which would enjoy so much success outside the country and spark so much debate within its borders, underscores the decisive influence of the foreigner's perception in converting the bullfights into a national festivity. We do not here pretend to reduce a jumbled phenomenon to a mechanical cause-effect relationship. Clearly, the national festivity is no foreign invention; it emerged well before the romantic cliché took hold. However, we do believe that from the end of the eighteenth century and very particularly in the first half of the nineteenth century, the national festivity acquired its characteristic traits and became a constituent element in the deep-rooted romantic myth.

In constructing its modern national identity, Spain used as references the parameters of the most advanced countries in western Europe, especially France and England. This implied an awareness of a relative situation of backwardness and inferiority that was explicitly assimilated and even magnified (the decadence cliché, for example). It generated a dynamic of insecurity, weakness and dependence on foreign opinion. Here fits the myth of Romantic Spain, with all its strength and its ambivalence: retrograde, coarse, violent, ignorant and fanatical on one side and authentic, passionate, lively, generous and valiant on the other. All these adjectives are applicable to bullfighting as the supreme expression of them all and to Romantic Spain by extension. In this context, bullfighting appeared as an original pastime, specifically Spanish and not found elsewhere. At the same time that it captivated the attention and curiosity of the visitor, it maintained a discourse regarding Spanish *difference*. This double-edged sword would be used for opposite aims: conservatives, Catholics, etc., wielded it to defend Spanish particularity in the European context, while progressives brandished it to combat Spanish backwardness.

In this way, bullfighting became a symbolic element that distinguished Spain from the rest of the world. The taurine ritual is as Spanish as the 'oriental' architecture of the Alhambra in Granada and the Giralda Tower in Seville, Don Quixote and Sancho Panza, the bandits of Sierra Morena, the gypsies of Sacromonte (Granada), the landscape of Ronda (Málaga), the water carriers of Madrid or the monastery of El Escorial. In the festivity, Spanish history and tradition fuse to become the clichés as they are seen from the outside. For many, the bullfights generate a morbid attraction reminiscent of the *Autos de fe* (religious executions) or the garrotte (with its atrocious parallelism with the point of the sword in the bull). The ceremony of the bullring seems to preserve an echo of the ritualistic ceremonies of the Inquisition, with its mix of solemnity and popular participation. Blood plays an essential role in all of them, becoming a characteristic feature of Spanishness.

The bullfight also represents the Spanish conception of existence as a cruel game, a tragedy, a mockery. Everything about the festivity has a symbolic aura. Thus, for example, the bullfighter is the vulnerable hero, both victim and executioner, a being who dies or kills but never loses his dignity. Dignity is something the Spaniard must never allow himself to lose. In the theatre of Spain's Golden Age, they called it honour.

Ultimately, we are dealing with a cosmovision of Spain and Spanish culture that came to fruition externally and then worked its way inward. With varying degrees of reticence, and at times with open enthusiasm, the festivity was assimilated by the elites as a distinctively Spanish element. A discourse emerged that discovered in bullfighting the quintessential Spanish idiosyncrasy, which coincided in essence with the main lines of the 'romantic print'. As the twentieth century advanced, the aura of success surrounding novelists such as Blasco Ibáñez and even Hemingway began to fade and were substituted by others who would use updated versions of the same parameters. When bestselling authors Dominique Lapierre and Larry Collins embarked on a Spanish work, they chose bullfighting (of course!) as their topic. The sole protagonist of *Or I'll Dress You in Mourning* (1968) was the most famous bullfighter of the Francoist period: Manuel Benítez, *el Cordobés*. In their work, the national festivity constituted the supreme symbol of a singular country where life and death intertwine in a dramatic game: sun, blood, passion, fate, mourning, glory.

The aforementioned hypothesis could also explain the palpable decline of tauromachy when the discourse on Spanish difference unravelled. This occurred in tandem with the death of Franco and subsequent political and economic integration into Europe. However, it cannot be reduced to a question of political minorities or intellectual elites. The Spanish population has undergone accelerated urbanization since the decades of Francoist economic development, and has lost its traditional reference points. Meanwhile, youth are being educated in values less and less *authentically* Spanish, and more open to modern currents. In symbolic terms, bullfighting has receded in the inexorable wake of football and other mass spectacles or forms of entertainment.

It does not therefore seem likely that the taurine spectacle will be accepted and assimilated as a 'national festivity' by new generations of Spaniards. Currently, tauromachy appears to pertain more to the past than to the future. However, the palpable decline in bullfighting as a grand mass spectacle does not necessarily imply its disappearance, at least in the short run. There are still hundreds of thousands of enthusiasts, especially in areas such as Andalusia. The decline alluded to is not incompatible with the preservation and even potentiation of certain symbols, such as the bull itself, which has been elevated to an icon that at times replaces the national coat of arms on the flag.

The clear waning of the festivity in empirical terms has not hindered its reactivation as a subject of debate and political manipulation, always on the increasingly more questionable basis of whether bullfighting should continue as a 'national festivity' or at least as a symbol of Spanishness. This explains why Catalan nationalists succeeded in banning bullfighting throughout Catalonia. However, as we have said, as the bullfights are losing this standing, the bull as a symbol of Spain is gaining prominence in the most varied political, cultural and sports contexts. Spanish modernity has frequently been described as an updating of taurine symbols: Pedro Almodóvar's films (*Matador*, 1986, for example) have played a key role in this, and taurine symbols are heavily used in promoting the 'Spain brand' in general. Tourism has not forgotten the attraction of bulls, though they are often peddled in twisted or embarrassing ways. Daily life and language in the most diverse media is also rife with taurine references. This reality should not be undervalued; it is perceptible to any observer and seems compatible with indifference to, or even rejection of, bullfighting.

Spain is losing ground as the country of bullfights as the *fiesta nacional*, but it is still considered the country for *fiesta* – in all its ambiguity – and this *fiesta* clearly includes bullfighting. Unlike neighbouring countries, concerts and other modern spectacles are held in bullrings, with their open *tendido* seating serving as postmodern stands and their golden sand covered with carpets, lights and special effects. Meanwhile, motor tourists are surprised by the enormous billboards in the form of a black bull that dominate the landscape. These vintage advertisements for a well-known Spanish brandy remain as icons of the Spanish countryside. In the south, Andalusian cities cultivate a passion for bullfighting; in the north, the Pamplona *Sanfermines* are still going strong as one of the most famous taurine festivities in the world.

Undoubtedly, the bull continues to play a relevant, iconic role in the Spanish context; though its virtue as an identitary emblem is questionable. It shares the plight of other conventional symbols, such as the national anthem, the flag or commemorative monuments. Many Spaniards neither embrace nor identify with these symbols but look upon them with a profound, historically influenced sense of rejection.

Rafael Núñez Florencio is a historian and philosopher who has extensively written on historic and literary topics, and published several monographs, articles and book reviews in journals and newspapers. His most recent books are *El peso del pesimismo. Del 98 al desencanto*

(Madrid, 2010) and (alongside Elena Núñez González) *¡Viva la muerte! Política y cultura de lo macabro* (Madrid, 2014).

Notes

1. Manuel Machado, 'La fiesta nacional', in Cossío (1959: 129).
2. Núñez Florencio (2001).
3. Sousa (1928); Casares Herrero (1935); Arriba and Romaguera (1949); Henríquez (1951); Martínez Salvatierra (1961); Aulestia (1967); López Valdemoro de Quesada (1985 [1899]); Abarquero Durango (1988).
4. Henry Kamen, 'Consideraciones sobre la fiesta nacional', *El Mundo*, 11 August 2010.
5. Sánchez Álvarez-Insúa (2006: 907).
6. Núñez Florencio (2010).
7. Shubert (1999).
8. Andreu (2008).
9. Maeztu (1997: 142).
10. Costa (1913: 5).
11. Baroja (1979: 159, 222).
12. Verhaeren and Regoyos (1983).
13. Gutiérrez-Solana (2004: 155–57, 263–68; 1998).
14. Noel (1967: 161–62).
15. Unamuno (1965: 55–66).
16. Vicent (2001).
17. Jesús Mosterín, 'La España negra y la tauromaquia', *El País*, 11 March 2010.
18. Cambria (1974: 242–43).
19. Ortega y Gasset (1962: 141).
20. Abad de Santillán (1917: 75).
21. Pérez de Ayala (1925 [1918]: 179, 185–86, 259–64).
22. Tierno Galván (1961: 53–77).
23. López Rinconada (1996); Claramunt López (2006); Urrutia (1974).
24. See Mingote (1975).
25. Boix (2011: 138).
26. Marzal (2010).
27. Ríos Mozo (1971: 13).
28. See Cossío (2007), as well as Cossío (1995), for the abridged version.
29. González Troyano (1988); Moreno Galván (1960); Lasker (1976); Amorós (1993).
30. Mariatc Cobaleda, 'El simbolismo del toro en la obra poética de Miguel Hernández', http://www.miguelhernandezvirtual.es/new/files/Actas_II_Pre sentacion/17mariat.pdf; R. Fernández Palmeral, 'El toro en la obra de Miguel Hernández', *Perito Literario-Artístico*, Revista de Literatura y Arte Alicantino, May 2005. http://www.revistaperito.com/.
31. Bergamín (1981: 39–42).
32. Amorós (1999: 13–16, 21–23).

Chapter 10

Sports and the Spanish Nation

Alejandro Quiroga

On 21 June 2000, the Spanish National Football Team played one of its most memorable matches in history. In the last game of the group phase of the European Football Championship in Belgium and the Netherlands, the Spanish team needed to beat Yugoslavia to go on to the quarter-finals. In minute 92, the team was losing 3–2. What occurred in the following minutes was one of the most spectacular comebacks in international football history. In minute 93, the referee called a penalty in Spain's favour, and Gaizka Mendieta calmly scored from the spot to tie it up. Two minutes later, Pep Guardiola in centre field passed to Ismael Urzáiz, who set up the shot for Alfonso Pérez to score with a half-volley. With this goal *in extremis*, Spain won the game and moved on to the quarter-finals. The Spanish press described the team's comeback as 'racial': the victory, a 'demonstration of caste and courage', was won because the team had channelled their legendary 'fury'.[1] The game hadn't been won through good playing and goal-scoring opportunities, but by 'epic ferocity and self-respect'.[2]

Four days later, Spain battled France in the quarter-finals. In the final moments of the game, the French retained a 2–1 advantage, but in minute 90 the Italian referee Pierluigi Collina awarded Spain a penalty shot. Raúl González grabbed the ball, placed it at the spot, and with a too-strong shot sent it over the crossbar. Once again, Spain had fallen in the quarter-finals of a major tournament. Now, the Spanish press spoke of a 'sad, pitiful' farewell due to 'bad luck', unfair 'treatment by chance' and 'misfortune'.[3] The defeat was blamed on a historical 'curse' that kept Spain from ever going beyond the quarter-finals. Enrique Ortego wrote poetically for *ABC* newspaper: 'The present is written with the same pen as the past, and the future will always end the same. Spain once again returns home after the quarter-finals. The semi-finals are our own particular Everest'.[4] 'You can't fight destiny', declared Javier Gascón in *El Mundo Deportivo*.[5]

In the span of four days, the Spaniards had gone from distinguishing themselves for their ferocity and caste to being the sad victims of historical misfortune that barred them from standing among the greatest in Europe. Whether 'history' carries more weight than missed penalty kicks in football is certainly up for debate; however, here we are mainly interested in the press commentary on these two games. The reactions provide a clear example of the narrative that developed around Spaniards in relation to sports in the twentieth century. This discourse portrayed Spanish athletes, and by extension the Spanish people, as passionate, fierce and courageous beings. Caste and fury were the 'natural' expressions of a national identity, here projected through sports. In the same way and with no apparent contradiction, this narrative overflowed with pessimism and fatalism when addressing failures. Spaniards were frequently described as sad figures, victims of dark fate and uncontrollable historical forces rather than their own incompetence.

In recent years, the idea of nation as narrative has become popular among historians. This interpretation views a nation as a set of metaphors and images that are created and recreated through discourse. These emerged at the end of the eighteenth century: master narratives that created a national past for different territories and political communities throughout the world.[6] In Europe, Enlightenment historians were the first to create a modern national narrative that eventually spread and was recreated by journalists, politicians and academics throughout the nineteenth century. These master narratives of the nation were mainly passed down through textbooks, news and novels found in schools, homes and cultural centres.[7] With the rise of mass society in early-twentieth-century Europe, a new popular historiography took shape as the past and national myths were spread through magazines, newspapers, cinema, radio and eventually television. These popular representations of the past were usually clear, simplified, unidimensional and quite effective in creating a national image.[8]

Sports played a critical role in shaping national narratives, language and myths during the twentieth century.[9] With the advent of the modern Olympic Games in 1896 and the increasing popularity of a variety of international competitions in the early twentieth century, the notion emerged that athletes had a 'national style' that somehow reflected the identity of the country they represented. The association between national teams and national identities perpetuated itself through media repetition and narrative that emphasized the 'typical' style of different

countries. This was complemented by the elevation of athletes to legendary myth status. Thus, the great teams and sports heroes of the past
became associated with an ensemble of national traits set in a patriotic
narrative that appealed to a sense of collective belonging. Matches and
teams were interpreted as expressions of 'intrinsic' national characteristics: qualities the teams would always possess by virtue of having
possessed them in the past. Spain's national men's football team forged
the myth of 'Spanish fury' in the 1920 Antwerp Olympics, which became the reference for the Spanish 'authentic and national style', reflecting by extension the traits of the Spanish people.

These master sports narratives mainly propagated through the media, creating a 'culture of a nationality' by portraying national teams as
a set of national attributes, associating athletes with stereotypes in the
written press, on the radio and on television.[10] This perpetuated a set of
narratives and shared cultural values that reinforced popular perceptions of national unity. Sports helped generate and transmit a master
narrative for Spanish identity, while supplying images and representations of other national collectives. However, a failure narrative arose
alongside the fury myth, which reinforced fate, bad luck and injustice as part of the national identity in the dominant twentieth-century
narrative. Here, I shall analyse how sports generated and perpetuated
Spanish national identity in the twentieth century, examining the narrative combination of attributing successes to Spanish fury but recurring to fatalism when explaining failures. The first section examines
the period from 1900 to 1936, the second covers Francoism, and the
third analyses the transformations in the national sports narrative
from 1977 to 2000.

The Rise of Mass Society (1900–1936)

The practice of sports increased in Spain as mass society became consolidated. Urban development along with changing consumption patterns and labour conditions among the middle and working classes
generated more 'free time' in the early twentieth century. As leisure
became commercialized, sports developed into a form of mass entertainment. In Spain, a definite sports system emerged between 1900 and
1936. Cycling, boxing and especially football appealed across social
strata and became mass spectacles while basketball, athletics, rugby
and hockey – which were more popular among the bourgeoisie – experienced less growth.[11] The increasing relevance of sports as mass entertainment gave rise to specialized sports press and increased sports

coverage in daily newspapers.[12] Sports became another stage for narrating the Spanish nation, complementing the work of historians, writers and teachers.

Sports identities originally developed in local spheres and enthusiasts were devoted to their neighbourhood, town or city football, cycling or rowing clubs before regional or national teams existed (though they generated no real conflict of interests).[13] Clubs played in provincial and regional leagues, while regional teams usually played friendly games against other regional teams. Sometimes, regional teams would play against clubs, city teams or even national teams. For example, the Catalan and French football teams contended on 21 February 1912 and Catalonia played against Spain in Barcelona on 13 March 1924.[14] In Spain, the 1915 Prince of Asturias Cup was among the first nationally organized football competitions for regional teams.[15] During the 1920s and 1930s, regional teams became quite popular in football and other sports such as hockey, cycling and horse racing.

Regarding regional sports and national identities, the *Mancomunitat,* or Commonwealth of Catalonia, worked to 'Catalanize' sports from its creation in 1914 until its abolition in 1925. Basque nationalism also used sports for propaganda. Significantly, King Alfonso XIII linked the monarchy with sporting events and the Primo de Rivera dictatorship encouraged physical exercise to improve the race and promote patriotic Spanish values. Regional teams were not generally considered a threat to Spanish unity, nor did regional sports identities conflict with Spanish identity. This compatibility among local, provincial, regional and national identities in pre–Civil War Spain illustrates the 'multiple identities' that could easily overlap in an individual.[16] In the decades prior to the Franco dictatorship, the devoted Barça fan could be emotionally committed to the Catalan regional squad, while publicly supporting the Spanish national football team.

The associations between teams, national traits and Spanish identity were wrought from men's football clubs. The myth of 'Spanish fury' is bound up in the origins of the Spanish national team. In 1920, the Spanish Football Federation formed the first national squad to represent Spain at the Olympic Games in Antwerp. The team won a silver medal, along with commentaries in the foreign press regarding their brusque, unsophisticated style. The French daily *L'Auto* first used the term *fury* in reference to the Spanish Olympic team, with the headline 'Denmark defeated by Spanish fury'.[17] Other newspapers quickly appropriated it, with clearly negative connotations. H. Hollander, a journalist for the Dutch daily *De Telegraaf,* used the word often to describe the Spanish team's brutality on the field. The Dutch and Belgian press asserted that this savagery defined more than the football team, it responded to the Spanish national trait that the Spanish *Tercios* of Flanders had demonstrated militarily centuries earlier during the 1576 Sack of Antwerp. In truth, the abundant attributions of 'fury' and 'brutality' reflected the seizing of an opportunity to project Spain's 'Black Legend' – a key myth in Belgian and especially Dutch national discourse – onto the Spanish team.

The Spanish press, however, quickly turned 'fury' into a complement. Galician journalist Manolo de Castro covered the Antwerp Games and was the first to positively associate 'fury' with the Spanish team in the weekly *Madrid-Sport*. De Castro (called Handicap), along with two other colleagues, was a national team manager and an occasional linesman in Spanish matches. He reported how the Belgian press believed 'fury' to be what distinguished the Spanish team from others.[18] He emphasized the team's capacity to combine 'hard, fiery, furious play' with a more 'deliberate and precise' style, but only the first traits stuck. Accordingly, the Spanish team's superiority in the match against the Netherlands was attributed to 'our classic fury' in confronting the less energetic Dutch team.[19] Sweden's attempt to intimidate the Spanish team also failed, as they were 'defeated by the macho Spanish players'. Spain's silver medal reflected the 'great love the footballers felt for their country as they stepped onto the football pitches in Brussels and Antwerp, and to their enthusiasm and bravery as they played their fast, scientific match'.[20]

Later that year, Handicap's compiled articles and memories from the event were published in a book, *Las gestas españolas en el football Olímpico de Amberes*, which reinforced the benign use of 'fury'. 'Brutality' and 'savagery' underwent similar redefinition as courage and virility. In 1924, renowned reporter Juan Deportista published a book that constituted the first attempt to conceptualize 'Spanish fury' in the world of sports. For Deportista, it expressed a display of 'ferocity and pride' in a typically Spanish 'desperate struggle', adding a touch of southern passion to a game invented by the English.[21] Assisted by a sizable publicity campaign, the book became a bestseller and the 'fury' took hold in sports media and even general newspapers. In 1929, a sports weekly titled *Furia Española* was launched in Barcelona.

As triumphant Spanish fury established itself, the national sports narrative acquired a certain negativity regarding defeat. Accordingly, on the dark side of Spanish fury, fate and unjust referees constituted both the cause of and explanation for defeat. In the Antwerp Olympics, Spain won every match except the one against Belgium. Manolo de Castro's article justified the defeat as a combination of bad luck – a 'tragic afternoon' for the Spaniards – and a 'negligent or partial referee' who conceded a goal to the Belgians from a 'scandalously off-sided position'.[22] Luis Argüello, the treasurer for the Spanish Royal Football Federation, echoed that the Spanish team had lost 'because they *had to lose*'. He blamed the 'tourist referee' for the annulling of 'two goals, which would have tied the score'.[23] A *Madrid-Sport* editorial asserted that if 'misfortune had not fallen upon us, we would have certainly been in first place'.[24] This fatalistic discursive cement hardened four years later in the 1924 Paris Olympics, when Spain – the crowd favourite – was eliminated in the first match, losing 1–0 to Italy. The one goal was in fact scored by the Spaniard Pedro Vallana in his own goal in minute 84. The Spanish press blamed the referee:

> The reputation for *Spanish fury* was too intimidating and had to be contained at any cost. Our team did not seem *furious,* on the contrary, the game was rather meek. But even playing poorly, we couldn't be beaten! However, the referee was on the field for a reason, and finding no opportunities to punish our team, he opted to let anything the Italians did go by, and *they set a new record for playing dirty.* Believing us stupid and himself *impartial,* he resorted to calling midfield fouls against us and ignoring the Italians when they did the same (which they did several times) in the penalty area.[25]

Spain: the victim of cruel fate for scoring an own goal, and of a referee who had collaborated in the Italian victory, rewarding Italian knavery rather than Spanish chivalry. This quixotic discourse – defeated but honourable – became a longstanding Spanish stereotype that was reinforced in the Amsterdam Olympics. In 1928, the International Olympic Committee requested that only amateur players be sent to the games. The Spanish Football Federation complied and sent a team composed entirely of non-professional players. Upon arriving, they learned that most teams had some professional players as well. After defeating Mexico 7–1, the Spanish team went up against the Italian team, which included several well-known professional players. By minute 15, Spain was winning, but the match ended in a draw because 'adversity once again decided to torment our enthusiastic representatives'.[26] The Italians won the subsequent tiebreaker match 7–1, and some reporters again blamed the referees. *La Vanguardia* declared that 'in the first half the referee already began to favour the Italians, who scored several goals off-sides'.[27]

The 'fury and failure' narrative extended to international success and failure in basketball, boxing and even cycling. These sports could also reflect national courage and virility or misfortune and manoeuvres by envious foreigners.[28] The great success of this narrative in the early twentieth century is partially attributable to its good fit with national and international stereotypes that had been operative since the end of the nineteenth century, portraying the Spanish people as a passionate, hot-blooded, masculine and impulsive race. After the First World War, a new discourse of virility elevated the modern, healthy and athletic man. Sports became an excellent expression of new masculinity and a means for social expansion; and fury quickly became an expression of virility among the Spanish population during the 1920s.[29] Likewise, fatalism in sports was an extension of a nationalism with a historical penchant for grumbling and moaning. This too was evident during the last decades of the nineteenth century, when the country specialized in lamenting its national misfortunes.[30] The colonial Disaster of 1898 only accentuated this tale of national woe and self-pity, which found its way into artistic and literary circles, schools and especially the press.[31] Primo de Rivera's dictatorship tried to paint a brighter image of Spain, but the Spanish clichés of passion and racial virility persisted, combined with large doses of pessimism and fatalism, especially in the 1920s.[32]

Sports became more politicized during the Second Spanish Republic. They also gained popularity as leisure became increasingly commercialized and associationism grew among the urban middle class and women.[33] The fury and failure discourse remained intact during this democratic period and was even perpetuated by opposing political ideologies. During the 1934 FIFA World Cup in Italy, the correspondent from the Catholic daily *El Debate* praised the advances of Fascist Italy and how players gave the fascist salute before each game.[34] *El Socialista*, however, understood how football could manipulate the masses. It published an editorial that directly accused Mussolini of rigging the World Cup in order to feed victorious football imagery to the Italian proletariat. By distracting them from the country's economic issues, they would more easily succumb to manipulation, even slavery.[35] Ideological differences aside, Spanish newspapers continued the narrative of fury and persecution by the referees throughout the World Cup.[36] When Spain met Italy in the quarter-finals on 31 May 1934, seven Spanish players were injured and the match ended in a draw. Reportedly, the Belgian referee Louis Baert let the Italians get away with a great deal of violence, and conceded their goal after an attack on the Spanish goalkeeper Ricardo Zamora. However, when Ramón de la Fuente evaded four rival players to score a goal, it was declared off-side. The next day, after Swiss referee René Marcet nullified a controversial goal from Spain, Italy won the rematch 1–0.

The Spanish press united in their outrage over the partiality of the referees and the violence of the Italians. After the first match against Italy, *El Socialista* lauded the Spanish team's 'great enthusiasm for the fight', but declared them powerless against 'a referee who wanted the Blue Eleven to win at all costs'.[37] Following the rematch, *El Socialista* accused the referee Marcet of 'undoubtedly receiving the same orders as the first referee. From the very beginning of the game our boys could see they would not be winning this match, because the man was willing to frustrate any advances that would jeopardize the Italians' game.'[38] *El Debate* spoke of fury while praising the chivalry and heroism of the Spanish team, which had valiantly resisted both the Italians and the referee. Though Spain had been eliminated in the 'battle of Florence', the team was awarded an 'indisputable moral triumph' in the press.[39] The image of quixotic chivalry in defeat continued to accompany the spread of Spanish fury.

The Franco Dictatorship (1936–75)

Like their Italian and German counterparts, when the Francoists rose to power after the Spanish Civil War they brutally imposed a fascist-type regime that saw sports as a vehicle for nationalistic indoctrination. The Falangist-controlled National Sports Delegation instituted a new sports regime directed by General José Moscardó. From the outset, Moscardó understood that sports had to be subordinated to the state as a key to strengthening the race. He intended to create compulsory biological files to track the physical development of all Spaniards.[40] The regime established three types of sports entities. First were the national federations for regulated sports that organized formal leagues through sports clubs in different categories. Second were sports related to the single party, *F.E.T. y de las JONS*, a blatant plagiarism of Nazi and Italian institutions, with their own practices and tournaments. These incorporated sections from Falange, such as the Youth Front, the Women's Section and the Spanish Collegiate Trade Union. Third, and much less relevant, were military sports, which enjoyed a degree of autonomy and incorporated physical education into the military.[41]

In contrast with General Moscardó, who insisted on promoting amateur sports, the 1940s and 1950s saw the expansion of sports –predominantly football – as mass events. The Francoists had been harnessing the propagandistic potential of football since the Civil War, when the Rebels created their national team in the Basque Country and debuted against Real Sociedad in San Sebastián in December 1938.[42] After the war, Moscardó made some changes: the national team exchanged their traditional red kits for Falangist blue, clubs were filled with single-party officials and players were required to salute and sing *Cara al Sol* before every match, in an attempt to turn football stadiums into a sort of patriotic cathedrals for worshipping the nation and the New State.[43] Germany, Italy, Vichy France, Portugal and Switzerland invited Spain to their friendly matches – complete with speeches on fascist brotherhood and anti-communist struggle – leaving little doubt regarding Franco's loyalties or his regime's moral standing during the Second World War.

From the outset, Francoism incorporated the fury myth into its national narrative, propagating it as an expression of Spanish ferocity and courage. With its irrational, occasionally violent connotations, *fury* became a favourite term in the Francoist press. It 'proved' the existence of specifically Spanish racial traits, perpetuated the inferiority of women and enhanced the regime discourse regarding Spanish regeneration. In a Europe dominated by Nazis, and as the Falange reached full power in Spain, the Francoist regime created a racial image of the Spanish athlete that complemented the chivalrous honour and vehemence that the media had associated with fury prior to the Civil War. However, Francoist nationalism in sports did not necessarily attempt to eliminate all regional expressions. Instead, the Francoist press attempted to establish Basque traits as primordially Spanish, and traditional Basque sports as a sample of quintessential Spanishness.[44] Regional teams continued to play against each other in almost all sports after the Civil War, including football matches between Catalonia and Castile.[45] The cycling Tour of Catalonia had been cancelled in 1937 and 1938 due to the fighting, but quickly resumed in 1939. Like Nazi Germany and Fascist Italy, Francoist Spain allowed some regional representation, so long as it posed no threat to national unity.[46]

With the fall of the Third Reich, Falangist influence diminished in Franco's advisory cabinets and the dictatorship underwent cosmetic changes to distance itself from its former German and Italian allies. The fascist salute was abandoned in September 1945 and the Spanish national team returned to wearing red kits in 1947. However, the dictatorship continued to use football for popular indoctrination: the Francoist press presented Spanish sports triumphs as victories for the regime, as new methods of mass communication made football increasingly relevant in society. During the 1940s and 1950s, the press would often begin talking about international matches about two weeks prior, collect copious amounts of information the day of the event and review it for days after. Radio broadcast of international games allowed the regime to reach millions of people in bars, cafés and homes. The propagandistic NO-DO (News and Documentaries) newsreels also included abundant reports on matches, taking Francoist and national team discourse to viewers across the country. With this powerful combination of written press, radio and the NO-DO, the dictatorship could keep football matches (and their corresponding nationalist narrative) in people's minds for weeks. The repetition of football news had an important cumulative effect that increased the impact of official messages in the minds of the Spanish people.

This 'nationalizing media accumulation process' gave individuals more references to the Francoist nation, both in public (the radio at the café or the NO-DO at the cinema) and private (the newspaper and transistor radio in the sitting room) spheres.[47] The performance of the national team in the 1950 World Cup in Brazil perfectly illustrates this process and how the Francoist regime appropriated the team's victories. After beating Chile 2–0 and the United States 3–1, Spain defeated England with a goal by Telmo Zarra and placed among the four best teams. In the days prior to the game, the English and Spanish press had been stirring up passions with allusions to the privateering activities of Sir Francis Drake and Britain's colonial decadence, respectively.[48] The game was broadcast on radio, and journalist Matías Prats immortalized Zarra's winning goal. The newspapers spoke of the match in epic terms for days and the victory was replayed in the NO-DOs for months. To the journalists who had dared to doubt the possibility of a Spanish victory, Armando Muñoz Calero, president of the Spanish Football Federation, declared: '[Our players] were filled with such faith and patriotism, they rose above all envy. Clearly they were only thinking of our great nation, with the best Commander in the world.'[49]

The myth of fury remained as an abiding, central element in regime discourse throughout the 1950s. During the Brazil World Cup, the press praised the combination of historic fury and 'an impressive show of technique and team play' in the match against England.[50] The press also linked sports victories to great national historical feats. English piracy and the former Spanish Empire in the Americas surfaced in matches against 'treacherous Albion'; when France, Turkey or Belgium were defeated, 2 May 1808, the Battle of Lepanto and the *Tercios* of Flanders were recalled, respectively.[51] Direct association of historical feats with the national football team established a continuous narrative between patriotic acts of the past and present-day sports using Francoist nationalist imagery. The myth of fury remained operative as the regime appropriated the victories of Real Madrid in the 1950s.

When they became champions of Europe for the first time in June 1956, Catalan Football Federation President Agustín Pujol attributed their victory to 'the most refined technique, combined with the traditional traits of Spanish football: courage and fury'.[52] It is common knowledge that the dictatorship attempted to use Real Madrid's European victories to reduce its international isolation, and that the team benefited from the regime's support. By mid-decade, Real Madrid had become an unofficial ambassador for Spain – and Francoism by extension – in an arrangement the directors, trainers and players fully understood.[53]

The dictatorship continued to use mass media implacably in its later years to transmit its patriotic message, and football remained the regime's preferred instrument. However, methods changed with social transformations and the expansion of television. Television – and televised matches – contributed decisively to the 'nationalizing media accumulation process'. Television not only enhanced the nationalizing process, it also multiplied the audience for Francoist discourse with its narrative regarding Spain and Spanish national traits. Transmission of football games to the small screen also affected newspapers, which began to include more pages on football and further increased its social relevance. By the mid-1960s, the print run for Spanish sports dailies outnumbered that of the general newspapers.[54]

Francoism systematically used Televisión Española (TVE) to broadcast its nationalist narrative through sporting events from the 1960s on,[55] as was clearly illustrated during the 1964 European Football Championship. The semi-finals and finals were held in Spain, and the dictatorship demonstrated full awareness of the propagandistic potential of television. The matches were broadcast directly by Eurovision and Intervision to reach the largest possible number of viewers. *Marca* newspaper stated that the most important aspect of Spain's victory over the USSR in the final on 21 June 1964 was that 'millions and millions of Spaniards' had seen it on television.[56] To strengthen patriotic sentiment in the 'internal market', TVE retransmitted the match on 29 June to 'allow fans to relive the triumph of Spanish football'.[57] For Franco, who watched the final in the Santiago Bernabéu stadium, the victory was that Spanish 'unity and patriotism' had appeared on television screens in 'many countries across the world'.[58] Of course, this national unity excluded the losers of the Civil War. José Antonio Elola Olaso, national delegate for physical education and sports, reminded everyone that this victory had occurred while 'celebrating 25 years of peace'[59]. The daily newspaper *ABC* left no room for misinterpretation:

After 25 years of peace, the applause resounds as authentic and eloquent support for the spirit of 18 July. I would say that popular, intentional and enthusiastic support for the state has never been as high as in this quarter-century, born from victory over communism and its comrades.... Spain becomes more orderly, mature and coherent every day, as a people, advancing in solidarity towards economic, social and institutional development.[60]

The myth of fury was more present than ever in the 1964 European Football Championship. Spain had defeated the Soviets through strength, ferocity and courage. 'The second half could only have ended in victory thanks to the team's fury', declared *Marca*. Comparisons to the 'epic of Antwerp' became commonplace, indicating the degree to which fury remained a primordial narrative in the pantheon of Francoist national myths. Journalists described how the 1964 players 'finished off corners like Belauste' had in the 1920 Olympics, or how Marcelino's goal 'must have made those who had been in Antwerp weep with emotion and consolation'.[61] Spanish national coach José Villalonga uncannily predicted: 'If until now we have always referred to the feat of Antwerp ... I believe our team's achievements today may perhaps become exemplary for the next forty-four years.'[62]

Meanwhile, broadcasting of league matches between Real Madrid and FC Barcelona and TVE retransmission of the Spanish national team's all-time best games became a household tradition on 30 April and 1 May each year. The dictatorship offered more football in a crude attempt to counteract protests on International Worker's Day.[63] As football success declined during late Francoism, the dictatorship appropriated other sports to project its nationalist narrative: the triumphs of Manolo Santana and Manuel Orantes in tennis, Federico Martín Bahamontes and Luis Ocaña in the Tour de France, the international titles of boxers Pepe Legrá, Pedro Carrasco and José Manuel Ibar 'Urtain', Paco Fernández Ochoa's Olympic gold in skiing, and the 1973 victories of Real Madrid and the national basketball team. These all served as platforms for the dictatorship to exalt national grandeur and perpetuate the 'One, Great and Free' political narrative along with a cultural narrative that defined the Spanish people as passionate, quixotic, *toreros* – the envy of foreigners.[64]

Francoism perpetuated the failure narrative by playing the victim to explain Spain's poor international athletic performance. Defeat was usually attributed to bad luck and unfair referees, reflecting Spanish pessimism and the Francoist persecution complex. When England defeated Spain in the 1968 European Football Championship quarter-finals, team manager Domingo Balmanya declared that the final score of 1–0 was unfair, that the referee had favoured the British and that he was happy because 'the team played to win the game with great courage and good will but lost in the most unfortunate way, by a solitary goal scored five minutes before the end of the match'.[65] These explanations were repeated three years later when Spain and the USSR battled for leadership of their division during the qualifying phase of the 1972 European Football Championship. The Spanish team badly needed to win in Seville after having lost the match in Moscow, but a 0–0 tie eliminated them from the Championship. Alongside arbitration errors, the daily paper *AS* blamed Spain's traditional misfortune for the loss:

> We needed to win ... but, unfortunately – and never has that word been more appropriately used in football – the ball did not want to enter Rudakov's goal, a goalkeeper who not only rivals the legendary Yachin, but who is also shamelessly allied with the goddess Fortune, who ensured that the ball did not enter the Soviet goal even when it got past Rudakov.[66]

During Francoism, fatalism became a sort of self-fulfilling prophecy in Spanish sports. In blaming bad luck and referees, Spain failed to properly analyse its deficiencies, namely a lack of investment and sports facilities. Placing responsibility beyond human control both strengthened the national failure narrative and dismissed any critique of the regime's sporting policies. Spain's poor infrastructures, and performance, remained unchanged. In the final days of Francoism, media sources not controlled by the regime dared to expose the pathetic state of Spanish sports teams and the fact that fate was used as an excuse for failure in the national narrative. A November 1975 article in the magazine *Don Balón* described the situation of Spanish sports: 'very few instructors, very scant and poor sports facilities, where the Law on Physical Education is scarcely applied, but plenty of windbag managers who continue to harp on the idea that all we need is luck'.[67]

The commentary demonstrated that Francoist narrative did not entirely fool the public, and questioned the effectiveness of Franco's nationalizing methods. Forty years of an imposed image of Spain and an official idea of nation combined with the regime's moral, cultural and political disrepute – especially amongst the youth – had altered national sentiment. People held 'Spanishness' in such disregard that identification of the political and cultural elite with a collective Spain proved problematic during the early days of the transition to democracy, particularly in Catalonia and the Basque Country. However there were limits to the nation's loss of prestige: social changes during late Francoism – the creation of a modern consumer society, the expansion of television, new forms of entertainment and mass tourism – had a significant homogenizing impact and served as informal nationalization methods that were detached from official state media and means.[68] From this perspective, sports and especially football became effective nationalizers, though in a more cultural than political sense. Similarly, many Spaniards had developed sentimental ties to the Spanish nation that did not necessarily involve political acceptance of the dictatorship. The daily experience of the Spanish people differed greatly from the official messages and narrative, so Francoist propaganda proved rather ineffective in fostering support for the regime. Though most Spaniards stayed informed through Francoist press, radio and television, in the final years many developed a democratic, anti-authoritarian political stance that completely opposed official propaganda.[69] Some Spaniards had somehow learned to distinguish between the 'sporting nation' of athletes in international competitions and the 'official nation' of Francoism.

The Parliamentary Monarchy (1977–2000)

With the return of democracy to Spain, popular sports expanded, infrastructures improved, associationism increased, and people showed greater interest in sporting events. The new political system fostered strong support for sports in the final decades of the twentieth century with a constitutional mandate requiring public authorities to promote sports. It sought to 'create' democratic citizens and project Spain internationally as a modern country. Public administrations in Spain's Autonomous Communities collaborated with private institutions (professional leagues, federations, associations) to organize great sporting events such as the 1982 FIFA World Cup and the 1992 Olympic Games in Barcelona, achieving unprecedented international recognition.[70] Political and structural changes in Spanish sports ran parallel to international changes in media. During the 1980s and 1990s, the European press discovered the direct relation between sports content and sales. In Spain, this resulted in a considerable increase in radio and television hours dedicated to sports.[71] The 'nationalizing media accumulation process' accelerated, promoting a Spanish identity linked to sports. With the exception of media controlled by sub-state nationalists, most Spanish media symbolically contributed to constructing an image of the nation through sport.[72]

The fury and failure narrative, however, persisted in the new democratic Spanish identity under construction. Though reference to fury had significantly declined, probably in reaction to Francoist overuse of the term, it endured as a Spanish trait in national sports narratives. In November 1977, when Spain played against Yugoslavia in the so-called Battle of Belgrade, the match became infamously brutal; Juan Gómez quarrelled with the spectators and was hit with a bottle. Yet Spain won 1–0 and qualified for the Argentina World Cup. *El Mundo Deportivo* applauded the moment: 'hats off for our team's fury, cool-headedness, integrity and opportunism in the face of such provocation'.[73] Spain's 12–1 victory over Malta in December 1983 provided another opportunity to cite genius, courage and fighting spirit. The *ABC* headlines hailed it as 'the return of Spanish fury', stating that 'this wave of goals was celebrated throughout Spain as a historic feat, like the goals of Zarra or Marcelino'.[74] Linking the match to former great victories established continuity with the past and reinforced the Spanish narrative of passionate, courageous fighters. The players' comments also connected national identity and gameplay: 'we've shown our *genio* [fiery temperament] and proven we are Spanish', defender José Antonio Camacho declared.[75] In a flurry of stereotypes, *El Mundo Deportivo* stated that Seville's special luck, the *duende sevillano,* had 'restored the image of our national team to its former glory, and the "Spanish spirit" that seemed lost to the ages'.[76] President Felipe González grasped the importance of the victory and personally phoned the players to congratulate them, attempting to associate the socialist government with Spain's triumph as thousands of citizens poured onto the streets of Seville and Madrid to celebrate.[77]

The failure narrative that highlighted misfortune and persecution by referees remained as the flip side of Spanish temper and gallantry in sports. When Spain lost to France in the 1984 European Football Championship final, victimism returned to the national forefront. According to *La Vanguardia*, the game was lost when 'Platini scored after a non-existent foul with the help of the Spanish goalkeeper, who had the ball in his hands and dropped it. The "clever" Czech referee Christov, painfully aware that the match was being played in Paris, only made the game more difficult for Spain.' *El Mundo Deportivo* declared more blatantly, 'a joke of a goal robbed us of the title. The referee was undoubtedly the best French player!'[78] Self-pitying indignation was patent; one daily from Barcelona even bordered on xenophobia with its article 'Christov I, King of the Frogs': 'It is as we feared. These French are such oafs that even in a place called the *Parc des Princes* they act like crooks, for if last night's game was not a crime, then Mitterand himself should provide an explanation. Undeniably, the most French Frog on the field was dressed in black!'[79]

Throughout the 1990s, allusions to fate and referee injustice remained quite common. The commentary on the 1994 World Cup quarter-finals between Spain and Italy, where the Italians won with a goal three minutes before the end of the game and the referee ignored a clear penalty on behalf of Luis Enrique, whose nose had been nose broken by Mauro Tassotti's elbow, clearly illustrates the permanence of this narrative of failure due to external factors.[80] It fit perfectly with the Spanish narrative of failure as a nation, which was fashionable among intellectuals, university professors, politicians and the press during the 1980s and 1990s.[81] In an article titled 'National-footballism', sociologist Enrique Gil Calvo spoke of the importance of the sport for Spain, 'the only European State which for various reasons has failed to create a true national identity'.[82] Other countries possessed a wide range of emotionally charged patriotic symbols, but Spain was different:

Since Spain lacks a national culture, the national football team is almost the only symbol (along with the other Olympic teams) capable of expressing a common collective identity and filling citizens with emotion by giving them the feeling of being members of one same collective. That is why football is so important in Spain, with no love or faith in the homeland, only faith in football and love for our national team make us proud to be Spanish.[83]

Gil Calvo accurately underscored the importance of football for nationalizing the masses in Spain, but overlooked how the narrative of failure also helped shape the Spanish national identity. Pessimism and fatalism were two key national features by which Spaniards defined themselves, so embedded in the Spanish identity that they successfully forged a national culture.

During the 1980s and 1990s, the fury and failure narrative began to erode in sports. Identifying Spaniards with passion and force reflected a certain primitivism, backwardness and male bravado that conflicted with the 'modern European Spain' that the socialist – and later conservative – governments so eagerly pursued. With the tennis victories of Arantxa Sánchez Vicario and Conchita Martínez in the 1980s and 1990s, fury extended to women; these sports celebrities were often presented as examples of courage and Spanish spirit. However, the fury discourse was not actually 'feminized', rather, these female champions were 'masculinized' in a country where female sports received minimal media attention. Spain's entry in the European Economic Community, along with the 1992 Olympic Games, World Expo and other international events, promoted an image of Spain as a normal, even modern, country. The 1992 Olympics best illustrate a deliberate state investment to project a modern, cosmopolitan Spain to both a national and international audience. It worked: survey research indicated that, in association with sports, Spaniards had internalized this image of a dynamic, open and modern Spain.[84]

Fury fit awkwardly as a defining feature of the national character in this new historical context; and its flip side, the failure myth, began to be questioned in the late twentieth century. In the late 1990s, some historians began to reject the idea of Spain as a historical anomaly and presented the national past as something normal within Europe. Success in sports – the Barcelona Olympics, Miguel Indurain in the Tour de France, Spanish tennis players in the Roland Garros tournament and the European Cups won by the FC Barcelona and Real Madrid in the 1990s – were explained as signs of a modernizing country competing on a level playing field with its European neighbours.[85] Even in failure, the explanation no longer involved a lack of fury. After Spain beat Bulgaria 6–1 in the 1998 World Cup in France – a victory both complete and useless, as the national team was still eliminated – the newspaper *El País* declared that Spaniards lacked not fury, but a winning attitude, as a national trait.[86] To some degree, the Spanish press was simply reproducing the Spanish loser-mentality stereotype that the British press was fostering. Apparently, something psychic or mental kept Spain from winning and made Spaniards underperform in great sporting events. Those who looked beyond pseudobiology and determinism found cause in the black forces of history. This chapter began with how some journalists explained Spain's elimination by France in the 2000 European Football Championship as being less about missed penalty kicks in the last minute and more about something incalculable: 'It is always the same. It's as though tradition has an irreversible influence and the national team trips over the same stone.'[87]

The fury and failure narrative was mainly linked to the Spanish national football team, which normally failed to meet expectations. As Spanish teams – even Spanish football clubs – began to enjoy international success in basketball, handball, cycling, tennis, golf and motorbiking, the narrative of fury and failure lost meaning. Modernity and normality have effectively eroded these myths in Spanish sports, though they lingered on in football. Despite the complimentary or alternative identities generated by football clubs, the surveys, television audiences and stadium attendance indicated that the social significance and public support of the Spanish national football team remained strong throughout the 1980s and 1990s.[88] Though support was weaker in Catalonia and the Basque Country, the strong identification of Spaniards with the national football team confirms: the continuity of multiple identities in sports, and that informal symbols of Spanishness carried no obvious Francoist connotations and were more easily assimilated than official symbols after the return to democracy.[89]

Conclusion

In Spanish sports, the fury-fatalism duo emerged in the 1920s. It projected stereotypes already established in literature, art and journalism, remaining relatively unchanged throughout the twentieth century. The impact of the narrative grew in tandem with the increasing significance of sports as a Spanish pastime and with the nationalizing media accumulation process. In the 1920s and 1930s, the fury myth fit easily in a Europe that defined national characteristics as a mix of racially and culturally immutable elements. Fatalism, misfortune and unfair referees were welcomed in a Spain identified with a *Mater Dolorosa* since the prior century, a society that in the first decades of the twentieth century had assimilated its failure, incapacity and backwardness. The fury myth combined well with Francoism: playing into the racism of the regime and the quixotic Spanish nature that the Civil War victors sought to emphasize. Fatalism and unfair referees served the victimism of the Francoist national narrative: an isolated regime that rationalized economic and social backwardness as foreign envy. The fury myth lost strength as the country modernized, but sporting success was still explained by recurring to Spaniards as *Don Quixote* figures fighting against the elements and overcoming adversity. In the post-Franco democracy, the narrative of sporting – and national – failure gradually faded as Spaniards embraced the image of a modern, normal country.

In the first decade of the twenty-first century, national football failures such as the 2002 World Cup and the 2004 European Football Championship generated an uncomfortable tension with the discourse of a successful, modern European nation. As in the 1990s, this tension did not exist in other sports: success in tennis, cycling, motorbiking, golf, handball or even club-level football fit well with the advanced, self-confident Spain that was being marketed politically and culturally.[90] Internationally, the image of Spain was linked to modernity through sports,[91] a perception that helped redefine the fury myth and the fatalistic connotations surrounding the Spanish national identity. Triumph in the 2008 and 2012 European Football Championships and the 2010 World Cup made victimism implausible and the beloved fatalism that had been so useful in creating a national identity of failure became irrelevant. Those titles crowned the political and cultural process of reaffirming Spanishness that began in the late twentieth century. In the last decade, we have shifted from a certain 'patriotic bulimia' based on fatalistic, lukewarm identification with sports figures to a sort of 'nationalist obesity' that massively exalts Spanishness.

Alejandro Quiroga is a Reader in Spanish History at Newcastle University. He specializes in the study of national identities and nationalisms. His most recent book is *Football and National Identities in Spain* (Basingstoke, 2013). He is also the author of *The Reinvention of Spain: Nation and Identity Since Democracy* (Oxford, 2007) (with Sebastian Balfour) and *Making Spaniards: Primo de Rivera and the Nationalization of the Masses, 1923–1930* (Basingstoke, 2007), and has edited *Right-Wing Spain in the Civil War Era* (London, 2012) and *Católicos y patriotas. Religión y nación en la Europa de entreguerras* (Madrid, 2013).

Notes

1. *ABC*, 22 June 2000; *El Mundo Deportivo*, 22 June 2000; *La Vanguardia*, 22 June 2000.
2. *ABC*, 22 June 2000.
3. *ABC*, 26 June 2000; *El Mundo Deportivo*, 26 June 2000.
4. *ABC*, 26 June 2000.
5. *El Mundo Deportivo*, 26 June 2000.
6. Berger (2007).
7. Berger (2011).
8. Paletschek (2011: 3–5).
9. MacClancy (1996).
10. Crolley and Hand (2002: 8).
11. Bahamonde (2011).
12. Castañón (1993: 45, 49).
13. Giulianotti (1999: 33).
14. *El Mundo Deportivo*, 14 March 1924.
15. *Cuadernos de Fútbol*, September 2009.
16. Díez Medrano and Gutiérrez (2001: 757).
17. Martialay (2000: 287–88).
18. *Madrid-Sport*, 16 September 1920.
19. Salazar (1996: 24–26).
20. *Madrid-Sport*, 16 September 1920.
21. Deportista (1924: 16, 20, 27).
22. *Madrid-Sport*, 9 September 1920.
23. *Madrid-Sport*, 16 September 1920.
24. *Madrid-Sport*, 9 September 1920.
25. *ABC*, 2 June 1924.
26. *La Vanguardia*, 5 June 1928.

27. *La Vanguardia*, 5 June 1928.
28. *La Vanguardia*, 3 May 1935 and 5 May 1935.
29. Uría (2008: 141–43).
30. Álvarez Junco (2001: 567–84).
31. Núñez Florencio (2010: 55–90).
32. Quiroga (2008: 303–5).
33. Pujadas (2011: 125–167).
34. *El Debate*, 31 May 1934 and 1 June 1934.
35. *El Socialista*, 2 June 1934.
36. *El Debate*, 1 June 1934.
37. *El Socialista*, 1 June 1934.
38. *El Socialista*, 2 June 1934.
39. *El Debate*, 2 June 1934.
40. *Marca*, 21 December 1938.
41. Santacana (2011: 210–11).
42. *Marca*, 21 December 1938.
43. González Aja (2002: 183).
44. *Marca*, 3 January and 18 January 1939.
45. *Marca*, 18 March 1941; *ABC*, 17 March 1942.
46. Núñez Seixas and Umbach (2008); Cavazza (2006).
47. Quiroga (2015: 514).
48. *El Alcázar*, 4 July 1950.
49. *Marca*, 3 July 1950.
50. *Marca*, 3 July 1950.
51. Sanz Hoya (2012: 423).
52. *ABC*, 14 June 1956.
53. Duke and Crolley (1996: 35–36).
54. Fernández Santander (1990: 14, 242).
55. González Aja (2011: 337–40).
56. *Marca*, 22 June 1964.
57. *ABC*, 26 June 1964.
58. Franco Salgado-Araujo (2005: 563).
59. *Marca*, 22 June 1964.
60. *ABC*, 23 June 1964.
61. *Marca*, 22 June 1964.
62. *Marca*, 22 June 1964.
63. Shaw (1987: 221).
64. *La Vanguardia*, 21 July 1966 and 10 July 1974; *AS*, 10 September 1975; *ABC*, 5 October 1973 and 24 July 1973.
65. *La Vanguardia*, 4 April 1968.
66. *AS*, 28 October 1971.
67. Cited in Sixte Abadía (2011: 362).
68. Sanz Hoya (2012: 428).
69. Sevillano (2000: 36, 210–11).
70. Bodin (2011: 465–66).
71. López López (2011: 393–432).
72. Crolley and Hand (2002: 123).

73. *El Mundo Deportivo*, 1 December 1977.
74. *ABC*, 22 December 1983.
75. *ABC*, 22 December 1983.
76. *El Mundo Deportivo*, 22 December 1983.
77. *La Vanguardia*, 22 December 1983.
78. *Mundo Deportivo*, 28 June 1984.
79. *Mundo Deportivo*, 28 June 1984.
80. *El Mundo Deportivo*, 10 July 1994.
81. Archilés (2011).
82. *El País*, 13 June 1998.
83. *El País*, 13 June 1998.
84. Bodin (2011: 451–53).
85. Solís (2003: 146).
86. Crolley and Hand (2002: 112–13).
87. *ABC*, 26 June 2000.
88. Sanz Hoya (2012: 430).
89. Núñez Seixas (2010: 134).
90. Quiroga (2013: 110–15).
91. MacFarland (2008: 607–14).

Chapter 11

Music and Spanish Nationalism

Sandie Holguín

Most historians of nationalism have avoided the topic of music, leaving it to ethnomusicologists, folklorists or even cultural studies scholars, to sort out the ephemeral art that historians have difficulty lassoing. But to study the impact of nationalism on music – or music on nationalism – requires a broader understanding of the larger forces at work contributing to nationalist fervour. In Europe specifically, the effects of modernization and industrialization created anxiety among residents, who worried that they were losing their cultural uniqueness to these dislocating forces. People who feared an encroaching cultural homogenization began to define, cultivate and promote forms of culture that they deemed suitably national. Others worked to limit the 'viruses' of foreign and mass culture in order to preserve what they saw as an authentically national culture linked directly to a country's soil or heartland. By the end of the nineteenth century, and certainly within the confines of the twentieth, numerous cultural strands were circulating and competing for the greatest number of adherents, including folk, official, mass, regional and avant-garde cultures. But just because some cultural movements had many admirers, does not mean that they were deemed authentically national. In fact, nationalists of all stripes often railed against mass, regional and avant-garde cultures for stripping away the foundations of national cultures' identities.[1]

In Spain, these battles to define and promote a national identity through cultural projects appeared in debates over music and musical performances over the course of the twentieth century. Given the numerous musical movements and groups that emerged in this period and given the limits of space, this essay cannot pretend to be completely comprehensive. There were, however, certain patterns that emerged by the end of the nineteenth century: tensions surfaced between people who sought a music that looked to the past, which, they hoped, could act as a bulwark against modern, foreign cultures, and those who promoted a synthesis of 'cosmopolitan' modern music with more traditional regional styles already found in Spain. By the latter part of the Franco regime, however, promoters of a Spanish national music found themselves treading carefully between the two positions.

The Musical Landscape before 1898

The nineteenth century saw slow and uneven industrial and urban development in Spain, with cities like Bilbao and Barcelona taking the economic lead and attempting to pull sclerotic Madrid into the modern era. With the development of these industrial cities came an influx of workers ready to work in factories and workshops and an increasing number of people from the middling and professional classes flexing their new economic muscle. As in the rest of Europe, Spanish cities housed a growing population that began to inhabit new spaces of sociability made possible by the creation of cheap and plentiful entertainment and increased leisure time. During the late-nineteenth century, cafés, bars, taverns, opera houses, theatres, *cafés conciertos*, *cafés líricos* and *cafés cantantes* dotted the Spanish urban landscape, and different social classes segregated themselves among the various forms and spaces of entertainment.[2]

Because Madrid was the capital city and housed the royal court, all major musical performances passed through there, and in Madrid, the court and aristocracy played their role as patrons of official culture. They sponsored the ballet, the symphony and the opera, and they generally accepted the musical trends passed onto them by France, Italy, Germany and Russia. While the aristocratic elites were considered the cultural tastemakers in Spain, the growing middle classes began to compete for that mantle as urban entertainment became more subject to the commercial marketplace. Despite receiving aristocratic patronage, opera and symphonic orchestras never attained the national stature visible in France, Germany and Russia because the Spanish State lacked the financial and ideological wherewithal to subsidize a similar national musical culture. Instead, in Spain popular forms of national music filled the vacuum left by the State. And it was within this changing economic landscape of the nineteenth century that a decidedly self-consciously Spanish musical form emerged: the *zarzuela*.[3]

In Madrid, the *zarzuela* materialized as a Spanish alternative to the Italian opera. By the late-nineteenth century, it became the musical theatre of choice, as performances became more subject both to the whims and needs of the commercial marketplace. The music tended towards short set pieces and the musical numbers often borrowed from traditional Spanish folk dances and songs and often included a chorus that represented 'the Spanish people'. Towards the close of the century, the music and settings tended to focus on Andalusia and Madrid, cementing the reputation of the *zarzuela* as *the* form that remained authentically Spanish. The plots revolved around romantic and usually historical themes, the lyrics reflected Spanish nationalistic and sometimes jingoistic impulses, and the staging leaned towards the spectacular. *Zarzuela's* popularity crashed after the events of 1898 and structural changes in the theatrical world.

While *zarzuela* dominated in Madrid, *wagnerismo* washed over Europe and flooded the Spanish borders. *Wagnerismo* represented another approach to the question of music and nationalism. As developed by the German Richard Wagner, the opera functioned as a total or synthetic work of art. The architecture of the theatre, the drama itself, the dance, the music, the sets – all had to be conceived by the composer as an organic whole in order to induce a mystical response from the audience who were compelled to identify with the *Volk* myths performed on stage. Wagner's aesthetic theories and the application of these theories to his operas represented the pinnacle of musical nationalism in Germany. The question, then, was, could Spanish composers apply his ideas on Spanish soil? Catalonia answered 'yes', but in places like Madrid, opinions were solidly mixed. *Wagnerismo* seemed to be yet another foreign import that prevented Spanish composers from charting their own path towards national greatness.

In contrast to the more formal performances of lyrical theatre, other forms of mass culture began to arise in this period, and they would be resounding successes during the pre–Civil War era. The (male) working and middle classes often imbibed their music with their food and drink, leading to the popularity of *cafés conciertos* and *cafés cantantes,* which, especially in the latter case, had the reputation of encouraging vices such as excessive drinking and whoring. The *cafés cantantes,* which often featured flamenco performers, increased dramatically in urban soundscapes all over Spain by the late nineteenth century, and the popularity of these locales would have the double effect of incurring the wrath of social reformers and scolds, and of cementing Spain's national identity as an Andalusian one in the minds of foreigners everywhere.[4]

Popular culture – that is, rural, folkloric culture – was deemed to be in decline during this period, but, as happened in other industrial countries, cultural nationalists began to look to the countryside to define and rejuvenate the Spanish musical scene. Two people, especially, contributed to the fashioning of a distinctly national musical style: Antonio Machado Álvarez (*Demófilo*) and Felipe Pedrell. Although not a musician himself, Demófilo, was one of the founders of folklore studies in Spain. He collected and disseminated folk tales and songs from around Spain, both as a writer and a teacher. By tracking down the lyrics to songs from his native Andalusia and publishing them, he provided an intellectual *imprimatur* to the music of the Gypsies and the folk culture of Andalusia. Pedrell, the eminent composer from Catalonia, studied Continental European classical and folk music histories and then spent much of his lifetime researching Spanish liturgical, classical and folk music traditions. He lobbied for the creation of a national music that incorporated Spanish folk music into modern operatic and symphonic compositions. Concerned that Spanish composers created derivative music and would therefore never be taken seriously by international audiences and critics, he actively implored Spanish composers to draw on the rich and diverse traditions of Spanish folk music to breathe new life into stale compositions.[5]

And so it was that on the eve of 1898, the musical scene in much of Spain was in flux. The *zarzuela* flourished, as did the wildly popular *cafés cantantes*. Fewer spectators attended the opera, and folk music appeared to be disappearing or becoming irrelevant. Once the United States quickly and decisively defeated Spain in 1898, the next few decades witnessed multiple debates across the political spectrum over the meaning of Spanish identity and the causes of Spain's decline. Music was not immune to these debates. In fact, some people saw the opportunity to shape Spanish national identity by moulding the musical tastes of Spanish audiences while others took a more active approach to eliminate musical forms that they deemed foreign.

The Crisis of Spanish Music and the Nation (1898–1939)

After Spain's defeat in the Spanish-American War, many questioned how a once-grand empire could tumble so ignominiously. Spain's social critics suggested at least three paths towards Spain's regeneration, which could be applied to almost any perceived problem: (1) look to industrialized, modern western Europe as a model to emulate; (2) shut out all foreign elements and concentrate on distinctly Spanish history and traditions as a road to salvation; (3) capture those qualities that appear beneficial in modern western Europe and synthesize them with

Spanish traditions to create a stronger, more vibrant Spain. Each of these models had its counterpart and promoter in the world of music and performance.

Two musical forms took hits from regenerationist critics immediately following '*el desastre*', namely, *zarzuela* and flamenco. With *zarzuela*, complaints tended towards the ideological, whereas those lodged against flamenco leaned towards the moral. Regenerationists across Spain seized on the *zarzuela*'s nationalistic lyrics and increasingly risqué stagings as a symptom of Spain's degeneration. Music and theatre critics of this period complained bitterly about the *zarzuela*'s role in the decline of Spanish cultural life, and they seized on the *zarzuela*'s nationalistic lyrics, the Spanish stereotypes and the vacuousness of its plots and musical arrangements to distance themselves from the State that had failed everybody in 1898. By 1909, this genre receded from the forefront of mass culture. Instead, the masses thronged to new forms of musical entertainment, much of it foreign born. Flamenco, on the other hand, while achieving cross-class popularity in both Spain and abroad, became a target of both progressives' and conservatives' ire.

For Spanish progressives, flamenco – which they often linked indistinguishably with bullfighting – symbolized the weight of tradition and of Spain's backwardness in the modern world. Novelists such as Emilia Pardo Bazán and Pío Baroja, intellectuals such as Miguel de Unamuno and Joaquín Costa and journalists such as Gaspar Núñez de Arce and Eugenio Noel railed against the Spanish mania for flamenco and what we might now call the 'flamenco lifestyle', which they dubbed *flamenquismo*. This included the love of the bullfight, the imitation of torero and/or flamenco dancers' dress, an adoption of 'gypsified' slang, and frequent attendance at *cafés cantantes*. For these regenerationists, the Spanish craze for *flamenquismo* hampered reformers' attempts to bring Spain into the modern scientific and industrial era. Instead of concentrating on the poor educational system or the lack of infrastructure in Spain, Spanish newspapers filled their pages with the latest bullfighting event or flamenco entertainment. The *antiflamenquistas* commented on how *flamenquismo* reflected Spaniards' lack of culture, laziness, vulgarity, frivolity and downright immorality.[6]

For the Catholic Church and other conservatives, the *cafés cantantes*, along with just about any other form of modern entertainment that included music that could be construed as sexually suggestive, represented the absolute decline of Spanish morality, and therefore, of the Spanish nation. The spaces of flamenco performances often occupied neighbourhoods that one might call vice-ridden, and it attracted audiences across class lines. The owners, performers and some of the audiences came from the uncontrollable working classes, and the establishments themselves gave off the air of complete disorder and vice: the spectacle of the *café cantante* included women of uncertain moral status and drunken clients and performers. These entertainments were hidden in dark alleyways, limited to interior spaces, and access to these performances came only at the very late hours of the night. In fact, numerous attempts to regulate *cafés cantantes* began at the end of the nineteenth century and stretched into the twentieth. Certain reformers in the Catholic Church lumped *cafés cantantes* together with prostitution and pornography, and urged the abolition of all these pursuits, for they did not conform to the teachings of the Church, nor by extension, to the Catholic identity of the Spanish nation.

The other complaint most consistently lodged against both the *zarzuela* and flamenco is that they had no redeeming social value. They functioned solely as commercial enterprises that catered to the values of the lowest common denominator. Regenerationist critics of music desired music that would elevate the consciousness of the Spanish people. Only then would change occur in Spain's social and political realm. For these critics, the *zarzuela* and flamenco symbolized the Spanish government's substitution of bread and circuses (well, really just circuses) for any real and desperately needed reform of the Spanish nation. Despite social reformers' wishes to the contrary, audiences did not stop attending these spectacles. As World War I approached, the *zarzuela* became the purview of the bourgeoisie. Flamenco bars flourished, although not as much as at the beginning of the century. Instead, it permuted into the hybrid *opera flamenco*, and many flamenco dancers and singers became international superstars and part of a wide commercial nexus that seemed antithetical to the 'pure and authentic' flamenco that aficionados cherished.

World War I would soon transform the musical landscape and mass culture in urban Spain, and for many, it was a transformation to be loathed. Spain did not participate in the Great War, so performers found in Spain a refuge from the violence and scarcity that befell them in their home countries. The incursion of foreigners brought novel forms of entertainment that eventually made their way across Spain, so that by the 1920s, places like Barcelona and Madrid became crossroads for the cosmopolitan musical trends hitting cities everywhere in the industrialized world. Cabarets, dance halls, jazz clubs and variety shows scattered across the urban land- and soundscape. The cuplé, a Spanish version of the risqué cabarets of continental Europe, made inroads into Spain's cities. Spaniards began to learn the newest dance numbers, including the tango and the Charleston, and they showed off their steps in dance halls and cafés. Black musicians played for white audiences, and men and women held each other close, sometimes provocatively, while gliding across the dance floor. Needless to say, this influx of foreign forms of music and dance alarmed Spanish social critics who viewed this new music as a contagion that infected the Spanish nation.

No group was more horrified by this musical invasion than the Church and its most fervent supporters. A response typical of Catholic critics came from Manuel Herrera y Ges, a columnist for the Carlist Catholic daily *El Siglo Futuro*. Contrasting what he witnessed in Catalonia, musical celebrations rooted in region (the sardana) and musical entertainment rooted in the United States (jazz bands), he declared one 'art' and the other 'noise', respectively. The author complimented the musicians and sardana dancers for their rhythm, form and overall harmony: 'In the music and dance there is art, beauty, emotion and, above all, decency.' In contrast, he accused the jazz-band celebrants, who carried on their festivities in the more hidden interiors of the barrios, of fomenting disharmony and sexual license. To him, the musicians all seemed to be playing different musical numbers at the same time: 'Such confusion breaks out that there is no way to understand it.' Worse, this type of music served only to cover up the sexual shenanigans of the spectator-dancers: 'Men and women can pair up, embracing each other shamelessly, and they pretend to follow the music with epileptic contortions.' Herrera y Ges concluded his article in a manner that Catholic newspapers would frequently replicate: 'There is no art, nor beauty, nor emotion; only noise, the dulling of the senses, brutalization, immorality. Disgusting!'[7] So repulsive was this new music to the Catholic hierarchy, that groups like Catholic Action would sponsor conferences and run campaigns throughout the 1930s and 1940s to rid Spain of this 'foreign trash'.

Neoclassical Music and the Avant-Garde

At the turn of the century, a small group of Spanish composers who are etched into the Spanish classical music canon – Enrique Granados, Isaac Albéniz and Manuel de Falla – produced musical innovations that heeded Pedrell's call to distil the 'essence' of the Spanish folk tradition in their compositions.[8] More importantly, they began a process of musical cross-fertilization with French and Russian composers in their attempts to create a distinctly Spanish music. Although the aforementioned Spanish composers began their training with Felipe Pedrell and imbibed his philosophy of creating a national music, they eventually felt the need to leave the suffocating atmosphere of the Spanish musical establishment and travelled to Paris to expand their musical repertoire. They composed works that linked them to their land of birth, but Falla made the biggest international name for himself, and it is to him we now turn to understand how how his modernist music transitioned from an *españolismo* located in Andalusia to a universalism developed out of Castile.

Falla resided in Paris from 1907–14 and moved in musical circles influenced by Claude Debussy that included European composers such as Maurice Ravel and Igor Stravinsky. Falla fell under the spell of Debussy's modernist music and sought ways to incorporate Debussy's style into his own. Debussy, on the other hand, had become enamoured of the 'Spanish Gypsy music' he had heard performed at the Universal Expositions held in Paris in 1889 and 1900. His encounters with the flamencoized Spanish music in Paris convinced him that Spanish music had something of the exotic to offer the world, and he persuaded Falla to assimilate echoes of that Gypsy music into Falla's compositions.

When the war reached France, Falla moved back to Spain and began what would become a very fecund musical period that began as a sort of homage to Andalusia, but that ended with a rejection of that region for his musical idiom. In collaboration with María Martínez Sierra, Falla wrote the score for *El Amor Brujo*. In composing it, he synthesized Andalusian folk songs and rhythms with those of French modernist music. He also cast 'real Gypsies' in his work, most notably the flamenco dancer Pastora Imperio, who, although not trained formally in dance, lent an indigenous authenticity to Falla's concert hall work. Although this work succeeded internationally, it fell flat for most Spanish critics because they believed it too French and devoid of Spanish soul.

Falla's music would soon be imbued with 'Russian spirit' after the arrival in Spain of the Russian ballet in 1916, and of Stravinsky in the 1920s. Falla, like the Russian composer Mikhail Glinka, believed that Russians and Spaniards shared a musical link through something broadly defined as the Orient. The innovative works performed by the Russian ballet provided inspiration for Falla's next big work, while for some of the Russians who were on this tour and subsequent ones, the Spanish music they witnessed in *cafés cantantes* enriched their own choreographic imaginations. This cross-cultural fertilization resulted in Falla's *El sombrero de tres picos*, a modernist work put together with the collaboration of some of the finest artists of the avant-garde: Falla wrote the score, basing it on the novel by Pedro Antonio de Alarcón;

Pablo Picasso created the 'cubist' sets; the Russians Leonid Massine and Sergei Diaghilev choreographed.

When *El sombrero de tres picos* premiered in London right after the war (1919), and soon after in Paris, it was a grand success. Critics in these countries praised Falla for his use of the modernist idiom to secure an accurate portrayal of the 'Spanish race', the 'Spanish temperament' and the 'Spanish character'. By incorporating versions of Spain's regional music and dances into the story, and by including Picasso's sets with images out of a bullfight that was never part of the original novel, Falla and his collaborators presented foreign spectators with a modernist take on *españolismo*, and the foreigners lapped it up. Spaniards, however, did not.

After the Madrid premiere in 1921, critical reviews were decidedly mixed, if not downright bad. Many critics were outraged by the reinterpretation of a well-loved, traditional Spanish novel. They found the modernist aesthetics clashed too greatly with the traditional story line, that Falla had been too influenced by the musical traditions of France and Russia, and therefore had stripped the very Spanish story of its national essence. Others liked its modernist bent because they imagined that it diminished the work's Spanishness. The majority disliked the work, both because it seemed too shocking for traditional audiences and too generic to be a national treasure. According to them, the characters were stock clichés, the sets too generic, the dances redolent of Andalusia, yet not Andalusian enough. Finally, there were some who perceived in this work a great strength: the ability to maintain elements of Spanish national identity while appealing to a more universal audience. It is this synthesis that Falla would now work to achieve, and he would try to do this by moving from a stylized Andalusia to a more universal and yet truly Spanish Castile.

Falla's shift from Andalusia to Castile occurred most irrefutably in his work, *El retablo de Maese Pedro*. Taken from Cervantes's *Don Quixote*, Falla's *Retablo* employed Castilian-based folksongs and melodies in the context of a canonical Spanish text. He impressed both domestic and international critics with his skilful appropriation and reinterpretation of a national treasure. On 29 March 1924, critic Juan del Brezo wrote in *La Voz*, 'Today Falla extends his view to the pure national essences.... He turns his eyes toward the central meseta and ... by moving away from the flamenco and Gypsy rhythms, Falla ... creates the most convincing and distinctly Spanish work.'[9] Falla had achieved that delicate balance that some regenerationists had called for: the synthesis of Spanish tradition with European modernity. In doing so, he created something fresh but still recognizably Spanish.

The Second Republic's Quest for
a National Musical Culture (1931–36)

With the advent of the Second Republic, important figures from the Republican-Socialist coalition worked to unify the citizens of the badly fractured Spanish nation by exposing them to important Spanish traditional and contemporary works in music, literature and art. Official Spain tried once again to include Spanish citizens in the body politic through programs like the *Misiones Pedagógicas* and the creation of the Junta Nacional de Música.[10]

The *Misiones Pedagógicas* was a government-sponsored program charged with bringing both elite and popular urban culture to the peasants in the countryside. The *Coro y Teatro del Pueblo* featured prominently in the *Misiones Pedagógicas* program. With the goal of bringing the theatre to the people, the *misioneros* – volunteers mostly from Madrid's universities – performed the plays outdoors, usually in public plazas. They interspersed their theatrical performances with songs and ballads derived from folk traditions.

The director of the theatre's chorus, Eduardo Martínez y Torner, aided in recreating many of these songs. He headed the Division of Musicography and Folklore in Madrid's Centro de Estudios Históricos, compiling, classifying and recording traditional folk songs and ballads, and reconstructing the music for ballads from the sixteenth and seventeenth centuries. He sought to trace the roots of Spanish folk songs and those of elite culture to discover their commonalities and reach some understanding of the spiritual character of the Spanish people. Admitting no real separation between folk and official music, he argued instead that all Spanish music shared elements of a greater organic whole.

In this spirit, Torner and his chorus sang and danced the many regional songs that he had collected in his studies, 'giving back' the songs that belonged to the people and linking them to the common musical culture of the Spanish elites. He opposed Castilianizing the music and lyrics and, instead, insisted on recreating and performing songs in their original regional tongues. Therefore, the choral performances not only celebrated regionalism but also revealed the tensions between centralized and regional cultures in the policies of the Second Republic. The theatrical experience of the Coro y Teatro del Pueblo reconciled many elements, making the whole greater than the sum of its parts and incorporating the periphery into the centre. At the end of their performances, the *misioneros* handed out the song lyrics and sometimes the scores of the music they had just performed, thus codifying and officially legitimating folk songs that had once been passed down the generations through oral tradition.

Back in Madrid, more formal attempts were made to create and promote a national music for Spain, such as the creation of the Junta Nacional de Música y Teatros Líricos. One of the organization's mandates was to put recent works into production and then export them as part of Spain's national patrimony.[11] Despite the republic's good intentions, the plans to create a national musical theatre had to be jettisoned with the beginning of the war in July 1936.

When the Civil War ended in 1939, Spain's musical soundscape transformed. Many *cafés cantantes* were forced to close down. Plans to create a national theatre stalled until later in the Franco regime and many of the prized performers and music critics of the 1920s and 1930s went into exile by the close of the war, draining the country of much of the talent that had formed part of the Silver Age of Spanish culture. It was now up to the Franco regime to encourage musical forms that represented the values of the war's victors.

Music under the Franco Regime

Just as the revolutionary Left before the Civil War viewed cultural artefacts and the performing arts as intrinsic to a society's transformation, so too did the revolutionary and conservative Right. The Right strove to create a musical culture that would channel the revolutionary tendencies of the working classes into acceptable avenues. While the Franco regime never adhered to some strict definition of fascism, it most assuredly brought elements of fascist aesthetics and ideology to the table with a heaping dollop of Catholicism. This fusion of hyper-nationalism with conservative Catholicism – known as National-Catholicism – coloured all aspects of Spanish life, including the cultural sphere. Two pillars of the Franco regime – the Church and the Falange – worked on campaigns to purify Spanish culture and to remake it according to the tenets of National-Catholicism. For the early years of the Franco regime, this meant that flamenco would play a much less prominent role as a symbol of Spanishness, and other regional folk songs and dances would prevail.

The Nationalists handsomely rewarded the Catholic hierarchy for its support during the war, handing the reins of morality over to the Church's leadership. The Church worked to eliminate the perceived foreign virus of modernity that had permeated Spanish borders since 1789. Nowhere was this clearer than in the cultural sphere, especially in the realm of entertainment. The Catholic establishment censored entertainments such as movies, plays and festivals, and regulated (mainly female) sexuality and dress. As noted earlier, the Spanish Catholic Church had fulminated against the loose morals brought on by the modern age. Whereas before the war, the Church could only denounce these transgressors of Catholic morality, after the war, it had full license to prosecute them. The Permanent National Office of Vigilance over Entertainment became the umbrella organization for Catholic groups to monitor, criticize and sanction entertainment, especially with respect to their suitability for women and minors.

Although films and plays underwent the greatest scrutiny by Catholic officialdom, dance and its musical accompaniment also fell under their purview. The modern dances and music that had been so popular with the masses in the years preceding the Civil War became something to regulate severely, if not ban outright. Various sub-organizations of Catholic Action held campaigns, such as the Austerity and Morality Campaign, to warn young women and girls, especially, of the dangers of modern music. The problem, according to these organizations, was that pure Spanish dance had been perverted and/or lost by the influx of foreign ideas: 'The boiling cuplés, shameless and pornographic, came to us from abroad; the tangos, brittle, agonizing … and sensuous, came to us from abroad; epileptic jazz, jungle-like, Aborigines with the taste of papaya and the smell of the pigsty, came to us from abroad.'[12] Other Catholics wrote tracts that covered similar territory, emphasizing modern music's role in eliciting sinful behaviour among unmarried couples. While condemning most dances, all of these tracts made exceptions for Spain's regional folk music and dance, underscoring the wholesomeness of the rhythms and dances. This music received praise because the sexes rarely mixed and the dancers moved about in graceful steps out in the open, in public plazas. Therefore, in most instances, the Catholic establishment endorsed the recuperation of Spain's regional dances, costumes and songs, hoping that such a move would cure Spain of the foreign infection that had decimated its national culture and its women's modesty.

The Promotion of the Folkloric

The Franco regime could not survive by repression alone. From a Nationalist's point of view, one of the major causes of Spain's troubles in the pre–Civil War period was its fissiparous nationalism. Creating a strong, unitary nationalism became a top priority for the regime. This nationalist ideology appeared in the usual places, in schools, through church teachings, in political speeches and so on. But it was also encouraged in the cultural sphere, through mass spectator sports and spectacles such as football and bullfighting, and through sanitized musical entertainments that could bind people across region and class.

The most successful of these cultural creations came from the Sección Femenina (Women's Section, SF) of the single party Falange, who appropriated and transformed folklore to achieve national regeneration. The SF had already begun to think about this issue before the Civil War had ended. Their project of national recuperation, the Coros y Danzas de España, remains one of the most important legacies of the SF. What may have seemed like a hare-brained idea when its founder, Pilar Primo de Rivera, imagined it in 1939 became internationally recognized by the 1950s. It began first as a means to achieve domestic unification, and later as a platform for cultural diplomacy. In addition to performing at many official functions within Spain, the Coros y Danzas featured representatives in such international organizations as the United Nations, UNESCO and the International Federation of Folkloric Groups.[13]

The Coros y Danzas served many purposes, but for Pilar these groups operated primarily to unify Spain. The organizers of the Coros y Danzas tied music and dance to the people and to the land from which they had sprung. Pilar Primo de Rivera had an almost mystical conception of music, including it as a sacred prong in a Holy Trinity that also incorporated 'National Syndicalist doctrine', and 'the land'. She imagined music as the great facilitator of national unity, and she conceived of the Coros y Danzas as a representation of unity in plurality: 'When in Castile they also know the sardana and they know [how] "the chistu" [Basque flute] is played, when one understands all of the depth and philosophy found in Andalusian song, instead of knowing about it through the little *zarzuela* venues … when fifty or sixty thousand voices are united to sing the same song, then, yes, we will have attained unity among men and among the lands of Spain.'[14] In this context, regional diversity became unproblematic because the Coros y Danzas articulated a way to domesticate political regionalist aspirations in the service of the Spanish State.

In addition to its contributions towards the expression of Spanish unity in diversity, the Coros y Danzas promoted values near and dear to fascist and Catholic hearts. Regional dances embodied the characteristics of their requisite lands and the authentic expression of their peoples, which meant that the dances themselves were not 'exotic' or 'foreign'; the songs and dances represented the expression of the group, not the individual. Finally, by researching, preserving and performing these songs and dances, the organizers of the Coros y Danzas prided themselves on recovering a world almost lost to modernity and disseminating these performances to the greater world.

In 1942, the SF began organizing first provincial, then regional and then national competitions to pick the best exemplars of traditional regional songs and dances. From 1942–76, the SF held about twenty of these contests in Spain. According to Pilar Primo de Rivera, what began as 3,000 participants in 1942 eventually peaked at around 60,000. When the first national competition began to be publicized, newspapers parroted the SF's nationalistic messages. *ABC* exclaimed that the SF held these contests to 'bring to the public consciousness Spain's great folkloric beauty when so many exotic dances and foreign songs try to supplant it'.[15]

The Coros y Danzas at first seemed destined to fulfil domestic educational purposes only. That is, folklorists and performers strove to educate the Spanish populace about their own folkloric traditions that the SF perceived to be threatened by modernity. It helps to remember that the SF viewed themselves as menders of the national fabric that had been riven both by modernity and civil war. Their dissemination of Spanish folklore would therefore aid in national reconciliation.

A voyage to Argentina in 1948 launched the Coros y Danzas to international success and became a way for the SF to reconnect with an exiled people, re-establish cultural links with Spain's historic imperial subjects and become cultural ambassadors for the Franco regime. In the memoir she wrote towards the end of her life, Pilar spoke of the SF's need to spread its ideology to the greater world, and most especially, to the Hispano-American world. She expressed this desire to renew the broken cultural, linguistic, historical and religious bonds between the 'Mother Country' and the former colonies.

During their tours through Latin America, every move the Coros y Danzas made was cultivated to remind Spaniards, Spanish exiles and Latin Americans of the historical and cultural bonds that no one could rend asunder. During stops along that tour and subsequent ones, the performers provided both symbolic and explicit links between Spain and Latin America through the conduits of colonialism and Catholicism, and then attempted to strengthen these bonds through language and music. For example, in 1949, while in Lima Peru, the Coros y Danzas placed flowers on the grave of the conquistador Francisco Pizarro on their way out to Chile. While in Santiago, Chile, they attended a mass at the Church of San Francisco, and placed flowers on a marker commemorating another conquistador, Pedro de Valdivia. Whenever possible, it seems, the Coros y Danzas attended masses and placed themselves in locations that would make Latin Americans and exiled Spaniards see the historical and cultural links between the Mother Country and its former colonies. In fact, the leaders of the SF made no attempt to hide their neocolonial longings. Pilar spoke of music's power to unite peoples from distant lands: 'For this reason the Falange, which is, above all, unity, has preferred music, better than any other way, to unite our spirits, and the part of music most accessible to everyone has been chosen: singing. Song, which we [Latin] Americans and Spaniards sing in the same language.' She blithely compressed time, history and space in order to (re)incorporate the defunct Spanish Empire into the new Spanish State: 'So then the sea that separates us will be only an accident of geography, that will serve to bring and carry back and forth the culture of your Republics and of our Patria.'[16] Music, in other words, might conquer where armies could not. With a strong belief in the power of music to heal all manner of wounds, the Coros y Danzas used its troupes to break down the barriers remaining between hostile nations and Spain, and exiled Spaniards and the Franco regime.

Another chief goal of the international tours was didactic. The Coros y Danzas sought to disabuse foreigners especially of their erroneous conceptions of Spain's history, traditions and people. With an essentialized understanding of geography, the SF always connected the regional songs and dances to the land, holding steadfastly to the notion that one could not separate the songs, rhythms and steps of each region's music from the land from which they sprung. Tired of the old saw that Spain was Andalusia (and vice-versa), the Coros y Danzas took every opportunity to puncture that myth, even as they sometimes reinforced that Andalusian exoticism. And while foreign audiences may have accepted the diversity of Spanish folklore, in the end they almost always favoured the dynamic foot stamping and syncopated rhythms of the Andalusian/flamenco *zapateados* performed by the women from Andalusia.

From the 1950s on, this foreign preference for flamenco over folklore had important consequences for the Franco regime and for the state of Spanish music in general, for it was in the 1950s that Spain's tourism boom began, and it would need flamenco to generate cash for the Spanish State. This fact did not escape officials' attention. In his 1953 plan for how best to promote tourism in Spain, Carlos González Cuesta wrote, 'Tourists looks for comfort and ease in their travels ... good food ... and Spanish stereotypes: Bulls, flamenco dance, singing, Gypsies.... We have to resign ourselves for tourism purposes to be a country of stereotypes, for the day that we [stop] we will have lost ninety per cent of the reason for being a tourist attraction.'[17] Although Spanish elites and promoters of official culture often disliked flamenco because of its commercialism that catered to the 'base' tastes of the masses, flamenco's distinctly commercial appeal eventually persuaded those in power to hitch their wagon to that money-making star. To save face, cultural promoters of the regime ended up playing a sort of double game by projecting simultaneously conflicting identities of Spain to foreign and domestic audiences. The Ministry of Tourism promoted both a stereotypical Spain as exemplified by Manuel Fraga's 'Spain is Different' campaign, and a Spain of diversity, that had something for every kind of tourist – hunter, skier, sunbather and art enthusiast.

This double game and the multiple renderings of Spain's national identity really emerged most obviously during the 1964–65 New York World's Fair. Inside the Spanish Pavilion, the Ministry of Tourism mounted an exhibit that included posters, films, photographs and samples of artisanal products from various regions of Spain. The series of images and products were portable enough to be carried on tour around the world and demonstrated to the world once and for all how much variety Spain had to offer the tourist. But it was the music that often lured the spectators in.

Individual dance stars rotated in and out of the Pavilion over the course of two years, but two types of performances remained constant throughout the Pavilion's tenure: the Coros y Danzas and professional flamenco dancing. The prominence of both these types of dance in the Spanish Pavilion reflected the Franco regime's decision to project on the one hand, a Spanish identity that was rural, timeless, folkloric and unified by regional plurality (the Coros y Danzas) and, on the other hand, a national identity that the regime (rightly) imagined that tourists wanted: an Andalusian-based Spain represented by orientalized, exotic flamenco dancers and singers. In Spain itself, however, the regime presented the Coros y Danzas as the cultural victor over the hearts and minds of Spaniard and foreigner alike.

In New York, the Coros y Danzas performed daily in the patio of the Pavilion, becoming the conduit through which the Spanish government displayed and softened for foreigners its most important and oppressive institutions, the military and the Catholic Church. The Coros y Danzas were trotted out for special occasions related to Spain and the World's Fair. They paraded along Fifth Avenue during 'Spain Week', a week coinciding with Columbus Day. They greeted a Spanish naval training ship with traditional sailing and fishing songs when it docked at Pier 86 and then met the naval cadets the next day when they attended mass at St. Patrick's Cathedral. By their mere physical proximity to representatives of the Spanish military and Spanish Church, the Coros y Danzas transformed symbolically into the representatives of Spanish culture.

The Spanish press continued to portray the Coros y Danzas as the reflection of a multicultural Spain that was greater than the sum of its parts and more representative of the entire country than Andalusia. The Coros y Danzas enabled 'spectators to see a Spain that is not only Andalusia, but also Extremadura, Aragon, the Basque Country ... and all these regions of Spain'.[18] More importantly, the Spanish press understood the financial rewards of displaying a friendly, colourful Spain to willing audiences. Given that there were over ten million visitors to the Fair, and that many of those visitors would visit the Spanish Pavilion, the hope was that Spain would see the financial returns through tourism (which it did).

The dances performed in the Teatro Español, mainly flamenco and some forms of Spanish classical dance, appeared to be aimed at giving audiences what they wanted and what they expected Spanish music to be. The main performers were the international stars Manuela Vargas, Antonio Gades and Rosa Durán, and the majority of the dances showcased the variety of dances we call flamenco. Although the performers certainly expected audiences to become caught up in flamenco's syncopated rhythms, the shows' organizers also appeared to want to educate audiences about the meaning and roots of flamenco music, even if the history of flamenco and Spanish dance was crafted to suit promotional ends. They achieved this education through the booklets that accompanied both Antonio Gades's and Rosa Durán's Tablao Zambra programs, which taught audiences the meanings of the various flamenco songs and dances.

The program for Tablao Zambra projected foreign stereotypes of Andalusian orientalism, while still trying to give audiences formalized ways of seeing the dance. It drew on stereotypes of Andalusia and explained the music's pull for classical composers such as Debussy and Falla. Then it explained how the Tablao Zambra, founded in Madrid in 1954, functioned as a way for spectators to hear 'pure', authentic flamenco songs and dances that were in danger of being lost. Concerned with the notion of authenticity, the Spanish Ministry of Tourism thus promoted a (non-existent) ur-flamenco untainted by modern mass culture, and pushed flamenco's historical roots many centuries back, rather than to the nineteenth century where they belonged. Finally, the program stuck to an orientalizing script that worked well with foreigners, linking flamenco's history to the 'primitive' songs and dances of 'oriental peoples'.[19]

The Spanish government offered spectators at least two versions of Spain through music and dance, one diverse but unified, timeless and rural, and the other exotic and mystical. The Spanish government may have wanted to present foreigners with a more complex vision of the Spanish nation, one that demonstrated great regional variation, but they undercut this vision by relegating the Coros y Danzas to amateur status. Instead, they gave the public what it wanted, the exoticism of flamenco, and in doing so, Andalusia once again became synonymous with Spain. Whereas in the early years of the Franco regime, most flamenco performers were ignored by the Francoist press as reminders of a Spain corrupted by the vice and commercialism of modernity, by the late 1950s, they were promoted alongside other more 'folkloric' acts like the Coros y Danzas of the SF. Documentary and archival evidence seems to indicate that after the 1950s, the Coros y Danzas served as propaganda for domestic purposes, while the flamenco performances were thrown in to appease and attract foreign audiences. The tourism and image producers under the Franco regime realized that they could play both narratives out at once, Spain as multiregional and Spain as Andalusia, without harming anyone in the process. In the end, business concerns trumped ideology.

The Waning of a National Music:
Late- and Post-Francoist Spain

In conjunction with the Spanish tourist boom, the rise of a consumer society within Spain during the 1960s also broke down musical barriers. With increased numbers of Spanish citizens owning transistor radios, television sets and records, and with the influx of tourists from other lands, Spaniards were increasingly exposed to the international youth culture that championed rock and roll as its anthem. Rebellious rock proved to be much more attractive to Spanish youth than the didactic Coros y Danzas or the watered-down flamenco in Benidorm and Ibiza. With a country beginning to rebel against the constraints imposed by decades of political and religious authoritarianism, rock and roll seemed much more fitting for a country on the eve of transition and reconfiguration.

The youth of Spain also began to compose their own versions of folk music that differed profoundly from those imposed by the State. Following the patterns set by folk protest singers like Bob Dylan and Joan Baez, folk singers like Victor Manuel and Ana Belén began writing and singing politically tinged folksongs that protested the Franco regime. Other musicians began writing and performing in their regional languages as a way to distance themselves from the official language of the State, singers such as Lluís Llach and María del Mar Bonet, who were most associated with the Catalan folk movement, *La Nova Cançó*. Performing in Catalan, Basque or Galician became a distinctly political act in the waning years of the Franco regime and in the transition to democracy.[20]

When the transition to democracy was finally completed, so ended any form of national music. The Coros y Danzas disbanded by 1977. Like the Spanish nation itself, which had become increasingly decentralized through the creation of numerous autonomous states, music became simultaneously decentralized and internationalized. Musicians and other musical performers exhibited loyalties to their own regions – see, for example, the showcasing of Catalan musical talent during the 1992 Olympics in Barcelona. Catalans, Galicians and Basques composed music in their native tongues, and places like Andalusia began to capitalize on their flamenco traditions by setting up research centres for flamenco, creating international flamenco contests, and receiving recognition from UNESCO for its contribution to the Intangible Cultural Heritage of Humanity. At the same time, musical performers in Spain borrowed from other musical genres around the world – hip-hop, jazz, world music – to create new musical syntheses for domestic and international audiences.

Spanish elites had begun the twentieth century in a state of cultural anxiety, looking for ways to use music to bind the nation together. Many had tried to prevent modern and foreign music from crossing its borders, but music – ephemeral sound – could not be so easily dissuaded. Despite the numerous attempts to freeze Spain into some pastoral folk vision of the past, modernity did eventually impose itself on the country, and with it came a kaleidoscope of music that broke down national borders and became part of the globalizing process that is still with us today.

Sandie Holguín is an associate professor of modern European cultural and intellectual history at the University of Oklahoma. A specialist in modern Spanish history, she is currently writing *The Soul of Spain? Flamenco and the Construction of National Identity, 1800–1975*, which explores how regional nationalists, Spaniards, and foreigners grappled with flamenco culture as a symbol of Spanish national identity.

Notes

1. A few works have begun to grapple with music and nationalism. See Evans (2000); White and Murphy (2001); Applegate and Potter (2002); Bohlman (2004); Frolova-Walker (2007); Kelly (2008); Jackson and Pelkey (2005). Here are but a few important works on theories of nationalism and on Spanish nationalism: Anderson (1983); Hobsbawm and Ranger (1992); Smith (1996); Billig (1995); Alvarez Junco (2001); Núñez Seixas (1999).
2. Gómez-García Plata (2005); Salaün (2001); Steingress (2006); Serrano (1989).
3. Much of this discussion of the *zarzuela* comes from Young (2016).
4. For discussions of Andalusia as Spain, see Álvarez Junco (1994); Storm (2014).
5. Martí (1997).
6. Alvarez (2007).
7. M. Herrera y Ges, 'Crónica de arte: arte y ruido', *El Siglo Futuro,* 23 August 1928.
8. This section owes a great deal to the work of Hess (2001).
9. Cited in Hess (2001: 228).
10. For a discussion of the *Misiones Pedagógicas,* see Holguín (2002); Mendelson (2005: 93–124).
11. Sopeña Ibáñez (1958: 184).
12. Romeral (1939).
13. Casero García (2000); García Serrano (1953); Ortiz (1999).
14. Primo de Rivera (1942: 20–21).
15. 'Primer Concurso nacional de Coros y Danzas de la Falange Femenina', *ABC,* 19 June 1942.
16. Primo de Rivera (1942: 131).
17. See C. González Cuesta, 'Estudio sobre la propaganda turística y su cuantía', 1953, Archivo General de la Administración, Alcalá de Henares, Sección Cultura, 49.04, Box 18520.
18. E. Meneses, 'Visite con Blanco y Negro la Feria de Nueva York', *Blanco y Negro,* 16 May 1964, pp. 53–56.
19. Cruz Novillo et al. (1964).
20. Van Liew (1993).

Chapter 12

A More Spanish Spain
The Influence of Tourism on the National Image

Eric Storm

For many foreigners, Spain is the country of flamenco, bullfighting, the Alhambra and sangria. While many Spaniards do not see themselves reflected in these stereotypes, it is clear that the identity of a country is not generated exclusively by the images its inhabitants have of their own nation, nor – we have to admit – is it entirely determined from abroad. The collective identity of a nation is in fact the product of a complex interaction between its native people and those from abroad. And perhaps the field in which this interaction is most immediate is that of tourism.[1] Foreign travellers go to a country hoping that their hosts will satisfy their expectations. At the same time, the tourism sector wishes to attract customers, and in its advertising tries to present an attractive image of the country that takes into account the assumed desires of potential travellers. However, this relationship between visitors and hosts becomes more complicated, because there are also travellers from within the country who have their own demands, and a range of official authorities that intervene in matters associated with tourism, so that political factors begin to play an important role.

In the case of Spain, one can see that this interaction between different actors, each with their own intentions and interests, has been very complex. Foreign tastes for the popular culture of Spain's gypsies, the legacy of Al-Andalus or bullfighting, for example, have not fitted very well with the desire of many Spaniards to see themselves as a civilized Western people. Equally, the efforts made by successive governments to encourage cultural tourism in the interior of the country have not been able to prevent tourists from seeking sun and beaches on a massive scale along the Mediterranean coast, where they have also expected to enjoy the cliché Spain of guitars and castanets. Hence, the images that foreign visitors have of the nature, culture and historic heritage of Spain have been very different from those held by its inhabitants themselves. People from outside Spain, moreover, have tended to see it as a uniform entity, while those within the country focus above all on its great internal variety. Nor have ideas on Spanish identity always been the same. There has been a clear historical evolution on this point, and to understand current clichés it is necessary to study this complex and dynamic process in its different stages, beginning with the nineteenth century.

The Nineteenth Century and the Restoration

In the nineteenth century, no official body charged with promoting tourism existed, and so, strictly speaking, there was no official tourism policy on the part of the state. Nor were the numbers of travellers very great, and a large part of what 'tourism' did exist did not have any implications for national identity, since it was primarily a cosmopolitan phenomenon. This could be seen, for example, in the popularity of spas, and in the development of the first bathing resorts from mid-century onwards. Their principal clientele was drawn from the aristocracy and international *haute bourgeoisie,* and beach towns – like Brighton, Ostend or San Sebastián – adopted a similar cosmopolitan style, whether in the architecture of their luxury hotels, in entertainment (casinos, balls) or in gastronomy (with French cuisine).

Nevertheless, there was also another tradition of tourism, that of the cultural traveller. Beginning in the Age of Romanticism, British, French, German and American travellers had started to discover the beauty of Spain and its art. What attracted them, too, was precisely those things that distinguished Spain from the international canon: the legacy of Arabic civilization in Al-Andalus, and popular traditions such as bullfights, gypsy dances and religious processions. Through the work of these travellers, as well as through the new travel literature and theatre, opera and painting, the cultural elites of Western countries gradually formed their own idea of what Spanish national identity was like. The classic example of this imagining of Spain by Romantic travellers was *Carmen*, which began life as a story written by Prosper Mérimée in 1845 about the passionate tragic love affair of a Seville gypsy. It was adapted for the theatre and then in 1875 by Georges Bizet as an opera, which was immensely successful and created an enduring stereotype of the Spanish woman from the lower classes.[2]

Although Spanish authorities and elites tended to be annoyed by this exotic, primitive image of their country, at times they too employed the stereotypes formed by foreign travellers to represent Spain on the international stage. This was seen most particularly at world fairs. The Spanish Pavilion in the Paris exhibition of 1878, for example, was clearly inspired by the Alhambra and other masterpieces of Moorish architecture in Andalusia. However, portraying oneself as exotic, and identifying Spain with a Muslim past, also had its disadvantages, and for the international exhibition in Paris in 1900 Spain built a pavilion in the ornate plateresque style of the sixteenth century, which, as a Spanish version of the European Renaissance, seemed more suitable for impressing an international audience in a dignified manner. The message was that Spain had taken part in the international modernity of that era (the Renaissance), and given it its own, distinctive national touch (plateresque decoration).[3] This solution satisfied public opinion at home, but it was clear that a strikingly exotic building attracted attention much more than a structure that could scarcely be recognized as 'Spanish' by the average visitor. At the 1900 show, for instance, one attraction that was far more spectacular than the official Spanish pavilion was *L'Andalousie au Temps de Maures* (Andalusia in the Time of the Moors), an exhibit filling a 5,000-square-metre plot that was created by a French private company.[4]

Thus, many of the romantic clichés about Spain, its monuments, landscapes, primitive traditions and its inhabitants that had been formulated during the first half of the nineteenth century continued, to a great extent, to determine the image maintained of the country outside its borders. Although the numbers of travellers had grown considerably thanks to railways and steam ships, and later cars, buses and aeroplanes, its principal attractions were still the traditional bathing resorts like San Sebastián and Santander, the monuments from the Muslim era in Andalusia, the imperial city of Toledo and lastly Madrid, with the glories of the Prado Museum.

Domestic tourism followed the same traditional patterns as cosmopolitan tourism. However, the improvement in means of transport did facilitate the emergence of a new phenomenon, *excursionismo*, hiking and discovering the countryside, which began to gain popularity above all in Catalonia and Madrid. While hiking and mountain walking were part of an international fashion, in Spain they also had a clearly nationalistic component, since the main destinations were the most spectacular historic and natural monuments in the country. Little by little, the *excursionistas* diversified their attentions, turning towards lesser monuments in villages and typical landscapes, contributing thereby to the construction of new regional and local identities. This relationship with regionalism was most obvious in the case of Catalonia. In Catalan hiking associations, which were not drawn from a restricted elite and for whom, consequently, the principal means of communication was Catalan, the interest shown in the regional and local heritage was intimately linked to the growth of a strong collective identity. This was one reason why the mountain and monastery of Montserrat became established as a sacred location for the Catalanist movement. In Madrid, the Sierra de Guadarrama mountain range northwest of the city became the favourite area for hiking, although Toledo also attracted a growing number of visitors. As a result, both became symbols of a new Castilian identity.[5]

In response to this new demand for whatever was traditional and typical, some of the people in the villages and provincial cities visited by walkers and rural explorers began to offer handicrafts, regional dishes, accommodation in distinctive buildings and staff in traditional dress. The invention of regional gastronomy, for example, was reflected in cookery books, which from the 1920s began to classify Spanish cuisine according to different regions. The dictatorship of Primo de Rivera confirmed the growing interest in the country's native produce by creating, at the request of winegrowers in La Rioja, Spain's first *denominación de orígen* (designation of origin) for wines – a system that was itself, of course, a French invention – and by publishing a *Guía del Buen Comer Español. Inventario y Loa de la Cocina Clásica de España y sus Regiones* (Guide to Good Eating in Spain: Inventory and Eulogy of the Classic Cuisine of Spain and its Regions).[6]

In the same first decades of the century, the Spanish State had also begun to concern itself with tourism, doing so before the majority of European countries. It was precisely the meagre numbers of foreign visitors that led the government to take measures to encourage a promising sector of the economy and correct mistaken ideas of Spain as a country that was primitive and inhospitable.[7] Hence, in October 1905, a Liberal government created a National Commission for the Promotion of Tourism, which in 1911 became the Comisaría Regia de Turismo y Cultura Artística (Royal Office for Tourism and Artistic Culture). Marquis Benigno de la Vega Inclán was appointed its first commissioner, and, despite the fact that it had to operate virtually without a proper budget, it succeeded in initiating some significant projects.[8]

Its activities were orientated towards encouraging cultural tourism, and thereby also stimulating Spanish national pride. This could be seen for example in the creation of the Casa del Greco museum in Toledo and the Casa de Cervantes in the great writer's former home in

Valladolid, both of which can be regarded as educational monuments devoted to two key figures in Spain's cultural heritage. The Comisaría also published itineraries for tours of historic cities such as Segovia or Ávila, monuments of the standing of El Escorial or impressive landscapes such as those of the Sierra Nevada. In addition, it also commissioned museum catalogues, the production of a great number of postcards and the publication of a collection of small-format books in three languages titled *El Arte en España* (Art in Spain). By means of all these activities, it contributed to formulating and confirming the conventional canon of the historical, artistic and natural heritage of Spain, which gave a privileged position to the identification of 'Spain' with Castile and Andalusia.[9]

However, the royal commissioner did not only interest himself in a glorious national past, fine arts and majestic scenery, but also demonstrated enormous concern for regional popular culture. Hence, when the Marquis de la Vega Inclán initiated the building of the future Paradores in 1926 – state-run luxury hotels in locations away from traditional tourist routes – it was decided that several would be build in regional styles so that they might be better suited to the local climate, landscape and traditions. It was also proposed to serve travellers the best of local dishes and produce, and equip the staff with traditional dress.[10]

This cultural regionalism, which in this case clearly served to provide local roots for Spanish identity and demonstrate the diversity that could exist within the fundamental unity of the fatherland, also emerged in the renovation of the district of Santa Cruz in Seville, carried out between 1912 and 1920. This historic medieval quarter was in a very bad state, and aroused scarcely any interest. Then, thanks to the intervention of the Comisaría, it was made more *Sevillano* than ever. We can even speak of the invention of a tradition: squalid, insanitary alleys were converted into the archetype of a Seville *barrio*. Streets were recobbled and cleaned, with new street lamps and name plaques, and gardens and intimate little squares created, all in the most typical Andalusian style. Even the majority of its newly built houses, constructed in the new regionalist style, were more 'typical' than the existing buildings, producing a historical pastiche that in the long term has enjoyed astonishing success. Other cities initiated similar projects, as in, for example, the creation of the characteristic 'Gothic Quarter' of Barcelona.[11]

The nationalism of the Comisaría Regia de Turismo was openminded, liberal and secular. However, under the impact of the First World War, the Russian Revolution and the growing strength of the labour movement in Spain, this cosmopolitan liberal nationalism lost impetus, and many politicians and intellectuals began to reconsider their position. The growing importance of a National-Catholic ideology also made itself felt in tourism policy during these years. In 1918, for example, Covadonga, where the Asturian King Pelayo was believed to have won his first victory against the Muslims in 722, and Ordesa in the Pyrenees, associated with the initial stages of the *Reconquista* in Aragon, were chosen as Spain's first national parks. Both areas have exceptional scenery, but perhaps more important than their natural beauty was their historic significance, since both were linked to the beginnings of Spain's 'Reconquest' from Muslim rule, and so could be considered cradles of a Catholic Spanish nation.[12]

The central state and the Royal Commission did not act alone. In some cases, local authorities and elites also collaborated in the work of promoting cultural tourism – of the kind that involved wealthier travellers – by making Spain more Spanish. Perhaps the best example was, again, the city of Seville. In 1910, a competition for the façades of new buildings was organized, which favoured buildings in a '*Sevillano*' style. It was a great success, and within a few years Andalusian 'regionalism' became the dominant style in Seville, and not just in the district of Santa Cruz. Between around 1916 and 1932, about half of the new buildings erected in the city could be described as regionalist in style. Consequently, thanks to its architects and craftsmen, Seville as a whole became more *Sevillano* than it had ever been previously. Similarly, when in the same year of 1910, the decision was taken to organize an Ibero-American Exhibition in the city – which would eventually be held, after long postponements due mainly to the First World War, in 1929 – Seville's principal regionalist architect, Aníbal González Álvarez, was appointed to design the main buildings for the event, such as the magnificent Plaza de España, because it was felt that his plans for the project would form 'an authentically Spanish, and eminently regional, ensemble'. As would equally be very clear in the final results – with the 'Avenue of the Race', the Plaza de América and above all the Plaza de España itself, with its benches representing all Spain's provinces, busts of its foremost national heroes and bridges representing the historic kingdoms of Castile, León, Aragon and Navarre – cultural nationalism could also be made use of as a showcase and a special attraction to draw in the largest possible number of visitors.[13]

However, creating a traditional image of one's own collective identity was not the only option. The organizers of the International Exhibition in Barcelona, held in the same year as the Seville fair, 1929, chose to follow the opposite path. Catalonia preferred to use the occasion to portray itself as a modern and cosmopolitan region. The event had initially been conceived as an exhibition dedicated entirely to the ultra-modern industry of electricity, and had been scheduled for 1917. The majority of the new buildings required were to be built in the new, sober international neoclassical style known in its Catalan variant as *noucentisme*, a play on the double meanings of the word *nou* (both 'new' and 'nine'), as the style of the new century in the 1900s. However, since the organizers understood that they could not compete in terms of modernity with San Francisco, which was due to hold an ambitious international exposition in 1915, they decided to add something that the Americans did not have: the historic and artistic treasures of Spain – which were to be exhibited in the new 'National Palace' at the top of the hill of Montjüic – and its wealth of popular traditions, which would be shown off in a special avenue devoted to 'Types of Spanish Life'. In the final design of the Exhibition, this avenue became the *Pueblo Español* (Spanish Village), a collection of careful reproductions of tra- ditional vernacular architecture from all the regions of Spain that is still today one of Barcelona's best-known tourist attractions. Unfortu- nately, by the time it was finally possible to inaugurate the Exhibition in 1929 – since it too had suffered long delays, due to the World War and political problems – *noucentisme* no longer seemed so modern, and it was the Weimar Republic that presented itself as the most ad- vanced of all countries, providing the celebrated Barcelona Pavilion by Ludwig Mies van der Rohe, a landmark of the new architectural func- tionalism.[14] Even so, this evident zeal for presenting one's community to the world in an ultra-modern style would also be characteristic of democratic Spain during the final decades of the century.

Dictatorship, Republic and Civil War

Tourism did not initially figure in the list of priorities of General Primo de Rivera, and after he seized power in a coup d'état in 1923, there were few immediate changes in the tourism policy of the government. It was not till two years later that the dictator decided that the cen- tral government should take over the reins of both the Ibero-American Exhibition in Seville and the Barcelona Exhibition, since both proj- ects, which had begun as local initiatives, were not making sufficient progress. Subsequently, since the regime then felt itself responsible for the two exhibitions, which could enhance its international prestige, it decided to professionalize the administration of tourism, taking as a model the Italian Ente Nazionale per la Industria Turistica. Hence, in

April 1928 it replaced the Comisaría Regia with the Patronato Nacional de Turismo (National Tourism Trust), which had its own proper budget, and even opened seven offices abroad.[15]

The creation of the Patronato Nacional de Turismo certainly signified a radical change of course. The new body concerned itself with every dimension of modern tourism: hotels, the training of professional staff, advertising, catalogues, guidebooks, reliable statistics and the creation of official tourist information centres. In addition, instead of focussing solely on the nation's artistic and historical heritage, it also set out to present Spain as a modern country. In its first report issued in 1930, the organization insisted on 'the political importance for Spain that it should be known not just as an immense museum ... but also as a modern people open to all kinds of initiatives and suggestions, however advanced they may be'. This was most clearly manifested in the Patronato's advertising posters, which no longer solely portrayed traditional characters in folkloric dress, but also modern tourists in the latest fashions. Use was even made of highly modern designs inspired by cubism, futurism and art deco.[16]

While the Primo de Rivera dictatorship had tried to associate itself with technological and economic modernization, the Second Republic inaugurated in 1931 wished to show itself to the world above all as a country that was advanced in political and cultural terms. Equally, although the tourism administration had less money at its disposal than a few years earlier, the republic also introduced certain novelties. In the first place, it wished to democratize domestic tourism by organizing trips for schools, and introducing a *cartilla turística* (tourist card) that enabled the less well-off to save money by buying transport tickets and accommodation at reduced prices. The new government also proposed to direct travellers' attention towards less-visited regions, and began the decentralization of tourism administration by delegating responsibility for Catalonia to the Catalan autonomous government in 1932.[17]

Perhaps the most drastic change was in the image of the country that official bodies wished to transmit. What mattered most to the left-wing governments was not so much to reach an international audience in order to promote tourism but to address the ordinary people. They wished to fortify the legitimacy of the republic by showing it to be a modern state that was working in favour of all citizens, providing, for example, greater funding for primary education and public libraries. In this they did not only make efforts to enable workers to have leisure time and travel for holidays, but also introduced measures to bring the national heritage closer to ordinary people, organizing the famous

Misiones Pedagógicas (Educational Missions) of young volunteers who toured the most deprived areas of the country. Through film and slide shows, a 'travelling museum' with copies of famous paintings, concerts and performances by theatre groups such as *La Barraca*, the government introduced the milestones of Spanish high culture to even the remotest villages.[18]

This recognition of the importance of culture and of extending it as broadly as possible was also visible during the Civil War. The Republican government did as much as it could to protect the artistic and monumental heritage under its control, and even evacuated the greatest artistic treasures from areas close to the battlefronts. It also mobilized avant-garde writers and artists, to endow itself with an aura of cultural and political modernity. In 1937, for example, the Second International Congress of Anti-Fascist Writers was held in a Madrid under siege by Franco's troops. Picasso was named honorary director of the Prado Museum, and shortly afterwards he painted his *Guernica* for the Spanish Pavilion in the Paris International Exhibition, in which space was also provided for the autonomous governments of Catalonia and the Basque Country.[19]

The rightist or 'nationalist' side in the war, for its part, presented itself as a traditional authoritarian state that protected the established order, religion and private property, although it also had fascist aspects. Franco and his supporters paid less attention to the protection of the national heritage, and preferred traditionalist artists to the avant-garde. However, while both warring camps were highly active in promoting their cause abroad, only Franco's government in Burgos decided to make use of tourism, organizing a set of 'war routes' to exhibit the achievements of their 'National Crusade' to an international public. In effect, the regime's new Servicio Nacional de Turismo (National Tourism Service) acquired twenty buses in the United States for the purpose, and in July 1938 the first tourists were able to enjoy a guided tour of the battlefields. By the war's end a few thousand foreigners, in general people already sympathetic to the nationalist cause, had toured these 'Itineraries of Spanish Heroism'.[20]

Francoism

With the war over, Franco and his regime did not show any great interest in encouraging international tourism. The *Rutas de Guerra* had been a success and continued in operation, renamed 'National Routes'. However, with the exception of these organized tours, the propaganda value of which was highly regarded, the government did not look well upon the uncontrolled arrival of foreign travellers. Even in 1950, a Francoist minister still declared his scepticism regarding the benefits that tourism could bring to Spain, asking, 'Why would we want a few foreigners coming in and showing us their hairy legs?'[21] What was of most concern to the regime was the potential dangers tourism could bring, for both national security and the moral health of the population. Hence many obstructions were placed in the way of travellers, from strict border controls to rigid regulation of travel agencies and currency exchange facilities and the *tríptico* (three-part) form that travellers had to carry with them at all times and show at hotels in order to control their movements.[22] Francoist tourism policy thus had many similarities with that of its ideological enemy, the Soviet Union, where Intourist accompanied and exercised vigilance over all foreign visitors.

Nevertheless, the tourism administration that Franco had established during the war continued to function. The National Tourism Service became the Dirección General de Turismo (General Directorate of Tourism), which remained – following the example of Nazi Germany – part of the Press and Propaganda Sub-Secretariat of the Interior Ministry. Its officials quite soon took their first steps towards professionalizing the tourism sector, and as early as August 1939 they recommended adapting food served in hotels to international tastes, avoiding 'regional concoctions' with 'excessively strange characteristics or strong dressings unknown outside of Spain', though without ceasing to serve classic Spanish dishes such as 'paella, *cocido madrileño*, or Spanish omelette'. At the end of the 1940s and in the first years of the next decade, the desire to escape from international isolation and economic necessity – felt above all in the shortage of foreign currency – provided the main stimulus for those who looked at international tourism from a more pragmatic viewpoint.[23]

As to domestic tourism, there were no such ideological obstacles, but rather the opposite. In this regard, the regime clearly followed the pattern set by Fascist Italy and Nazi Germany, encouraging *excursionismo* and group tours around the country through the various organizations included in its official single party (*Movimiento*). In the tours and outings organized by the Youth Front, Women's Section and Spanish University Union, patriotic exultation and political indoctrination formed part of the programme. In addition, in 1939 the regime created an organization specifically for the purpose of providing leisure for workers, the Obra Sindical 'Educación y Descanso' ('Education and

Rest' Union Foundation), which not only concerned itself with sports, theatre performances and concerts but also organized excursions and holidays for its members, which officially numbered over five million. Catholic tourism also enjoyed the support of the regime. Encouragement was given, for example, to the pilgrimage to Santiago de Compostela, especially during the Holy Years, when 25 July, the Day of St James, fell on a Sunday. In 1952, also, Barcelona attracted a million visitors to the thirty-fifth International Eucharistic Congress.[24]

What the regime wished to show off during these years was above all the great monuments of Spain's glorious past, and its venerable popular traditions. Hence the preferred destinations were the historic cities of the interior, while the tourist calendar was preferentially organized around the main saints' days and religious or folkloric holidays, with a special focus on *Semana Santa* (Holy Week) and the bullfighting season. Encouragement was also given to excursions into the world of nature. Hunting and fishing, after all, were Franco's favourite hobbies. This policy was so successful that drastic measures had to be taken on some hunting estates to prevent the extinction of certain species. A different fate befell the bastions of high culture, such as the great art museums and the royal palaces, which from 1950 were opened to the public as part of the *Patrimonio Nacional* (National Heritage). The high cost of admission to the museums and palaces made it clear that the regime had less regard for the country's artistic treasures, and made no effort to extend knowledge of them.[25]

If Spain were to escape from its international ostracism, after 1945 it was no longer advisable to place too much emphasis on the regime's most openly fascist aspects. Folklore and traditional dress, songs and dances, in contrast, offered ideal neutral, depoliticized terrain. In addition, these clichéd images were also what the great majority of tourists were interested to see, as the authorities were well aware. A competition for promotional ideas launched by the new Ministry of Information and Tourism in 1953 made it clear that Spain's primary asset was its *tipismo*, its most traditional character. One of the participants in the competition expressed this with complete candour, declaring that 'the tourist wants amenities and ease of travel, comfort in hotels, good food at the restaurant, better wine, and *españoladas* [a usually derogatory term for any cliché of Spanishness]: bulls, dance, Flamenco, singing, Gypsies ... Sevilla, Córdoba, Granada.... We must resign ourselves, where tourism is concerned, to being a country of *pandereta* [tambourines].' Consequently, in 1957, the Ministry launched an advertising campaign with the slogan 'Spain is Different', associating the country with exoticism. More than ever, folklore, bulls, flamenco and cliché images of Andalusia represented Spain in the brochures and posters distributed abroad.[26]

The Francoist policy of using tourism to propagate the traditionalist values of the regime while imposing iron control on the movements of foreign travellers eventually failed, since during the 1950s the government found itself obliged to liberalize the tourism industry and its supervision of the flow of visitors. With the devaluation of the peseta in 1959, which more or less coincided with the introduction of the first charter flights and the emergence of mass tourism in the countries of western Europe, tourism became an economic sector of crucial importance. The number of foreigners visiting Spain initiated a vertiginous ascent in the 1960s, rising from 4 million in 1959 to 34 million by 1973. The great majority of these tourists, however, were not interested in the kind of tourism promoted by the regime, but only wanted sun and sand, which thanks to the new economic policy were accessible at very competitive prices. The only meeting point between the new mass tourism and Francoism was in folklore, although this was no longer the main attraction, but only an extra way of passing the time – in the shape of an outing to a typical village, a donkey ride or a flamenco show in a bar – as part of a holiday by the beach.[27]

The gradual opening-up of the regime entered a new phase with the appointment in 1962 of Manuel Fraga Iribarne as minister of information and tourism. He very quickly began to develop a more active policy for promoting the regime both at home and abroad. In 1964, for example, he oversaw the celebration of '25 Years of Peace' since Franco's victory in 1939, stressing most of all the order that reigned in the country and the contribution the regime had made to international peace. The Ministry's programmes also presented Spain as a modern country in which the regime guaranteed stability, effective planning and economic growth, one in which there was no need to democratize the government, since 'Spain is Different'. Fraga also modernized Spain's image as a tourist destination. As early as 1961, allusions to Andalusian clichés and exoticism were largely replaced in official promotional material by more specific images of Spain's regional diversity, although they still primarily portrayed local *fiestas* and traditional customs and handicrafts. In brochures, Spain was now presented as a *continente turístico*, a place with so many diverse regions that it offered as wide a variety of experiences as a continent, and one of the Ministry's publications highlighted the regional diversity of Spanish gastronomy. For the New York World's Fair in 1964, Fraga not only presented Spain as a country with both folklore and technological advances, but also provided a sensational display of works of art, which even included paintings by Miró and Picasso.[28]

This policy of presenting the country as a 'unity in diversity' was perhaps addressed more to a domestic than an international public, since at this time the Catalan and Basque movements had been re-emerging with renewed energy. It is possible that it was thought within the Ministry of Information and Tourism that giving recognition to a certain degree of cultural diversity might take away part of the discontent felt at the centralism of the State ruled from Madrid. In the television series *Conozca usted España* (roughly, 'Know your Spain'), broadcast with great success between 1966 and 1969, the Ministry explicitly set out to encourage domestic tourism, with the implication that this would stimulate mutual understanding and the integration of the different regions of the country. This policy probably had fewer implications for the image of Spain abroad, since the advertising produced by commercial travel agencies – which was quantitatively far more important than the equivalent material distributed by the Ministry of Information and Tourism – continued to rely on national clichés like bulls and flamenco.[29]

Nevertheless, the emphasis given to folkloric images had begun to lose ideological weight. For both the regionalist cultural activists of the early twentieth century and the majority of Francoists of the older generation, the popular traditions of the countryside had been a true expression of the spirit of the people, and therefore represented the most authentic part of the nation. This valuable inheritance from the past had to be protected and preserved. However, the reality was very different. In many places around Spain, traditions were presented – as in the flamenco shows on the Catalan Costa Brava – that originated in other regions and had nothing to do with local customs. An early demonstration of the fact that many Spaniards were fully aware that they were disguising themselves to appeal to foreigners was the famous film *Bienvenido, Mr Marshall* (Welcome, Mr Marshall), made in 1953 when the Franco regime was negotiating its first agreement with the United States to receive economic aid in return for providing military bases. Thinking they are going to be visited by some US representatives, the inhabitants of a Castilian village decide to dress up as Andalusians with flamenco dresses and cardboard Cordoban hats and put up fake whitewashed walls, all to satisfy the Americans' supposed appetite for the exotic. In 1964, the Ministry of Information and Tourism itself admitted openly that folklore had become a mere marketing tool. In a tourist guide that was published in eleven languages, visitors were warned, 'something that irritates most Spaniards is corny "Spanishery".... Don't say "toreador" for *torero* or *matador,* or keep on about Carmen and that just to show how well up you are on things Spanish. "Spanishery" is a business mounted by certain Spaniards with an eye to the more ingenuous tourist.' The preservation of genuine traditions had turned into the commercialization of national stereotypes, which could be seen not only in the huge numbers of flamenco shows or *tablaos* along the coast but also in the conscious adoption of Spanish stereotypes by popular singers like Manolo Escobar and Julio Iglesias.[30]

For both national and international publics, Fraga Iribarne also wanted to associate tourism with progress and openness. This was applied quite literally in the so-called *destape* (uncovering) – the relaxation of prudish restrictions on clothing and other areas of everyday life – which was openly favoured by a Fraga who wanted a 'joyful, miniskirted Spain'. With the enormous success of tourism – by 1964, Spain had become the foremost tourist destination in the world, ahead of France and Italy – this became the symbol par excellence of the country's modernity. Fraga did not fail to take advantage of any opportunity to proclaim the successes of the regime, as when Spain's millionth tourist was met with cameras and a press reception at the airport. The NO-DO, or *Noticiario-Documental,* the official newsreel that was shown in all Spanish cinemas before the main feature, also began to give more attention to tourism, associating it with the economic miracle and the modernization of the country. The minister hoped that this would make Spaniards feel proud of their country, one so beloved by foreign visitors.[31]

This peaceful invasion of tourists had unanticipated effects as well. One, for example, was that the expansion and modernization of the tourist sector did away with the local flavour and real character of many localities along the Spanish coast. Picturesque villages like Benidorm or Torremolinos were rapidly transformed into modern cities of concrete. The displacement of tourism from the interior to the coast brought consequences for Spain's reputation abroad. In place of a country of monumental cities and diverse landscapes appealing to a select number of travellers, its profile was now dominated by the image of Mediterranean costas with beaches full of sunbathers. Paella and sangria replaced the Spanish omelette and sherry, and Don Juan won out over Carmen. While in the nineteenth century, European male writers had fantasized about passionate, sensual dark-eyed women like Carmen, in the new era the myth of the 'Latin lover' or Iberian *macho* gained ground. This was in part due to the numbers of Spanish men who, drawn by the fame and supposedly loose morals of the *Suecas* (Swedish girls, though it could be extended to any blonde northern European woman), seduced a Nordic beauty on the beach. Although there were no doubt Spanish women who had relationships with blonde men, the Spanish collective imagination was dominated by the coupling of the Iberian macho and the *Sueca*. This was shown, for example, in the new film genre of 'Celtiberian sex comedies', like those featuring Alfredo Landa and Manolo Escobar. Although the apparently daring images they showed of promiscuity, adultery and semi-naked bodies seemed to go against the strict Catholic morality that was still proclaimed by the regime, parodies of the new sexual relationships like *Las Estrellas están Verdes* (The Stars are Green, 1971) or *Manolo la Nuit* (1973) could in a subtle way also feed national pride. In them, the Iberian macho generally occupied a lowly position such as that of a waiter or hotel clerk, but managed to invert the hierarchy by conquering the tourist. Moreover, in general, in the end normality was re-established when Don Juan went back to his home village and married a good Spanish girl.[32]

Democracy

The economic crisis of 1974, which ended the period of continuous tourism growth in Spain, and the transition to democracy that was initiated in 1975 provided an opportunity to reconsider the tourism model that prevailed in the country. One important change was the decision to transfer responsibilities over tourism to the autonomous regions. Although the new autonomous institutions took some time to function effectively, in general their response to the ending of the first tourism boom was to diversify the range of activities on offer, stimulating, for example, rural and cultural tourism to adapt to a less-standardized demand. A modern equivalent was also provided for traditional *fiestas,* and Lloret de Mar, Ibiza and Marbella, each with its own particular public, became new symbols of international nightlife. Overall, however, the area in which the transition brought a total break with the past was the manner in which Spain was presented to the outside world. While the Franco regime had preferred a traditional, folkloric image of Spain, the first democratic governments wanted to give an image of a country that was modern, democratic and cosmopolitan.[33]

This desire to present Spain as a modern European country was still more marked during the governments of the Socialist Party, the PSOE, from 1982 to 1996. By 1983, the Ministry of Transport, Tourism and Trade had already chosen an emphatically modern design by Joan Miró as a standard logo for all the tourism promotion of the state, the famous semi-abstract sun in red, yellow and black, with the single word *España* beneath it.[34] At the same time, the governments of Felipe González, like the leaders of the Second Republic before them, wished to show off the new face of the country. They did so not just abroad but also in an educational manner to the public at home, most especially by extending facilities to allow access to the achievements of international high culture for the broadest possible public. This modernizing policy culminated in 1992, when Seville celebrated its Expo '92, Barcelona hosted the Olympic Games and Madrid was European Capital of Culture.

The Olympics confirmed Barcelona's new status as an innovative cultural centre, which it had acquired in large part thanks to its policy of urban renovation. Thus, the decaying industrial district of Poble Nou was turned into a stylish Olympic village, and the old port was elegantly reconnected with the city. Some of the main buildings for 1992 were entrusted to international star architects: thus, Norman Foster built the Collserola tower above the city, Frank Gehry created the *Peix d'Or* (Golden Fish), a striking sculpture outside the Olympic Village, and the Catalan Ricardo Bofill designed the new airport terminal. However, the one figure that, in the following years, would emerge as another international symbol of this ultra-modern Spain – like Pedro Almodóvar in cinema or Ferran Adrià in cuisine – was the Valencian Santiago Calatrava. His Olympic Communications Tower on Montjuïc is a good example of his spectacular architecture based on futuristic technology. Thanks to all these transformations, Barcelona became a fashionable destination for city trips.[35]

The Universal Exposition (or Expo) in Seville in 1992 was staged to commemorate the five-hundredth anniversary of the Discovery of America, and like the Barcelona Olympics was characterized by a post-modern aesthetic. The new high-speed train, the AVE, transported passengers in record time from Madrid to Seville, where by crossing over Calatrava's new Alamillo Bridge they could reach the exhibition site on the island of La Cartuja, with its various pavilions that, also, had nearly all been created in ultra-modern styles. However, after the Expo closed, the subsequent promised conversion of the island into a technology park was a failure. The best example of the spectacular renovation of an industrial city in Spain was Bilbao. Calatrava and Foster both made their contributions, with a bridge and new metro stations, respectively. The icing on the cake, though, in the reconversion of the former industrial zone beside the River Nervión, was Frank Gehry's Guggenheim Museum. This spectacular deconstructivist building transformed the city into an internationally famous tourist destination.[36]

Moreover, the new democratic Spain did not only present itself to the world as a modern and cosmopolitan country, but also as a very varied whole. The new autonomous regions were now able to create profiles for themselves as separate tourist destinations, and this diversity also came to the fore in 1992. During the Barcelona Olympics, for example, Catalan symbols were omnipresent. In addition, too, Spain's national past was also portrayed in a more diverse manner. With the Expo, the government sought to revive and emphasize Spain's historic links with the countries of Latin America, and it also staged a major exhibition of Arab art and culture in Granada, and included a special programme, *Sefarad '92* (from the old Hebrew name for Spain), that gave wide-ranging attention to the country's Jewish legacy through exhibitions, publications, concerts and conferences.[37]

All of which does not mean that the old familiar Spanish traditions no longer played any part at all. One could say that Madrid managed to improve its international image by appealing above all to its traditions and artistic past. The city was conclusively established as the prime showcase for the national artistic heritage. In 1986, the Museo Nacional Centro de Arte Reina Sofía first opened its doors as a giant space for contemporary art, and from 1992 it exhibited Picasso's *Guernica*. The same year of 1992 also saw the inauguration of the Museo Thyssen-Bornemisza on the nearby Paseo del Prado, so that with the already-existing Prado Museum the three formed a real 'Art Avenue' of stunning art museums, to which would soon be added the renovated Atocha railway station. The Thyssen, the station and later the Prado itself were all subtly renovated by Rafael Moneo, the star architect of the capital. Nevertheless, the mayor of Madrid for the Partido Popular from 1991 to 2003, José María Álvarez del Manzano, had another idea of tradition, insisting that the municipal orchestra play *pasodobles* and *zarzuelas* (tunes from Spanish operettas) in the opening ceremony of Madrid's season as European Cultural Capital.[38] This intervention well reflected the change that had taken place in the perception of Spanish folklore. While at the beginning of the century it had been progressive intellectuals who had salvaged and promoted popular traditions, by the 1990s they had become commercial products that appealed above all to certain right-wing politicians, as well as to a substantial ordinary public.

Conclusion

To sum up, we can say that the field in which there has been most continuity with regard to perceptions of Spain from outside has been in the expectations of foreign tourists. The role of pioneers was played by the travellers of the Romantic era, who set out looking for a country that was exotic, primitive and different, and found a European Orient in Andalusia with its Arab monuments, gypsy dances and strange celebrations. Flamenco and bulls, the joy of the *fiesta* and picturesque traditional villages in large part still define the country's image for foreigners. Nevertheless, in the course of the last hundred years there have been substantial changes. There has been a clear growth, for example, in the interest shown in the folklore of other regions, which to some degree has diversified the image of Spanish popular culture. There has continued to be a certain predilection for the monuments of Al-Andalus, but other landmarks of Spain's historic and cultural heritage have also seen a rise in foreign interest. Recently, in addition, avant-garde culture, from *Guernica* to the Bilbao Guggenheim, has attracted a growing number of foreign visitors. However, the one area that has seen the most profound transformation has been the radical change in the type of leisure that tourists prefer. Until the middle of the twentieth century, a select number of travellers visited, above all, the traditional bathing resorts of the north coast and the historic cities of the interior; from around 1950 onwards, in contrast, huge masses of people began to head towards the Mediterranean coast in search of heat and pleasure. From a rather exotic European country with an interesting historic heritage, Spain became a cheap destination for sun and sand.

Within Spain, this demand from abroad produced a variety of reactions. While they did not focus exclusively on the cliché Spain of the tambourine, the different Spanish authorities understood that it was advisable to present a traditional picturesque image of the country if they wanted to attract the largest number of foreign visitors. At the same time, however, the interest shown by domestic travellers in the popular culture of the countryside was also clearly increasing, beginning with the hikers at the turn of the century. People no longer visited only the great monuments of the past or the most spectacular landscapes, but also wanted to see characteristic villages, handicrafts and folk traditions and enjoy regional dishes. With the creation of the state-owned chain of Parador hotels, the encouragement given to regionalist architecture, the renovation of the old quarters of cities, the introduction of designated origins for wines and the publicity given to regional gastronomy and folklore the various authorities of the first decades of the century acknowledged the importance of these trends. It was from this point on that Spain began to become more Spanish, Andalusia more Andalusian and Seville more *Sevillano*.

Until Franco's arrival in power, this new interest in folklore also had a clear participatory element, since it included popular culture and those who produced it as an integral part of the Spanish nation, which up to that point had been defined principally by reference to great works of its high culture and historic heritage. During the Second Republic and in the democratic era that began in the 1970s, recognition has been given to the fundamental diversity of the country, with a decentralization of tourism administration and an effort to make international high culture and the landmarks of the national heritage reach the widest possible public. Under Franco, in contrast, the only regional diversity displayed in public was in folklore, which lost, in addition, its emancipatory dimension.

As to the historic heritage, the different regimes did everything they could to satisfy the foreign taste for the exotic, facilitating access to the main monuments of Spain's Islamic past. However, they also sought to preserve and publicize other aspects of the historic legacy, generally those connected with the medieval *Reconquista,* the Discovery of America or Spain's 'Golden Age' in the sixteenth and seventeenth centuries. New sites were even invented to evoke historical memories, as in the Casa del Greco and the Casa de Cervantes. In this regard, the preferences of conservative regimes like that of Franco were very different from those of democratic governments, which in 1992, for instance, gave attention not only to the feats of Columbus but also to Spain's Muslim and Jewish legacies. There were also major differences in the ways contemporary culture was employed to promote the country abroad. While the Second Republic and later democratic governments used avant-garde art to give a modern image of the country, the Restoration and the Franco regime placed more emphasis on tradition.

Another matter that has always concerned Spanish authorities has been the image of Spain as a backward nation. Every government, without exception, has wished to correct this harmful representation by demonstrating the modernity of the country. However, this could be done in very different ways. The *Comisaría Regia* of the Restoration wished to meet the new cultural tastes of a select cosmopolitan public. The dictatorship of Primo de Rivera focussed above all on improving infrastructure in order to give an image of technological modernity. The Second Republic preferred to present Spain as a country that was advanced in the fields of politics and culture. From 1957, Franco followed once again the model of Primo de Rivera, showing off an efficient modernizing regime, while after 1975, the new governments returned to the republican model, presenting Spain as a democratic country fully integrated in Europe and combining spectacular architecture with the innovative urban renewal schemes of Barcelona or Bilbao.

However, what has been the ultimate impact of all these changes on the image of Spain? The most striking aspect of the era that lasted up until the 1940s was that the national imaginary of Spain was produced by and for the Western cultural elites. The vision of Spain held by foreigners was determined above all by travel literature, novels, theatre, the opera and the press. Travellers also played their part, confirming many of the existing clichés. Those Spanish intellectuals and politicians who attempted to modify or to some extent adapt these images formed part of the same cosmopolitan European elite, and in large part shared the same tastes and fashions.

From the 1950s, the masses arrived. From then on it was this mass tourism and the new communications media, radio, cinema and television that largely determined the image of Spain. If previously it had above all been intellectuals who had invented and propagated the principal national and regional myths and symbols, now it was business and marketing. And, while in the earlier period many intellectuals had believed in the existence of a national character that it was important to preserve and cultivate, nowadays the great majority of their contemporary equivalents disdain banal stereotypes. Today it is the mass public that has begun to consume and show their preferences for national clichés, both the foreign tourists who buy typical souvenirs and the large sector of the public within Spain who sing the kitsch anthem *¡Que viva España!* to celebrate victories in sports.

Eric Storm lectures in European History at Leiden University. His research interests include Spanish history and the construction of national and regional identities in Europe. He is author of *La cultura del progreso. Pensamiento político en la España del cambio de siglo* (Madrid, 2001), *The Culture of Regionalism: Art, Architecture and International Exhibitions in France, Germany and Spain, 1890–1939* (Manchester, 2010) and *The Discovery of El Greco: The Nationalization of Culture versus the Rise of Modern Art, 1860–1914* (Brighton, 2016). He has also co-edited *Region and State in Nineteenth-Century Europe* (Basingstoke, 2012).

Notes

1. Storm (2014).
2. Charnon-Deutsch (2004).
3. Bueno (1989).

4. Méndez Rodríguez (2008).
5. Moreno Garrido (2004: 58–63); Marfany (1995: 293–307).
6. Afinoguénova (2014).
7. Pack (2006: 25–27).
8. Menéndez Robles (2007); Moreno Garrido (2004: 108–16, 151–57).
9. Storm (2016); Menéndez Robles (2007: 162–231); Moreno Garrido (2004: 204–19, 240–52).
10. Menéndez Robles (2007: 178–203). The example given was that of country hotels in California: Moreno Garrido (2004: 119–20).
11. Moreno Garrido (2004: 221–29); Cócola Gant (2013).
12. Moreno Garrido (2004: 252–71); Boyd (2002).
13. Storm (2010: 208–15).
14. Storm (2010: 198–203).
15. Moreno Garrido (2007: 117–25).
16. Moreno Garrido (2004: 140, 147); Afinoguénova (2007: 50–53).
17. Correyero and Cal (2008: 181–83, 197–98, 224).
18. Holguin (2002).
19. J. Álvarez Lopera (1982); Shubert (1999: 134).
20. Holguin (2005).
21. Unnamed minister, quoted in a letter from José Luis Ochoa, Spanish Ambassador in Uruguay, 21 April 1970; quoted in Pack (2006: 43).
22. Pack (2006: 43; see also 34–35, 43–57).
23. Pack (2006: 35, see also 39–57).
24. Molinero (2005: 144–51); Moreno Garrido (2007: 172–80, 283–87); Pack (2006: 153–55).
25. Moreno Garrido (2007: 171–76).
26. Pack (2006: 69, 68–72); Hernández Ramírez (2008: 74–82).
27. Pack (2006; 83–104); Moreno Garrido (2007: 207–10, 240).
28. Crumbaugh (2009: 29–33, 41–67); Pack (2006: 147–51); Afinoguénova (2010: 420–24); Shubert (1999: 146).
29. Afinoguénova (2010: 425–26); Pack (2006: 152).
30. Crumbaugh (2009: 8, 67–86); quote in Pack (2006: 151).
31. Crumbaugh (2009: 94); Pack (2006: 140–42).
32. Crumbaugh (2009: 87–108) and Nash (2015).
33. Moreno Garrido (2007: 256–66, 314–18, 336–45).
34. Crumbaugh (2009: 135–6, note 2).
35. Hargreaves (2000); Adagio (2004: 69–70, 74–82).
36. Adagio (2004: 82–87, 90–98).
37. Hargreaves (2000: 97–106); Morgan (1999).
38. Morgan (1999: 65).

Bibliography

Abad de Santillán, Diego. 1917. *Psicología del pueblo español*. Madrid: Imprenta de F. Peña.

Abadía i Naudí, Sixte. 2011. 'Deporte, ciudadanía y libertad: la Transición en España y el deporte, 1975–1982.' In *Atletas y ciudadanos. Historia social del deporte en España*, ed. Xavier Pujadas. Madrid: Alianza, 357–92.

Abarquero Durango, Rosario. 1988. *El toro, el caballo y el hombre como intérpretes de la fiesta nacional*. Madrid: Barlovento.

Adagio, Carmelo. 2004. 'Il PSOE e la Gestione dei Grandi Eventi del 1992.' *Spagna Contemporanea* 25: 69–100.

Afinoguénova, Eugenia. 2007. 'El discurso del turismo y la configuración de una identidad nacional para España.' In *Cine, imaginario y turismo. Estrategias de seducción*, ed. Antonia del Rey-Reguillo. Valencia: Tirant lo Blanch, 33–63.

———. 2010. '"Unity, Stability, Continuity": Heritage and the Renovation of Franco's Dictatorship in Spain, 1957–1969.' *International Journal of Heritage Studies* 16, no. 6: 420–24.

———. 2014. 'An Organic Nation: State-Run Tourism, Regionalism, and Food in Spain, 1905–1931.' *Journal of Modern History* 86, no. 4: 743–79.

Afinoguénova, Eugenia, and Jaume Martí-Olivella, eds. 2008. *Spain is (Still) Different: Tourism and Discourse in Spanish Identity*. Lanham: Lexington Books.

Alcalá Zamora, Niceto. 1930. *Conferencia de D. Niceto Alcalá Zamora pronunciada en el Teatro de Apolo, de Valencia, el dia 13 de abril de 1930*. Madrid: Imprenta de Juan Pérez, 54–56.

Altamira, Rafael. 1900–1911. *Historia de España y de la civilización española*. 4 vols. Madrid and Barcelona: Gustavo Gili.

———. 1917. *España y el programa americanista*. Madrid: Editorial América.

———. 1998. *Psicología del Pueblo Español* [1902]. Madrid: Biblioteca Nueva.

Álvarez, Sandra. 2007. *Tauromachie et flamenco, polémiques et clichés: Espagne, fin XIXe–début Xxe*. Paris: L'Harmattan.

Álvarez Chillida, Gonzalo. 1996. *José María Pemán. Pensamiento y trayectoria de un monárquico (1897–1941)*. Cádiz: Universidad de Cádiz.

Álvarez Junco, José. 1994. 'España: El peso del estereotipo.' *Claves de Razón Práctica* 48: 3–12.

———. 2001. *Mater Dolorosa: La idea de España en el siglo XIX*. Madrid: Taurus.

———. 2005. *Alejandro Lerroux: El emperador del Paralelo*. Madrid: Síntesis.

————. 2011. *Spanish Identity in the Age of Nations*. Manchester: Manchester University Press.

Álvarez Lopera, José. 1982. *La política de bienes culturales del gobierno republicano durante la Guerra Civil Española*. Madrid: Ministerio de Cultura.

Álvarez Pérez, Antonio. 1966. *Enciclopedia intuitiva-sintética-práctica*. Valladolid: Miñón.

Amorós, Andrés. 1993. *Escritores ante la fiesta (de Antonio Machado a Antonio Gala)*. Madrid: Egartorre.

————. 1999. *Toros, cultura y lenguaje*. Madrid: Espasa.

Anderson, Benedict R. 1983. *Imagined Communities: Reflections on the Origin and Spread of Nationalism*. London: Verso.

Andrade Blanco, Juan A. 2012. *El PCE y el PSOE en (la) Transición. La evolución ideológica de la izquierda durante el proceso de cambio político*. Madrid: Siglo XXI.

Andreu Miralles, Xavier. 2008. 'De cómo los toros se convirtieron en fiesta nacional: los "intelectuales" y la "cultura popular (1790–1850)".' *Ayer* 72: 27–56.

————. 2009. 'Retrats de família (nacional): discursos de gènere i de nació en les cultures liberals espanyoles de la primera meitat del segle XIX (1808–1850).' *Recerques* 58–59: 5–30.

Antich, José. 1994. *El Virrei. És Jordi Pujol un fidel aliat de la Corona o un cavall de Troia dins de la Zarzuela?* Barcelona: Planeta.

Applegate, Celia, and Pamela Potter, eds. 2002. *Music and German National Identity*. Chicago: University of Chicago Press.

Archilés, Ferran. 2008. 'Vivir la comunidad imaginada. Nacionalismo español e identidades en la España de la Restauración.' *Historia de la educación* 27: 57–85.

————. 2011. 'Melancólico bucle. Narrativas de nación fracasada e historiografía española contemporánea.' In *Estudios sobre nacionalismo y nación en la España contemporánea*, eds Ismael Saz and Ferran Archilés. Zaragoza: Prensas Universitarias de Zaragoza, 245–330.

Aresti, Nerea. 2010. *Masculinidades en tela de juicio. Hombres y género en el primer tercio del siglo XX*. Madrid: Cátedra.

————. 2014. 'A la nación por la masculinidad. Una mirada de género a la crisis del 98.' In *Feminidades y masculinidades. Arquetipos y prácticas de género*, ed. Mary Nash. Madrid: Alianza, 47–74.

Aróstegui, Julio. 2006. 'Traumas colectivos y memorias generacionales: el caso de la guerra civil.' In *Guerra Civil. Mito y memoria*, eds Julio Aróstegui and François Godicheau. Madrid: Marcial Pons, 57–93.

Arriba, Víctor de, and Julio Romaguera. 1949. *Álbum de la fiesta nacional. Recopilación gráfica y literaria de la fiesta española*. Barcelona: Gráficas Rex.

Asensio, Eugenio. 1976. *La España imaginada de Américo Castro*. Barcelona: El Albir.

Augusteijn, Joost, and Eric Storm, eds. 2012. *Region and State in Nineteenth-Century Europe: Nation-Building, Regional Identities and Separatism*. Basingstoke: Palgrave.

Aulestia, Salvador. 1967. *La fiesta de los toros o la fiesta nacional española. Versión filosófica, mítica, esotérica y teúrgica de la fiesta, reveladora de sus aspectos más profundos y trascendentes.* Barcelona: Scholtz.

Ayala, Francisco. 1944. *Razón del mundo. La preocupación de España.* Buenos Aires: Ayala.

Azaña, Manuel. 1966. *Obras completas.* Mexico City: Oasis.

———. 1990. *Obras completas,* vol. II. Madrid: Giner.

———. 1997. *Diarios, 1932–1933: Los cuadernos robados.* Barcelona: Crítica.

Bagehot, Walter, ed. 2010. *La Constitución Inglesa* [1867]. Madrid: Centro de Estudios Políticos y Constitucionales.

Bahamonde, Ángel. 2011. 'La escalada del deporte en España en los orígenes de la sociedad de masas, 1900–1936.' In *Atletas y ciudadanos,* 89–123.

Balfour, Sebastian, and Alejandro Quiroga. 2007. *The Reinvention of Spain: Nation and Identity since Democracy.* Oxford: Oxford University Press.

Ballester, Josep. 1992. *Temps de quarentena. Cultura i societat a la postguerra al País Valencià (1939–1959).* Valencia: Tres i Quatre.

Ballesteros Beretta, Antonio. 1919–41. *Historia de España y su influencia en la Historia Universal.* 12 vols. Barcelona: Salvat.

Banti, Alberto M. 2005. *L'onore della nazione. Identità sessuali e violenza nel nazionalismo europeo dal XVIII secolo alla Grande Guerra.* Turin: Biblioteca Einaudi.

Barea, Arturo. 2002. *The Forging of a Rebel* [1951]. Introduction by Nigel Townson. London: Granta Books.

Baroja, Pío. 1979. *El árbol de la ciencia.* Madrid: Alianza.

Beller, Manfred, and Joep Leerssen, eds. 2007. *Imagology: The Cultural Construction and Literary Representation of National Characters. A Critical Survey.* Amsterdam: Rodopi.

Bergamín, José. 1981. *La música callada del toreo.* Madrid: Turner.

Berger, Stefan. 2007. 'The Power of National Pasts: Writing National History in Nineteenth- and Twentieth-Century Europe.' In *Writing the Nation: A Global Perspective,* ed. Stefan Berger. Basingstoke: Palgrave Macmillan, 30–62.

———. 2011. 'Introduction: Narrating the Nation. Historiography and Other Genres.' In *Narrating the Nation: Representations in History, Media and the Arts,* eds Stefan Berger et al. Oxford and New York: Berghahn Books, 1–16.

Bilbao, Félix. 1916. *Orientaciones femeninas.* Valencia: Librería Religiosa de María Belenguer.

Billig, Michael. 1992. *Talking of the Royal Family.* London: Routledge.

———. 1995. *Banal Nationalism.* London: Sage.

Blasco Herranz, Inmaculada. 2003. *Paradojas de la ortodoxia. Política de masas y militancia católica femenina en España (1919–1939).* Zaragoza: PUZ.

Bodin, Dominique. 2011. 'Inclusión social y práctica deportiva.' In *Atletas y ciudadanos,* 433–66.

Bohlman, Philip V. 2004. *The Music of European Nationalism: Cultural Identity and Modern History.* Santa Barbara, CA: ABC-CLIO.

Boix, Salvador. 2011. *Toros sí. Una defensa razonada.* Madrid: Temas de Hoy.

Bourdieu, Pierre. 1997. *Capital cultural, escuela y espacio social.* Mexico City: Siglo XXI Editores.

Box, Zira. 2010. *España, año cero. La construcción simbólica del franquismo.* Madrid: Alianza.

Boyd, Carolyn P. 1997. *Historia patria: Politics, History, and National Identity in Spain, 1875–1975.* Princeton, NJ: Princeton University Press.

———. 2002. 'The Second Battle of Covadonga: The Politics of Commemoration in Modern Spain.' *History & Memory* 14, no. 1–2: 37–64.

Breuilly, John. 1985. *Nationalism and the State.* Manchester: Manchester University Press.

Bueno, Gustavo. 1996. *El mito de la cultura.* Barcelona: Prensa Ibérica.

———. 2005. *España no es un mito. Claves para una defensa razonada.* Madrid: Temas de Hoy.

Bueno Fidel, María José. 1989. 'Arquitectura y nacionalismo. La imagen de España a través de las exposiciones universales.' *Fragmentos* 15–16: 58–70.

Bussy-Genevois, Danièle. 1995. 'Les visages féminins de l'Espagne ou la réprésentation introuvable.' In *Femmes, Nations, Europe,* ed. Marie-Claire Hoock-Demarle. Paris: Publications de l'Université de Paris 7 Denis Diderot, 25–39.

Caine, Barbara, and Glenda Sluga. 2000. *Género e Historia. Mujeres en el cambio sociocultural europeo, 1780–1920.* Madrid: Narcea.

Cambria, Rosario. 1974. *Los toros, tema polémico en el ensayo español del siglo XX.* Madrid: Gredos.

Campos Pérez, Lara. 2010. *Los relatos de la nación. Iconografía de la idea de España en los manuales escolares (1931–1983).* Madrid: Centro de Estudios Políticos y Constitucionales.

Cannadine, David. 1983. 'The Context, Performance and Meaning of Ritual: The British Monarchy and the "Invention of Tradition", c. 1820–1977.' In *The Invention of Tradition,* eds Eric Hobsbawm and Terence O. Ranger. Cambridge: Cambridge University Press, 101–64.

Cánovas del Castillo Antonio. 1997. *Discurso sobre la nación. Ateneo de Madrid, 6 de noviembre de 1882.* Introduction by Andrés de Blas. Madrid: Biblioteca Nueva.

Capel Martínez, Rosa M. 1986. *El trabajo y la educación de la mujer en España (1900–1930).* Madrid: Ministerio de Cultura.

Carretero y Nieva, Luis, et al., eds. 1952. *Las nacionalidades españolas: edición ampliada y anotada por Anselmo Carretero y con prólogo de Pedro Bosch-Gimpera.* Mexico City: Intercontinental.

Carrión, Ignacio. 1976. *Querido señor Rey ... (cartas al Rey de los niños españoles).* Madrid: Ediciones 99.

Casanova, Julián. 2005. *La Iglesia de Franco.* Barcelona: Crítica.

Casares, Maria. 1981. *Residente privilegiada.* Barcelona: Argos Vergara.

Casares Herrero, Emilio. 1935. *De la fiesta nacional. Estudio del toro de lidia.* Valladolid: Tip. Manolete.

Casero García, Estrella. 2000. *La España que bailó con Franco.* Madrid: Nuevas Estructuras.

Casquete, Jesús, and José Luis de la Granja. 2012. 'Ikurriña.' In *Diccionario ilustrado de símbolos del nacionalismo vasco,* eds Santiago de Pablo et al. Madrid: Tecnos, 508–31.

Casquete, Jesús, and Ludger Mees. 2012. 'Movimientos sociales, nacionalismo y símbolos.' In *Diccionario ilustrado,* 15–32.

Castañón, Jesús. 1993. *El lenguaje periodístico del fútbol.* Valladolid: Universidad de Valladolid.

Castro, Américo. 1948. *España en su Historia.* Buenos Aires: Losada.

———. 1954. *La realidad histórica de España.* Mexico City: Porrúa.

Cavazza, Stefano. 2006. 'El culto de la pequeña patria en Italia, entre centralización y nacionalismo: De la época liberal al fascismo.' *Ayer* 64: 107–19.

Cenarro Lagunas, Ángela. 2006. *La sonrisa de Falange. Auxilio Social en la guerra civil y en la posguerra.* Barcelona: Crítica.

Charnon-Deutsch, Lou. 2004. *The Spanish Gypsy: The History of a European Obsession.* University Park: Penn State University Press.

Christian Jnr, William A. 1999. 'Religious Apparitions and the Cold War in Southern Europe.' *Zainak* 18: 65–86.

Clara, Josep. 2001. 'Represión, intolerancia y consolidación de los protestantes catalanes en la postguerra. El ejemplo de Girona.' *Anales de Historia Contemporánea* 17: 301–23.

Claramunt López, Fernando. 2006. *República y Toros (España, 1931–1939).* Madrid: Dédalo.

Clark, Christopher, and Wolfram Kaiser, eds. 2003. *Culture Wars: Secular-Catholic Conflict in Nineteenth-Century Europe.* Cambridge: Cambridge University Press.

Cleminson, Richard, and Francisco J. Vázquez García. 2011. *Los invisibles. Una historia de la homosexualidad masculina en España (1850–1939).* Granada: Comares.

Cócola Gant, Agustín. 2013. 'The Invention of the Barcelona Gothic Quarter.' *Journal of Heritage Tourism* 9, no. 1: 18–34.

CON ESPAÑA. 2001. *Con España en el corazón. Primer discurso de la Corona y los mensajes navideños del rey, 1975–2000. Edición conmemorativa del 25 aniversario de la Corona.* Madrid: Galaxia Gutenberg / Círculo de Lectores.

Correyero, Beatriz, and Rosa Cal. 2008. *Turismo: la mayor propaganda de Estado. España: desde sus inicios hasta 1951.* Madrid: Visión Libros.

Cortes Generales de España, eds. 1980. *Constitución Española. Trabajos parlamentarios.* Madrid: Cortes Generales.

Cossío, José María de. 1959. *Los toros en la poesía* [1931]. 3rd edition. Madrid: Espasa-Calpe.

———. 1995. *Los toros.* 2 vols. Madrid: Espasa-Calpe.

———. 2007. *Los toros.* 30 vols. Madrid: Espasa-Calpe.

Costa i Deu, Joan, and Modest Sabaté. 2006. *La nit del 6 d'Octubre a Barcelona* [1935]. Valls: Cossetània.

Costa, Joaquín. 1913. *Costa contra los toros. Costa por el árbol. Costa y el desastre.* Zaragoza: Ateneo Costista.

Crexell, Joan. 1998. *Català a l'escola. Les campanyes populars sota el franquisme.* Barcelona: La Magrana.

Crolley, Liz, and David Hand. 2002. *Football, Europe and the Press*. London: Frank Cass.

Crumbaugh, Justin. 2009. *Destination Dictatorship: The Spectacle of Spain's Tourist Boom and the Reinvention of Difference*. Albany: State University of New York Press.

Cruz, Rafael. 2006. *En el nombre del pueblo. República, rebelión y guerra en la España de 1936*. Madrid: Siglo XXI.

———. 2009. 'El sabor fúnebre de la política española entre 1876 y 1940.' In *Políticas de la muerte: Usos y abusos del ritual fúnebre en la Europa del sigo XX*, eds Jesús Casquete and Rafael Cruz. Madrid: Catarata, 73–106.

———. 2005. 'Old symbols, New Meanings: Mobilising the Rebellion in the Summer of 1936.' In *The Splintering of Spain: Cultural History and the Spanish Civil War, 1936–1939*, eds Chris Ealham and Michael Richards. Cambridge: Cambridge University Press, 159–76.

Cruz Novillo, José María, et. al. 1964. *Zambra, Tablao Flamenco*. Madrid: Orbe.

Cruz Orozco, José Ignacio. 2001. *El Yunque Azul. Frente de Juventudes y sistema educativo: Razones de un fracaso*. Madrid: Alianza.

Cuesta Bustillo, Josefina. 2006. '"Las capas de la memoria": Contemporaneidad, sucesión y transmisión generacionales en España (1931–2006).' *Hispania Nova* 7 (hispanianova.rediris.es/7/dossier/07d009.pdf).

De Francisco, Andrés. 2012. *La mirada republicana*. Madrid: Los Libros de la Catarata.

De la Cueva Merino, Julio. 1994. *Clericales y anticlericales: El conflicto entre confesionalidad y secularización en Cantabria, 1875–1923*. Santander: Universidad de Cantabria.

———. 2000. 'Católicos en la calle: la movilización de los católicos españoles, 1899–1923.' *Historia y Política* 3, no. 1: 55–79.

De Pablo, Santiago, et al., eds. 2012. *Diccionario ilustrado de símbolos del nacionalismo vasco*. Madrid: Tecnos.

De Pablo, Santiago. 2007. 'La lingua basca durante la Dittatura franchista: Repressione, resistenza e identità nazionale.' *Storia Contemporanea in Friuli* 37/38: 123–44.

Del Pozo Andrés, Mª Mar 2000. *Currículum e identidad nacional. Regeneracionismos, nacionalismos y escuela pública (1890–1939)*. Madrid: Biblioteca Nueva.

———. 2007. 'La construcción de la identidad nacional desde la escuela: el modelo republicano de educación para la ciudadanía.' In *Construir España. Nacionalismo español y procesos de nacionalización*, ed. Javier Moreno-Luzón. Madrid: Centro de Estudios Políticos y Constitucionales, 207–32.

Del Valle, José, ed. 2013. *A Political History of Spanish: The Making of a Language*. Cambridge: Cambridge University Press.

Del Valle, José, and Luis Gabriel-Steehman. 2004. 'Lengua y mercado: El español en la era de la globalización económica.' In *La batalla del idioma. La intelectualidad hispánica ante la lengua*, eds. José del Valle and Luis Gabriel-Steehman. Madrid and Frankfurt: Iberoamericana/Vervuert, 253–63.

Delgado Gómez Escalonilla, Lorenzo. 2003. 'La política latinoamericana de España en el siglo XX.' *Ayer* 49: 121–60.

Demolins, Edmundo. 1899. *En qué consiste la superioridad de los Anglo-Sajones*. Valladolid: Imprenta Castellana.

Deploige, Jeroen, and Gita Deneckere, eds. 2006. *Mystifying the Monarch: Studies on Discourse, Power, and History*. Amsterdam: Amsterdam University Press.

Deportista, Juan. 1924. *Furia española. De la Olimpiada de Amberes á la de París*. Madrid: Renacimiento.

Díez Medrano, Juan, and Paula Gutiérrez. 2001. 'Nested Identities: National and European Identity in Spain.' *Ethnic and Racial Studies* 24, no. 5: 753–78.

Dreyfus-Armand, Geneviève. 2000. *El exilio de los republicanos españoles en Francia: De la guerra civil a la muerte de Franco*. Barcelona: Crítica.

Duarte, Àngel. 1997. 'La esperanza republicana.' In *Cultura y movilización en la España contemporánea*, eds. Rafael Cruz and Ledesma M. Pérez. Madrid: Alianza, 169–99.

———. 2008. 'Il repubblicanesimo recuperato. La ripresa del discorso repubblicano nella Spagna di oggi.' *Memoria e Ricerca* 27: 169–86.

———. 2009. *El otoño de un ideal. El republicanismo histórico español y su declive en el exilio de 1939*. Madrid: Alianza.

Duke, Vic, and Liz Crolley. 1996. *Football, Nationality and the State*. Harlow: Longman.

Espinosa de los Monteros, María. 1920. *Influencia del feminismo en la legislación contemporánea*. Madrid: Reus.

Evans, Nicholas M. 2000. *Writing Jazz: Race, Nationalism, and Modern Culture in the 1920s*. New York: Garland.

Fabra Ribas, Antonio. 1975. *La semana trágica*. Madrid: Seminarios y Ediciones.

Fagoaga, Concha. 1986. *El sufragismo en España: análisis de las fuentes hemerográficas*. Madrid: Universidad Complutense de Madrid.

Fajardo Spínola, Luis. 2009. *¿Hacia otro modelo de Estado? Los socialistas y el Estado autonómico*. Cizur Mayor: Thomson Reuters/Civitas.

Fernández, Antonio. 1948. *Enciclopedia práctica (grado medio)*. Barcelona: Miguel A. Salvatella.

Fernández, Carlos. 2000. *Casares Quiroga, una pasión republicana*. Sada/A Coruña: Ediciós do Castro.

———. 1990. *El fútbol durante la Guerra Civil y el franquismo*. Madrid: San Martín.

Ferrer i Gironés, Francesc. 1985. *La persecució política de la llengua catalana*. Barcelona: Edicions 62.

Flor, Vicent. 2012. *Noves glòries a Espanya. Anticatalanisme i identitat valenciana*. Catarroja: Afers.

Franco Salgado-Araújo, Francisco. 2005. *Mis conversaciones privadas con Franco* [1976]. Barcelona: Planeta.

François, Etienne, and Hagen Schulze, eds. 2002. *Deutsche Erinnerungsorte*. 3 vols. Munich: Beck.

Freire, Andrés. 2009. *Las paradojas de la 'normalización' del gallego.* Madrid: FAES.

Freitas, María Pilar. 2008. *A represión lingüística en Galiza no século XX.* Vigo: Xerais.

Frolova-Walker, Marina. 2007. *Russian Music and Nationalism: From Glinka to Stalin.* New Haven, CT: Yale University Press.

Fuertes Muñoz, Carlos. 2012. 'La nación vivida: Balance y propuestas para una historia social de la identidad nacional española bajo el franquismo.' In *La nación de los españoles. Discursos y prácticas del nacionalismo español en la época contemporánea,* eds Ismael Saz and Ferran Archilés. Valencia: PUV, 279–300.

Fundación Santa María. 1992. *La sociedad española de los 90 y sus nuevos valores.* Madrid.

Gallego, Ferran. 2008. *El mito de la Transición. La crisis del franquismo y los orígenes de la democracia (1973–1977).* Barcelona: Crítica.

Gallofré, Maria Josepa. 1991. *L'edició catalana i la censura franquista (1939–1951).* Barcelona: Publicacions de l'Abadia de Montserrat.

Galvani, Victoria. 1982. *El Rey y la Comunidad Iberoamericana. La filosofía y las tesis del iberoamericanismo de España en el reinado de Juan Carlos I.* Madrid: Fundación CIPIE.

Ganivet, Ángel. 1897. *Idearium español.* Granada: Lit. Viuda e Hijos de Sabatel.

García Isasti, Prudencio. 2004. *La España metafísica. Lectura crítica del pensamiento de Ramón Menéndez Pidal (1891–1936).* Bilbao: Euskaltzaindia.

García Serrano, Rafael. 1953. *Bailando hasta la Cruz del Sur.* Madrid: Gráficas.

Geisler, Michael E., ed. 2005. *National Symbols, Fractured Identities: Contesting the National Narrative.* Lebanon, NH: University Press of New England.

Gimeno de Flaquer, Concepción. 1900. *Evangelios de la mujer.* Madrid: Librería Fernando de Fe.

Giulianotti, Richard. 1999. *Football: A Sociology of the Global Game.* Oxford: Polity Press.

Gómez-García Plata, Mercedes. 2005. 'El género flamenco estampa finisecular de la España de pandereta.' In *La escena española en la encrucijada, 1890–1910,* eds. Serge Salaün et al. Madrid: Fundamentos, 101–24.

González, Magdalena. 2009. 'La generación herida. La guerra civil y el primer franquismo como seña de identidad en los nacidos hasta el año 1940.' *Jerónimo Zurita* 84: 87–112.

González Aja, Teresa. 2002. 'La política deportiva en España durante la República y el franquismo.' In *Sport y autoritarismos. La utilización del deporte por el comunismo y el fascismo,* ed. Teresa González Aja. Madrid: Alianza, 169–202.

———. 2011. '"Contamos contigo". Sociedad, vida cotidiana y deporte en los años del desarrollismo (1961–1975).' In *Atletas y ciudadanos,* 323–53.

González Anleo, Juan. 1999. 'La religiosidad española: presente y futuro.' In *La Iglesia en España, 1950–2000,* ed. Olegario González de Cardedal. Madrid: PPC, 11–57.

González Cuevas, Pedro Carlos. 1997. 'El rei taumaturg (la fabricació de Joan Carles I).' *L'Avenç* 212: 37–42.

González Troyano, Alberto. 1988. *El torero héroe literario.* Madrid: Espasa.

Gutiérrez Ravé, José, ed. 1955. *Habla el Rey. Discursos de Don Alfonso XIII.* Madrid: Iruma.

Gutiérrez Solana, José. 1998. *La España negra.* Granada: La Veleta.

———. 2004. *Obra literaria,* vol I. Madrid: Fundación Santander Central Hispano.

Hargreaves, John. 2000. *Freedom for Catalonia? Catalan Nationalism, Spanish Identity and the Barcelona Olympic Games.* Cambridge: Cambridge University Press.

Haro Tecglen, Eduardo. 1997. *Diccionario Político.* Barcelona: Planeta.

Henríquez, José. 1951. *Toros. La fiesta nacional española.* Barcelona: Tipismo de España.

Hermet, Guy. 1985. *Los católicos en la España Franquista,* vol. 1: *Los actores del juego politico.* Madrid: Centro de Investigaciones Sociológicas.

Hernández Ramírez, Javier. 2008. *La imagen de Andalucía en el turismo.* Seville: Centro de Estudios Andaluces.

Herrero Rodríguez de Miñón, Miguel. 2004. 'El sentido histórico de la Monarquía como forma de Estado (cómo sacar provecho del artículo 1,3 de la Constitución).' *Cuadernos de Historia del Derecho,* special issue, 147–61.

Hess, Carol A. 2001. *Manuel de Falla and Modernism in Spain: 1898–1936.* Chicago: University of Chicago Press.

Hobsbawm, Eric J., and Terence O. Ranger, eds. 1992. *The Invention of Tradition.* Cambridge and New York: Cambridge University Press.

Holguin, Sandie. 2002. *Creating Spaniards: Culture and National Identity in Republican Spain.* Madison: University of Wisconsin Press.

———. 2005. '"National Spain Invites You": Battlefield Tourism during the Spanish Civil War.' *American Historical Review* 110, no. 5: 1399–426.

Humlebaek, Carsten. 2015. *Spain: Inventing the Nation.* London: Bloomsbury.

Ibárruri, Dolores. 1979. *El único camino.* Barcelona: Bruguera

Iglesias, Carmen, ed. 1999. *Símbolos de España.* Madrid: Centro de Estudios Políticos y Constitucionales.

Iribarren, Jesús, ed. 1974. *Documentos colectivos del episcopado español, 1870–1974.* Madrid: Biblioteca de Autores Cristianos.

Isnenghi, Mario. 1996. *I luoghi della memoria. Simboli e miti dell'Italia unita.* Rome: Laterza.

———. 1997. *I luoghi della memoria. Personaggi e date dell'Italia unita.* Rome: Laterza.

Jackson, Jeffrey H., and Stanley C. Pelkey, eds. 2005. *Music and History: Bridging the Disciplines.* Jackson: University Press of Mississippi.

Jardón, Manuel. 1993. *La 'normalización' lingüística, una anormalidad democrática.* Madrid: Siglo XXI.

Jiménez Losantos, Federico. 1995. *Lo que queda de España. Con un prólogo sentimental y un epílogo balcánico.* Madrid: Temas de Hoy.

Juliá, Santos. 2003. 'Echar al olvido. Memoria y amnistía en la Transición.' *Claves de Razón Práctica* 129: 14–24.

———. 2004. *Historias de las dos Españas.* Madrid: Taurus.

———. 2010. *Vida y tiempo de Manuel Azaña (1880–1940).* Madrid: Taurus.

Kelly, Barbara L., ed. 2008. *French Music, Culture, and National Identity, 1870–1939*. Rochester, NY: University of Rochester Press.

Kolár, Pavel, and Milos Rezník, eds. 2012. *Historische Nationsforschung im geteilten Europa, 1945–1989. Festschrift für Miroslav Hroch*. Cologne: SH Verlag.

Kreis, Georg, ed. 2010. *Schweizer Erinnerungsorte*. Zürich: Verlag Neue Zürcher Zeitung.

Landes, Joan B. 2001. *Visualizing the Nation: Gender, Representation, and Revolution in Eighteenth-Century France*. Ithaca, NY, and London: Cornell University Press.

Lapierre, Dominique, and Larry Collins. 1968. *Or I'll Dress You in Mourning*. New York: Simon & Schuster.

Lasker, Linda Gail. 1976. *El tema de los toros en la novelística española contemporánea*. New York: Abra.

Lodares, Juan Ramón. 1999. *El paraíso políglota*. Madrid: Taurus.

———. 2002. *Lengua y patria*. Madrid: Taurus.

López Facal, Ramón. 2000. 'La nación ocultada.' In *La gestión de la memoria. La Historia de España al servicio del poder*, ed. Juan Sisinio Pérez Garzón. Barcelona: Crítica, 111–59.

López García, Ángel. 1985. *El rumor de los desarraigados*. Barcelona: Anagrama.

———. 2006. *Babel airada. Las lenguas en el trasfondo de la supuesta ruptura de España*. Madrid: Biblioteca Nueva.

López López, Bernat. 2011. 'Impacto social y cultural del deporte en la España del bienestar: televisión, consumo y deporte mediático, 1982–2000.' In *Atletas y ciudadanos*, 393–432.

López Rinconada, Miguel Á. 1996. *Los toros y la guerra de Cuba. Las corridas benéfico-patrióticas (1895–1898)*. Madrid: Egartorre.

López Valdemoro de Quesada, Juan G. 1985. *El espectáculo más nacional* [1899]. Madrid: Coculsa.

Lowe, Sid. 2010. *Catholicism, War and the Foundation of Francoism: The Juventud de Acción Popular in Spain, 1931–1939*. Brighton: Sussex University Press.

MacClancy, Jeremy. 1996. 'Sport, Identity and Ethnicity.' In *Sport, Identity and Ethnicity*, ed. Jeremy MacClancy. Oxford: Berg, 1–20.

MacFarland, Andrew. 2008. 'Introduction: Sport, Mass Consumerism, and the Body in Modern Spain." *Sport in Society: Cultures, Commerce, Media, Politics* 11, no. 6: 607–14.

Maddens, Bart, and Kristine Vanden Berghe. 2003. 'The Identity Politics of Multicultural Nationalism: A Comparison between the Regular Public Addresses of the Belgian and the Spanish monarchs (1990–2000).' *European Journal of Political Research* 42: 601–27.

Maeztu, Ramiro de. 1997. *Hacia otra España*. Madrid: Biblioteca Nueva.

Marcilhacy, David. 2010. *Raza hispana. Hispanoamericanismo e imaginario nacional en la España de la Restauración*. Madrid: Centro de Estudios Políticos y Constitucionales.

Marfany, Joan-Lluís. 1995. *La cultura del catalanisme. El nacionalisme català en els seus inicis*. Barcelona: Empúries.

Marías, Julián. ed. 2000. *25 años de reinado de Juan Carlos I*. Madrid: Planeta.

Marichal, Juan. 1995. *El secreto de España. Ensayos de historia intelectual y política*. Madrid: Taurus.

Mar-Molinero, Clare. 1996. 'The Role of Language in Spanish Nation-Building.' In *Nationalism and the Nation in the Iberian Peninsula: Competing and Conflicting Identities*, eds Clare Mar-Molinero and Angel Smith. Oxford and Washington, DC: Berg, 69–87.

Marsland, David. 2001. 'National Symbols.' In *Encyclopaedia of Nationalism*, ed. Athena S. Leoussi. London: Transaction Publishers, 220–22.

Martí, José Luis. 1997. 'Folk Music Studies and Ethnomusicology in Spain.' *Yearbook for Traditional Music* 29: 107–40.

Martín, José Luis, and Philip Pettit. 2010. *A Political Philosophy in Public Life: Civic Republicanism in Zapatero's Spain*. Princeton, NJ: Princeton University Press.

Martialay, Félix. 2000. *¡¡¡Amberes!!! Allí nació la furia española*. Madrid: Real Federación Española de Fútbol.

Martínez Salvatierra, José. 1961. *Los toros. La fiesta nacional española*. Barcelona: Sayma.

Marzal, Carlos, ed. 2010. *Sentimiento del toreo*. Barcelona: Tusquets.

Massot i Muntaner, Josep. 1996. *El primer franquisme a Mallorca. Guerra civil, repressió, exili i represa cultural*. Barcelona: Publicacions de l'Abadia de Montserrat.

Mayordomo Pérez, Alejandro, and Juan M. Fernández Soria. 1993. *Vencer es convencer. Educación y política: España, 1936–1945*. Valencia: Universitat de València.

Mendelson, Jordana. 2005. *Documenting Spain: Artists, Exhibition Culture, and the Modern Nation, 1929–1939*. University Park: Penn State University Press.

Méndez Rodríguez, Luis. 2008. *La imagen de Andalucía en el arte del siglo XIX*. Seville: Centro de Estudios Andaluces.

Menéndez Pidal, Ramón. 1941. *Manual de Gramática histórica española*. 6th edition. Madrid: Espasa-Calpe.

———. 1971. *Los Españoles en la Historia* [1959]. Madrid: Espasa-Calpe.

Menéndez Reigada, Albino G. 2003. *Catecismo patriótico español* [1937]. Barcelona: Península.

Menéndez Robles, María L. 2007. *El Marqués de la Vega Inclán y los orígenes del turismo en España*. Madrid: Ministerio de Industria, Turismo y Comercio.

Menéndez-Pidal de Navascués, Faustino. 1999. 'El Escudo.' In *Símbolos de España*, ed. Carmen Iglesias, 15–373.

Michonneau, Stéphane, and Xosé M. Núñez Seixas, eds. 2014. *Imaginarios y representaciones de España durante el franquismo*. Madrid: Casa de Velázquez.

Mingote, Antonio. 1975. *Las fiestas nacionales*. Madrid: Myr.

Molinero, Carme. 2005. *La captación de las masas. Política social y propaganda en el régimen franquista*. Madrid: Cátedra.

Monge y Bernal, José. 1936. *Acción Popular: (Estudios de biología política)*. Madrid: Sáez Hermanos.

Monteagudo, Henrique. 2013. 'Spanish and the Other Languages of Spain in the Second Republic.' In *A Political History of Spanish*, 106–22.

Montero Díaz, Julio, et al. 2001. *La imagen pública de la monarquía. Alfonso XIII en la prensa escrita y cinematográfica.* Barcelona: Ariel.

Montero García, Feliciano. 2000. *La Acción Católica en el franquismo: Auge y crisis de la Acción Católica especializada.* Madrid: UNED.

Montero Moreno, Antonio. 1961. *Historia de la persecución religiosa en España 1936–1939.* Madrid: Biblioteca de Autores Cristianos.

Moral, Felix. 1998. *Identidad regional y nacionalismo en el Estado de las Autonomías.* Madrid: Centro de Investigaciones Sociológicas.

Morales Moya, Antonio. 1993. 'Historia de la Historiografía española.' In *Enciclopedia de Historia de España*, vol. VII, ed. Miguel Artola. Madrid: Alianza, 583–684.

Morcillo, Aurora G. 2000. *True Catholic Womanhood: Gender Ideology in Franco's Spain.* Illinois: Northern Illinois University Press.

———. 2010. *The Seduction of Modern Spain: The Female Body and the Francoist Body Politic.* Lewisburg, PA: Bucknell University Press.

Moreno Galván, Francisco. 1960. *Los toros en la literatura contemporánea.* Madrid: Taurus.

Moreno Garrido, Ana. 2004. 'Turismo y nación. La identidad nacional a través de los símbolos turísticos (España 1908–1929).' PhD thesis, Universidad Complutense de Madrid.

———. 2007. *Historia del turismo en España en el siglo XX.* Madrid: Síntesis.

Moreno-Luzón, Javier. 2004. 'Entre el progreso y la Virgen del Pilar. La pugna por la memoria en el centenario de la Guerra de la Independencia.' *Historia y Política* 12: 41–78.

———. 2006. 'De agravios, pactos y símbolos. El nacionalismo español ante la autonomía de Cataluña (1918–1919).' *Ayer* 63: 119–51.

———. 2012. *Modernizing the Nation: Spain during the Reign of Alfonso XIII. 1902–1931.* Brighton: Sussex Academic Press.

———, ed. 2013. 'Dossier: Imaginarios nacionalistas en el primer tercio del siglo XX.' *Hispania. Revista Española de Historia* 73, no. 244: 313–524.

Moreno-Luzón, Javier, and Xosé M. Núñez Seixas, eds. 2013. *Ser españoles. Imaginarios nacionalistas en el siglo XX.* Barcelona: RBA.

Morgan, Tony. 1999. '1992: Memories and Modernities.' In *Contemporary Spanish Cultural Studies*, eds. Barry Jordan and Rikki Morgan-Tamosunas. London: Arnold, 58–67.

Munson, Elizabeth. 2000. 'Regenerando a la mujer, regenerando España.' *Foro hispánico. Revista hispánica de Flandes y Holanda* 18: 43–54.

Muñoz Soro, Javier. 2003. 'Entre la memoria y la reconciliación. El recuerdo de la República y la guerra en la Generación de 1968.' *Historia del Presente* 2: 83–110.

Narváez, María V. 2009. *La imagen de la mujer en la guerra civil. Un estudio a través de la prensa gaditana (1936–1939).* Cádiz: Quorum Editores.

Nash, Mary. 2006. *Rojas, Las mujeres republicanas en la Guerra Civil.* Barcelona: Taurus.

―――. 2015. 'Mass Tourism and New Representations of Gender in Late Francoist Spain: The *Sueca* and Don Juan in the late 1960s.' *Cultural History* 4, no. 2: 136–62.

Noel, Eugenio. 1967. *Escritos antitaurinos*. Madrid: Taurus.

Nora, Pierre, ed. 1984. *Les lieux de mémoire. I. La République*. Paris: Gallimard.

―――. 1986. *Les lieux de mémoire. II. La Nation*. Paris: Gallimard.

―――. 1992–94. *Les lieux de mémoire. III. Les France*. Paris: Gallimard.

Núñez Florencio, Rafael. 2001. *Sol y Sangre. La imagen de España en el mundo*. Madrid: Espasa Calpe.

―――. 2010. *El peso del pesimismo. Del 98 al desencanto*. Madrid: Marcial Pons.

Núñez Seixas, Xosé M. 1994. 'Galeguismo e cultura durante o Primeiro Franquismo (1939–1960): Unha interpretación.' *A Trabe de Ouro* 19: 99–117 and 20: 85–103.

―――. 1999. *Los nacionalismos en la España contemporánea (siglos XIX y XX)*. Barcelona: Hipòtesi.

―――. 2001. 'What is Spanish Nationalism Today? From Legitimacy Crisis to Unfulfilled Renovation (1975–2000).' *Ethnic and Racial Studies* 24, no. 5: 719–52.

―――. 2006. *¡Fuera el Invasor! Nacionalismos y movilización bélica durante la Guerra Civil Española, 1936–1939*. Madrid: Marcial Pons.

―――. 2010. *Patriotas y Demócratas. El discurso nacionalista español después de Franco*. Madrid: Los Libros de la Catarata.

―――. 2014. 'La región y lo local en el primer franquismo.' In *Imaginarios y representaciones de España durante el franquismo*, eds Stéphane Michonneau and Xosé M. Núñez Seixas. Madrid: Casa de Velázquez.

Núñez Seixas, Xosé M., and Maiken Umbach. 2008. 'Hijacked Heimats: National Appropriations of Local and Regional Identities in Germany and Spain, 1930–1945.' *European Review of History – Revue européenne d'histoire* 15, no. 3: 295–316.

Ofer, Inbal. 2009. *Señoritas in Blue: The Making of a Female Political Elite in Franco's Spain*. Sussex: Sussex Academic Press.

Orensanz, Aurelio. 1974. *Religiosidad popular española, 1940–65*. Madrid: Editora Nacional.

Ortega y Gasset, José. 1922. *España invertebrada. Bosquejo de algunos pensamientos históricos*. Madrid: Espasa-Calpe.

―――. 1931. *Rectificación de la República*. Madrid: Revista de Occidente.

―――. 1962. *La caza y Los toros*. Madrid: Espasa-Calpe.

Ortiz, Carmen. 1999. 'The Uses of Folklore in the Franco Regime.' *The Journal of American Folklore* 112, no. 446: 479–96.

Ostolaza, M. 2007. 'La nación española en el País Vasco, 1875–1931: el papel de la escuela.' In *El País Vasco y España: Identidades, nacionalismos y Estado (siglos XIX y XX)*, eds Luis Castells et. al. Bilbao: Universidad del País Vasco, 163–84.

Ovejero, Félix, José Luis Martín and Roberto Gargarella, eds. 2003. *Nuevas ideas republicanas: Autogobierno y libertad*. Barcelona: Paidós Ibérica

Özkirimli, Umut. 2000. *Theories of Nationalism: A Critical Introduction*. London: Palgrave.

Pack, Sasha D. 2006. *Tourism and Dictatorship: Europe's Peaceful Invasion of Franco's Spain*. Basingstoke: Palgrave Macmillan.

Paletschek, Sylvia. 2011. 'Introduction: Why Analyse Popular Historiographies?' In *Popular Historiographies in the 19th and 20th Centuries*, ed. Sylvia Paletschek. Oxford and New York: Berghahn Books, 3–15.

Pan-Montojo, Juan, ed. 1998. *Más se perdió en Cuba. España, 1898 y la crisis de fin de siglo*. Madrid: Alianza.

Pasamar, Gonzalo. 2010. *Apologia and Criticism: Historians and the History of Spain, 1500–2000*. Oxford et al.: Peter Lang.

Payne, Stanley. 1999. *Fascism in Spain 1923–77*. Madison: Wisconsin University Press.

Peña López, Juan Manuel, and José Luís Alonso González. 2004. *La Guerra Civil y sus banderas: 1936–1939*. Madrid: Agualarga.

Pérez Bustamante, Ciriaco. 1939. *Síntesis de historia de España*. Madrid: Ediciones Españolas.

———. 1940. *La fundación de un imperio (España en América)*. Madrid: Redención.

———. 1941. *Historia de España y la civilización española*. Madrid: Yagües.

———. 1942. *Historia del Imperio español*. Madrid: García Enciso.

Pérez de Ayala, Ramón. 1925. *Política y toros: ensayos* [1918]. Madrid: Renacimiento.

Pérez Díaz, Víctor. 1993. *The Return of Civil Society: The Emergence of Democratic Spain*. Cambridge, MA: Harvard University Press.

Pérez Garzón, Juan Sisinio. 2000. 'La creación de la *Historia de España*.' In *La gestión de la memoria*, 63–110.

Pike, Frederick B. 1971. *Hispanismo, 1898–1936: Spanish Conservatives and Liberals and their Relation with Spanish America*. Notre Dame, IN, and London: University of Notre Dame Press.

Pinto Cebrián, Guillermo. 1999. *Historia de los actos solemnes vinculados a la bandera de España (bendición y juramento de fidelidad). Reflexiones sobre su ceremonial, simbología y tradición*. Oviedo: Universidad de Oviedo.

Piqueras, José A., and Manuel Chust, ed. 1996. *Republicanos y repúblicas en España*. Madrid: Siglo XXI.

Powell, Charles T. 1991. *El Piloto del Cambio. El rey, la monarquía y la transición a la democracia*. Barcelona: Planeta.

Preston, Paul. 1978. *The Coming of the Spanish Civil War: Reform, Reaction and Revolution in the Second Republic*. London: Macmillan.

Primo de Rivera, Pilar. 1942. *Discursos, circulares, escritos*. Madrid: Sección Femenina de F.E.T. y de las J.O.N.S

Pujadas, Xavier. 2011. 'Del barrio al estadio. Deporte, mujeres y clases populares en la Segunda República, 1931–1936.' In *Atletas y ciudadanos*, 125–67.

Quiroga Fernández de Soto, Alejandro. 2007. *Making Spaniards: Primo de Rivera and the Nationalization of the Masses, 1923–30*. London: Palgrave Macmillan.

————. 2008. *Haciendo españoles. La nacionalización de las masas en la dictadura de Primo de Rivera (1923–1930).* Madrid: Centro de Estudios Políticos y Constitucionales.

————. 2013. *Football and National Identities in Spain: The Strange Death of Don Quixote.* Basingstoke: Palgrave-Macmillan.

————. 2015. 'Spanish Fury: Football and National Identities under Franco.' *European History Quarterly* 45, no. 3: 506–29.

Radcliff, Pamela B. 1997. 'La representación de la nación. El conflicto en torno a la identidad nacional y las prácticas simbólicas en la Segunda República.' In *Cultura y movilización en la España Contemporánea*, 305–25.

————. 2009. 'La historia oculta y las razones de una ausencia. La integración del feminismo en las historiografías de la transición.' In *El movimiento feminista en España en los años 70*, eds Carmen Martínez et al. Madrid: Cátedra, 53–70.

Raguer, Hilari. 2001. *La pólvora y el incienso: La iglesia y la Guerra Civil española, 1936–1939.* Barcelona: Península.

Real Academia de la Historia, ed. 2003. *Veinticinco años de Reinado de S.M. Don Juan Carlos I.* Madrid: Real Academia de la Historia/Deloitte.

Ríos Mozo, Rafael. 1971. *El intelectual y el toreo.* Seville: Univ. de Sevilla.

Rodrigo, Javier. 2008. *Hasta la raíz. Violencia durante la guerra civil y la dictadura franquista.* Madrid: Alianza.

Rodríguez, Miguel. 2004. *Celebración de 'la raza'. Una historia comparativa del 12 de octubre.* Mexico City: Universidad Iberoamericana.

Rodríguez Centeno, Juan Carlos. 2003. *Anuncios para una guerra. Política y vida cotidiana en Sevilla durante la Guerra Civil.* Sevilla: NosDo/Ayuntamiento de Sevilla.

Rolland, Denis, et al. 2001. *España, Francia y América Latina. Políticas culturales, propagandas y relaciones internacionales, siglo XX.* Paris: L'Harmattan-CSIC.

Romeral, Flores del. 1939. *Contra el cine inmoral – Lo extranjerizante.* Zaragoza: Octavio y Peláez.

Romero Ferrer, Alberto. 2012. *Escribir 1812. Memoria histórica y literatura.* Sevilla: Fundación José Manuel Lara.

Romero Maura, Joaquín. 2000. *La romana del diablo. Ensayos sobre la violencia política en España.* Madrid: Marcial Pons.

Romero Samper, Milagrosa. 2005. *La oposición durante el franquismo*, vol. 3: *El exilio republicano.* Madrid: Encuentro.

Ruiz García, Maribel, and Fernando Martínez López, eds. 2012. *El republicanismo de ayer a hoy. Culturas políticas y retos de futuro.* Madrid: Biblioteca Nueva.

Salaün, Serge. 1990. *El cuplé (1900–1936).* Madrid: Espasa-Calpe.

————. 2001. 'La sociabilidad en el teatro (1890–1915).' *Historia Social* 41: 127–46.

Salazar, Bernardo de. 1996. *La Selección a través de sus crónicas.* Madrid: El País-Aguilar.

Salomón Chéliz, Pilar. 2005. 'Las mujeres en la cultura política republicana: religión y anticlericalismo.' *Historia Social* 53: 103–18.

——. 2009. 'Republicanismo e identidad nacional española: la República como ideal integrador y salvífico de la nación.' In *Discursos de España en el siglo XX,* eds Carlos Forcadell et al. Valencia: Publicacions Universitat de València, 35–64.

Salvador, Gregorio. 1987. *Lengua española y lenguas de España.* Barcelona: Ariel.

Sánchez Álvarez-Insúa, Alberto. 2006. 'Toros y sociedad en el siglo XVIII. Génesis y Desarrollo de un espectáculo convertido en seña de identidad nacional.' *ARBOR. Ciencia, Pensamiento y Cultura* CLXXXII, no. 722: 893–908.

Santacana, Carles. 2011. 'Espejo de un régimen. Transformación de las estructuras deportivas y su uso político propagandístico, 1939–1961.' In *Atletas y ciudadanos,* 205–32.

Sanz Hoya, Julián. 2012. 'De la azul a "La Roja". Fútbol e identidad nacional española durante la dictadura franquista y la democracia.' In *La nación de los españoles,* 410–36.

Sanz-Bachiller Izquierdo, Mercedes. 1940. *Mujeres de España.* Madrid: Afrodisio Aguado.

Sarasola, Ibon. 1976. *Historia social de la literatura vasca.* Madrid: Akal.

Saz, Ismael. 2003. *España contra España. Los nacionalismos franquistas.* Madrid: Marcial Pons.

Schaser, Angelika. 2007. 'The Challenge of Gender: National Historiography, Nationalism, and National Identities.' In *Gendering Modern German History: Rewriting Historiography,* eds Karen Hagemann and Jean H. Quataert. New York and Oxford: Berghahn Books, 39–62.

Seco Serrano, Carlos. 1988. *Juan Carlos I. El Rey que Reencontró América,* Madrid: Anaya.

Sepúlveda, Isidro. 2005. *El sueño de la Madre Patria. Hispanoamericanismo y nacionalismo.* Madrid: Marcial Pons / Fundación Carolina.

Serrano, Carlos. 1989. 'Cultura popular / Cultura obrera en España alrededor de 1900.' *Historia Social* 4: 21–31.

——. 1999. *El nacimiento de Carmen. Símbolos, mitos y nación.* Madrid: Taurus.

Sevillano Calero, Francisco. 2000. *Ecos de papel. La opinión de los españoles den la época de Franco.* Madrid: Biblioteca Nueva.

——. 2007. *Rojos: La representación del enemigo en la Guerra Civil.* Madrid: Alianza.

Shaw, Duncan. 1987. *Fútbol y franquismo.* Madrid: Alianza.

Shubert, Adrian. 1999. 'O Franquismo vai à feira. O regime franquista, as feiras mundiais e as imagens da nação.' *Penélope* 21: 131–56.

——. 1999. *Death and Money in the Afternoon: A Social History of the Spanish Bullfight.* New York: Oxford University Press.

Simons, Ludo, et al., eds. 1998. *Nieuwe Encyclopedie van de Vlaamse Beweging.* 3 vols. Tielt: Lannoo.

Smith, Anthony D. 1996. 'The Origins of Nations.' In *Becoming National: A Reader,* eds Geoff Eley and Ronald Grigor Suny. New York: Oxford University Press, 106–30.

——. 1999. *Myths and Memories of the Nation.* Oxford: Oxford University Press.

————. 2009. *Ethno-symbolism and Nationalism: A Cultural Approach*. New York: Routledge.

Solis, Leon. 2003. *Negotiating Spain and Catalonia: Competing Narratives of National Identity*. Bristol: Intellect Books.

Sopeña Ibáñez, Federico. 1958. *Historia de la música española contemporánea*. Madrid: Rialp.

Sopeña Monsalvo, Andrés. 1994. *El florido pensil. Memoria de la escuela nacionalcatólica*. Barcelona: Crítica.

Sousa, Claudio. 1928. *La Fiesta Nacional, o análisis moral y social de las corridas de toros*. Badajoz: Joaquín Sánchez.

Steingress, Gerhard. 2006. … *Y Carmen se fue a París: Un estudio sobre la construcción artística del género flamenco (1833–1865)*. Córdoba: Almuzara.

Storm, Eric. 2010. *The Culture of Regionalism: Art, Architecture and International Exhibitions in France, Germany and Spain, 1890–1939*. Manchester and New York: Manchester University Press.

————. 2014. 'Overcoming Methodological Nationalism in Nationalism Studies: The Impact of Tourism on the Construction and Diffusion of National and Regional Identities.' *History Compass* 12, no. 4: 361–73.

————. 2016. *The Discovery of El Greco: The Nationalization of Culture versus the Rise of Modern Art*. Brighton: Sussex Academic Press.

————. 2017. 'La nacionalización del hogar en España.' *Journal of Iberian and Latin American Studies* (forthcoming).

Tejerina, Benjamín. 1992. *Nacionalismo y lengua. Los procesos de cambio lingüístico en el País Vasco*. Madrid: Siglo XXI.

Thomas, Maria. 2013. *The Faith and the Fury: Popular Anticlerical Violence and Iconoclasm in Spain, 1931–1936*. Brighton: Sussex University Press.

Tierno Galván, Enrique. 1961. *Desde el espectáculo a la trivialización*. Madrid: Taurus.

Townson, Nigel, ed. 1994. *El republicanismo en España: (1830–1977)*. Madrid: Alianza.

————. 2002. *La República que no pudo ser: La política de centro en España (1931–1936)*. Madrid: Taurus.

Traverso, Enzo. 2007. *El pasado, instrucciones de uso. Historia, memoria, política*. Madrid: Marcial Pons.

Tuñón de Lara, Manuel. 1961. *La España del siglo XIX (1808–1914)*. París: Club del Libro Español.

————. 1966. *La España del siglo XX*. París: Librería Española.

————. 1967. *Historia y realidad del poder. El poder y las élites en el primer tercio de la España del siglo XX*. Madrid: Cuadernos para el Diálogo.

————. 1969. *Medio siglo de cultura española (1885–1936)*. Madrid: Tecnos.

————. 1970. *Historia del movimiento obrero español*. Barcelona: Labor.

————. 1973. *Metodología de la Historia Social de España*. Madrid: Siglo XXI.

————, ed. 1980–1991. *Historia de España*. Barcelona: Labor.

Tusell, Javier, and José Calvo. 1990. *Giménez Fernández: precursor de la democracia española*. Sevilla: Mondadori – Diputación Provincial de Sevilla.

Ucelay-Da Cal, Enric. 1994. 'Prefigurazione e storia: la guerra civile spagnola del 1936–39 come riassunto del passato.' In *Guerre fratricide. Le guerre civili in Età Contemporanea,* eds Gabriele Ranzato and Alain Corbin. Turin: Boringhieri, 193–220.

Unamuno, Miguel de. 1965. *Escritos de toros.* Madrid: Arges.

———. 2005. *En torno al casticismo* [1895]. Madrid. Cátedra.

Uría, Jorge. 2008. 'Imágenes de masculinidad. El fútbol español en los años veinte.' *Ayer* 72, no. 4: 121–55.

Urrutia, Julio de. 1974. *Los toros en la guerra española.* Madrid: Editora Nacional.

Valls Montes, Rafael. 1992. *La Derecha Regional Valenciana (1930–1936).* Valencia: Institució Alfons el Magnànim.

Van Ginderachter, Maarten, and Marnix Beyen, eds. 2012. *Nationhood from Below: Europe in the Long Nineteenth Century.* Basingstoke: Palgrave Macmillan.

Van Liew, Maria. 1993. 'The Scent of Catalan Rock: Els Pets' Ideology and the Rock and Roll Industry.' *Popular Music* 12, no. 3: 245–61.

Varela, Javier. 1999. *La novela de España. Los intelectuales y el problema español.* Madrid: Taurus.

Varela Suárez-Carpegna, Joaquín. 2009. *La Constitución de 1876.* Madrid: Iustel.

Verhaeren, Emile, and Darío Regoyos. 1983. *Viaje a la España negra.* Palma de Mallorca: Olañeta.

Vicens Vives, Jaume. 1952. *Aproximación a la Historia de España.* Barcelona: Centro de Estudios Históricos Internacionales.

———. 1954. *Notícia de Catalunya.* Barcelona: Destino.

———. 1957–59. *Historia social y económica de España y América.* 5 vols. Barcelona: Teide.

Vicens Vives, Jaume, and Montserrat Llorens. 1958. *Industrials i polítics del segle XIX.* Barcelona: Teide.

Vicent, Manuel. 2001. *Antitauromaquia.* Madrid: Aguilar.

Vidal-Quadras, Alejo. 1993. *Cuestión de fondo.* Barcelona: Montesinos.

Vilar, Sergio. 1976. *La oposición a la dictadura: Protagonistas de la España democrática.* Barcelona: Ayma.

Villares, Ramón. 2001. 'O Republicanismo na España Contemporánea.' In *El Republicanismo coruñés en la historia,* eds Grandío Seoane et al. A Coruña: Concello de A Coruña, 51–54.

Vincent, Mary. 1996. *Catholicism in the Second Spanish Republic.* Oxford: Clarendon.

———. 2005. '"The Keys of the Kingdom": Religious Violence in the Spanish Civil War, July–August 1936.' In *The Splintering of Spain,* 68–92.

———. 2007. *Spain 1833–2002: People and State.* Oxford: Oxford University Press.

———. 2009. 'Expiation as Performative Rhetoric in National-Catholicism: The Politics of Gesture in Civil War Spain.' *Past and Present* 203, suppl. 4: 235–56.

Vinyes, Ricard. 2002. *Irredentas. Las presas políticas y sus hijos en las cárceles franquistas.* Madrid: Temas de Hoy.

White, Harry, and Michael Murphy, eds. 2001. *Musical Constructions of Nationalism: Essays on the History and Ideology of European Musical Culture 1800–1945*. Cork: Cork University Press.

Young, Clinton D. 2016. *Music Theater and Popular Nationalism in Spain, 1880–1930*. Baton Rouge: Louisiana State University Press.

Yuval-Davis, Nira. 1997. *Gender and Nation*. London: Sage.

Zabaltza, X. 2003. 'Lengua, territorio y conciencia nacional en España (1839–1975).' PhD thesis, Universidad Pública de Navarra.

Zamora Bonilla, Jesús. 2011. 'Discursos irresponsables y retóricas intransigentes.' In *Palabras como puños,* ed. Fernando del Rey Reguillo. Madrid: Tecnos, 523–95.

Zimdars-Swartz, Sandra. 1991. *Encountering Mary: Visions of Mary from La Salette to Medjugorje*. Princeton, NJ: Princeton University Press.

Zugasti, Ricardo. 2007. *La forja de una complicidad. Monarquía y prensa en la Transición española (1975–1978)*. Madrid: Editorial Fragua.

Zulaika, Joseba. 1988. *Basque Violence: Metaphor and Sacrament*. Reno: Nevada University Press.

Index